U0744949

中國—东盟法律评论

2013年 第3卷 · 第1期

China–ASEAN Law Review   Volume III Oct.2013 Number 1

■ 张晓君　主编
　Zhang Xiaojun　Editor–in–Chief

■ 中国法学会中国—东盟法律研究中心　主办
　Sponsored by China–ASEAN Legal Research Center

厦门大学出版社　国家一级出版社
XIAMEN UNIVERSITY PRESS　全国百佳图书出版单位

中國—东盟法律评论

韩桥生

Bình luận pháp luật Trung quốc - Asean.

越南—中国—东盟法律信息咨询中心主任陈大兴用越南文字为
《中国—东盟法律评论》题写刊名

Journal Undang Undang Asean-China

冯正仁

马来西亚联邦法院前大法官、第五届"中国—东盟法律合作与发展高层论坛"
组委会主席冯正仁先生以马来语为《中国—东盟法律评论》题写刊名。

東埔寨司法部大臣昂翁·瓦塔纳用高棉语为《中国—东盟法律评论》题写刊名

中国一东盟法律研究
中心：

法学之花盛开！

徐步
驻东盟大使
二〇一四年九月七日

中国—东盟法律研究中心理事会人员名单

■ 中国

名誉理事长

陈冀平	中国法学会党组书记　中国法学会常务副会长

理事长

张鸣起	中国法学会副会长

副理事长

余远牧	重庆市法学会会长
谷昭民	中国法学会对外联络部主任
付子堂	西南政法大学校长
罗东川	最高人民法院民四庭庭长

理事

杨丽艳（女）	西南政法大学国际经济法教授
沈四宝	上海财经大学国际经济法教授
慕亚平	中山大学区域法教授
王　瀚	西北政法大学国际私法教授
唐青阳	重庆行政学院教授
张晓君	西南政法大学投资法教授
刘想树	西南政法大学国际私法教授
赵万一	西南政法大学民商法教授
许明月	西南政法大学经济法教授
卢代富	西南政法大学经济法教授
谭宗泽	西南政法大学行政法教授
王玫黎	西南政法大学国际公法教授
陈忠林	重庆大学刑法教授
陈云东	云南大学法学院教授
董　石	司法部驻深圳办事处主任，法学博士
陈　敏	中国海商法协会秘书长

秘书长

张晓君	西南政法大学国际法学院院长

《中国—东盟法律评论》顾问委员会委员

■**中国** （中方）

张鸣起	中国法学会副会长
余远牧	重庆市法学会会长
谷昭民	中国法学会对外联络部主任
张国林	西南政法大学党委书记
付子堂	西南政法大学校长
吴志攀	北京大学常务副校长
杨国华	商务部条法司副司长
王　瀚	西北政法大学副校长

■**东盟国家** （按字母顺序排列）

占·索斯威	柬埔寨司法部国务秘书
克拉罗·阿莱兰诺	菲律宾司法部总检察长
王科林	文莱仲裁协会会长
哈利芬·东巴	印度尼西亚最高法院院长
麦特瑞·苏塔帕古	泰国中央知识产权与国际贸易法院院长
索托尼·穆罕达利	印度尼西亚最高法院大法官
冯正仁	马来西亚联邦法院大法官
温·敏特	缅甸总检察长办公室副主任
扎伦·叶宝和	老挝司法部部长

Advisory Committee

■China

Zhang Mingqi	Vice-president of China Law Society
Yu Yuanmu	President of Chongqing Law Society
Gu Zhaomin	Director-General of China Legal Exchange Center
	Director of the Department for Overseas Liaison of China Law Society
Zhang Guolin	Secretary of CPC of Southwest University of Political Science and Law
Wu Zhipan	Vice-Chancellor of Beijing University
Fu Zitang	Chancellor of Southwest University of Political Science and Law
Yang Guohua	Deputy Director of the Department of Treaty and Law, Ministry of Commerce of P. R. C.
Wang Han	Vice-Chancellor of Northwest University of Politics and Law

■ASEAN Countries (List in Alphabetical Order)

Chan Sotheavy	Secretary of State of Ministry of Justice of Cambodia
Claro A. Arellano	The Prosecutor General of Department of Justice of Philippines
Colin Ong	President of Arbitration Association of Brunei Darussalam
Harifin A. Tumpa	President of the Supreme Court of Indonesia
Maitree Sutapakul	Chief Judge of the Central Intellectual Property and International Trade Court
Soltoni Mohdally	Senior Justice of Supreme Court of Indonesia
Tan Sri James Foong	Justice of the Federal Court of Malaysia
Win Myint	Deputy Director General from the Office of the Prosecutor General of Myanma
Chaleuan Yapaoher	Minister of the Ministry of Justice, Lao PDR

目 录

Contents

编 者 按

　　《中国—东盟法律评论》第 3 卷第 1 期为东盟国家投资和仲裁法律制度专刊,包括中国及东盟投资法律制度、中国及东盟投资仲裁机制、中国及东盟商事仲裁机制、中国—东盟自贸区法律机制等内容,收录了来自中国、印度尼西亚、新加坡、马来西亚、泰国、越南、菲律宾、缅甸、老挝、柬埔寨等十国法律法学界共计 12 篇文章,反映了中国及东盟国家法律法学界人士对本区域经贸合作及法制发展中存在问题的前沿性研究成果。

　　西南政法大学国际法学院院长张晓君教授,孙南翔博士生与缅甸联邦最高法院研究室主任 Yin Yin Han 合作撰写了《缅甸仲裁法研究及中国经验》一文,解读了缅甸投资仲裁和商事仲裁制度,比较了《中国仲裁法》与《缅甸仲裁法》,提出了中国商事仲裁实践可供缅甸仲裁法完善的借鉴经验。缅甸联邦总检察长办公室助理署长 Khin Khin Phyu 和缅甸联邦最高法院官员 Win Khin Moe Sint 合作撰写了《中国—东盟自贸区法律框架下缅甸投资仲裁机构与机制研究》一文,该文介绍了《缅甸仲裁法》、《缅甸外商投资法》以及《联合国国际贸易委员会规则》和《纽约公约》,在阐明上述法律和条约之间的关系后,作者认为当前缅甸法律革新是在中国—东盟自贸区的法律框架内探索仲裁机制完善的有利尝试。

　　在《菲律宾外国投资法研究》中,菲律宾司法部助理国家公诉员 Xerxes U. Garcia 先生介绍了菲律宾政府颁布和实施的关于外国投资法律,具体列述了菲律宾现行法律中禁止外资进入的行业、外资股权最高限于 25% 的行业、外资股权最高限于 30% 的行业和外资股权最高限于 40% 的行业。同时,该文还介绍了菲律宾的商事仲裁实践并得出菲律宾投资法律机制的自由程度较高的结论。菲律宾司法部检控律师 Herbert Calvin P. Abugan 与菲律宾最高法院 lucas P. Bersamin 大法官办公室法庭检察长 Karla A. Funtila-Abugan 合作撰写了《菲律宾仲裁制度及其解决国际投资争端的方法》,认为菲律宾有历史悠久的涉外法律和政策，正积极建立并完善非讼纠纷解决机制，以期在国际舞台上扩大菲律宾的影响力。

在《老挝促进外商直接投资的法律政策》中，老挝司法部官员 Viengphet Sengsongyialorfaichon 介绍了老挝吸引外商投资的法律及其他相关政策，作者认为外商投资促进了老挝的经济增长和社会发展。对东道国而言，外商投资的长期性决定了资本的稳定性。因此，吸引外商投资是老挝长期经济发展计划中的重要组成部分。在《中国—东盟自由贸易区法律框架下的老挝投资仲裁机构与机制》中，老挝最高人民法院官员 Phongphana Lvangamoth & Chansouk Khahphou 认为投资仲裁是解决民商事纠纷的重要方式。老挝政府试图通过仲裁解决机制来补充司法系统的缺陷。在比较 WTO《争端解决规则及程序的谅解》和中国—东盟自由贸易协定下的纠纷解决程序后，该文认为老挝理论界和实务界应重视在国际机制下私人主体与国家的互动作用。

柬埔寨司法部法律教育和传播局公正司法项目主席 Kim Bora 和柬埔寨司法部国际关系局外交事务副处长 Chea Karona 合作撰写了《论柬埔寨的商事仲裁法和国家仲裁中心》，作者介绍了柬埔寨的法律环境、商事仲裁法、柬埔寨国家仲裁中心及与该中心组织和运作相关的附属法令，作者认为柬埔寨在政治、经济和社会等领域需要进一步地改变，因为在外国投资者寻找投资机会时，商事仲裁法和国家仲裁中心对于提高柬埔寨的国家形象具有至关重要的作用。

在《马来西亚仲裁的一般规定以及对于马来西亚仲裁终局裁决的案例分析》中，马来西亚高等法院律师 Chan Szu Fu 和 Wong Keat Ching 介绍了2005 年《马来西亚仲裁法案》以及可适用于马来西亚仲裁的国际条约，并对马来西亚法院作出的关于国家及司法管辖权纠纷的六个案件进行具体案例分析，并得出马来西亚法院对待仲裁裁决以及仲裁协议效力上做法相对一致的结论。

在《作为替代性争端解决方式的仲裁：以印度尼西亚为视角》中，印度尼西亚东努沙登加拉省勒姆巴塔岛地区法院法官 Marcellino Gonzales S. 和印度尼西亚南苏拉威西省望加锡地区法院法官 Makmur Mukhtar Supu 在介绍印尼的仲裁体系、印尼仲裁结构后，系统梳理了印尼的仲裁实践，并建议印尼仲裁法应参考借鉴《联合国国际贸易法委员会国际商事仲裁示范法》，以期能与相关国际公约相协调。同时，印尼地区法院的法官需要深入了解仲裁的含义和本质。

在《中国—东盟自贸区法律框架下新加坡的投资仲裁机构和机制》中，新加坡李欣阳律师认为新加坡是东盟成员,也是中国—东盟自贸区的缔约国。然而,东盟国家并没有统一的法律和法律体系。新加坡有着普通法传统,拥有完整的法律框架,并且大量采用了国际通行的实践做法。基于此,新加坡适合建设东盟仲裁中心,以便更好地解决东盟国家的商事和投资争端。

在《越南商业仲裁法概述》中,越南的 Nguyen Phuoc Bao Tri 详细介绍了越南法律体系的基本框架、投资领域的国际条约、对外国投资争端仲裁的法律认可及外国仲裁裁决在越南承认和执行的规则与程序,作者认为越南通过更优的仲裁立法以鼓励外国投资是必要的。新《越南商事仲裁法》给予了外国投资者在解决与当地企业纠纷方面更多的保障,尤其是新法与相关国际协议和公约相符。

泰国知识产权和国际贸易中央法院案例开发与国际事务部外交关系官员 Ornjira Nithichayanon 与泰国知识产权和国际贸易中央法院诉讼部民事案件立案局法律官员 Vera Mungsuwan 合作撰写了《中国—东盟自由贸易区的法律框架下泰国投资仲裁机构和机制》,作者认为泰国鼓励使用替代性纠纷解决方式,以便争议各方和平解决争端。相比于法院诉讼,替代性纠纷解决程序更方便且灵活,并为双方当事人提供有利的结果。因此,作为替代性纠纷解决方式,在泰国,仲裁机制应被广泛使用。

《中国—东盟法律评论》编辑部
2013 年

Editor's Note

Investment and arbitration legal system issues in ASEAN countries are the main subjects of the third volume of the *China-ASEAN Legal Review* (CALR), including Investment Law of China and ASEAN countries, the investment arbitration intuitions of China and ASEAN countries, the commercial arbitration intuitions of China and ASEAN countries, and legal mechanism in CAFTA. The *CALR* presents twelve articles collected from China, Indonesia, Singapore, Malaysia, Thailand, Vietnam, Philippines, Myanmar, Laos and Cambodia. Those papers to a great extent reflect latest research achievements of China and ASEAN countries' academics and practitioners on local and regional economic and trade cooperation problems.

In the article "Commercial Arbitration in Myanmar and China's Experience", Professor Zhang Xiaojun, the Dean of International Law School in Southwest University of Politics and Law, Ms. Yin Yin Han, the research Director of the Union of Myanmar Supreme, and Mr. Sun Nanxiang, the Ph. D-candidate of Southwest University of Politics and Law, introduce the Myanmar Investment Arbitration and Commercial Arbitration Institutions, after comparing PRC Arbitration Law with Myanmar Arbitration Act, the authors suggest that as a new Arbitration Law in Myanmar is drafting, China's experience could be valuable to some degree. In the article "Investment Arbitration Institution and Mechanism in Myanmar under the Legal Framework of China-ASEAN Free Trade Area", Ms. Khin Khin Phyu, Assistant Director of the Union Attorney General's Office of Myanmar, and Ms. Win Khin Moe Sint, the staff officer of Supreme Court in Myanmar Union, specifically describe Myanmar

Arbitration Law, Myanmar Foreign Investment Law and New York Convention, etc., after clarifying the relationship between those laws and treaties above, the authors believe that the current legal reform in Myanmar is an exploration in legal dispute settlement, in order to meet the demand of China-ASEAN Free Trade Agreement.

In the article "Philippine Laws Regulating Foreign Investments", Mr. Xerxes U. Garcia, the Prosecutor of Department of Justice in Philippines, introduces laws and regulations on foreign investment in Philippines, specifically enumerated the existing prohibitions and restrictions on foreign investment. Meanwhile, the article also describes the commercial arbitration experience in Philippines. In the article "The Philippine Arbitration System and Its Approach to Resolving International Investment Disputes", Atty. Herbert Calvin P. Abugan, Prosecution Attorney Ⅱ at the Department of Justice of the Philippines, and Atty. Karla A. Funtila-Abugan, Court Attorney Ⅳ under the Office of Associate Justice Lucas P. Bersamin of the Supreme Court of the Philippines, argue that the Philippines has a long history of foreign relations. The Philippines is improving alternative dispute resolution mechanism, which would expand its influence around the world.

In the article "Foreign Direct Investment in Lao PDR", Viengphet Sengsongyialorfaichon, the official of the Ministry of Justice in Laos, introduces the law and policies to attract foreign investment. Without doubts, foreign investment would promote economic growth and social development in Laos. Therefore, the policy to attract foreign investment is included in long-term economic development plan of Laos. In the article "Investment Arbitration Institution and Mechanism in Laos under the Legal Framework of China-ASEAN Free Trade Area", the author regards investment arbitration settlement as the most important court in solving civil and commercial disputes. The government of Lao PDR has endeavored to improve the court system by arbitration settlement mechanism and treaties. In comparison with WTO dispute settlement mechanism and China-ASEAN Free Trade Agreement after the dispute settlement procedures, the author suggests that Laos should improve the interaction between private sector and the state.

In the article "Commercial Arbitration Law and National Arbitration Center of Kingdom of Cambodia", Mr. Kim Bora, Chief of House of Justice of Access to Justice Project in Ministry of Justice in Cambodia, and Ms. Chea Karona, Deputy Bureau Chief of Foreign in Ministry of Justice in Cambodia, believe that Cambodia has undergone sweeping changes, not only in the field of politics and security, but also in the country's economic and social landscape. Therefore, Commercial Arbitration Law and National Arbitration Center are important for improvement of Cambodia's standing among investors looking for opportunities in the Kingdom of Cambodia.

In the article "General Provisions on Arbitration in Malaysia and Case Analysis on the Finality of Arbitration Awards in Malaysia", Chan Szu Fu, Partner in Cheong De Vries & Co. and Wong Keat Ching, Advocate & Solicitor in High Court of Malaya, introduce general provisions on arbitration in Malaysia under the Arbitration Act 2005 as well as international arbitration treaties applicable to Malaysia. And then, the authors describe six cases decided by the Malaysian Courts involving arbitration matters from various countries and jurisdictions, which shows the consistent approach adopted by Malaysian Courts in giving effect to arbitration awards and agreements to arbitrate.

In the article "Arbitration as an Alternative Dispute Resolution in Indonesia", Marcellino Gonzales S. the judge on District Court of Lembata Island in Indonesia, and Makmur Mukhtar Supu, explain the Indonesian arbitration institutions and the arbitration functions. The authors suggest the Indonesian arbitration law should modify according to the UNCITRAL Model. Meanwhile, the Indonesian District Court judge should master the spirit and procedure of commercial arbitration.

In the article "Investment Arbitration Institution and Mechanism in Singapore under the Legal Framework of China-ASEAN Free Trade Area", Li Xinyang, an attorney in Singapore, states that Singapore is a member of ASEAN and the contracting states of China-ASEAN Free Trade Area. Moreover, Singapore has a common law tradition and a comprehensive legal framework, as well as the extensive experience of international arbitration. Therefore, Singapore is able to be the location of ASEAN Arbitration Center, which aims to address the commercial and investment disputes peacefully.

In the article "An Overview of Law on Commercial Arbitration in Vietnam", Nguyen Phuoc Bao Tri, provides an overview of law on commercial arbitration in Vietnam in conjunction with agreement in which Vietnam and China entered into in order to protect investors by promoting the arbitral mechanism in resolving the dispute. Furthermore, the author believes new Vietnam Commercial Arbitration Law offers the freedom to resolve private disputes.

In the article "Investment Arbitration Institution and Mechanism in Thailand under the Legal Framework of China-ASEAN Free Trade Area", Ornjira Nithichayanon, foreign relations officer in the Central Intellectual Property and International Trade Court in Thailand, and Vera Mungsuwan, legal officer in the Central Intellectual Property and International Trade Court in Thailand, recognize Thailand has encouraged the use of Alternative Dispute Resolution in order to settle the dispute before the parties submitting their cases to be tried by the Court. ADR process is much easier and more convenient than normal litigation in Court. Therefore, arbitration is one of the alternative dispute resolutions widely used in Thailand.

Editorial Board of China-ASEAN Law Review
2013

论柬埔寨的商事仲裁法和国家仲裁中心

Kim Bora* & Chea Karona**
任仪 译

摘要 本文主要是在"中国—东盟"合作框架下,为研究"东盟自由贸易区的法律变革与合作"项下的国际会议项目所作的前期准备。本文主要涉及以下内容:概述、柬埔寨的背景环境、商事仲裁法、柬埔寨国家仲裁中心及与中心组织和运作相关的附属法令。

柬埔寨在政治和安全领域以及国家经济和社会面貌上都已经发生了巨大的变化。因此,在投资者寻找投资机会的过程中,商事仲裁法和国家仲裁中心对于提高柬埔寨的国家形象具有至关重要的作用。

关键词 商事仲裁法 国家仲裁中心

缩写表

ADR	Alternative Dispute Resolution 非诉讼争端解决程序(可替代纠纷解决方式)
CAMFEBA	Cambodian Federation of Employers and Business Associations 柬埔寨雇主联盟和商业协会
GMA	Garment Manufacturers Association of Cambodia 柬埔寨服装制造商协会
LAC	Labor Arbitration Council 劳动仲裁委员会
NAC	National Arbitration Center 国家仲裁中心

---

* 柬埔寨司法部法律教育和传播司项目首席官员。
** 柬埔寨司法部国际关系司外事处副处长。

RGC   Royal Government of Cambodia 柬埔寨王国政府
UNCITRAL   United Nations Commission on International Trade Law 联合国国际贸易法委员会
WTO   World Trade Organization 世界贸易组织

一、概述

柬埔寨于 2005 年加入世界贸易组织(WTO)。自那时起,随着争端解决在现代贸易经济发展过程中的重要性逐渐提高,商事仲裁法(CAL)作为一揽子改革中的重点方案被正式提出。

2006 年,柬埔寨国民议会通过了商事仲裁法;该法遵循国际惯例,建立了一套私人解决商事纠纷的仲裁体系。此外,该法规定在商务部的主持下建立一个国家仲裁中心(NAC)。2009 年 7 月 24 日,在与商界及发展伙伴代表协商后,部长级理事会通过了关于柬埔寨国家仲裁中心组织和运作的附属法令。

商事仲裁或商业性 ADR 服务主要包括调解、和解、仲裁以及这些方式的混合。国家仲裁中心的主要目的在于为商界提供一个除法院(诉讼)之外的争端解决途径,以期更加迅速、低廉、明确、公平地解决纠纷。

二、柬埔寨的背景环境

(一)经济环境

自 2000 年至 2013 年的十多年间,柬埔寨的年平均经济增长率高达 6.5%[①],柬埔寨经历了一个经济快速扩张期。这已经引发了柬埔寨国家、人民和经济的重大结构性转变。人口增长已经放缓,国家城市化水平提高。随着大范围的社会效益的增强,贫困已经显著减少。社会经济正在从以农业为基础向以工业和服务业为主发展。2012 年出现了本土的证券交易所。出口量几乎是从无到有,占据了 GDP 的近 70%[②],外国直接投资的显著增加使得

[①] http://www.cbre.com.kh/2012/06/sees-cambodian-economic-growth-012/.

[②] 柬埔寨发展资源研究所。

柬埔寨不再依赖经济援助。尽管当前的全球经济危机对许多领域(包括服装业和建筑业)都造成了显著的不利影响,柬埔寨政府仍旧致力于发展适宜本国和国际投资的商业环境。

(二)法律和司法环境

1993 年,由于诺罗顿·西哈努克亲王的统治,柬埔寨转变为了"柬埔寨王国"。随后,在 1993 年的自由选举中,柬埔寨建立起了由两位总理(一位来自旧政府,一位来自民主党的代表)组成的政府领导。新的宪法于 1993 年 9 月由参议院颁布,1993 年宪法包括 14 个章节共 139 条。

柬埔寨实行省或市级法院为一审法院的单一的司法体系。无论争议的性质或大小,这些省或市级法院拥有对所有案件的管辖权。上诉案件由位于首都的上诉法院管辖。再次上诉有可能会由最高法院行使管辖权,最高法院是对除选举案件、宪法案件以外争议的最高上诉法院。

柬埔寨商事争端解决的法律框架发展十分迅速。新的民事诉讼法典和民法典分别于 2006 年和 2007 年颁布。民事诉讼法典已被执行;一旦完成过渡性安排,实质性的民法典也将被执行。目前,关于建立商业法庭的建议正在进一步的立法商讨中。

由于意识到快速解决商事争端的重要性,柬埔寨于 2006 年 3 月颁布了商事仲裁法。该法遵照联合国贸易法委员会的范例并受到了好评。尽管该法没有明确提及调解,但它允许当事方以调解作为一种自愿的方式来解决争端(第38 条)。

积极的一面是,商事仲裁法和民事诉讼法典为仲裁程序中的法院的司法管辖权提供了限制性标准。因此,法律规定:法院应将与仲裁协议有关的争端提交进行仲裁(第 8 条);适格的仲裁庭有权依其管辖权作出裁决(第 24 条);在符合联合国贸易法委员会示范法规定的情形下,法院不得撤销或拒绝执行仲裁庭的裁决(第 44 条、第 46 条)。这些规定被民事诉讼法典第 353 条进一步强化,该条重申了限制法院越权对仲裁案件进行管辖的规定。

三、商事仲裁法

商事仲裁法颁布于 2006 年,包括如下 9 个章节共 47 条:

第一章　总则

1.宗旨及适用范围

•本法的宗旨是依照当事方的意愿,公正、迅速地解决商事争端,保护当事方的正当法律权利和利益,促进经济的健康发展。

•本法不得因某一争端可以提交仲裁或其他争端解决程序解决,或因某些争议不得提交仲裁解决而影响柬埔寨其他法律的执行。

2.定义和解释规则

•"仲裁"是指任何仲裁,不论是否是由常设仲裁机构进行的。

•"仲裁庭"由独任仲裁员或一组仲裁员构成。

•"法院"是指主权国家司法体系的组成部门或机构。

•"仲裁协议"是当事方订立的,同意将就双方之间某一特定法律关系中已经产生或将要产生的争端提交仲裁解决的协议,无论该协议是否以合同的形式订立。

•除本法第36条外,凡本法规定允许当事方自行决定某一问题的,当事方有权将这种意思自治权授予第三方(这里的"第三方"包括机构)。

•凡本法规定涉及当事方均同意或可能会同意的事实的,或者以其他任何方式提及当事方之间的协议的,该协议包括该协议中的任何规则。

•除本法第33条(a)款和第40条(a)款外,凡本法规定涉及诉讼的,该规定同样适用于反诉;凡本法规定涉及抗辩的,该规定也适用于对反诉的抗辩。

•一项仲裁具有"国际性",如果

仲裁协议的当事方在协议订立时营业地位于不同国家的;或

仲裁协议任何一方的营业地位于本国境外的;

当事方明确同意仲裁协议的标的涉及一个以上国家的。

3.书面通知的接收

•如果书面通知被递交给收件人,或通知被递交至收件人营业地、惯常居住地或收件地址,则应视为该通知已送达收件人;如果在合理查询后仍未出现上述情况,如果通知被送至收件人最后为人所知的营业地、惯常居住地或收件地址,则视为通知已送达收件人。

•本法第3条不适用于诉讼程序。

4.异议权的放弃

•如果一方已经知道另一方没有履行本法的规定或仲裁协议项下的义务,但在仲裁程序中并未立即提出或在限定的期限内提出对不履行义务的异议,则应被视为已放弃其提出异议的权利。

5.法院干预的限度

•除非本法另有规定,应由本法规制的争端均不受法院干预。

6.其他授权法院对仲裁进行监督协助的职能

• 本法第 19(3)条,第 19(4)条,和第 19(5)条,第 21(3)条,第 22 条和第 24(3)条中所规定的职能,应由法院(商事法院、上诉法院或最高法院)或国家仲裁中心执行。

第二章　仲裁协议

7.定义及仲裁协议的形式

• 仲裁协议包括合同中的仲裁条款或单独提交的仲裁协议。

• 仲裁协议应当为书面形式。如果它被包含在当事方签署的文件或交换的信件中,或以其他方式提供协议记录的电子通信方式等,或在申诉状和答辩状交换过程中一方提出仲裁而另一方未提出反对的,均视为仲裁协议的书面形式。合同中涉及的文件包含仲裁条款的,也视为仲裁协议,只要合同是书面的且该相关文件构成该合同的一部分。

8.仲裁协议及诉诸法院的实质性申诉

• 如果一方当事人在不晚于其提交第一次实质性申诉时提出要求,法院在审理涉及仲裁协议的争端时,应当指示当事人仲裁,除非法院认定仲裁协议无效或实际不能履行。

• 即使上述提及的诉讼程序已经开始,仲裁程序仍然可以开始或继续;在仲裁开始前,法院应将争端移交仲裁庭解决。

9.仲裁协议及法院的临时措施

• 在仲裁程序开始前或程序进行中,仲裁协议的当事方不得向法院申请临时保护措施或请求法院批准采取此类措施。

第三章　国家商事仲裁中心

10.国家仲裁中心

• 独立的国家仲裁中心应当在商务部的主持下建立。国家仲裁中心的宗旨是:

• 通过柬埔寨的仲裁方式推动商事纠纷的有效解决;

• 为柬埔寨仲裁案件的管理建立必要的基础设施和规则,只要争端方在仲裁协议中明确规定将争端提交中心。

11.仲裁员

• 仲裁员,无论是柬埔寨人或外国人,都应当在中心进行注册。国家仲裁中心有义务对仲裁员的资质进行鉴定,并公布当年的仲裁员名单。该名单不是绝对的,当事方可以选择该名单之外的人担任其案件的仲裁员。

12.仲裁员的资质

· 被获准成为国家仲裁中心成员的自然人和法律实体是:

· 已在中心注册的仲裁员;

· 商会;

· 柬埔寨律师协会;以及

· 由工商业者、实业家、商人和服务提供者组成的社团。

· 仲裁中心会员申请应当由不少于7人组成的仲裁中心执行委员会审议决定。执行委员会成员任期三年,可以连选一次。

13. 商会和专业协会

· 商会可以在金边建立仲裁中心。由工商业者、实业家、商人和服务提供者组成的社团可以建立自己的仲裁机构以解决其成员间以及其成员与第三方之间的纠纷。

14. 全国商会专业人员的管理

· 国家仲裁中心由下述机构进行管理:

· 中心大会;以及

· 执行办公室。

· 大会应具备以下职能或职责:

· 依仲裁中心主席的要求,或经执行理事会大多数成员的要求,每年至少开会1~2次;

· 选举执行理事会;

· 检查执行理事会的年度报告;

· 审定仲裁中心的财务预算;

· 确定仲裁成本和费用;

· 审定与中心运作和仲裁有关的规则的修订及管理办法的制定;

· 履行中心组织和运作附属法令中所规定的其他职责。

15. 大会

· 大会应当由自然人成员和法律实体代表成员出席。

16. 执行理事会的组成

· 国家仲裁中心执行理事会由大会成员选举产生。执行理事会主席由国家仲裁中心主席担任。

17. 国家仲裁中心的组织和运作

· 国家仲裁中心的组织和运作应依照附属执行法令的规定。

第四章　仲裁庭的组成

18. 仲裁员的人数

- 当事方有权自行决定仲裁员的人数。仲裁员的人数应当是奇数。

- 若当事方未作此决定,则仲裁员人数为 3 个。

19. 指定仲裁员

- 仲裁员的指定应遵照以下规定:

- 非经当事方同意,任何人不得以其国籍原因而使其丧失担任仲裁员的资格。

- 根据本条第(4)、(5)款的规定,当事方可以约定指定仲裁员的程序。

- 依据本法第 6 条的规定,依本条第(3)、(4)款规定向法院(商业法院、上诉法院或最高法院)或国家仲裁中心提起的争端不得上诉。本法第 6 条所规定的法院(商业法院、上诉法院或最高法院)或国家仲裁中心在指定仲裁员时,应充分考虑当事方所要求的仲裁员的资质以最大限度地确保仲裁员的独立性和公正性。在指定国际仲裁中单一仲裁员或第三仲裁员时,依据本法第 19 (1)条的规定,本法第 6 条所规定的法院(商业法院、上诉法院或最高法院)或国家仲裁中心应当考虑指定拥有非当事方国籍仲裁员的适当性。

20. 仲裁员回避的依据

- 有可能会被指定的仲裁员应当对任何可能有损其公正性和独立性的事件或情形进行披露。自被指定为仲裁员至整个仲裁程序中,被指定的仲裁员应当毫不迟疑地向当事方披露上述事件或情形,除非当事方已经知晓上述事件或情形。

- 只有在有损于仲裁员公正性和独立性的情形确实存在,或仲裁员不具备当事方所要求的资质的情况下,仲裁员才会遭受质疑。若当事方在其指定或参与指定后发现存在上述情形的,当事方有权质疑由其指定或参与指定的仲裁员。

21. 仲裁员回避的程序

- 根据本条第(3)款的规定,当事方有权约定质疑仲裁员的程序。

- 若当事方未能达成上述约定,意欲质疑仲裁员的一方应当在其得知仲裁庭组成后的 15 日内,或在得知本法第 20(2)条规定的情形后,将写明质疑原因的书面报告送达仲裁庭和另一当事方。除非被质疑的仲裁员自行退出或经另一当事方同意,质疑应由仲裁庭裁定。

- 若在当事方约定的程序或本条第(2)款规定的程序中质疑均未成功,提出质疑的一方可以在收到反对质疑通知后的 30 日内,要求本法第 6 条所规定的法院(商业法院、上诉法院或最高法院)或国家仲裁中心对质疑作出裁定,当事方对该裁定不得上诉;在该裁定尚未作出前,仲裁庭可以继续仲裁程序并作出裁决。

22.无法或不能进行仲裁

· 如果仲裁员在法律上或事实上不能履行其职能,或因其他原因不能及时履行职能,该仲裁员自行退出或经当事方同意,该仲裁员的职能终止。另外,如果表明存在与上述情形相反的证据,任一当事方均可以要求本法第6条所规定的法院(商业法院、上诉法院或最高法院)或国家仲裁中心对职能的终止作出裁定,当事方对该裁定不得上诉。

· 若依照第21(2)条的规定仲裁员自行退出或经当事方同意,该仲裁员的职能终止,这并不意味着承认本条或第20(2)条中涉及的理由的有效性。

23.替代仲裁员的指定

· 凡依据本法第21条、第22条的规定终止仲裁员职能的,应依照本法第19条的规定指定替代仲裁员。

第五章 仲裁庭的管辖权

24.仲裁庭就其管辖权问题的权能

· 仲裁庭可以对其管辖权问题作出裁定,包括针对是否存在仲裁协议以及对仲裁协议效力的质疑。因此,构成合同一部分的仲裁条款应当被视为区别于合同其他条款的独立协议。合同无效的裁定不得影响仲裁条款的法律效力。

· 当事方应在提交答辩书之前对仲裁庭的管辖权提出抗辩。当事方对管辖权的抗辩权不应因其指定或参与指定仲裁员而受到减损。在仲裁程序中,一旦出现仲裁庭超越其管辖权行事的情况,当事方应立即提出抗辩。无论在何种情形下,只要仲裁庭认为是合理的,仲裁庭可以允许推迟提出抗辩。

· 在对本条第(2)款涉及的抗辩进行裁定的过程中,依据案件事实,仲裁庭可以将其作为先决问题处理,也可以将其作为裁决的一部分。若仲裁庭将上述抗辩作为先决问题裁定,仲裁庭享有管辖权。各当事方在收到该裁定后的60日内可以向本法第6条规定的法院提出申诉,法院作出裁定后不得上诉;在该裁定尚未作出前,仲裁庭可以继续仲裁程序并作出裁决。

25.仲裁组决定采取临时措施的权力

· 除非各当事方另有约定,经一当事方请求,在确有必要的情况下,仲裁组可以裁定允许一方采取临时保护性措施。仲裁组可以要求采取措施的一方提供适当的担保。

第六章 仲裁程序规范

26.公平对待各当事方

· 各当事方应当被平等对待,且享有同等的诉讼权利,包括其陈述的权利。

27.程序规则的确定

· 当事方有权同意或不同意仲裁庭在审理案件时遵循的程序。

· 若当事方对审理程序未达成一致意见,仲裁庭可以根据本法的规定依其认为适当的程序进行审理。仲裁庭享有的权力包括对证据的接受、证据相关性及重要性的认定。

28.仲裁地

· 当事方可以自行约定仲裁地点。当事方无约定的,可以在充分考虑案件事实(包括当事方之间的协议)的情况下确定仲裁地。

· 尽管有本条第(1)款的规定,除非当事方另有约定,仲裁庭可以在其认为有利于当事方协商解决争端的任何地点进行审理,听取证人、专家、当事方的陈述,对设备、财产、文件等进行检验。

29.仲裁程序的开始

· 除非当事方另有约定,某一争端的仲裁程序自被申请人接到仲裁请求时开始。

30.仲裁语言

· 当事方可以约定仲裁程序中适用一种或几种语言。当事方没有约定的,由仲裁庭决定所用语言。

· 仲裁庭可以要求各方将文字性的证据翻译为由各方约定或仲裁庭决定的仲裁语言。

31.申请书和答辩书

· 在由当事方约定或仲裁组决定的一段合理期限内,仲裁申请人应当说明事实、争议点、所寻求的救济措施以支持其仲裁申请;被申请人应当就申请人的申请提出抗辩,除非当事方对此类陈述的内容另有约定。当事方可以提交任何其认为与之相关的文件或证据。

· 除非当事方另有约定,任何一方都可以在仲裁程序中对其申请书或答辩书进行补充或修改,除非仲裁组认为允许这种延迟修改是不合理的。

32.开庭和书面审理程序

· 除非当事方有相反的约定,仲裁庭有权决定以开庭的方式出示证据或进行口头辩论,或者以书面审理的方式对文件或其他实质性材料进行审理。然而,除非当事方约定不以开庭的方式审理,经一当事方请求,仲裁庭应当在仲裁程序中的适当的阶段进行开庭审理。

　　·关于对材料、货物、其他财产或文件进行审查的开庭或会议,仲裁庭应充分地提前通知各当事方。

　　·一个当事方提供给仲裁庭的所有陈述、文件或其他信息都应当通知另一当事方。任何仲裁庭可能据以作出裁决的专家报告或证据文件都应当通知给另一方。

　　33.当事方的违约

　　·申请人未能依照本法第31(1)条的规定提交申请陈述的,仲裁组应当裁定终止程序。

　　·被申请人未能依照本法第31(1)条的规定提交抗辩书的,仲裁组应当继续仲裁程序,且不得将此作为采纳申请人主张的依据。

　　·一方当事人未能出庭应诉或提交书面证据的,仲裁组可以继续审理并依据已有的证据作出裁决。

　　34.仲裁庭指定的专家

　　·仲裁庭可以指定一个或多个专家针对特定问题向仲裁庭进行汇报。

　　·除非当事方另有约定,经一方当事人请求或仲裁庭认为确有必要的,仲裁庭可以要求当事方向专家提供相关信息,或向专家提供获得相关信息的渠道,包括相关文件、货物或财产。

　　35.获取证据过程中的法庭援助

　　·仲裁庭或经仲裁庭批准的一方当事人可以向有管辖权的法院(商业法院,上诉法院或最高法院)申请法庭援助以获取证据。法院(商业法院,上诉法院或最高法院)可以在其权能范围内,依照证据提取规则执行上述请求。

　　第七章　作出裁决及程序终止

　　36.解决实质性争端可适用的规则

　　·当事方可以约定仲裁庭审理争端时适用的法律。任何对一国法律或法律体系的指引都应当被详细分析;除非有明确的表示,法律的指引只涉及一国的实体法而不是其冲突法。

　　·当事方没有约定的,仲裁庭应当适用其认为最合适的法律。

　　·只要经当事方的明确授权,仲裁庭应当依善良原则和善地解决争端并充当友好调解人的角色。

　　·在任何案件中,仲裁庭都应当充分考虑仲裁协议的规定、贸易惯例和交易习惯。

　　37.仲裁员作出裁决

　　·在仲裁员人数大于一人的仲裁程序中,裁决依多数人意见作出。

38.争端的解决

• 经双方当事人的请求,在正式的仲裁程序开始之前,仲裁庭可以与当事方就是否能够达成无偿授产安排进行商讨;

• 若当事方认为可以达成,则仲裁庭可以以其认为适当的方式向当事方提供援助。

• 若当事方在正式的仲裁程序开始之前或在此过程之中解决了争端,仲裁庭应裁定终止仲裁程序;经当事方请求,仲裁庭可以将争端解决条件以仲裁裁决的形式记录下来。

• 应当依照本法第39条的规定制定附有双方同意条件的裁决,并声明该文件是一项裁决。该文件与其他仲裁裁决具有相同的法律地位和法律效力。

39.仲裁裁决的形式和内容

• 仲裁裁决应当以书面形式作出并由仲裁员签名。在有多个仲裁员的仲裁程序中,只要说明漏签的原因,有大多数仲裁员签名的裁决也具有效力。

• 仲裁裁决应当说明作出裁决所依据的理由,除非当事方同意可以没有裁决理由或裁决是依照本法第38条的规定作出的经当事方同意的有条件的裁决。

• 裁决应当以各方约定的方式将仲裁的成本分摊给各当事方,仲裁成本包括仲裁员费用和杂项费用;若当事方没有约定的,应当以仲裁庭认为适当的方式进行费用分摊。若当事方有约定或仲裁庭认为适当的,裁决可以规定给予胜诉当事方合理的律师费用。

• 依照本法第28(1)条的规定,仲裁裁决应当写明日期和仲裁地点。仲裁裁决应当被视为在上述地点作出的。

• 裁决作出后,应当依照本条第(1)款的规定,经仲裁员签字后递交给各当事方。

40.程序的终止

• 仲裁程序依仲裁裁决、和解协议或仲裁庭依本条第(2)款作出的终止命令而终止。仲裁庭在下列情况下应签发终止令:

• 仲裁申请人撤回申请,除非被申请人提出反对且仲裁庭认为争端的解决关系到其法律利益;

• 当事方同意终止程序;

• 仲裁庭因其他原因认为继续仲裁程序无意义或不可能。

• 仲裁庭依照本法第41条和第42(4)条的规定发布终止仲裁程序的指令。

41.对裁决的修正和解释以及补充裁决

• 应当在收到裁决后 30 日内作出,除非当事方对该期限另有约定。

• 一方当事人可以要求仲裁庭对仲裁裁决中的计算错误,书写、印刷错误或其他类似性质的错误进行纠正,同时通知另一当事方。

• 一方当事人可以要求仲裁庭对仲裁裁决中的某一特定问题或部分进行解释和阐述,同时通知另一当事方。若仲裁庭认为该要求是合理的,应当在接到请求后 30 日内给予解释和阐述。该解释和阐述构成裁决的一部分。

• 仲裁庭可以在其签发裁决之日起 30 日内,自行纠正本条第 1(a)款规定的错误。

• 除非当事方另有约定,在收到仲裁裁决后的 30 日内,当事方在通知另一方当事人之后,可以请求仲裁庭就其已提出仲裁申请但未经审理的事项作出补充裁决。若仲裁庭认为该要求是合理的,应当在接到请求后 30 日内作出补充裁决。

• 若经要求且通知当事方,仲裁庭可以延长其依本条第(1)、(3)款进行纠正、解释、阐述或作出补充裁决的期限。

• 仲裁庭进行纠正、解释、阐述或作出补充裁决应适用本法第 39 条的规定。

第八章　裁决的追索权、承认和强制执行

42.仲裁裁决的撤销申请

• 对于追索权、仲裁裁决的承认和强制执行的司法管辖权由柬埔寨上诉法院享有。

43.最终司法管辖权

• 柬埔寨最高法院拥有最终司法管辖权,当事方在收到上诉法院裁决后仍不满的,可以在收到上诉法院裁决后 15 日内向最高法院上诉。

44.仲裁裁决的撤销申请

• 当事方只能依照本条第(2)、(3)款的规定向法院提交撤销申请以对抗仲裁裁决。

• 只有在下述情况下,仲裁裁决有可能被上诉法院或最高法院裁定撤销:

• 当事方超过自收到仲裁裁决后 30 日期限的,或者当事方提交了本法第41 条的申请后的 30 日内,不能提交撤销申请。

• 上诉法院或最高法院在收到撤销申请后,经一方当事人申请或其认为适当的情形下,可以裁定中止撤销程序,在规定的中止期间内,仲裁庭可以重新仲裁或采取消除撤销裁决依据的行为。

45.裁决的承认和执行

·无论仲裁地位于哪一国家,仲裁裁决应当被视为具有法律约束力;经向有管辖权法院的书面申请,应当依照本条和本法第 44 条的规定执行仲裁裁决。

46.拒绝承认或执行的理由

·经一方当事人请求,若当事人向上诉法院提供了下列关于拒绝承认或执行仲裁裁决的证据:

·第 7 条规定的仲裁协议的一方当事人无行为能力的;或依据当事方的约定依照柬埔寨的法律,上述仲裁协议无效的;或

·作出申请的一方当事人并未提前就仲裁员或仲裁程序的指定向另一方发出通知,或不能有效地陈述其案情;或

·裁决涉及的争端不在仲裁协议约定的范围内,或者裁决超出了仲裁协议的约定范围,如果关于已提交仲裁的争端的裁决能够与未提交仲裁的争端的裁决区分开来,仅撤销未提交仲裁的争端的裁决;或

·仲裁组的组成或仲裁程序没有依照当事方的约定进行,或当事方没有约定时,未依照仲裁地法律的规定进行;或

·依据裁决作出地的法律,裁决还未对当事方产生法律约束力,或裁决被撤销或被裁决作出地法院裁定中止;或

·上诉法院认为依照柬埔寨法,仲裁所涉及的争议不能通过仲裁来解决;或

·裁决的承认会导致对柬埔寨公共政策的减损。

第九章 最终条款

47.废止

·商业仲裁章节中与本法不一致的规定一律被废止。

四、国家仲裁中心

为了能够通过商事仲裁解决商事纠纷,正如商事仲裁法规定的那样,政府发布了一项关于国家仲裁中心的组织和运作的附加法令。在与私人代表商讨附加法令的过程中,逐步形成了一项有利于中心高效和可持续运作的法令。

诚然,主要的商业团体包括柬埔寨商务协会联盟、柬埔寨服装制造协会和政府—私营部门论坛、法律、税收和治理工作组都积极地参与到了附加法令的讨论过程中来。其中,私营部门对制定附加法令和国家仲裁中心建立过程的

参与,是保证中心能够符合商业团体需要的关键因素。私营部门越来越倾向于选择利用国家仲裁中心来解决商事纠纷。

法律、附加法令和国家仲裁中心旨在促进仲裁的发展、培训仲裁员、在柬埔寨提供商事仲裁服务。国家仲裁中心正是在商务部的主持下建立的。建立国家仲裁中心的规定如下,见附加法令第三章:

• 商务部委任由 12 名来自不同政府机构和私营部门的代表组成的"发起与选举委员会"(附加法令第 45 条)。

• 该委员会由商务部代表担任主席,并公布了以创世成员身份加入国家仲裁中心的机会和最大限额为 60 名的候选人名单(第 47 条)。

• 至少 50 名候选人可以被推选参加由商务部组织的培训,顺利完成培训的候选人可以成为国家仲裁中心的成员(第 49 条)。

• 代表私营部门的商会和其他组织可以补充指派在国家仲裁中心大会有选举权的代表(第 34 条)。

• 国家仲裁中心大会的举办以及执行理事会的成立意味着国家仲裁中心的建立。

• 国家仲裁中心执行理事会任命一位执行秘书负责中心的日常工作。

五、关于国家仲裁中心组织和运作的附加法令

商事仲裁法颁布于 2009 年,共 9 章:

• 第一章　总则
• 第二章　地位和职能
• 第三章　结构
• 第四章　经费
• 第五章　首次仲裁员选举
• 第六章　过渡条款
• 第七章　最终条款

六、结论

柬埔寨的实践说明法律改革是国民经济发展的强大推动力。柬埔寨王国政府将继续致力于遵循依照联合国国际贸易法委员会范本而制定的商事仲裁法的内容;附加法令保证了国家仲裁中心的独立性,得到了来自律师、商务部

各部门、司法部各部门、法律和司法改革议会、司法部门和广大私营部门的支持。

柬埔寨为商业团体提供了一个除诉讼之外的另一种建立在劳动仲裁经验之上的更迅速、更低廉、更公平的争端解决途径,为高效解决争端、吸引投资提供了良好的环境。

在东亚—太平洋地区投资迅速增长的背景下,柬埔寨的商事仲裁法和国家仲裁中心对于国内及国际商业的发展具有重要的意义。

Commercial Arbitration Law and National Arbitration Center of Kingdom of Cambodia

Kim Bora* & Chea Karona**

Abstract　　This paper is prepared for Program of International Conference on "Legal Reform and Cooperation of CAFTA" under China-ASEAN cooperation. It describes some information such as: Background, Cambodia Context, Commercial Arbitration Law, National Arbitration Center, and Sub-decree on the Organization and Functioning of National Arbitration Center.

Cambodia has undergone sweeping changes, not only in the field of politics and security, but also in the country's economic and social landscape. Therefore, Commercial Arbitration Law and National Arbitration Center are important for improvement of Cambodia's standing among investors looking for opportunities in the Kingdom of Cambodia.

Keywords Commercial Arbitration Law and National Arbitration Center

Acronyms

ADR　　　　　Alternative Dispute Resolution

CAMFEBA　　Cambodian Federation of Employers and Business Associa-

---

* Chief of House of Justice of Access to Justice Project, Department of Legal Education and Dissemination, Ministry of Justice and

** Deputy Bureau Chief of Foreign Affairs, International Relation Department, Ministry of Justice.

tions
GMA   Garment Manufacturers Association of Cambodia
LAC   Labor Arbitration Council
NAC   National Arbitration Center
RGC   Royal Government of Cambodia
UNCITRAL   United Nations Commission on International Trade Law
WTO   World Trade Organization

I. Background

Cambodia has joined World Trade Organization (WTO) in 2005. Then, as the important role that dispute resolution plays in the development of a modern trading economy, a Commercial Arbitration Law (CAL) was included as a priority in this package of reforms.

The CAL was passed by Cambodia's National Assembly in 2006; establishing a framework for the private arbitration of business disputes that follows international practices. The law also envisages a National Arbitration Center (NAC), established under the auspices of the Ministry of Commerce. Following consultations with representatives of the business community and development partners, a Sub-decree on the organization and functioning of a National Arbitration Center was passed by the council of ministers on July 24, 2009.

The purposes of this commercial arbitration or commercial ADR services are understood to include mediation, conciliation and arbitration, as well as combinations of these practices. Specially, the NAC's goal is to offer the business community an alternative to the courts for the resolution of disputes, solving them more quickly, inexpensively, confidently, and fairly.

II. Cambodia Context

A. Economic Context

Cambodia has experienced a period of rapid economic expansion, with growth averaging 6.5％[1] over the 10 years period from 2000 to 2013. This has translated into major structural changes for the country, its people and the economy. Population growth has slowed and the country has become more urbanized. Poverty has been reduced significantly, with improvements in a range of social outcomes. The economy is modernizing from an agricultural base with industry and service sectors deve loping. Construction has grown and the development of banking and insurance sectors can be observed. The local stock exchange is practice in 2012. Exports have increased from almost nothing to 70％[2] of GDP and significant flows of foreign direct investment are making the country less aid-dependent. Although the current global economic crisis is having a significant impact on a range of sectors, including garment and construction, the Royal Government of Cambodia (RGC) continues to focus on the development of a business environment that will encourage both local and international invest-ment.

1. http://www.cbre.com.kh/2012/06/sees-cambodian-economic-growth-012/.

2. Cambodia Development Resource Institute.

B. Legal and Judicial Framework

In 1993, Cambodia had been changed its form into Kingdom of Cambodia because of the reign of Samdech Norodom Sihanouk. After, Cambodia set up its own government leading, free election in 1993, by two prime ministers in which one from the old government and another from democracy party's representative. However, the constitution is promulgated by senate in September, 1993 have 14 Chapters and 139 Article.

Cambodia has a unitary judiciary with courts of first instance at the provincial/municipal level. These courts have jurisdiction over all cases regardless of the nature or magnitude of the dispute. Appeals are heard by an Appeals Court, which sits in the capital. A further appeal may be made to the Supreme Court, which is the highest appellate court in all except electoral and constitutional matters.

The regulatory framework for commercial dispute resolution in

Cambodia is evolving rapidly. A new civil code and a code of civil procedures were promulgated in 2007 and 2006, respectively. The civil procedures code is now in force and the substantive civil code will enter into force once transitional arrangements have been completed. A proposal for the establishment of a commercial court is currently before the government and further legislation

Recognizing the need for more effective commercial dispute resolution systems, Cambodia enacted the CAL in March 2006. This law follows the UNCITRAL model and is generally considered to be of acceptable quality. Although the law does not specifically refer to mediation, it allows for mediation to occur as a way to facilitate the voluntary settlement of disputes (Article 38).

On the positive side, both the CAL and the civil procedures code provide for the standard limitations on the jurisdiction of the court with regard to arbitral proceedings. Thus the Law instructs courts to refer matters which are the subject of an arbitration agreement to arbitration (Article 8); provides the arbitral tribunal with the competence to rule on its own jurisdiction (Article 24); and limits the power of the courts to set aside or refuse to enforce an award in the instances specified in the UNCITRAL model law (Articles 44 & 46). These provisions are reinforced by Article 353 of the civil procedures code, which restates the requirement to enforce restrictions on courts to hear the merits of cases subject to arbitration.

Ⅲ. Commercial Arbitration Law

The *Commercial Arbitration Law* (CAL) promulgated in 2006 and has 9 chapters and 47 articles as below:

Chapter Ⅰ General Provision

1. Purpose and Scope of Application

• The purpose of this law is to facilitate the impartial and prompt resolution of commercial disputes in accordance with the wishes of the parties, to safeguard the legal rights and interests of the parties, and to promote the sound development of the economy.

• This Law shall not affect any other law of the Kingdom of Cambodia by virtue of which certain dispute may be submitted to arbitration or other dispute resolution procedures, or by virtue of which certain disputes may not be submitted to arbitration.

2. Definitions and Rules of Interpretation

• "Arbitration" means any arbitration whether or not administered by a permanent arbitral institution.

• "Arbitral tribunal" means a sole arbitrator or a panel of arbitrators.

• "Court" means a body or organ of the judicial system of a state.

• "Arbitration agreement" is an agreement by the parties to submit to arbitration all or certain disputes which have arisen or which may arise between them in respect of a defined legal relationship, whether contractual or not.

• Where a provision of this law, except Article 36 of this Law, leaves the parties free to determine a certain issue, such freedom includes the right of the parties to authorize a third party, including an institution, to make that determination.

• Where a provision of this Law refers to the fact that the parties have agreed, or that they may agree, or in any other way refers to an agreement of the parties, such agreement includes any rules referred to in that agreement.

• Where a provision of this Law, other than in Articles 33(a) and 40 (a), refers to a claim, it also applies to a counter-claim, and where it refers to a defense, it also applies to a defense to such counter-claim.

• An arbitration is "international" if

• The parties to an arbitration agreement have their places of business in different states at the time of the conclusion of that agreement; or

• One of the following places is situated outside the state in which the parties have their places of business;

• The parties have expressly agreed that the subject matter of the arbitration agreement relates to more than one country.

3. Receipt of Written Communications

• Any written communication is deemed to have been received if it is delivered to the addressee personally, or if it is delivered at his place of business, habitual residence or mailing address; if none of these can be found after making a reasonable inquiry, a written communication is deemed to have been received if it is sent to the addressee's last known place of business, habitual residence or at the last known address of the addressee.

• The provisions of Article 3 of this Law do not apply to communications in court proceedings.

4. Waiver of Right to Object

• A party who knows that any provision of this Law from which parties may derogate, or any requirement under the arbitration agreement, has not been complied with, and yet proceeds with the arbitration without stating his objection to such non-compliance without undue delay or, if a time limit is provided therefore, within such period of time, shall be deemed to have waived his right to object.

5. Extent of Court Intervention

• In matters governed by this Law, no court shall intervene except where so provided in this Law.

6. Court of other Authority for Certain Functions of Arbitration Assistance Supervision

• The functions referred to in Articles 19(3), 19(4), and 19(5); 21 (3); 22; and 24 (3) of this law shall be performed by the Court (Commercial, or Appeal, or Supreme) or National Arbitration Center.

Chapter Ⅱ Arbitration Agreement

7. Definition and Form of Arbitration Agreement

• Arbitration agreement includes an arbitration clause in a contract or a separate submission agreement.

• The arbitration agreement shall be in writing. An agreement is in writing if it is contained in a document signed by the parties or in an exchange of letters, or other means of electronic telecommunication which provide a record of the agreement, or in an exchange of statements of claim and defense in which the existence of an agreed is alleged by one party and not denied by another. The reference in a contract to a document containing an arbitration clause constitutes an arbitration agreement, provided that the contract is in writing and the reference is such as to make the clause part of the contract.

8. Arbitration Agreement and Substantive Claim before Court

• A court before which an action is brought in a matter which is the subject of an arbitration agreement shall, if a party so requests not later than when submitting his first statement on the substance of the dispute, refer the parties to arbitration unless it finds that the agreement is null and void, inoperative or incapable of being performed.

• Where an action referred to in paragraph (1) of this Article has been brought, arbitral proceedings may nevertheless be commenced or continued and the court shall refer the issue to the arbitration, while it is pending before the arbitration.

9. Arbitration Agreement and Interim Measures by Court

• It is not incompatible with an arbitration agreement for a party to request, before or during arbitral proceedings from a court an interim measure of protection and for a court to grant such measure.

Chapter Ⅲ National Center of Commercial Arbitration

10. National Arbitration Center

• An independent National Arbitration Center (NAC) shall be established under the auspices of Ministry of Commerce. The objectives of the National Arbitration Center are:

• To promote settlement of commercial disputes by means of arbitration in Cambodia;

• To create the necessary infrastructure and rules for the administration of arbitration cases in the Kingdom of Cambodia, where an express agreement of disputing parties to refer disputes to National Arbitration Center;

11. Arbitrators

• The Khmer natural person or foreigner who is arbitrator shall register with the National Arbitration Center. The National Arbitration Center shall have an obligation to determine the arbitrators' qualification and shall make the public announcement of arbitrators' list yearly. The list is not absolute; the parties are free to choose the arbitrator outside that list.

12. Qualification of Members of Arbitrators

• The natural person and legal entity to be permitted as a member of the National Arbitration Center are:

• An arbitrator who has registered his/her name with the National Arbitration Center;

• The Chamber of Commerce;

• The Bar of the Kingdom of Cambodia; and

• The Association that comprises of businessman, industrialist, merchant and services provider.

• The application to be a member of the National Arbitration Center shall be determined by the Executive Board of the National Arbitration Center that comprises not more than seven (7) members. The term of each member is three (3) years and may re-elect for one more term.

13. The Chamber of Commerce and Chamber of Professions

• The Chamber of Commerce may establish an arbitration center in Phnom Penh. The Association that comprises of businessman, industrialist, merchant and services provider may establish its own arbitral institution for disputes arising among its members; and between its members and third party.

14. Management of National Chamber of Professions

• The National Arbitration Center shall be governed by:

• A General Assembly; and

• An Executive Office.

• The General Assembly shall have inter alia functions and duties:

• To meet one or twice per year at the request of the Chairman of the National Arbitration Center or at the request of the majority members of Executive Board;

• To elect the Executive Board;

• To inspect the annual report of Executive Board;

• To approve the financial budget of National Arbitration Center;

• To determine the fees and costs of arbitration;

• To approve the amendment of rules and regulations that related to the operation of National Arbitration Center and functioning of arbitration; and

• To fulfill other functions and duties that determined in the Sub-decree of the organization and functioning of National Arbitration Center.

15. The General Assembly

• The General Assembly shall be attended by the members who are natural persons and a representative of each legal entity.

16. Composition of Executive Board

• The Executive Board that manages the National Arbitration Center shall be elected among its members by the General Assembly. The Chairman of Executive Board shall be the Chairman of the National Arbitration Center.

17. Organization and Functioning of National Arbitration Center

• The organization and functioning of National Arbitration Center shall be determined by implementing Sub-decree.

Chapter Ⅳ Composition of Arbitral Tribunal

18. Number of Arbitrations

• The parties are free to determine the number of arbitrators. The number of arbitrators shall be odd number.

• Failing such determination, the number of arbitrators shall be three (3).

19. Appointment of Arbitrations

• The appointment of arbitrator shall determine as follows:

• No person shall be precluded by reason of his nationality from acting as an arbitrator, unless otherwise agreed by the parties.

• The parties are free to agree on a procedure for appointing the arbitrator or arbitrators, subject to the provisions of paragraphs (4) and (5) of this Article.

• A decision on a matter entrusted by paragraph (3) or (4) of this Article to the Court (Commercial, or Appeal, or Supreme) or National Arbitration Center as specified in Article 6 of this Law shall be subject to no appeal. The Court (Commercial, or Appeal, or Supreme) or National Arbitration Center as specified in Article 6 of this Law, in appointing an arbitrator, shall have due regard to any qualifications required of the arbitrator by the agreement of the parties and to such considerations as are likely to secure the appointment of an independent and impartial arbitrator. In the case of a sole or third arbitrator in an international arbitration, the Court (Commercial, or Appeal, or Supreme) or National Arbitration Center as specified in Article 6 of this Law shall take into account as well the advisability of appointing an arbitrator of a nationality other than those of the parties as specified in Article 19(1) of this Law.

20. Ground for Challenge

• When a person is approached in connection with his possible appointment as an arbitrator, he shall disclose any circumstances likely to give rise to justifiable doubts as to his impartiality or independence. An arbitrator, from the time of his appointment and throughout the arbitral proceedings, shall without delay disclose any such circumstances to the parties, unless they have already been informed of them by him.

• An arbitrator may be challenged only if circumstances exist that give rise to justifiable doubts as to his impartiality or independence, or if he does not possess qualifications agreed to by the parties. A party may challenge an arbitrator appointed by him, or in whose appointment he has participated, only for reasons of which he becomes aware after the appointment has been made.

21. Challenge Procedure

• The parties are free to agree on a procedure for challenging an arbitrator, subject to the provisions of paragraph (3) of this Article.

• Failing such agreement, a party who intends to challenge an arbitrator shall, within fifteen (15) days after becoming aware of the constitution of the arbitral tribunal or after becoming aware of any circumstance referred to in Article 20 (2) of this Law, sends a written statement of the reasons for the challenge to the arbitral tribunal and the other party or parties. Unless the challenged arbitrator withdraws from his office or the other party agrees to the challenge, the arbitral tribunal shall decide on the challenge.

• If a challenge under any procedure agreed upon by the parties or under the procedure of paragraph (2) of this Article is not successful, the challenging party may request, within thirty days after having received notice of the decision rejecting the challenge, the Court (Commercial, or Appeal, or Supreme) or National Arbitration Center as specified in Article 6 of this Law to decide on the challenge, which decision shall be subject to no appeal; while such a request is pending, the arbitral tribunal, including the challenged arbitrator, may continue the arbitral proceedings and make an award.

22. Failure or Impossibility to Act

• If an arbitrator becomes De Jure or De Facto unable to perform his functions, or for other reasons fails to act without undue delay, his mandate terminates if he withdraws from his office or if the parties agree on the termination. Otherwise, if a controversy remains concerning any of these grounds, any party may request the Court (Commercial, or Appeal, or Supreme) or National Arbitration Center as specified in Article 6 of this Law to decide on the termination of the mandate, which decision shall be subject to no appeal.

• If, under this Article or Article 21(2), an arbitrator withdraws from his office or a party agrees to the termination of the mandate of an arbitrator, this does not imply acceptance of the validity of any ground referred to in this Article or Article 20(2).

23. Appointment of Substitute Arbitrator

• Where the mandate of an arbitrator terminates under Article 21 or 22 of this Law, a substitute arbitrator shall be appointed according to Article 19 of this Law.

Chapter Ⅴ Jurisdiction of Arbitral Tribunal

24. Competence of Arbitral Tribunal to Rule on Its Jurisdiction

• The arbitral tribunal may rule on its own jurisdiction, including any objections with respect to the existence or validity of the arbitration agreement. For that purpose, an arbitration clause that forms part of a contract shall be treated as an agreement independent of the other terms of the contract. A decision by the arbitral tribunal that the contract is null and void shall not entail Ipso Jure the invalidity of the arbitration clause.

• A plea that the arbitral tribunal does not have jurisdiction shall be raised not later than the submission of the statement of defense. A party is not precluded from raising such a plea by the fact that he has appointed, or participated in the appointment of, an arbitrator. A plea that the arbitral tribunal is exceeding the scope of its authority shall be raised as soon as the matter alleged to be beyond the scope of its authority is raised during the arbitral proceedings. The arbitral tribunal may, in either case, admit a later plea if it considers the delay justified.

• The arbitral tribunal may rule on a plea referred to in paragraph (2) of this Article either as a preliminary question or in an award on the merits. If the arbitral tribunal rules as a preliminary question that it has jurisdiction, any party may request, within thirty(30) days after having received notice of that ruling, the court specified in Article 6 to decide the matter, which decision shall be subject to no appeal; while such a request is pending, the arbitral tribunal may continue the arbitral proceedings and make an award.

25. Power of Arbitral Panel to Order Interim Measures

• Unless otherwise agreed by the parties, the arbitral panel may, at the request of a party, order any party to take such interim measure of protection as the arbitral panel may consider necessary in respect of the subject matter of the dispute. The arbitral panel may require any party to provide appropriate security in connection with such measure.

Chapter Ⅵ Conduct of Arbitral Proceedings

26. Equal Treatment of Parties

• The parties shall be with equality and each party shall be given a full opportunity to present his case, including representation by any party of his choice.

27. Determination of Rule of Procedure

• The parties are free to agree or disagree on the procedure to be followed by the arbitral tribunal in conducting the proceedings.

• Failing such agreement, the arbitral tribunal may, subject to the provisions of this Law, conduct the arbitration in such manner as it considers appropriate. The power conferred upon the arbitral tribunal includes the power to determine the admissibility, relevance, materiality and weight of any evidence.

28. Place of Arbitration

• The parties are free to agree on the place of arbitration. Failing such agreement, the place of arbitration shall be determined by the arbitral tribunal having regard to the circumstances of the case, including the agreement of the parties.

• Notwithstanding the provisions of paragraph (1) of this Article, the arbitral tribunal may, unless otherwise agreed by the parties, meet at any place it considers appropriate for consultation among its members, for hearing witnesses, experts, or the parties, or to conduct inspection to equipment, property or other documents.

29. Commencement of Arbitral Proceedings

• Unless otherwise agreed by the parties, the arbitral proceedings in respect of a particular dispute commence on the date on which a request for that dispute to be referred to arbitration is received by the respondent.

30. Language

• The parties are free to agree on the language or languages to be used in the arbitral proceedings. Failing such agreement, the arbitral tribunal shall determine the language or languages to be used in the proceedings.

• The arbitral tribunal may order that any documentary evidence shall be accompanied by a translation into the language or languages agreed upon by the parties or determined by the arbitral tribunal.

31. Statements of Claim and Defense

• Within the period of time agreed by the parties or determined by the arbitral panel, the claimant shall state the facts supporting his claim, the points at issue and the relief of remedy sought, and the respondent shall state his defense in respect of these particulars, unless the parties have otherwise agreed as to the required elements of such statements. The parties may submit with their statements all documents they consider to be relevant or may add a reference to the documents or other evidence they will submit.

• Unless otherwise agreed by the parties, either party may amend or supplement his claim or defense during the course of the arbitral proceedings, unless the arbitral panel considers it inappropriate to allow such amendment, having regard to the delay in making it.

32. Hearings and Written Proceedings

• Subject to any contrary agreement by the parties, the arbitral tribunal shall decide whether to hold oral hearings for the presentation of evidence or for oral argument, or whether the proceedings shall be conducted on the basis of documents and other materials. However, unless the parties have agreed that no hearings shall be held, the arbitral tribunal shall hold such hearings at an appropriate stage of the proceedings, if so requested by a party.

• The parties shall be given sufficient advance notice of any hearing and of any meeting of the arbitral tribunal for the purposes of inspection of materials, goods, other property or documents.

. All statements, documents or other information supplied to the arbitral tribunal by one party shall be communicated to the other party. Also, any expert report or evidentiary document on which the arbitral tribunal may rely in making its decision shall be communicated to the parties.

33. Default of a Party

• The claimant fails to communicate his statement of claim in accordance with Article 31(1) of this Law, the arbitral panel shall terminate the proceedings.

• The respondent fails to communicate his statement of defense in accordance with Article 31(1) of this Law, the arbitral panel shall continue the proceedings without treating such failure in itself as an admission of the claimant's allegations.

• Any party fails to appear at a hearing, or fails to produce documentary evidence; the arbitral panel may continue the proceedings and make the award on the evidence before it.

34. Expert Appointed by Arbitral Tribunal

• May appoint one or more experts to report to it on specific issues to be determined by the arbitral tribunal.

• May require a party to give the expert any relevant information, or to produce, or to provide access to, any relevant documents, goods or other property for his inspection. Unless otherwise agreed by the parties, if a party so requests, or if the arbitral tribunal considers.

35. Court Assistance in Taking Evidence

• The arbitral tribunal, or a party with the approval of the arbitral tribunal, may request from a competent Court (Commercial, or Appeal, or Supreme) assistance in taking evidence. The Court (Commercial, or Appeal, or Supreme) may execute the request within its competence and according to its rules on taking evidence.

Chapter Ⅶ Making of Award and Termination of Proceedings

36. Rules Applicable to Substance of Dispute

• The parties shall be free to agree upon the rules of law to be applied by arbitral tribunal to the merits of the dispute. Any designation of the law or legal system of a given state shall be construed, unless otherwise expressed, as directly referring to the substantive law of that state and not to its conflict of laws rules.

• Failing such an agreement by the parties, the arbitral tribunal shall apply the law that it considers appropriate.

• The arbitral tribunal shall decide ex aegu et bono or as amiable compositeur only if the parties have expressly authorized it to do so.

• In all cases, the arbitral tribunal shall take into account all the provisions of the arbitration agreement and also the usages of the trade and customs applicable to the transaction.

37. Decision Making by Panel of Arbitrators

• In arbitral proceedings with more than one arbitrator, any decision of the arbitral tribunal may be made by a majority of all its members.

38. Settlement

• Upon request by both parties, prior to commencement of formal arbitration proceedings, the arbitral tribunal may confer with the parties for the purpose of exploring whether the possibility exists of a voluntary settlement of the parties' dispute:

• If the parties determine that it does, the arbitral tribunal shall assist the parties in any manner it deems appropriate.

• If the parties settle the dispute prior to commencement of the formal arbitral proceedings, or in the course thereof, the arbitral tribunal shall terminate the proceedings and, if requested by the parties, may record the settlement in the form of an arbitral award on agreed terms.

• An award on agreed terms shall be made in accordance with the provisions of Article 39 of this Law, and shall state that it is an award. Such an award has the same status and effect as any other award on the merits of the case.

39. Form and Content of Award

• The award shall be made in writing and shall be signed by the arbitrator or arbitrators. In arbitral proceedings with more than one arbitrator, the signatures of the majority of all members of the arbitral tribunal shall suffice, provided that the reason for any omitted signature is stated.

• The award shall state the reasons upon which it is based, unless the parties have agreed that no reasons are to be given or the award is an award on agreed terms under Article 38 of this Law.

• The award shall allocate among the parties the costs of the arbitration, including the arbitrator(s) fee(s) and incidental expenses, in the manner agreed by the parties, or in the absence of such agreement, as the arbitrators deem appropriate. If the parties have so agreed, or the arbitrators deem it appropriate, the award may also provide for recovery by the prevailing party of reasonable counsel fees.

• The award shall state its date and the place of arbitration as determined in accordance with Article 28(1) of this Law. The award shall be deemed to have been made at that place.

• After the award is made, a copy signed by the arbitrators in accordance with paragraph (1) of this Article shall be delivered to each party.

40. Termination of Proceeding

• The arbitral proceedings are terminated by the final award, an agreed settlement, or by an order of the arbitral tribunal in accordance with paragraph (2) of this Article. The arbitral tribunal shall issue an order for the termination of the arbitral proceedings when:

• The claimant withdraws his claim, unless the respondent objects thereto and the arbitral tribunal recognizes a legitimate interest on his part in obtaining a final settlement of the dispute;

• The parties agree on the termination of the proceedings;

• The arbitral tribunal finds that the continuation of the proceedings has, for any other reason, become unnecessary or impossible.

• The mandate of the arbitral tribunal terminates with the termination of the arbitral proceedings, subject to the provisions of Articles 41 and 42 (4) of this Law.

41. Correction and Interpretation of Award, Additional Award

• Within thirty (30) days of the receipt of the award, unless another period of time has been agreed upon by the parties.

• With notice to the other party, a party may request the arbitral tribunal to correct in the award any errors in computation, any clerical or typographical errors, or any other errors of a similar nature.

• With notice to the other party, a party may request the arbitral tribunal to give an interpretation or amplification of a specific point or part of the award. If the arbitral tribunal considers the request justified, it shall provide the interpretation or amplification within thirty(30) days of receipt of the request. The interpretation or amplification shall form part of the award.

• Within no later than thirty (30) days after the issuance of award by the arbitral tribunal, the arbitration may correct the errors stated in paragraph 1(a) of this Article at its own initiatives.

• Unless otherwise agreed by the parties, within no later than thirty (30) days after receiving an award as to the claims, the party who has notified another party may request for additional awards presented in the arbitral proceeding but omitted from the award. If the arbitral tribunal considers the request justified, it shall make the additional award within thirty (30) days of receipt of the request.

• If it is required and by notifying the parties, the arbitral tribunal may extend the period of time with which it shall make a correction, interpretation, amplification, or additional award under paragraph (1) and (3) of this Article.

• The provisions of Article 39 of this Law shall apply to a correction, interpretation or amplification, or an addition to the award.

Chapter VIII Recourse, Recognition, and Enforcement of Arbitration Award

42. Application for Setting Aside as Exclusive Recourse against Arbitral Award

• The jurisdiction over recourse, recognition, and enforcement of arbitral award shall rest with the appellate court of the Kingdom of Cambodia.

43. Conclusive Jurisdiction

• The Supreme Court of Cambodia shall be the final jurisdiction to try counter claim of the party who is not satisfying with the decision of the appellate court within fifteen (15) days.

44. Application for Setting Aside as Exclusive Recourse against Arbitral Award

• Recourse to a court against an arbitral award may be made only by an application for setting aside in accordance with paragraphs (2) and (3) of this Article.

• An arbitral award may be set aside by the Appeal Court and Supreme Court only if:

• An application for setting aside may not be made after thirty (30) days have elapsed from the date on which the party making that application had received the award or, if a request had been made under Article 41 of this article within thirty (30) days, from the date on which that request had been disposed of by the arbitral tribunal.

• The Appeal Court and Supreme Court, when asked to set aside an award, may, where appropriate and so requested by a party, suspend the setting aside proceedings for a period of time determined by the Appeal Court and Supreme Court, in order to give the arbitral tribunal an opportunity to resume the arbitral proceedings or to take such other action as in the arbitral tribunal's opinion will eliminate the grounds for setting aside.

45. Recognition and Enforcement

• An arbitral award, irrespective of the country in which it was made, shall be recognized as binding and, upon application in writing to the competent court, shall be enforced subject to the provisions of this Article and Article 44 of this Law.

46. Grounds for Refusing Recognition or Enforcement

• At the request the party against whom it is invoked, if that party furnishes to the Appeal Court where recognition or enforcement is sought proof that:

• A party to the arbitration agreement referred to in Article 7 was under some incapacity; or the said agreement is not valid under the law to which the parties have subjected it or, failing, any indication by the parties, under the law of the Kingdom of Cambodia; or

• The party making the application was not given proper notice of the appointment of an arbitrator(s) or of the arbitral proceedings, or was otherwise unable effectively to present his case; or

• The award deals with a dispute not contemplated by or not falling within the terms of the arbitration agreement, or contains decisions on matters beyond the scope of the arbitration agreement, provided that, if the decisions on matters submitted to arbitration can be separated from those not so submitted, only that part of the award which contains decisions on matters not submitted to arbitration may be set aside; or

• The composition of the arbitral panel or the arbitral procedure was not in accordance with the agreement of the parties or, failing such agreement, was not in accordance with the law of the where the arbitration took place; or

• The award has not yet become binding on the parties in the country in which, or under the law of which, that award was made, or the award has been set aside or suspended by a court in the country which the award was made; or

• The Appeal Court finds that the subject matter of the dispute is, not capable of settlement by arbitration under the law of the Kingdom of Cambodia; or

• The recognition of the award would be contrary to public policy of the Kingdom of Cambodia.

Chapter Ⅸ Final Provisions

47. Abrogation

• Any provisions in commercial arbitration sector that are contrary to this Law shall be abrogated.

IV. National Arbitration Center

For the purpose of enabling businesses to resolve their disputes through commercial arbitration, the government, as set forth in the Commercial Arbitration Law, issued a Sub-decree on the organization and functioning of a National Arbitration Center. During the dialogue process with the private sector on the Sub-decree, there provided an adequate structure for an effective and sustainable NAC.

Importantly, major business groups, including the Cambodian Federation of Business Associations (CAMFEBA), the Garment Manufacturers Association of Cambodia (GMAC) and the Law, Tax and Governance Working Group of the Government-Private Sector Forum were actively involved in the consultation process on the Sub-decree. The participation of the private sector in the preparation of the Sub-decree, as well as in process of establishing the NAC, is a key factor for ensuring the NAC meets the needs of the business community. The increase of likelihood of private sector had chosen to utilize the NAC to resolve commercial disputes.

The Law and Sub-decree, the NAC has designed to have a leading role in promoting arbitration, training arbitrators and providing commercial arbitration services in Cambodia. The NAC is established under the auspices of the Ministry of Commerce. The provisions for the establishment of the NAC set out in Chapter 3 of the Sub-decree can be summarized as follows:

• The Ministry of Commerce appoints an "Inception and Selection Commission" comprising 12 members from various government agencies and private sector representatives (Article 45 of the Sub-decree).

• This commission, chaired by the representative of the Ministry of Commerce, announces the opportunity to join the NAC as a founding member and shortlists a maximum of 60 applicants (Article 47); Sub-decree on the organization and functioning of the NAC.

• At least 50 of these applicants will be selected to participate in a training course organized by the Ministry of Commerce, the successful completion of which will qualify them to become members of the NAC (Article 49).

• Chambers of Commerce and other organizations representing the private sector may appoint additional representatives who have a right to vote in the General Assembly of the NAC (Article 34).

• The NAC is established once a meeting of the general assembly of the NAC is held and a seven member Executive Board elected; and

• The Executive Board of the NAC then appoints a secretary general to take responsibility for the day-to-day management of the Center.

V. Sub-decree on the Organization and Functioning of a National Arbitration Center

The Commercial Arbitration Law (CAL) promulgated in 2009 and has 9 chapters as below:
• Chapter Ⅰ General Provisions
• Chapter Ⅱ Role and Functions
• Chapter Ⅲ Structure
• Chapter Ⅳ Funding and Recourses
• Chapter Ⅴ First Selection of Arbitrator
• Chapter Ⅵ Transitional Provisions
• Chapter Ⅶ Final Provisions

Ⅵ. Conclusion

Cambodia clearly demonstrates that legal reform is a great factor for national economic development. The RGC continues to focus on the Quality of law on commercial arbitration that is compliance with UNCITRAL model law, Sub-decree allows for an independent NAC, and support from lawyers, key ministries of Commerce and ministries of Justice, Council for Legal and Judicial Reform, the judiciary and a range of private sector actors for the establishment of an independent ADR center to give businesses greater confidence.

Cambodia made NAC to offer the business community an alternative to the courts for the resolution of disputes, solving them more quickly, inexpensively and fairly depend on experience through labor arbitration that have effective, efficient dispute resolution to build a better climate for Cambodia to attract investment.

Cambodia has CAL and NAC that would be extremely important for local and international businesses have been operated investment in this fast-growing region of east Asia-Pacific.

References:

Cambodia Development Resource Institute. Commercial Arbitration Law. Sub-decree on the Organization and Functioning of a National Arbitration Center. http://www. cbre. com. kh/2012/06/sees-cambodian-economic-growth-012/.

马来西亚仲裁的一般规定以及对于马来西亚仲裁终局裁决的案例分析

Chan Szu Fu* & Wong Keat Ching**

孙超 译

摘要 本文第一部分将介绍2005年仲裁法案中有关仲裁的一般规定以及可适用于马来西亚仲裁的一些国际条约。第二部分是涉及不同国家及司法管辖权问题下的由马来西亚法院作出裁决的六个案件的案例分析,这些案件涉及中东(埃及)、亚洲(中国)、欧盟、俄罗斯、东盟(老挝和泰国)以及在马来西亚成立的外国公司。这些案例彰显了马来西亚法院在对待仲裁裁决以及仲裁协议效力上的一致性做法。

关键词 2005年仲裁法案 马来西亚法院 投资 争端解决 仲裁协议 仲裁裁决

第一部分 马来西亚的仲裁

临时仲裁以及机构仲裁在马来西亚都很常见。国内事项的机构仲裁大多是由吉隆坡地区仲裁中心(KLRCA)受理的。而国际事项的机构仲裁经常因仲裁协议而选择由国际商会(ICC)以及伦敦国际仲裁院受理,而近些年来由新加坡国际仲裁中心以及香港国际仲裁中心受理国际性仲裁也成为较为普遍的选择。

---

* 马来西亚昌德·弗里斯事务所合伙人,大律师(中殿),马来亚高等法院辩护人及律师。

** 马来西亚祖尔拉菲克与合作伙伴律师事务所合伙人,马来亚高等法院辩护人及律师。

国内仲裁法

马来西亚 2005 年仲裁法案管辖仲裁地在马来西亚的仲裁活动。该法案是以联合国国际贸易法委员会 1985 年示范法为基础的。该法第三章规定了该法适用于国内及国际仲裁,并且仅在与本法第三部分的一些事项上有所不同,如:仲裁的合并或共同听证,高等法院对于初步法律问题的决定,对于高等法院关于法律问题的参考,上诉、仲裁的费用等。除非另有协议,在马来西亚作为仲裁地的国内仲裁其准据法应当为马来西亚的实体法。

国际仲裁协议

马来西亚是《纽约公约》的缔约国之一。2005 年法案的第 38 章规定国内仲裁或仲裁地在马来西亚的一项外国仲裁裁决应当受到本法的约束并且该项裁决应当能够在马来西亚执行。该章同时还规定"外国"的含义为,该国应为纽约公约的缔约国。

马来西亚同样也是《关于解决投资争端公约》(ICSID)的缔约国之一,并且投资争端解决公约法案在 1996 年开始施行。而且,马来西亚也是东盟《关于加强争端解决机制议定书》(越南议定书)的缔约国之一,这一议定书涵盖了东盟经济协议以及东盟 2007 年宪章(这一宪章是作为东盟争端解决的首要性框架协议出现的)。东盟成员之间的广泛的投资协议也提供了解决成员国与另一国投资者之间争端解决的机制。

1958 年相互执行裁决法案提供了一种可供选择的执行外国仲裁裁决的方法,即如果胜诉方可以将其仲裁裁决转换为具有司法管辖权的法院的一项判决,那么这样的仲裁裁决就将可以在该法案下得以执行。

2005 年法案还规定了仲裁准据法的问题:协议有规定的,按照双方协议;没有规定的,仲裁庭应当按照冲突法规则来确定仲裁准据法。

仲裁员的选择

2005 年法案允许争端方自行决定仲裁庭的结构以及聘任,可以依据任何可适用的仲裁规则来进行。

在 2005 年法案中关于仲裁员聘任程序的规定在该法的第 13 章。第 13 章与示范法第 11 条相一致,采用了两层方法来授予双方决定聘任仲裁员的程序的权利,也规定了在双方对于该程序不能达成一致时的处理机制。

2005 年仲裁法案规定,如果双方在仲裁协议中未就如何选聘仲裁员进行规定,或者没有达成一致,或者一方拒绝行使该项权利,那么吉隆坡地方仲裁中心主任将被授权决定选任仲裁员,并且他必须在 30 天之内行使这项权利,否则双方将有权诉诸法院来完成选任。

法院执行仲裁协议的方法

作为一般规则,法院尊重仲裁协议,并且不介入其中。为了赋予仲裁协议效力,根据 2005 年仲裁法案第 10 章的规定,法院一般会在涉及仲裁事项时发出中止令来暂停法庭中的行动。但是如果仲裁协议是无效的,或者不能被实施,或者双方事实上并没有争端,根据该法的相关规定是很难被施行的。

损害赔偿及利息裁决

损害赔偿是作为救济途径最为常见的一种形式。仲裁员可能会作出常规性的、专门性的以及惩戒性的损害赔偿裁决。该法第 33 章第 6 条规定,除非仲裁协议另有规定,仲裁庭可以对自裁决作出至裁决履行期间的任何一笔金钱裁决支付利息,并有权决定利率。

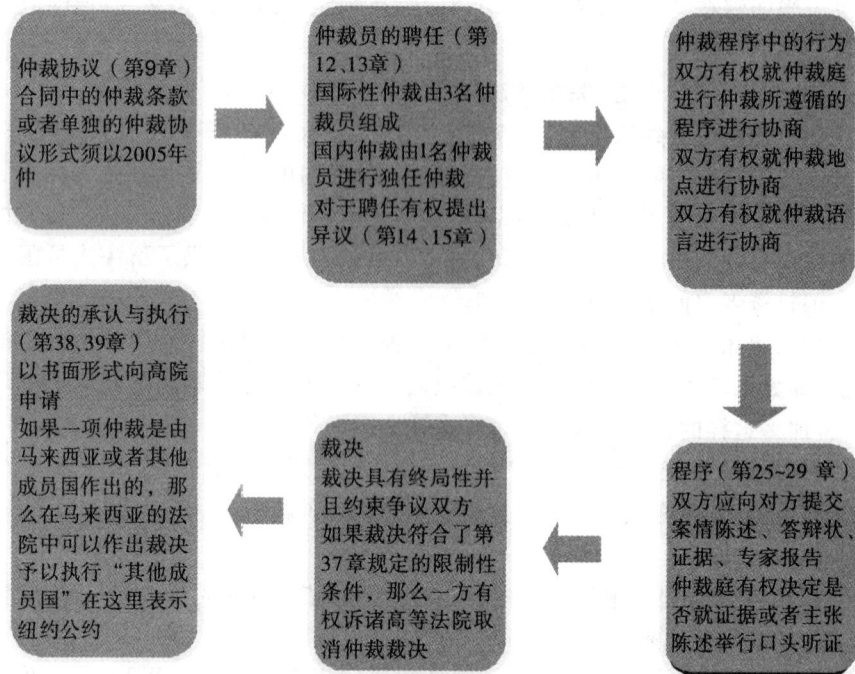

仲裁协议（第9章）
合同中的仲裁条款或者单独的仲裁协议形式须以2005年仲

仲裁员的聘任（第12、13章）
国际性仲裁由3名仲裁员组成
国内仲裁由1名仲裁员进行独任仲裁
对于聘任有权提出异议（第14、15章）

仲裁程序中的行为
双方有权就仲裁庭进行仲裁所遵循的程序进行协商
双方有权就仲裁地点进行协商
双方有权就仲裁语言进行协商

裁决的承认与执行（第38、39章）
以书面形式向高院申请
如果一项仲裁是由马来西亚或者其他成员国作出的,那么在马来西亚的法院中可以作出裁决予以执行"其他成员国"在这里表示纽约公约

裁决
裁决具有终局性并且约束争议双方
如果裁决符合了第37章规定的限制性条件,那么一方有权诉诸高等法院取消仲裁裁决

程序（第25~29章）
双方应向对方提交案情陈述、答辩状、证据、专家报告
仲裁庭有权决定是否就证据或者主张陈述举行口头听证

2005 年仲裁法法案条款概要

第二部分:在马来西亚进行终局性仲裁裁决的案例分析

取消马来西亚之外的仲裁裁决?

1. Twin Advance (M) Sdn. Bhd. v Polar Electro Europe BV［2013］7

MLJ 811 High Court（Pulau Pinang）

案情摘要：

原告与被告曾一致同意争端在新加坡进行仲裁。在发出传唤（以下称"传唤"）的同时，原告意图依据2005年仲裁法案（以下称"法案"）第37章第37条来撤销仲裁裁决。而被告方援引1980年高等法院规则第18条律令第19（1）规则进行抗辩，称马来西亚的高等法院既没有固有的管辖权也没有法律依据可以指引其驳回新加坡作出的裁决结果。

原告方辩称既然该法案的第38、39章赋予了法院承认并执行国内、国际仲裁裁决的管辖权，那么第37章应当被类推使用，即允许法院驳回在马来西亚以外作出的裁决。但是被告称，根据该法案第3章的明确规定，该法仅适用于以马来西亚为仲裁地的国内以及国外仲裁，因此第37条不能被援引来作为驳回处理马来西亚之外的仲裁裁决的依据。

判决同意被告方的申请并且不负担传唤所产生的诉讼费用：

（1）该法案第37章可以被援引适用于仲裁地在马来西亚的仲裁裁决，但不适用于仲裁地在马来西亚之外的仲裁裁决。法院固有的管辖权要求其不干涉仲裁领域，也不得剥夺原告方向新加坡高等法院申请驳回受理在新加坡作出的仲裁裁决的请求的权利。

（2）该法案的立法明确表明，第38、39章是被作为第3章的例外，不同并且独立于第37章的。如果第37章包含了驳回外国仲裁裁决的意思，那么法案中会明确进行表述。既然条文中没有明确表达，那么仲裁地的确定应当是依据这样的法律原则，即作出仲裁裁决之地，该地的法律是可以被适用并且是良法。

（3）法院应当排除通过行使其普遍性的或者"剩余"的权力，又或者其固有的管辖权来间接地改变该法案的实质性条款。新加坡是仲裁双方通过合同合意选择的仲裁地，那么新加坡必定是被双方作为后续各项有关该仲裁的争端的管辖权的所在地。而将仲裁地由新加坡改变为马来西亚并非法院的职责与职权范围。

（4）如果背离了仲裁裁决异议审理应由仲裁地法院审理这样一项被国际广泛接受的原则，那么也就背离了该法案的立法宗旨与目的，即达到国内与国际仲裁体制的统一。

2. Open Type Joint Stock Co. Efirnoye（"EFKO"）vs. Alfa Trading Ltd［2012］1 MLJ 685 High Court（Kuala Lumpur）

案情摘要：

原告是一家俄罗斯公司,与被告(马来西亚公司)签署了一份购买棕榈油制品的协议。根据该协议第 6 条("仲裁条款")的规定,双方同意双方的任何争端均通过仲裁方式进行解决。根据一项补充协议,仲裁条款被修改了。修改过的仲裁条款规定,如果申诉方是被告或者卖方,那么双方争端的最终解决应当由位于乌克兰的国际商事仲裁庭来负责;但是,如果申诉方为原告或者买方,那么双方争端的最终解决将由位于俄罗斯的国际商事仲裁庭来负责。这项合同在双方出现争端是发挥作用。被告在位于乌克兰的国际商事仲裁庭提出了仲裁申请,诉称原告方延迟给付棕榈油制品的运输费用及货款。而在该仲裁过程中,原告方提出了相应的反诉。原告方在位于俄罗斯的国际商事仲裁庭处提起仲裁申请,诉称被告方延迟放货。被告方对于原告方发起的程序提出了管辖权异议,并且主张在变更的仲裁条款中规定的可选择性路径应当以先提交仲裁一方的管辖权具有排他性的仲裁管辖效力进行理解。因此,根据相关条款的规定,被告方认为由于其先行向位于乌克兰的国际商事仲裁庭发出了仲裁申请,那么该仲裁庭也就相应具备了排他性的管辖权。在进行了最初抗辩后,被告方又向位于乌克兰的国际商事仲裁庭就原告提出的主张提起了反诉。尽管这一仲裁请求被提交到了位于乌克兰的国际商事仲裁庭,但位于俄罗斯的仲裁庭认为其依据仲裁条款的规定对该争议享有明确的管辖权。当位于俄罗斯的国际商事仲裁庭作出认可原告方的诉求的裁决后,被告方通过向俄罗斯仲裁法院上诉,要求撤销该项仲裁裁决,但俄罗斯仲裁法院驳回了被告方的诉求。

进而原告方依据 2005 年仲裁法案第 38 章要求承认并执行由俄罗斯国际商事仲裁庭作出的仲裁裁决。被告方认为该项申请所涉的仲裁的仲裁程序并不符合仲裁协议的规定,并且/或者这项仲裁裁决并不符合马来西亚的公共政策。被告方认为既然争端已经在乌克兰提起,那么后续的任何有关双方合同的诉求就应当在该项诉求之下被提起,而原告方后续在俄罗斯提起的仲裁程序是不符合合同中规定的程序要求的。被告方进一步主张,在俄罗斯解决的争端与在乌克兰解决的争端是完全相同的,那么任何一项裁决均可以在马来西亚得以执行,这就违背了马来西亚的公共政策。

判决同意原告方的申请及费用:

(1)俄罗斯仲裁庭已经充分考虑了被告方的诉求,即如果一方已经按照变更的仲裁条款选择了仲裁庭提起了仲裁程序,那么另一方就应当受到这项主张的司法管辖的约束。乌克兰以及俄罗斯的仲裁庭均没有支持被告方提出的解释,并且认为该条款应当按照其字面含义而被赋予效力。通过对该项变更的仲裁条款,两个仲裁庭作出的裁决以及双方的行为的考察,本院认为仲裁程序是符合法律要求的。而被告方选择性的解释将有悖于变更后仲裁条款明示的含义。

(2)俄罗斯仲裁庭的裁决表明,被告方在最初的异议后又在其管辖下向其提交了申请。既然被告方已经向俄罗斯仲裁庭提出了申请,那么其便不能再就管辖权问题提出异议。

(3)对俄罗斯仲裁庭裁决以及乌克兰仲裁庭裁决的"审查",清晰地表明尽管两项裁决涉及争端的合同是相同的,但其涉及的争端的主要问题是不同的。

当乌克兰仲裁庭的仲裁员们作出裁决时,他们明确声明由原告方在俄罗斯提起的仲裁请求不同于当下在乌克兰进行的仲裁。并且,两项诉求中都涉及了反诉问题,但并不彼此冲突。在这样的情形之下,被告方无法证明同一项争端由不同的仲裁庭作出了不同的裁决。正因如此,被告方主张的执行由俄罗斯仲裁庭作出的仲裁存在重大瑕疵,并且执行将会有损公共政策这一观点是错误的。违背公共政策的论点不应当被用来作为重新开启一项已经在仲裁中被解决的争端的伪装。

3. Infineon Technologies (M) Sdn. Bhd. vs. Orisoft Technology Sdn. Bhd. (previously known as Orisoft Technology Bhd) and another application [2011] 7 MLJ 539 High Court (Kuala Lumpur)

案情摘要:

该纠纷是有关一个三人仲裁庭作出的仲裁裁决的,原告是 Infineon,被告是 Orisoft,并且对原告方提起了反诉。原告方依据双方签署的"马来西亚工资与时间管理系统协议"的工作声明的第 26 条对被告提起了仲裁申请。被告方依据该条进行答辩,并聘请了 Chan Kok Chong 先生作为仲裁员,原告方聘请了 Dato Shaik Daud Ismail 先生作为仲裁员,双方仲裁员又共同聘请了 Low Beng Choo 女士作为第三位仲裁员。仲裁庭仲裁员的选任是由吉隆坡地区仲裁中心所规定的,这一规定是符合联合国国际商事仲裁中心规则的,并且是被记录在吉隆坡地区仲裁中心送达给首席仲裁员的有关首席仲裁员选任的往来信件之中的。参考这一临时规定,双方同意仲裁员的费用支付结构以及将 2005 年仲裁法案作为可援引的法律。由于该临时规定不符合吉隆坡地区仲裁中心规则 7(4)款的规定,该仲裁中心"指示"仲裁员撤销临时规定的第1 条。

作为回应,首席仲裁员称,该仲裁中心的主管以及该仲裁中心均无权向仲裁庭发出指示。首席仲裁员同样也以书面的方式通知了该仲裁中心的主管

(这份通知同样也送达到了双方律师),原告方未能遵守临时规定,首席仲裁员在该通知中强调仲裁庭已经通过案情听证会(show case hearing)进行了解决。此次听证是在原告方律师,Orisoft 的高管及其律师在场的情况下进行的。此后该仲裁庭对此作出了终局性裁决。仲裁庭认为 Infineon 一方未能提出对方违反或者不符临时规定的足够原因,并且其也未能在规定的时间内提交其主张。在这样的情况下,本院需要考察的就是,仲裁庭的仲裁程序是否正当以及吉隆坡地区仲裁中心的主管是否能够介入仲裁庭的裁决。该仲裁中心主管主张,主管所为是在确定仲裁开始的时间,并且由于仲裁中心有管理其提起仲裁的裁决的权利,包括对于仲裁员费用的支付,而这些是不得被提起异议的。由此看来,该中心管理仲裁的程序性事项,而非其实质。该中心及其主管的法律顾问向本院表明,尽管仲裁与诉讼是相互独立的两个程序,但在法院审理以上争议时,他们将会尊重法院作出的决定。Orisoft 主张,尽管双方在费用问题上没有争议,但该仲裁中心及其主管的行为构成了对仲裁实质性事项的影响,与此同时,应当认定该临时措施的违法性。本院同时也考虑了Infineon 申请撤销最终裁决,由于其不符合约定的程序,并且违反了正义性规则。

判决驳回原告方的诉求:

(1)机构仲裁在灵活性上不如临时仲裁,由于机构仲裁要受到特定机构在仲裁程序及行政上的管理,并且这些措施具体实施要受到该机构的监督。由于临时仲裁的基本原则,即自治以及对仲裁程序最少的干预,并且以仲裁庭作为对程序监督的主体,仲裁的环境会更加便利而不是受到更多的监管。

在机构仲裁的结构里,双方的自治性以及仲裁庭的自治性将会被轻易地剥夺,由于该结构主要是行政性的,这种观念是错误的。

(2)根据第 7(4)款规定,关于费用的确定,仲裁庭必须与该仲裁中心的主管进行商议,并且该主管在给予仲裁庭意见之前要先行与双方进行商议。预定的费用以及该中心的管理费用可能在例外、非寻常、不可预见的情形下被调整,但这些调整的自由裁量权在该中心的主管之手。鉴于以上,这些约束仲裁庭的强制性规则并没有被遵守。

(3)在保留仲裁庭自治性的意义上,本院认为允许仲裁中心主管保有介入仲裁庭指定的临时规则的广泛性权力,以保证这样的临时规则的正当性是正确的。这样的结论是符合 2005 年仲裁法法案的相关条款的。而在该纠纷中讽刺的是,虽然双方在费用上达成一致,在当原告方被该中心告知费用应当按照预定的进行时,其继而将这项争端诉诸仲裁庭并且没有在临时规定规定的时间内提交诉求。对原告方而言,其正当的诉求程序可能应当依据法案第35章第1条b款要求仲裁庭就该特定部分的临时规定给予解释。

(4)在考量仲裁庭的裁决是否存在错误之前,一项有关自然正义的正式要求被提出。仲裁庭违反了该中心规则第7条第4款的规定,由于其没有与仲裁中心主管商议便收取了交规则规定低的费用。对于仲裁的终局性裁决是否公平及正当,本院认为根据仲裁法的现行规定,法院不能去审查超越程序性的正当程序事项,由于考量特定裁决的公正性涉及实质利益,并且不是法院可以正当介入的议题。因此,依据法律与事实,并且考虑到双方提出的所有诉求,仲裁裁决应当被维持。

4. Government of the Lao People's Democratic Republic v Thai-Lao Lignite Co. Ltd. ("TLL"), a Thai Co. & Anor [2013] MLJU 165, High Court (Kuala Lumpur)

案情摘要:

本案的原告方是老挝政府(以下简称"老挝")。第一被告为 Thai-Lao Lignite Co, Ltd. (TLL),一家泰国公司,第二被告为 Hongsa Lignite Co Ltd (HLL),一家老挝公司。老挝政府与第一被告于 1992 年 5 月 29 日签署了一份采矿合同(第一份采矿合同),于同年 7 月 21 日签署了另外一份采矿合同(第二份采矿合同)。第一、二采矿合同被统称为采矿合同,在裁决中被称为"优先合同"。在仲裁程序中,原告方为被申诉方,而被告方为申诉方。

被告方(两家被告公司)是由一位泰国商人 Siva Nganthavee 先生创办的。其中,第二被告是由 Siva 先生于 1990 年与他的家庭成员及其控制的公司共同创办的。

两份采矿协议涉及的是位于泰老边境,老挝西北部洪沙特许地区的褐矿采集。第二份采矿协议修改了第一份采矿协议的采矿面积,特许开采地区由原来的 20 m² 扩展到了 60 m²。第二被告与老挝一家公司合并为 HLL 来开展褐矿在老挝的开采。HLL 75% 的股权由第二被告所有,25% 由老挝的政府机构所有。

为了更好地解决未来可能出现的争端,老挝政府与第二被告在第一份采矿协议中就争端解决条款达成了一致:

"第 31 条,争端解决:

一旦产生争端,双方应当友好协商解决。如果不能协商解决,那么该争端应当诉诸老挝经济调解委员会,或老挝法院,或国际经济纠纷解决组织。"

采矿协议的第二条即法律选择条款,本协议受老挝法律的调整。项目发展协议(PDA),是由 Siva 以及老挝政府进一步协商完成的。在项目发展协议(PDA)项下,老挝政府授予第一被告人一项特许权,在 Hongsa 建设发电厂来发电。这项计划将发出的电力卖给泰国国家所属的电力委员会(缩写为EGAT)。第二被告并没有签署这项协议。

项目发展协议(PDA)的第 14.1 条为其仲裁条款:

"第 14.1 条,仲裁:

(i)由该协议产生的任何争议,包括对于该协议的解释……任何一方可以将争端诉诸吉隆坡地区仲裁中心依照联合国国际商事仲裁规则……"

随后,Siva 先生设立了一家独立的老挝公司泰老电力有限公司(TLP),用以获得老挝的执照来建设和运营在老挝的电力设施。像这样重量级的工程,资金当然是关键。为了实施采矿项目协议以及电力工程项目协议,Siva 先生另外建立了一个公司来帮助泰老电力有限公司(TLP)解决银行贷款问题。这家公司叫作东南亚电力公司(SEAP)。Siva 先生的子公司以及关联公司情况如下:

1. TLL 是由 Siva 先生、其关联公司以及其家庭成员所有;

2. HLL 是由 75%TLL 以及 25%老挝政府机构所有;

3. SEAP 的 60%由 Siva 先生、他的关联公司以及其家庭成员所有,40%由 TLL 所有;

4. TLP 的 60%是由 SEAP 所有、40%由 TLL 所有。

原告指出 SEAP 以及 TLP 从未获得采矿协议以及老挝作为一方当事人的发展项目合同(PDA)项下的权利与义务。"

问题:

十年间,TLL 都未能将电力计划推进,而且随后亚洲金融危机又集中而至。曾经的东亚奇迹破灭,繁荣变成了爆炸。原告方为十年后的该问题描绘了一幅悲惨的图景:没有一瓦电被发出也没有一盎司的锡矿被开采!原告方在 2006 年 10 月 5 日终止了发展项目合同(PDA)。在 2006 年 10 月 11 日原告方终止了采矿协议。

但不乐观的结果还是发生了。被告方依据发展项目合同(PDA)中的仲裁条款发起了仲裁申请,并且对原告方错误地终止合同造成的实质性的损失提出了赔偿请求。TLL 以及 HLL 要求原告方承担其因错误地终止合同造成的损失(损失赔偿要求近 200,000,000 美元),其中包含了融资费用的补偿。

在 2008 年 6 月 26 日,TLL 与 HLL 向法院提起诉讼并要求给予临时救济。于是仲裁程序出现了一系列的时间节点,原告方在 2008 年 8 月 29 日针对申诉方诉求提交了答辩状；在 2009 年 2 月 20 日提交了开庭备忘录；于 2009 年 6 月 15 日提交了答辩备忘录；在 2009 年 9 月 14 日提交了结案备忘录并在 2009 年 11 月 4 日等。

原告方的此次诉求是基于两项主张。其一是管辖权。法院可以扩展其管辖权，但却错误地形式了其管辖权。另一个是法院针对 TLL 与 HLL 的不同的诉求收费标准相同，并且 HLL 并非 PDA 协议的签署方，这同样也违反了仲裁协议以及采矿协议关于管辖协议签署方的规定。

原告方的法律基础是法案第 37 章第 1 条 a 款第 4、5 项，该条 b 款第 2 项以及该章第 2 条 b 项的规定。

法院判决如下：

本院认为仲裁庭作出的判决一般而言应当是终局性并且具有约束性的，除非 2005 年仲裁法案第 37 章的条件被满足。并且法院对于仲裁裁决应当承担的是监督职能而非上诉职能。

对该仲裁裁决审查后，本院认为本院并不能够执行老挝法规制下的采矿协议以及同时受到老挝法以及纽约法规制下的 PDA 协议。两份协议关系紧密，因而很难决定两者之间谁应当成为援用的依据。

本案中有效的诉求仅为管辖权是否被超越。除非仲裁庭不能正当进行仲裁，双方依据 PDA 协议以仲裁协议在纠纷未解决的情况下，均应诉诸仲裁庭进行再次仲裁解决。

协议中的仲裁条款

5. TNB Fuel Services Sdn Bhd v China National Coal Group Corp [2013] MLJU 483，Court of Appeal (Putrajaya)

案情摘要：

在 2002 年，申诉方投标 Tanjung Bin 电力项目，来提供煤炭的供应。被告方提供的投标文件有：煤炭购买估价协议、标书、保函。

在 2012 年 12 月 4 日左右，被告方发标：

（1）一份 15 年期限的长期煤炭供应的完整标书。这份标书是由被告方的副总经理 Pan Wanze 签署的；

（2）保函的签发日期为 2002 年 12 月 2 日，由位于马来西亚的渣打银行为被告方提供 50 万马币的担保；

（3）煤炭供应的技术建议。

这份保函是由被告方的律师 William Randall 签署的，并且该律师的委任书是在 2002 年 11 月 26 日于香港由被申诉方进行公正的。这份委任书授权

Randall 代表被告方与上诉人协商煤炭供应合同事项。

上诉人接受了被告方的投标,并于 2003 年 11 月 18 日发出了中标通知书,其中包括:

(1)供应的形式和条件应当符合煤炭购买估价协议;

(2)被告方提供保函;

(3)被告方要聘请一位当地的代理人;

(4)被告方应在接到该中标通知书之日起 14 日内作出承诺。

被申诉方于 2003 年 12 月 18 日通过信函由 Zhou Dongzhou 作出了承诺,与此同时,由被告方代理人 William Randall,P. C. Yong 聘请了 Fasa Galian Sdn. 有限公司作为其当地代理。对该合同作出承诺后,被告方于 2004 年 5 月 15 日请求渣打银行提供 100 万马币的开业前保函给上诉人。渣打银行在保函表面重申,该保函是应我方客户(中煤能源集团公司)的请求签发的。

该保函应被告方的请求被延长过两次。上诉方称被告方违反合同未能供应合同规定的煤炭,而上诉方辩称此举是由于中国政府的政策变革所致。上诉方在 2009 年 8 月 13 日向申诉方发出仲裁通知书。而被告方则向位于 Shah Alam 地区的高等法院起诉,称双方之间并没有仲裁协议。并且被告方在法官作出禁止其进行仲裁的判决前申请并获得了单方面禁令。

该禁令于 2010 年 7 月 29 日通过双方的辩驳被确认了下来。但由于上诉方在上诉法院对单方面禁令提出上诉请求,因而该禁令便处于未决状态,而被告方的诉求由于其未能提供相应的保证金而被驳回。

由于被告方第一次起诉被驳回,仲裁庭于 2011 年 7 月 12 日被组建起来。而被告方于 2011 年 7 月 27 日向同一高等法院发出了与第一次几乎相同的诉求。而另一方面,上诉方根据法案第 10 章的相应规定申请中止诉讼程序,从而来支持仲裁的优先性。

双方于 2011 年 8 月 24 日由仲裁庭组织开启了准备会议。被告方对仲裁庭的管辖权提出了异议。该庭同意就被告方提出的管辖权异议作为一项初步议题举行听证。根据该庭的指示,双方应就初步议题交换诉求与证据。初步议题的听证时间从 2011 年 12 月 12 日持续至该月 16 日。但是,2011 年 8 月 25 日,被告方已经获得高等法院临时禁令。因此,仲裁庭确定的初步议题并不能够被听证。

2012 年 9 月 24 日,被告方获得了禁令申请。在同一判决中,法官驳回了附件 13 中的中止申请。本上诉是本庭同日作出的禁令许可及驳回的中止申请。

上诉庭判决如下：

将"仲裁协议"的新定义适用于本案事实,从而来决定第二次禁令申请是否应当被授予,应当根据双方书面的协议以及在该协议中援用的"仲裁协议",从而帮助本院确定双方认定的"仲裁协议"的定义。我们认为高院的法官据以考察被告方禁令申请的依据是1952年仲裁法法案而非本案应当适用的2005年仲裁法法案。我们认为高院是依据以下理由准予禁令申请的:

"本院通过对煤炭采购估价协议的审查发现,该协议虽然有仲裁条款,但该仲裁条款并不完整且并未经过双方签字。据此,本院认为原告方起诉合法。"

但本院认为上述禁令的许可没有援用到2005年法案第9节第5条的规定。

根据以上的原因,以及2005年法案第8章的规定,"任何法庭不得干预本法所涉及的问题,除非本法特别规定"。因此本庭驳回高等法院的签发的禁令申请,以及高院对原告作出的中止仲裁程序的命令。并且本院依据2005年仲裁法法案第10章决定中止编号为24-1925-2011的起诉请求。判决被告方承担15,000马币,包括本次的诉讼费用以及上诉方的上诉费用。本案的保证金退还于上诉方。

6. Ajwa for Food Industries Co (MIGOP) Egypt v Pacific Inter-link Sdn Bhd [2013] MLJU 689，Federal Court (Putrajaya)

案情摘要:

(1)被告方针对上诉方发起了两项仲裁申请,诉称上诉方未能送达书面协议项下的承诺的棕榈油制品,该协议中含有仲裁条款。

(2)上诉人在高院提起了两项单独的请求,驳回或者更改2010年4月13日依据马来西亚棕榈油提炼委员会仲裁与上诉规则作出的仲裁裁决。该协会作出如下裁决:(a)裁决上诉方向被告方给付2,261,100美元损失赔偿;(b)判决上诉方向被告方给付1,374,200美元损失赔偿。

(3)双方涉案的纠纷均没有正式的合同文本或记载。上诉方并不否认其向被告方购买产品这一事实。上诉方承认其合同的签订是通过电话协商以及电子邮件方式达成的。但是上诉方主张其间的合同并未涉及争端由该委员会进行仲裁的条款。

(4)仲裁庭的管辖依据为双方的书面销售合同。

(5)仲裁庭的另一管辖权依据为所谓的销售术语及条件标准(STC),该标准是在仲裁期间达成的,并且其中包含有被告方同意的仲裁条款。

(6)上诉方主张被告方所依据的销售合同中并不含有任何特别的争端解决条款。对于 STC,上诉方主张其是在仲裁期间达成的单独的协议,并且上诉方主张其并未见过且为同意签署。

(7)针对上诉方的案件,该仲裁庭并无管辖权,因为其并没有书面或其他形式的涉及销售事务争端解决的条款。

判决如下:

(1)2005 年仲裁法案中并未规定含有仲裁条款的协议一定是要经过签署的。针对本案,销售合同是书面的并且满足了该法案第 9 章第 4 条的规定。该协议囊括了含有仲裁条款的 STC,并且满足了该法案第 9 章第 5 条的要求。

(2)第 9 章第 5 条并未要求包含仲裁条款的 STC 作为附件或者被出版。只要其在文件中进行声明即满足该条的要求。因此,本院判决驳回两个上诉请求,并且维持上诉法院的判决。上诉方给付被告人 30,000 马币,保证金退还上诉人。

结论

以上六起案件涉及了不同的国家以及司法管辖区域,如中东(印度),亚洲(中国),欧洲,俄罗斯,东盟(老挝与泰国),也涉及在马来西亚的外国公司。

在 Twin Advance (M) Sdn. Bhd. vs. Polar Electro Europe BV 案中,一项驳回新加坡仲裁裁决的申请并没有得到支持。法院依据 2005 年仲裁法法案第 37 章规定可以援用该法的仲裁裁决要依据仲裁地在马来西亚。尤其是法院在作出判决时强调,"法院固有的管辖权不得被用来干预仲裁领域的管辖范围"。这点同样被 Open Type Joint Stock Co. Efirnoye ("EFKO") v Alfa Trading Ltd. 案所引用,马来西亚高等法院同意执行由俄罗斯仲裁庭作出的仲裁,因为双方对俄罗斯仲裁庭的管辖权并没有异议。马来西亚法庭还判决违反公共政策的诉求不应当被作为重启仲裁来解决问题的掩饰。

尽管在机构仲裁中,仲裁庭可能违反了行政性的临时规定,但如果仲裁庭的裁决已就仲裁申请中的实质问题作出裁决,那么法院便不能推翻仲裁裁决。

问题是:仲裁裁决在马来西亚法庭有可能被推翻吗?高等法院推翻仲裁裁决的依据被规定在仲裁法案第 37 章之中。因此,在 Government of the Lao People's Democratic Republic vs. Thai-Lao Lignite Co. Ltd., a Thai Co. & Another 案中,马来西亚高等法院推翻了一项仲裁裁决,并且判令双方依据仲裁协议再次进行仲裁,由于之前仲裁庭进行了超裁。这样,管辖权的诉求就被作为是一项没有被计划到的判决事项,或者未满足第 37 章第 1 节第 a

款第 4 项的规定。

最后,马来西亚的法庭,上诉庭以及州法庭迄今的判决认为仲裁条款应当在书面协议之中,但 2005 年仲裁法法案中并没有要求包含有仲裁条款的合同一定是要被签署的。这表明仲裁作为纠纷解决的一种手段是被马来西亚法庭所尊重的,并且双方也应当遵守其合同项下规定的仲裁条款。

可以预见在中国开放市场政策的情况下,中国—东盟自贸区中的各个成员的关系将会得到深化。马来西亚法庭一关的措施应当为外国投资提供好确定以及有信心的马来西亚法律平台。

General Provisions on Arbitration in Malaysia and Case Analysis on the Finality of Arbitration Awards in Malaysia

Chan Szu Fu[*] & Wong Keat Ching[**]

Abstract   The first part of this article introduces general provisions on arbitration in Malaysia under the Arbitration Act 2005 as well as international arbitration treaties applicable to Malaysia. The second part is a case analysis of 6 cases decided by the Malaysian Courts involving arbitration matters from various countries and jurisdictions, i. e. Middle East (Egypt), Asia (China), European Union, Russia, ASEAN (Laos and Thailand), and also foreign companies incorporated in Malaysia. These cases show the consistent approach adopted by Malaysian Courts in giving effect to arbitration awards and agreements to arbitrate.

Keywords   Arbitration Act 2005; Malaysia Courts; Investment; Dispute Resolution; Arbitration Agreement; Arbitration Award

Part 1: Arbitration in Malaysia

In Malaysia both ad hoc and institutional arbitrations are common. In-

---

* Partner, Cheong de Vries & Co; Barrister (Middle Temple); Advocate & Solicitor, High Court of Malaya.

** Partner, Zul Rafique & Partners; Advocate & Solicitor, High Court of Malaya.

stitutional arbitrations for domestic transactions are most popularly governed by the Kuala Lumpur Regional Center for Arbitration (KLRCA). International transactions provide for arbitration agreements governed usually by the International Chamber of Commerce (ICC) and the London Court of International Arbitration (LCIA), with the Singapore International Arbitration Center (SIAC) and the Hong Kong International Arbitration Center (HKIAC) becoming more common in recent years.

Domestic Arbitration Laws

The Malaysian *Arbitration Act* 2005 governs arbitration proceedings with the seat in Malaysia. The *Arbitration Act* 2005 is based on the UNCITRAL Model Law 1985. Section 3 of the *Arbitration Act* 2005 stipulates that the Act applies to both domestic and international arbitrations and differs only in relation to Part Ⅲ of the Act on matters such as consolidation of proceedings or concurrent hearings, determination of preliminary point of law by the High Court, reference on questions of law to the High Court, appeal, costs and expenses of arbitration.

For a domestic arbitration where the seat of arbitration is in Malaysia, the applicable law would be the substantive law of Malaysia, unless parties agree otherwise.

International Arbitration Treaties

Malaysia is a signatory to the New York Convention (Convention on the Recognition and Enforcement of Foreign Arbitral Awards 1958). Section 38 of the *Arbitration Act* 2005 provides that a domestic arbitration or an award from a foreign state (with the arbitration seat in Malaysia) shall be recognised as binding and shall be enforceable in Malaysia. Section 38 also provides that "foreign state" means a state which is a party to the New York Convention.

Malaysia is also a signatory to the Convention on the Settlement of Investment Disputes (ICSID Convention) and has enacted the Convention on Settlement of Investment Disputes Act in 1966. Further, Malaysia is a signatory of the ASEAN Protocol on Enhanced Dispute Settlement Mechanism 2004 (the Vientiane Protocol) which covers ASEAN economic agreements and the ASEAN Charter 2007 which is the overarching framework for dispute settlement in ASEAN. The Comprehensive Investment Agreement between members of ASEAN provides the dispute settlement mechanism in investment disputes between a member state and an investor of another member state.

The Reciprocal Enforcement of Judgments Act 1958 (REJA) provides for an alternative method of enforcing foreign arbitral awards whereby the successful party will convert his arbitral awards into a judgment of the court in the foreign jurisdiction. Thus an arbitral award which has been converted into a judgment can be enforced under REJA.

Section 30 of the *Arbitration Act* 2005 provides that the applicable law for international arbitration would be the law as agreed upon by the parties and where there is no such agreement, the arbitral tribunal shall apply the law determined by the conflict of laws rules.

Selection of Arbitrators

The *Arbitration Act* 2005 allows parties to decide on the composition and appointment of the arbitral tribunal subject to any rules of arbitration that may be adopted.

The procedure for appointment of arbitrators under the *Arbitration Act* 2005 is set out in Section 13 of the Act. Section 13 corresponds with Article 11 of the *Model Law* and adopts a two level approach to grant the parties the right to determine the procedure for appointment of arbitrators followed by a default mechanism if the parties fail to agree on the procedure.

Under the *Arbitration Act* 2005, where the parties fail to make provision for the appointment procedure in the arbitration agreement or if there is disagreement or if they refuse to exercise their rights to appoint a member of the arbitral tribunal, then the Director of the Kuala Lumpur Regional Center for Arbitration (KLRCA) is given the power to appoint the arbitrator and he has to do so within 30 days, failing which the parties could then proceed to court to have the appointment made.

The Courts' Approach towards Enforcement of Agreements to Arbitrate

The courts will as a general rule enforce agreements to arbitrate and therefore decline to interfere. To give effect to an agreement to arbitrate, the courts would normally grant a stay order to halt the action in court

pending reference to arbitration pursuant to Section 10 of the *Arbitration Act*
2005. Under the Act an arbitration agreement is unlikely to be enforceable
where the agreement is null and void, inoperative or incapable of being performed, or there is in fact no dispute between the parties.

Award of Damages and Interest

Damages are the most common form of remedy sought. The arbitrators
may award general, special and exemplary damages. Section 33(6) of the
Act provides that, unless otherwise provided in the arbitration agreement,
the arbitral tribunal may award interest on any sum of money ordered to be
paid by the award from the date of the award to the date of realisation and
determine the rate of interest.

Part 2: Case Analysis on Finality of Arbitration Awards in Malaysia

Setting Aside an arbitration award made outside Malaysia?

1. Twin Advance (M) Sdn. Bhd. v. Polar Electro Europe BV [2013] 7
MLJ 811 High Court (Pulau Pinang)

Summary:

The plaintiff and the defendant had consensually arbitrated a dispute in
Singapore. In the instant originating summons ("the summons") the
plaintiff sought to set aside the arbitration award ("the award") pursuant to
Section 37 37 of the *Arbitration Act* 2005 ("Act"). The defendant applied to
strike out the summons under order 18 rule 19(1) of the *Rules of the High
Court* 1980 on the ground the High Court in Malaysia had neither inherent
jurisdiction nor jurisdiction under the Act to set aside the Singapore-made
award. The plaintiff argued that since ss 38 and 39 of the Act gave the court
jurisdiction to recognise and enforce arbitration awards made both
domestically and by a foreign state, Section 37 should, by analogy, allow
the court to set aside an award which had been made outside Malaysia. The
defendant, however, said that since s 3 of the Act expressly provided for the
application of the Act only to domestic and international arbitrations where
the seat of arbitration was in Malaysia, it followed that s 37 could not be

invoked to set aside an award made outside Malaysia.

Held, allowing the defendant's application and striking out the originating summons with costs:

(1) Section 37 of the Act was applicable to an arbitral award where the seat of arbitration was in Malaysia but not where the seat was outside Malaysia. The inherent jurisdiction of the court also ought not to be invoked to intermeddle with the jurisdictional aspect of arbitration nor to allegedly do justice in the instant case when there was in fact no injustice as the plaintiff was at liberty to apply to the Singapore High Court to set aside the award made in Singapore.

(2) The intention of the Act was amply clear that Sections 38 and 39 were to be construed as exceptions to Section 3 of the Act and distinct and separate from Section 37. If Section 37 included the setting aside of an arbitral award of a foreign state the Legislature would have provided such express words in the section. In the absence of such express provision, the principle of law that the seat of arbitration was the place where challenges to an award were made remains applicable and good law.

(3) The court should exclude its general or residual powers or inherent jurisdiction to indirectly vary the substantive provisions of the Act. The seat or place of arbitration was intended and contractually agreed upon by the parties to be in Singapore. They must be taken to have chosen Singapore as the jurisdiction for any subsequent proceedings to challenge the award. It was not the court's role or function to rewrite their contract by converting the seat from Singapore to Malaysia.

(4) It was inconsistent with the Act's intent and purpose of achieving consistency between the international and domestic arbitral regimes if it departed from the internationally entrenched principle that the right to challenge an arbitral award, as distinct from the recognition of arbitration a-greements and recognition and enforcement of arbitral awards, ought to be in the courts of the place of arbitration.

2. Open Type Joint Stock Co. Efirnoye ("EFKO") v. Alfa Trading Ltd [2012] 1 MLJ 685 High Court (Kuala Lumpur)

Summary:

The plaintiff, a Russian company, entered into a contract to buy palm oil products from the defendant, a Malaysian company. Under clause 6 of this agreement ("the arbitration clause"), the parties agreed that any disputes that arose between them would be resolved by arbitration. Pursuant to an additional agreement, the arbitration clause was varied. The varied arbitration clause provided that if the complainant was the defendant or seller, then the dispute between the parties was to be passed for final resolution to the International Commercial Arbitration Court (ICAC) in Ukraine, but, if the complainant was the plaintiff or buyer, then the dispute was to be passed for final resolution to the ICAC in Russia. The contract between the parties was performed in part when disputes arose. The defendant filed an arbitration claim against the plaintiff in the ICAC in Ukraine complaining of a breach arising from late payment for the oil palm products supplied and delivered. This arbitration claim was defended by the plaintiff who filed a counterclaim in these proceedings. Subsequently, the plaintiff instituted an arbitration claim against the defendant in the ICAC in Russia for alleged breaches arising from late delivery of the oil palm products. The defendant took jurisdictional objections to the proceedings initiated by the plaintiff and submitted that the alternative venue clause in the varied arbitration clause, should be construed as providing exclusive jurisdiction of the arbitration tribunal to the party that was first to initiate arbitration in relation to the dispute that had arisen. Thus, the defendant contended that since it was the first to exercise the right to arbitration this resulted in the ICAC in Ukraine possessing exclusive jurisdiction to consider the dispute of the parties under the rules prevailing there. After this initial objection, the defendant filed a counterclaim to be considered together with the plaintiff's original claim. Notwithstanding the filing of another arbitral claim by the defendant in the ICAC in Ukraine, the Russian arbitral tribunal concluded that it had express jurisdiction by virtue of the varied arbitration clause. When the ICAC in Russia granted an award allowing the plaintiff's claim, the defendant applied by way of appeal to the Russian arbitral tribunal for a cancellation of the arbitration award, but the Russian arbitration court rejected the defendant's application. The plaintiff then proceeded with the present application for recognition and enforcement of the arbitration award issued by the ICAC in Russia pursuant to Section 38 of the *Arbitration Act* 2005 ("the Act"). The defendant objected to this application on the grounds that the arbitral procedure was not in accordance with the agreement of the parties, and/or the arbitration award was in conflict with the public policy of Malaysia. The defendant maintained that since it had already filed the Ukrainian claim, any further claim relating to the contract between the parties should be maintained under that claim and that by subsequently initiating arbitral proceedings in Russia the plaintiff had failed to adhere to the procedure stipulated in the contract. The defendant further submitted that the arbitration award determined in Russia amounted to the determination of an identical dispute to that determined in Ukraine thereby rendering any recognition of such an award contrary to public policy.

Held, allowing the plaintiff's application with costs:

(1) The issue raised by the defendant, namely that once a party had initiated arbitral proceedings in the forum of its choice under the varied arbitration clause, then the other party was bound to submit to that jurisdiction, had already been considered by the ICAC in Russia in great detail. Both the arbitration courts in Russia and Ukraine had disagreed with the interpretation put forward by the defendant and found that the clause was to be given effect as it was read. Having perused the varied arbitration clause, the findings and awards issued by the two arbitral tribunals and the conduct of the parties, this court found that the arbitral procedure was adhered to. The alternative construction forwarded by the defendant would be contrary to the express intention of the varied arbitration clause as objectively assessed.

(2) There was an express finding of the Russian arbitral tribunal that the defendant submitted to its jurisdiction after its initial objections. Since the defendant had submitted to the jurisdiction of the Russian tribunal, it was found that it ought not to seek to renege from that position by raising the jurisdiction issue again.

(3) It was also evident from a perusal of the Russian award and the Ukrainian award that the precise subject matter of the dispute between the

parties was different, although both disputes arose from the same contract.

When the arbitrators handed down the Ukrainian award they expressly stated that the arbitral proceedings initiated in Russia by the plaintiff were different from the issues dealt with in Ukraine. Further, both claimants in each of these proceedings had filed counterclaims, which were also not in conflict. In the circumstances, the defendant had failed to show that an identical dispute was decided by two tribunals resulting in two different decisions. As such, the defendant's contention that the enforcement of the arbitration award handed down by the ICAC in Russia was critically flawed and thus contrary to public policy was incorrect. The contravention of public policy argument ought not to be utilised as a guise to reopen settled matters in the arbitration.

3. Infineon Technologies (M) Sdn. Bhd. v. Orisoft Technology Sdn. Bhd. (previously known as Orisoft Technology Bhd) and another application [2011] 7 MLJ 539 High Court (Kuala Lumpur)

Summary:

The substance of the dispute concerned an arbitral award handed down by a three-man arbitral tribunal, where the claimant was Infineon and the respondent was Orisoft, which had counterclaimed against Infineon. Infineon commenced arbitration proceedings against Orisoft under clause 26 of the applicable statement of work executed between the parties for a project called "Malaysia Payroll and Time Management Systems Agreement". Orisoft, relying on clause 26, appointed its own arbitrator, Mr. Chan Kok Chong and Infineon appointed Dato Shaik Daud Ismail, and both arbitrators jointly appointed Ms. Low Beng Choo, as the third arbitrator. The appointment of the panel of arbitrators was confirmed by the KLRCA in accordance with Article 7(1) of the *UNCITRAL Rules*, and was recorded in the letter enclosing the letter of appointment of the presiding arbitrator sent by the KLRCA directly to the presiding arbitrator. Vide the interim order, the parties agreed, inter alia, on the arbitrators' fee structure and the application of the *Arbitration Act* 2005. As clause 1 of the interim order was made without compliance with rule 7(4) of the KLRCA Rules, the KLRCA "instructed" the arbitrators to revoke the above clause 1 of the order. In respond, the presiding arbitrator stated that neither the director nor the KLRCA had powers to issue directions to the arbitral tribunal. The presiding arbitrator also informed the director (with the letter copied to the solicitors for the parties) that as the claimant had failed to comply with the interim order, which according to the presiding arbitrator remained in force, the arbitral tribunal had fixed the matter for show cause hearing. The show cause hearing was held as scheduled with the presence of the solicitors of the claimant, the Managing Director of Orisoft and its solicitors. The arbitral tribunal then handed down its final award. The tribunal was satisfied that Infineon had failed to show sufficient cause for its breach or non-compliance of the interim order, in particular in regard to the filing of the points of claim within the stipulated time. In this context, the issues for the consideration of this court were whether there had been compliance with due process on the part of the tribunal, both formal and substantive, and whether the Director of the KLRCA could interfere with the arbitral tribunal. It was contended for the Director of the KLRCA that what the director did was to fix the date to hear the challenge, and this could not be objectionable in itself because the KLRCA administered the arbitration, including fees to be paid to arbitrators. In this regard, the KLRCA administered the procedural aspects of the arbitration, but not the merits. Counsel for the director and KLRCA did indicate to the court, during the course of submission on the above point, that the director and KLRCA would "respect" any decision rendered by this court, although both relied on absolute immunity from process. It was contended for Orisoft inter alia, that the conduct of the director and KLRCA constituted an interference with the subject matter of the arbitration and was tantamount to not recognising the validity of the interim order, despite the parties' agreement on the fees. The court also considered Infineon's application to set aside the final award essentially on the grounds of failure to comply with agreed procedure and breach of the rules of natural justice.

Held, dismissing plaintiff's case with costs:

(1) An institutionalised arbitration is less flexible than an ad hoc arbitration, since the arbitral tribunal will be subject to the administrative

and procedural rules of the particular institution, and a measure of supervision by the institution to ensure compliance with these rules. The environment will be more facilitative rather than supervisory in a substantive sense, since the cardinal principles of party autonomy and minimalist intervention in arbitral proceedings, coupled with the concomitant principle that an arbitral tribunal is a master of its own procedure. It cannot be a correct proposition that within the framework of an institutionalised arbitration, the autonomy of the parties, and that of the arbitral tribunal, can be so easily displaced by the arbitral institution, since the framework is in the main facilitative or administrative in nature.

(2) Rule 7(4) is mandatory in its requirement that when fixing its fees the arbitral tribunal must consult the Director of the KLRCA, and the Director may herself undertake consultations with the parties before giving advice to the arbitral tribunal. The scheduled fees and KLRCA's administrative charges may in exceptional or unusual or unforeseen circumstances be adjusted but that had to be at the discretion of the Director of the KLRCA. With respect, these mandatory provisions, by which the arbitral panel have undertaken to be bound, were not complied with.

(3) In the interest of preserving the autonomy of the arbitral panel, the court did believe it would be right to allow such a wide power to the director to interfere with an interim order made by the arbitral panel in the way it was sought to be done. The answer must surely lie with the provisions of the Arbitration Act 2005. The irony in this dispute was that both parties agreed on the fees, but the claimant, when told by the KLRCA that the fees should have followed the scheduled fees, then took issue with the arbitral panel and did not file the points of claim within the time stipulated in the interim order. The proper mode of challenge, should it be the intention of the claimant so to do, would be by resorting to, possibly, Section 35(1)(b) to request the arbitral panel to give an interpretation of this specific part of the interim order.

(4) As far as formal requirements of the rules of natural justice were concerned, no fault could be found in the decision of the arbitral panel. The arbitral panel itself was at fault in not complying fully with rule 7(4) of the

KLRCA Rules since it failed to discuss beforehand with the director the higher fees it sought to impose. On the question whether it would be fair and reasonable in the circumstances to allow the final award to stand, this court regretfully noted that the arbitration law, as it currently stands, does not allow this court to venture beyond procedural due process, since considerations of fairness of a particular decision of the arbitrators go to the merits and therefore were not a proper subject matter for this court to interfere. Therefore, on the facts and the law, and upon considering the full array of arguments by both counsel, the final award should stand.

4. Government of the Lao People's Democratic Republic vs. Thai-Lao Lignite Co. Ltd. ("TLL"), a Thai Co & Anor [2013] MLJU 165, High Court (Kuala Lumpur)

Summary:

The plaintiff here is the Government of Laos (Laos). The first defendant is Thai-Lao Lignite Co. Ltd. (TLL), a Thai company and the decond defendant is Hongsa Lignite Co. Ltd. (HLL), a Lao company. Laos and TLL had entered into a Mining Contract dated 29 May 1992 (1st Mining Contract) and subsequently on 21 July 1992, they entered into another Mining Contract (2nd Mining Contract). Subsequently Laos and TLL entered into a Project Development Agreement (PDA) dated 22 July 1994. The 1st and 2nd mining contracts are collectively referred to as the "mining contracts" and in the award as the "prior contracts". The plaintiff here was the respondent in the arbitration and the defendants here the claimants in the arbitration.

The defendants are companies formed by a Thai businessman named Mr. Siva Nganthavee ("Mr Siva"). TLL was formed in 1990 by Mr Siva together with his family members or the companies he controlled.

The two mining contracts involved the proposed mining of lignite in a concession area in the Hongsa region in the North-West of Laos along the Thai border. The 1st Mining Contract was amended by the 2nd Mining Contract to extend the concession area from 20 square meters to 60 square meters. TLL incorporated a Lao company in HLL to perform the lignite mining work in Laos. HLL was 75% owned by TLL and 25% owned by an agency of the Lao government.

In hoping for the best and yet being prepared for the worst, Laos and TLL in the 1st Mining Contract have agreed on a dispute resolution clause that reads:

"Article 31. Dispute Settlement:

Should there be any dispute, both parties shall discuss and agree to settle it well. Should it not be basically solved, the dispute shall be referred to the Laotian Board of Economic Conciliation or Laotian Court or International Economic Dispute Settlement Organisation. "

The mining contracts also contain a choice of law clause in Article 2 which states that the agreement would be governed by the law of Laos. As for the PDA, it was the fruition of further discussions between Mr Siva and Laos. Under the PDA, Laos granted TLL a concession to build a power plant at Hongsa to produce electricity. The plan was to sell the electricity to the Thai state-owned electricity board known by the acronym EGAT. The 2nd defendant is not a signatory to the PDA.

The PDA has its own arbitration clause in Article 14.1. It reads:

"Article 14.1: Arbitration.

(i) In the event a dispute arises out of this Agreement including any matters relating to interpretation of this agreement... either party may submit the dispute to arbitration conducted in Malaysia at the Kuala Lumpur Regional Center for Arbitration in accordance with the UNCITRAL Rules [...]"

Subsequently Mr Siva set up a separate Lao company, Thai-Lao Power Co Ltd (TLP) for the purpose of obtaining a Lao license to build and operate the power plant in Laos. For a project of this magnitude, capital was of course critical and crucial. As part of Mr Siva's corporate structuring to undertake the project under the mining contracts (the mining project) and the PDA (the power plant project), another company was incorporated for the purpose of arranging bank financing for TLP. It was called South East Asian Power Co. (SEAP). In the result the subsidiaries and associated companies in Mr Siva's stable appear as follows:

(1) TLL which was wholly owned by Mr. Siva and his associated

63

companies and family members；

(2) HLL which was owned 75% by TLL and 25% by an agency of Laos；

(3) SEAP which was owned 60% by Mr Siva and his associated companies and family members and 40% owned by TLL and

(4) TLP which was owned 60% by SEAP and 40% by TLL.

The plaintiff highlighted the point that SEAP and TLP never did acquire rights and obligations under the mining contracts as well as under the PDA to which Laos was a party.

Problem：

For 10 years, TLL was unable to move the power plant project forward and then the Asian financial crisis set in. What was often described as an East Asian economic miracle had become a meltdown; a boom became a bust. The plaintiff painted a pathetic picture of the problem that after a decade：not a watt of electricity was produced and not an ounce in weight of lignite was mined! The plaintiff sent a letter dated 5 October 2006 terminating the PDA. By another letter dated 11 October 2006, the plaintiff terminated the mining contracts.

The best did not happen but the worst did. Parties called into play and the defendants activated the arbitration clause in the PDA and claimed essentially for damages for wrongful termination of the PDA. TLL and HLL claimed close to USD 200 million in damages arising from the wrongful termination and it included an allowance for financing costs.

On 26 June 2008, TLL and HLL filed with the Tribunal a Statement of Claim and a Petition for Interim Relief. Thereafter the arbitration process proceeded inexorably with the various timelines being met with the plaintiff filing its initial pleading entitled "Statement of Defence, Opposition to the Petition for Interim Relief and Counterclaims" ("Statement of Defence") on 29 August 2008; the plaintiff filing its Opening Memorial on 20 February 2009; the plaintiff filing its Reply Memorial on 15 June 2009; the plaintiff filing its Closing Memorial on 14 September 2009 and culminating in the Tribunal issuing its Award on 4 November 2009.

The plaintiffs application in this Originating Summon (OS) to set aside the Award is mainly on two grounds. One is jurisdictional. It has the twin elements of the Tribunal exceeding its jurisdiction on the one hand and exercising its jurisdiction wrongfully on the other. The other ground is that of public policy in that the Tribunal breached the rules of natural justice in granting a "premium" of 10% of investment costs to TLL and HLL when both parties had submitted differently on it, quite apart from the fact that the Tribunal ordered the investment costs to be paid to non-parties to the PDA by taking into consideration the evidence of investment costs incurred by HLL, TLP and SEAP under the Mining Contracts and in that sense wrongfully exercising its jurisdiction over non-parties to the Arbitration Agreement. The statutory basis for the plaintiffs application is Section 37(1)(a)(iv) and (v), and Section 37(1)(b)(ii) and Section 37(2)(b) of the Arbitration Act 2005 (AA 2005).

The Court held as follows:

"I am conscious of the fact that an award of an Arbitral Tribunal is generally final and binding and can only be set aside on the limited grounds provided for in Section 37 of the AA 2005 for this purpose. I also remind myself that my powers are supervisory and not appellate in nature.

Having read the award, I cannot excise the part or portion which is attributable to claims under the mining contracts governed as it is under Laotian law, and the part or portion under the PDA, governed as it is partly under Laotian law and partly under New York law. It has been so comingled and computed together such that it is impossible to excise and extract that which should strictly stem from the PDA as opposed to that which has its source traceable to the mining contracts.

As the effective challenge is one of excess of jurisdiction, the whole award in the circumstance of the case, has to be set aside and I hereby so order. The dispute confining to the PDA and solely between the parties to the arbitration agreement is to be re-arbitrated before a new panel, resisting every temptation to traverse or transgress into the mining contracts which are governed by Laotian law. I also awarded costs of RM50,000.00 to the plaintiff. "

Incorporation of Arbitration Clause into an Agreement

5. TNB Fuel Services Sdn Bhd v China National Coal Group Corp [2013] MLJU 483, Court of Appeal (Putrajaya)

Summary:

In 2002, the appellant called for tenders for the long term supply of coal for its Tanjung Bin Power Project. The tender documentation provided to the respondent included the proforma Coal Purchase Contract, Bid Form, and Form of Bid Bond.

On or about 4th December 2012, the respondent submitted its bid which included:

(1) A duly completed Bid Form to supply coal for 15 years. This form was signed by the respondent's Deputy Managing Director, Mr. Pan Wanze;

(2) A Bid Bond dated 2nd December 2002, issued jointly by Standard Chartered Bank Malaysia Bhd and the respondent in the sum of RM 500,000.00; and

(3) Technical proposals for the supply of the coal.

The joint Bid Bond submitted by the respondent was signed by one William Randall who was the lawful attorney of the respondent, pursuant to a Power of Attorney issued by the respondent on 26th November 2002 duly notarized in Hong Kong. This Power of Attorney authorized Randall to negotiate a contract on behalf of the respondent to supply coal to the appellant.

The appellant accepted the respondent's bid and issued a Letter of Acceptance dated 18th November 2003 which included, inter alia, the following terms:

(1) That the terms and conditions of the supply shall be in accordance with the proforma Coal Purchase Contract;

(2) The respondent to provide a Bond for the due and proper performance of the contract;

(3) The respondent to appoint a local agent; and

(4) The respondent to acknowledge acceptance of the terms and conditions in the Letter of Acceptance within fourteen (14) days of the receipt of the Letter of Acceptance.

By its letter of 18 December 2003 signed by one Zhou Dongzhou, the respondent accepted the terms of the award and at the same time appointed a company known as Fasa Galian Sdn. Bhd, represented by its attorney William Randall and one P. C. Yong, as its local agent. After accepting the award of the contract, the respondent caused Standard Chartered Bank to furnish a Pre-Commencement Bond dated 15th March 2004 for the amount of RM 1 million in favour of the appellant. Standard Chartered Bank confirms to the face of this bond that it was issued "on behalf of and at the request of our client, China National Coal Group Corp" i. e the respondent.

This Pre-Commencement Bond was extended twice by the respondent. Both extensions included reference to the extensions having been effected at the request of the respondent.

According to the appellant, in breach of its obligations, the respondent then failed to supply the coal that it had promised the appellant for the said project citing changes in the policy of the Government of China. The appellant's response was to serve a Notice of Arbitration on the respondent on 13th August 2009. This caused the respondent to apply by way of Originating Summons to the High Court in Shah Alam OS No. 24-281-2010 ("the first OS") for a declaration that no "arbitration agreement" existed between the parties. It also applied and obtained an ex-parte injunction order before Justice Dato' Zaleha binti Yusof restraining the appellant from proceeding with the arbitration proceedings.

The ex-parte order was then confirmed inter-partes after arguments before Justice Dato' Zaleha binti Yusof on 29th July 2010. While the appellant's appeal to the Court of Appeal against the injunction order was pending, the first OS was struck off when the respondent failed to comply with an order for security costs.

Following the dismissal of the first OS, the arbitral tribunal was fully constituted on 12th July 2011. The respondent then filed a virtually identical Originating Summons in the High Court of Shah Alam on 27th July 2011 (OS 24-1925-2011-"the second OS") seeking similar orders as in its previous action and also an injunction application (Enc. 3) to once again injunct the arbitration proceedings. The appellant on the other hand filed a stay application (Enc. 13) under Section 10 of the Act to stay the respondent's action in favour of arbitration.

The appellant and the respondent attended the preliminary meeting fixed by the arbitral tribunal on 24th August 2011. The respondent informed the Tribunal that it was challenging the jurisdiction of the tribunal to hear the dispute that was brought to arbitration by the appellant. The Tribunal agreed to hear the respondent's jurisdictional challenge as a preliminary issue. Directions were given by the tribunal for parties to exchange pleadings and witness statements on the preliminary issue. A hearing date for the preliminary issue was fixed from 12th to 16th December 2011. However, on 25th August 2011, the respondent obtained an ad-interim injunction from Justice Dato' Zaleha binti Yusof pending the hearing of the respondent's injunction application. As a result, the preliminary issue before the Tribunal was never heard.

On 24th September 2012, the respondent's injunction application was granted by the Learned Justice Hadhariah binti Syed Ismail. In the same judgment, her Ladyship dismissed the stay application in Enclosure 13. This appeal is from the judgment of the Court of 24th September 2012 allowing the injunction and refusing stay.

The Court of Appeal held as follows:

Applying the new definition of "arbitration agreement" to the facts of this case, the application for the injunction in "the second OS" ought to have been determined based on an examination of all the documents exchanged between the parties to determine whether there was an agreement in writing and whether there was sufficient reference in this agreement to the document containing the "arbitration agreement" so as to entitle the Court to conclude that the "arbitration agreement" formed part of the agreement between the parties. With respect, the Learned High Court Judge, in our judgment, considered the merits of the respondent's application for the injunction on the basis of the Arbitration Act 1952 and not the Arbitration Act 2005, which ought to have been the case. We opine to this effect because of the following reasoning adopted by the Learned High Court Judge in allowing the application for the injunction restraining the appellant from proceeding with the pending arbitration:

"My own observation of the proforma Coal Purchase Contract which contained the arbitration clause but it is incomplete and do not have the signatures of the parties. The signing page is blank. On this ground alone, the plaintiff has a legitimate complaint."

With respect, in our judgment, the Learned Trial Judge erred in not considering the application for the injunction on the basis of Sub-section 9(5) of the Arbitration Act 2005 ...

··· For the reasons contained herein and the provisions of Section 8 of the 2005 Act which states that "No court shall intervene in matters governed by this Act, except where so provided in this Act", we allowed both appeals. The order of the High Court granting the injunction restraining the appellant from proceeding with the arbitration proceedings is hereby set aside. The order of the High Court refusing a stay of the pending arbitration proceedings is hereby set aside. We hereby order further proceedings in O-riginating Summons No. 24-1925-2011 be stayed pursuant to Section 10 of the Arbitration Act 2005. The respondent is hereby ordered to pay costs of RM 15,000 as costs here and below to the appellant in respect of both appeals. The deposit is hereby refunded to the appellant.

6. Ajwa for Food Industries Co. (MIGOP) Egypt vs. Pacific Inter-link Sdn. Bhd. [2013] MLJU 689, Federal Court (Putrajaya)

Summary:

(1) The respondent had initiated the two arbitration proceedings against the appellant alleging that the appellant had failed to take delivery of palm oil products which the appellant had ordered from the respondent pursuant to written contracts which contained arbitration clauses.

(2) Before the High Court the appellant filed two separate applications to set aside or vary two arbitration awards dated 13th April 2010 made by tribunals constituted under the Palm Oil Refiners Association of Malaysia ("PORAM") Rules of Arbitration and Appeal. The said PORAM awards are: o (b) Award in Arbitration Reference No. A296 which awarded damages in the sum USD 2,261,100.00 to the respondent; and o (c) Award in Arbitration Reference No. A272 which awarded damages in the sum USD 1,374,200.00 to the respondent.

(3) It is undisputed that parties had always dealt in an informal basis. The appellant did not dispute purchasing the products from the respondent. The appellant admitted that agreements were concluded through telephone conversations and email exchanges prior to any formal documentation being exchanged for confirmation. The appellant however contended that it never agreed to refer disputes to PORAM arbitration.

(4) The arbitral tribunal assumed jurisdiction relying on the Written Sales Contracts ("Sales Contracts").

(5) The arbitral tribunal also assumed jurisdiction relying on the so-called *Standard Terms and Conditions of Sale* ("STC") which the respondent had produced during the arbitration and which it alleged contained the arbitration clause which was agreed to by the appellant.

(6) The appellant alleged that the Sales Contracts which were relied on by the respondent did not contain any specific dispute resolution clause and in most cases, were unsigned. As for the *STC*, this was a separate document produced during the arbitration which the appellant contended it had never seen nor agreed to.

(7) It is the appellant's case that the PORAM tribunal has no jurisdiction to conduct the arbitral proceedings on grounds that there was no agreement, written or otherwise, to refer disputes arising from the sales transactions.

The Court held as follows:

(1) There is no requirement under the Arbitration Act 2005 that where a reference is said to be made to a document containing an arbitration clause in an agreement, that agreement must be signed. In the present case, it is clear that the contract of sale was in writing and satisfies the requirement of Section 9(4) of the Act. That agreement in writing incorporates the STC which contains the arbitration clause and satisfies the requirement of Section 9(5) of the Act.

(2) Section 9(5) of the Act does not require that the STC which contains the arbitration agreement being attached or published. It is sufficient that the incorporation is by notice in the document. In the result we would dismiss the two appeals with costs and affirm the decision of the

Court of Appeal. We award costs of RM 30,000 for the two appeals to the respondent. Deposit is to be refunded to the appellant.

Conclusion

The Six cases above involved dispute resolution from various countries and jurisdictions, i. e. Middle East (Egypt), Asia (China), European Union, Russia, ASEAN (Laos and Thailand), and also foreign companies incorporated in Malaysia.

In the case of Twin Advance (M) Sdn. Bhd. vs. Polar Electro Europe BV, an attempt for application to set aside the arbitration award by the Singapore arbitration was unsuccessful. The Court was under no doubt that Section 37 of the *Arbitration Act* 2005 (Malaysia) was applicable to an arbitral award where the seat of arbitration was in Malaysia but not where the seat was outside Malaysia. Notably, the Court held that "the inherent jurisdiction of the court ought not be invoked to intermeddle with the jurisdictional aspect of arbitration". The same applies in the case of Open Type Joint Stock Co. Efirnoye ("EFKO") vs. Alfa Trading Ltd, whereby the Malaysia High Court had allowed execution of the arbitration award by the Russia arbitral tribunal against the defendant on the grounds that the parties had agreed to be submitted to the jurisdiction of the Russian tribunal and ought not seek to renege from that position by raising the jurisdiction issue again. The Malaysia court further held that the contravention of public policy argument ought not to be utilised as a guise to reopen settled matters in the arbitration.

Even in the case of non-compliance of the interim order (as to the administrative charges) by the arbitral tribunal with the institutionalised arbitration (KLRCA), it would not constitute a ground for setting aside an arbitral award, so long as the arbitral panel had considered the arbitration claim on its merits.

The question is: would an arbitration award ever be set aside by the Malaysia courts? The power of the High Court to set aside an arbitral award is stated under Section 37 of the Arbitration Act 2005. Therefore, in the case of Government of the Lao People's Democratic Republic vs. Thai-Lao Lignite Co. Ltd. , a Thai Co. & Another, the High Court in Malaysia had set aside an arbitration award and ordered the arbitration agreement to be re-arbitrated before a new panel on the grounds that the arbitral panel had acted in excess of their jurisdiction. In that case, the jurisdictional complaint was regarding an award which dealt with a dispute not contemplated by or not falling within the terms of the submission to arbitration under Section 37(1) (a)(iv).

Last but not least, the Malaysia courts, in the Court of Appeal and Federal Court, held that so long as the arbitration clause is in writing and is incorporated into the agreement, there is no requirement under the Arbitration Act 2005 that where a reference is said to be made to a document containing an arbitration clause in an agreement, that agreement must be signed. This signifies that arbitration as an alternative dispute settlement mechanism is well recognised by the courts of Malaysia and that the parties shall be bound by their agreement to enter into arbitration.

It is foreseeable that the relationship between the participating countries in China-ASEAN Free Trade Area (CAFTA) shall be further enhanced in the light of adoption of open market policy by China. The consistent approach by the courts of Malaysia shall provide certainty and confidence in the laws of Malaysia, providing a good platform for foreign investments.

菲律宾外国投资法研究

Xerxes U. Garcia*

陈喆 译

菲律宾贸易工业部秘书 Gregory L. Domingo 在《外国投资者从另一个角度看菲律宾》一文中提到,"目前,外国投资者将其投资计划越来越多地置于菲律宾,并且这种基于双方互动的投资计划也包含了菲律宾的巨大利益"。关于利益,笔者将介绍菲律宾规制外国投资的相关法律。

国家有权制定独立的对外政策,在菲律宾这是一个根本的宪法和法律问题。就像其他国家首先考虑国家主权、领土完整、国家利益和民族自决权一样。与此原则一致,菲律宾政府颁布和实施了一些规制外国投资的法律。如:

1. 第 7042 号法案,即第 8179 号法案——外国投资法(1991),减少最低资本要求,规定最低注册资本为 20 万美元到 50 万美元。

2. 第 7721 号法案,规定开放外国银行进入菲律宾并放开其业务经营的范围。

3. 第 7652 号法案,即投资者租赁法,规定允许外国投资者租用土地,租期最长可达 50 年,还可延长 25 年。

4. 第 7718 号法案,即建设—经营—转让法(BOT 法),规定在某些项目中,可实施 BOT 项目,取消了对政府拨款、设置和政府税款和费用的限制,允许完全由外国所有的公司从事 BOT 项目。

5. 第 7888 号法案,授权菲律宾总统有权在多边金融机构的资产投资的情况下放宽综合投资法典下的国家要求,如在亚洲发展银行或者国际金融公司的资产投资。

在以上提到的法律中,菲律宾规制外国投资的首要法律就是共和国宪法第 7042 号,即外国投资法(1991)。共和国宪法 7042 号第 2 部分有如下规定:

---

* 菲律宾司法部检察官和第 6 期中国—东盟法律培训基地的东盟学员。

国家政策是吸引、促进和欢迎国外的个人、合伙企业、公司和政府包括他们的政治附属机构在国家宪法和有关法律允许国外投资范围内的、对促进国家工业化和社会经济发展有重大作用的行业进行生产性投资。下列行业鼓励外国投资:提高菲律宾人的生活水平并创造就业机会;提高农产品经济价值;增加菲律宾消费者的福利;扩大出口产品的范围、质量和数量,开拓国外市场;将有关技术转让到农业、工业和基础服务业。为主要服务于国内市场的企业补充资本和技术,也欢迎外国投资。

从以上规定我们可以看出,菲律宾的国家政策是鼓励外国投资的。外国投资有助于填补资金的不足,创造就业机会,促进发展,有助于菲律宾全面发展。外国投资的出口企业,在其产品和服务根据外国投资法有关条款规定未列入外国投资限制A清单和B清单规定范围的允许达到100%的所有权。但是,菲律宾法律规定了其在某些领域或者活动是有所保留的,并且有的领域或者活动是只能由菲律宾公民完全开展的。这个保留包括:(1)完全或者绝对保留给菲律宾人;(2)外国人的有限所有权。

绝对保留是指某些领域或者商业活动保留给菲律宾国民。而有限的外国所有权是指外国人的所有权或者外资只能达到特定的份额。为了更好地表明上述所提到的例外的领域,共和国宪法第7042号列明了保留给菲律宾国民的具体领域。这个表叫作外国投资限制表。其由两个清单组成:A清单和B清单。

A清单包括宪法和具体法律强制规定的保留给菲律宾国民的领域。

禁止外资进入的行业:

1.大众传媒(音像录制除外);

2.执照专业服务(法律特许的除外);

(1)工程

①航空工程

②农业工程

③化工工程

④民用工程

⑤电子工程

⑥电信和通信工程

⑦测量工程

⑧机械工程

⑨冶金工程

⑩采矿工程

⑪海上建筑和航海工程

⑫卫生工程

(2)医药和相关职业

①医生

②医药技术

③助产士

④护士

⑤营养和饮食

⑥验光师

⑦制药业

⑧物理治疗

⑨放射性治疗

⑩兽医

(3)会计

(4)建设

(5)刑事

(6)化学

(7)税务

(8)环境计划

(9)林业

(10)地理

(11)室内设计

(12)风景规划

(13)法律

(14)图书管理

(15)船员

(16)船上发动机管理

(17)管道控制

(18)糖制造

(19)社交工作

(20)教学(宪法第16条第14款;共和国宪法第5181号第一部分)

3.注册资本低于250万美元的商业零售;

4. 供电所；

5. 私人保安机构；

6. 小型矿业开采；

7. 菲内海、领海或专属经济区域的海洋资源的开发与利用；

8. 斗鸡业的所有、经营和管理；

9. 核武器及生化、放射性武器的生产、维修、仓储及分销；

10. 烟花炮仗及烟火器材。

外资股权最高限于 25% 的行业：

11. 私营对外劳务输出公司；

12. 菲地方政府出资的公共设施和维修合同（外国贷款或援助的招标项目除外）。

外资股权最高限于 30% 的行业：

13. 广告。

外资股权最高限于 40% 的行业：

14. 自然资源勘探、开发和利用（如与菲政府签有资金和技术援助协议，外资可拥有 100% 股权）；

15. 私人土地所有权（仅限以公司股权形式拥有）；

16. 公用事业（水、电）管理和运行；

17. 教育机构的所有、设立和管理；

18. 从事水稻、玉米的种植和加工；

19. SEC 管理的金融公司；

20. 为菲政府所有或控制的企业、公司、代理机构提供物资和商品的供货合同；

21. 深海商业捕捞；

22. 公寓所有权；

23. 各类资产、信誉及财产评估公司。

B 清单包括根据法律管理的行业和企业：

经菲国家特别部门批准，外资可在如下领域拥有 40% 的股权：

1. 经菲国家警察署批准，可从事火器、黑色火药、甘油炸药、爆破器材、望远镜及其他类似器材的生产、维修、仓储或生产过程中所需产品及配料的分销；

2. 经菲国防部门批准，外国投资可从事枪支弹药、军舰和军用船只以及类似设备和训练器材、配件的生产、维修、仓储或生产过程中所需产品及配料

的分销;

3. 危险药品的生产;

4. 菲法律允许的桑拿、蒸汽浴、按摩诊所等类似行业;

5. 赛马等非赌博形式的博彩业;

国内市场企业认缴资本不低于 2000 万美元,除非包含现金技术或者使用至少 50％的直接雇员,认缴资本可以减少到 1000 万美元。

由于鼓励外国投资是菲律宾的国家政策,菲律宾政府不仅允许外国投资者享有 100％的股权。为了进一步鼓励外国投资,菲律宾政府采取了一套鼓励经济活动的法律:

1. 行政命令第 226 号,即综合投资法典(1987),综合了关于投资的各项基本法律。对于本国和外国企业,若其经济活动属政府认定有助于经济发展的高度优先项目,本法案提出了一套范围广泛的优惠条件。

2. 共和国宪法第 7227 号,即 1992 年基础转换和发展法,规定了对位于苏比克湾自由港地区、克拉克经济特区及其延伸地区的企业激励措施。

3. 1995 年经济特区法,该法案是菲律宾国家为实现特定发展战略,通过采取措施有效地吸引生产性外国直接投资,在经济特区内发展农业加工业、工业、旅游业、娱乐业、商业、银行、投资及金融中心、工业房地产、出口加工业、自由贸易区,该法还成立了菲律宾经济区管理署,运营、管理、维持和发展经济特区。

为了更好地从事商业活动,每个商人所关心的不仅是投资可获得收益,他们也关心如何解决投资纠纷,如何保护投资以及他们的收益如何汇款。

由于在商业活动中发生纠纷是不可避免的,外国投资者考虑的不仅仅是在外国的竞争程度,还考虑解决商业纠纷的法律和规则。没有外国投资者愿意将自己的投资置于不利地位。并且,作为商人也是希望能够尽量避免诉讼的,因为诉讼通常不利于其生意。菲律宾已经建立了诉讼外纠纷解决机制。在纠纷进入诉讼程序前,私主体可以先寻求诉讼外纠纷解决方式。

除了建立了诉讼外纠纷解决机制,菲律宾法律也尊重当事方选择解决纠纷的方式的自由权。菲律宾民法典第 1306 款规定了"合同自由原则":

"当事方有权根据自己的意愿确定合同的条款、条件,只要其不违背法律、道德、习惯、公共秩序和国家政策。"

因此,假如一个私人合同的条款中规定了解决争端的方式,法院必须尊重其规定,并且当事方也应该受其约定的约束,遵守其商定的解决争端的方式。未经当事方同意,不得视合同无效。并且菲律宾民法典的第 1308 款中规定了

"相关合同"原则:"合同必须约束合同双方,其有效性和履行不能仅仅根据一方的意愿。"

除了以上内容,菲律宾还遵守了其对国际组织的承诺,在其宪法中规定了"合并原则"。这意味着接受国际法是菲律宾法律的一部分。其在宪法的第二部分的第 2 条中规定:"菲律宾,接受国际法作为其国内法的一部分的普遍原则,并且追求和平、平等、公正、自由。"为了达成其合并原则,菲律宾签署了一些国际协议和条约来解决外国投资者的问题。这些条约确定了外国投资者的"竞争水平"。

作为联合国的成员,菲律宾受《联合国国际贸易法委员会国际商事仲裁示范法》(1985 年 6 月 21 日)约束,并遵守《解决国家与他国国民间投资争端公约》以及《世界贸易组织争端解决机制》。

私人当事方争端的解决,适用以下法律:

1. 共和国宪法第 9285 号,即 2002 年替代性争端解决法;

2. 行政命令第 1008 号,即建设工业仲裁法;

3. 共和国宪法第 876 号,即仲裁法(适用于国内仲裁);

4. 菲律宾劳工法典。

除了关于解决争端的协议和条约,菲律宾还规定了双边条约的基本原则,包括:

1. 通过设立优惠的投资条件以促进各自经济的发展。

2. 最惠国待遇,规定缔约国的一方若给予第三国某种优惠待遇,缔约国的另一方即时获得相同的优惠待遇。

3. 征收条款规定,任何投资者在他国因国家紧急情况、改革、叛乱或者其他情况,东道国应给予其他国不低于给予第三国投资的优惠待遇

4. 投资转移条款,确保投资和回报从合同国的领土到其他国的自由转移。

5. 权利的债权转移条款。

菲律宾鼓励外国投资是其促进国家发展的一部分。菲律宾法律允许外国投资者享有 100% 的股权,并且出台了一系列鼓励外国投资的法律和命令。菲律宾法律还规定了"合同自由原则"等,并且菲律宾遵守了其对国家社会的承诺,有很好的声誉。

Philippine Laws Regulating Foreign Investments

Xerxes U. Garcia[*]

In the article entitled "Foreign Investors Take a Second Look at the Philippines", Honorable Secretary Gregory L. Domingo of the Department of Trade and Industry said "(T) here is tremendous interest in the Philippines right now from foreign investors based on the investment missions that are coming in droves and based on our interaction with them"[①]. In view of this interest, the author would like to part some of his knowledge and research regarding the laws in the Philippines that regulate foreign investments.

It is a basic and primordial constitutional and legal principle in the Philippines that the State shall pursue an independent foreign policy. In its relations with other states the paramount consideration shall be national sovereignty, territorial integrity, national interest, and the right of self-determination. [②] In consonance with this principle, the Philippine Government enacted and implementing several laws regulating foreign investments in the country. Some of these laws are as follows, to wit:

Republic Act No. 7042, as amended by *Republic Act No. 8179*—The *Foreign Investments Act of* 1991 —dwells on foreign investments without incentives; it reduced the minimum paid-in equity from US Dollars Five

---

* Prosecution Attorney at the Department of Justice of the Philippines.

① Article in InterAksyon. com, written by Ben Arnold O. de Vera, December 31, 2012, 10:44 P. M.

② Philippine Foreign Investment Brief, www. chanrobles. com.

Hundred Thousand (US $ 500,000) to US Dollars Two Hundred Thousand (US $ 200,000). [1]

Republic Act No. 7721—liberalized the entry and operations of foreign banks and financial institutions in the Philippines. [2]

Republic Act No. 7652— *The Investor's Lease Act* —grants to foreign investors the privilege of leasing private lands for a period of fifty (50) years [initial] which may be renewed for another twenty-five (25) years. [3]

Republic Act No. 7718— *The Build-Operate-Transfer Act* (BOT)— liberalized the implementation of the Build-Operate-Transfer Scheme in certain projects, eased the restrictions on government financing and setting and imposition of tolls and charges and wholly foreign-owned corporations are allowed to undertake certain projects under this scheme. [4]

Republic Act No. 7888—grants authority to the President of the Philippines to suspend the nationality requirement under the *Omnibus Investments Code* (Executive Order No. 226) in the case of equity investments by multilateral financial institutions like the Asian Development Bank [ADB] or the International Finance Corporation (IFC). [5]

Among these above-mentioned laws, the primary law that regulates foreign investment in the Philippines is *Republic Act No.* 7042 (*R. A.* 7042), otherwise known as the *Foreign Investment Act of* 1991, as amended by *Republic Act No.* 8179. Section 2 of *R. A.* 7042 states the State policy as follows:

"It is the policy of the State to attract, promote and welcome productive investments from foreign individuals, partnerships, corporations, and governments, including their political subdivisions, in activities which significantly contribute to national industrialization and socio-economic development to the extent that foreign investment is allowed in such activity

---

① Philippine Foreign Investment Brief, www. chanrobles. com.
② Philippine Foreign Investment Brief, www. chanrobles. com.
③ Philippine Foreign Investment Brief, www. chanrobles. com.
④ Philippine Foreign Investment Brief, www. chanrobles. com.
⑤ Philippine Foreign Investment Brief, www. chanrobles. com.

by the Constitution and relevant laws. Foreign investments shall be encouraged in the enterprises that significantly expand livelihood and employment opportunities for Filipinos; enhance economic value of farm products; promote the welfare of Filipino consumers; expand the scope, quality and volume of exports and their access to foreign markets; and/or transfer relevant technologies in agriculture, industry and support services. Foreign investments shall be welcome as a supplement to Filipino capital and technology in those enterprises serving mainly the domestic market. "

From the foregoing, it is, therefore, the national policy of the Philippines to encourage the placement of foreign investment. This is to fill in the capital gaps, to give additional employment opportunities to Filipinos, increase production and to help for the over all development of the country. It is the general rule in the Philippines that foreigners may own an interest in areas or business activities engaged in a domestic market enterprise[1] or export enterprise[2] to the extent of 100% of its capital. The exceptions to this rule, however, are those areas or activities reserved by the Constitution or specific laws to Filipinos or to entities wholly owned by Filipinos. This reservation is either (1) absolute or total reservation to Filipinos or (2) limited ownership/equity of foreigners.

Absolute reservation pertains to areas or business activities which only Filipinos or entities owned by Filipinos are allowed to engage. On the other hand, limited ownership pertains to areas or business activities where foreign ownership or equity is limited to a certain percentage. To have a better view on the areas covered by the aforementioned exceptions, *R. A.*

---

[1] Domestic Market Enterprise shall mean an enterprise which produces goods for sale, or renders services to the domestic market entirely or if exporting a portion of its output fails to consistently export at least sixty percent (60%) thereof. [Section 3, paragraph (e), *R.A.* 7042].

[2] Export Enterprise shall mean an enterprise wherein a manufacturer, processor or service (including tourism) enterprise exports sixty percent (60%) or more of its output, or wherein a trader purchases products domestically and exports sixty percent (60%) or more of such purchase. [Section 3, paragraph (e), *R.A.* 7042].

7042 provided for a list of areas or business activities that are reserved to Philippine nationals①. This list is called the Foreign Investment Negative List and has two (2) components, namely: "List A" and "List B".

Foreign investment under Negative List "A" are the areas or business activities where foreign ownership is limited by the Constitution or laws. The following are the areas or business activities under the Negative List "A"②, to wit:

No Foreign Equity

1. Mass Media except recording (Article XVI, Section 11 of the *Constitution*; *Presidential Memorandum Order* dated 4 May 1994).

2. Services involving the practice of licensed professions save in cases prescribed by law.

(1) Engineering

ⅰ. Aeronautical Engineering

ⅱ. Agricultural Engineering

ⅲ. Chemical Engineering

---

① The term "*Philippine national*" shall mean a citizen of the Philippines; of a domestic partnership or association wholly owned by citizens of the Philippines; or a corporation organized under the laws of the Philippines of which at least sixty percent (60%) of the capital stock outstanding and entitled to vote is owned and held by citizens of the Philippines; or a corporation organized abroad and registered as doing business in the Philippines under the Corporation Code of which one hundred percent (100%) of the capital stock outstanding and entitled to vote is wholly owned by Filipinos or a trustee of funds for pension or other employee retirement or separation benefits, where the trustee is a Philippine national and at least sixty percent (60%) of the fund will accrue to the benefit of Philippine nationals. Provided, that where a corporation and its non-Filipino stockholders own stocks in a Securities and Exchange Commission (SEC) registered enterprise, at least sixty percent (60%) of the capital stock outstanding and entitled to vote of each of both corporations must be owned and held by citizens of the Philippines and at least sixty percent (60%) of the members of the Board of Directors of each of both corporations must be citizens of the Philippines, in order that the corporation, shall be considered a "Philippine national". (as amended by *Republic Act No.* 8179).

② Pursuant to *Executive Order No.* 362, October 24, 1996, www. chanrobles. com.

iv. Civil Engineering

v. Electrical Engineering

vi. Electronics and Communication Engineering

vii. Geodetic Engineering

viii. Mechanical Engineering

ix. Metallurgical Engineering

x. Mining Engineering

xi. Naval Architecture and Marine Engineering

xii. Sanitary Engineering

(2) Medical and Allied Professions

i. Dentistry

ii. Medical Technology

iii. Midwifery

iv. Nursing

v. Nutrition and Dietetics

vi. Optometry

vii. Pharmacy

viii. Physical and Occupational Therapy

ix. Radiologic and X-ray Technology

x. Veterinary Medicine

(3) Accountancy

(4) Architecture

(5) Criminology

(6) Chemistry

(7) Customs Broker

(8) Environmental Planning

(9) Forestry

(10) Geology

(11) Interior Design

(12) Landscape Architecture

(13) Law

(14) Librarianship

(15) Marine Deck Officer

(16) Marine Engine Officer

(17) Master Plumbing

(18) Sugar Technology

(19) Social Work

(20) Teaching (Article XVI, Section 14 of the *Constitution*; Section 1 of R. A. No. 5181)

3. Retail Trade (*Republic Act No.* 1180)

4. Cooperatives (Chapter III, Article 26 of R. A. No. 6938)

5. Private Security Agencies (Section 4 of R. A. No. 5487)

6. Small-Scale Mining (Section 3 of R. A. No. 7076)

7. Utilization of marine resources in archipelagic waters, territorial sea, and exclusive economic zone (Article XII, Section 2 of the *Constitution*)

8. Ownership, operation and management of cockpits (Section 5 of Presidential Decree No. 449)

9. Manufacture, repair, stockpiling and/or distribution of nuclear weapons (Article II, Section 8 of the *Constitution*)

10. Manufacture, repair, stockpiling and/or distribution of biological, chemical and radiological weapons (various treaties to which the Philippines is a signatory and conventions supported by the Philippines) Domestic investments are also prohibited (Article II, Section 8 of the *Constitution*; Convention/Treaties to which the Philippines is a signatory)

Up to Twenty-Five Percent (25%) Foreign Equity

11. Private recruitment, whether for local or overseas employment (Articles 27 of Presidential Decree No. 4420)

12. Contracts for the construction and repair of locally-funded works except:

a. Infrastructure/development projects covered in *Republic Act No.* 7718, also known as the *Expanded BOT Law*; and b. Projects which are foreign-funded or assisted and required to undergo international competitive bidding (*Commonwealth Act* 541 as amended by Presidential Decree No. 1594; Letter of Instructions No. 630; *Republic Act No.* 7718)

Up to Thirty Percent (30%) Foreign Equity

13. Advertising (Article XVI, Section 11 of the *Constitution*)

Up to Forty Percent (40%) Foreign Equity

14. Exploration, development and utilization of natural resources (Article XII, Section 2 of the *Constitution*) [Full foreign participation is allowed through financial or technical assistance agreement with the President (Article XII, Section 2 of the *Constitution*)]

15. Ownership of private lands (Article XII, Section 7 of the *Constitution*; Chapter 5, Section 22 of *Commonwealth Act No.* 141)

16. Operation and management of public utilities Article XII, Section 11 of the *Constitution*; Section 16 of *Commonwealth Act No.* 146)

17. Ownership/establishment and administration of educational institutions (Article XIV, Section 2 of the *Constitution*)

18. Engaging in the rice and corn administration (Presidential Decree No. 194)

19. Financing companies regulated by the Securities and Exchange Commission (SEC) (Section 6, *Republic Act No.* 5980)

20. Contracts for the supply of materials, goods and commodities to government-owned or controlled corporation, company, agency or municipal corporation (*Republic Act No.* 5183)

21. Contracts for the construction of defense-related structure (e. g. , land, air, sea and coastal defense, arsenals, barracks, depots, hangars, landing fields, quarters, hospitals) (Commonwealth Act No. 541)

22. Project proponent and facility operator of a BOT project requiring a public utility franchise[(Article XII, Section 11 of the *Constitution*; Section 2(a) of R. A. No. 7718]

23. Private domestic and overseas construction contracts (*Republic Act No.* 4566; Section 14 of the *Constitution*)

On the other hand, Foreign Investment Negative List "B" are those areas or business activities wherein foreign investment or ownership is limited or reserved by reason of security (defense-related activities), public health and morals, and for the protection of "small and medium-sized domestic market enterprises"① with paid-in equity capital less than the equivalent of Two Hundred Thousand US Dollars(US＄200,000.00). The "small and medium domestic market enterprises" are reserved to Philippine nationals. The following are the specific areas or business activities under the Negative List "B"②, to wit:

Up to Forty Percent (40％) Foreign Equity

1. Manufacture, repair, storage, and/or distribution of products and ingredients used in the manufacture thereof requiring Philippine National Police (PNP) clearance:

a. Firearms (handguns to shotguns), parts of firearms and ammunition therefor, instruments or implements used or intended to be used in the manufacture of firearms

b. Gunpowder

c. Dynamite

d. Blasting supplies

e. Ingredients used in making explosives

f. Telescopic sights, sniperscope and other similar devices

2. Manufacture, repair, storage and/or distribution of products requiring Department of National Defense (DND) clearance:

a. Guns and ammunition for warfare

b. Nuclear weapons and ordnance

c. Military ordnance and parts thereof(*e. g.*, torpedoes, mines, depth-charger, bombs, grenades, missiles)

d. Gunnery, bombing and fire control systems and components

---

① Small and medium-sized domestic market enterprises with paid-in equity capital less than the equivalent of Two Hundred Thousand US Dollars (US＄200,000.00), are reserved to Philippine nationals: Provided, That if:(1) they involve advanced technology as determined by the Department of Science and Technology; or (2) they employ at least fifty (50) direct employees, then a minimum paid-in capital of One Hundred Thousand US Dollars (US＄100,000.00) shall be allowed to non-Philippine nationals. (Section 8, *R. A.* 7042).

② Pursuant to Executive Order No. 362, October 24, 1996, www. chanrobles. com.

e. Guided missiles/missile systems and components

f. Tactical aircraft (fixed and rotary-winged), components and parts thereof

g. Space vehicles and component system

h. Combat vessels (air, land, naval) and auxiliaries

i. Weapons repair and maintenance equipment

j. Military communications equipment

k. Night vision equipment

l. Stimulated coherent radiation devices, components and accessories

m. Biological warfare components

n. Armament training devices(*Republic Act No.* 7042, as amended by *R. A. No.* 8179)

3. Manufacture and distribution of dangerous drugs

4. Sauna and steam bathhouses, massage clinics and other like activities regulated by law because of risks they may impose to public health and morals.

5. Other forms of gambling, (*e. g.* , race track operation; racehorse ownership/importation)

Domestic market enterprises with paid-in equity of less than the equivalent of US $ 200,000. 00 unless they involve advance technology or they employ at least fifty(50) direct employees, the minimum paid-in capital will be reduced to US $ 100,000. 00.

Since it is the national policy of the Philippines to encourage foreign investment, the Government did not only allow 100% foreign ownership in selected areas and/or business activities. To further encourage foreign investment, there are laws enacted and executive orders issued which are not only regulatory in nature but also provide incentives to those foreign investments engaged in some chosen economic activities. Laws are as follows:

Executive Order No. 226—*The Omnibus Investments Code of* 1987 — sets forth the rules and parameters within which foreign investments in the Philippines may be made, with emphasis on the grant of incentives to certain sectors. ①

Republic Act No. 7227—The Bases Conversion and Development Act of 1992—sets forth the grant of incentives to industries and enterprises which establish their plants and offices within the Subic Bay Freeport Zone. ②

Republic Act No. 7916—The Special Economic Zone Act of 1995 — treats of incentives granted to industries and enterprises which situate their operation within Special Economic Zones. ③

Republic Act No. 7844—The Export Development Act of 1994— provides for incentives to business enterprises in the export industry. ④

Having in mind a glimpse of the laws that regulate foreign investment, it is imperative also to discuss some matters that are highly related and important in terms of business engagement. In engaging into any kind of business activity, every businessman's concern is not only the extent of his interest/equity and/or the benefits/incentives that he or his business may receive. It is a common and basic knowledge that investors have various concerns that are considered salient factors before he or she engage into a business. Some of these are matters concerning dispute resolution and enforcement of claims (whether through the process of court litigation or extra-judicial settlement), protection and repatriation of investment, and remittances of earnings, among others.

As disputes may always and inevitable arise in every business venture, foreign investors always take into consideration not only the level of competition in a particular foreign country but also the manner on how the laws and regulations in this country treat business disputes. For sure, no foreign investor would like to be in a disadvantage position regardless of how promising the income would be. Also businessmen, as much as possible, avoid court litigations for it is not always good for business. Fortunately,

---

① Philippine Foreign Investment Brief, www. chanrobles. com.

② Philippine Foreign Investment Brief, www. chanrobles. com.

③ Philippine Foreign Investment Brief, www. chanrobles. com.

④ Philippine Foreign Investment Brief, www. chanrobles. com.

the Philippines adheres to the so-called extra-judicial settlement of disputes. In fact, before a case is elevated or subjected to a full-blown trial in court, it is always the requirement that an extra-judicial effort to settle the dispute be exerted first by the private parties. Without exhaustion of this attempt to settle the dispute, the case is vulnerable for dismissal on the ground of being pre-mature.

Aside from the mandates of the law to undergo the processes of outside-of-the-court settlement before the court trial proper, the Philippine law also respects the autonomy of the parties to choose the mode and manner to settle disputes. Under the principle of "Liberality of Contracts" provided in Article 1306 of the *Civil Code* of the Philippines, it states:

"The contracting parties may establish such stipulations, clauses, terms and conditions as they may deem convenient, provided they are not contrary to law, morals, good customs, public order, or public policy. "

Hence, if a particular private contract has a stipulation regarding the manner and mode of settling disputes, the same is not only respected by the courts but also binding to both parties and must be followed. Suffice to say is that no contract of this kind can be rendered invalid, ineffective or inoperable without the consent and assent of the parties. Under the principle of "Mutuality of Contracts" provided in Article 1308 of the *Civil Code* of the Philippines, it states: "(T)he contracts must bind both contracting parties; its validity or compliance cannot be left to the will of one of them. "

Aside from the foregoing, the Philippines, as part of its commitment to the international community, included in its *Constitution* the "Doctrine of Incorporation". This means that the general accepted principles of international law are considered to be automatically part of the Philippine law. Article Ⅱ, Section 2, of the Constitution states that "(T) he Philippines XXX, adopts the generally accepted principles of international law as part of the law of the land and adheres to the policy of peace, equality, justice, freedom, and amity with all nations. "[1]As a realization to

---

① 1987 Philippine *Constitution*.

this doctrine of incorporation, the Philippines is a party-signatory of some international agreements and treaties that address foreign investors' concern. These agreements assure foreign investors of the so-called "On-the-Level Competition" in this country.

As a member of the United Nations, the Philippines is bound to follow the *Model Law* adopted by the U. N. Commission on International Trade Law (UNCITRAL) on June 21, 1985 for international commercial arbitration. The Philippines also adheres to the dispute settlement procedure provided by the *International Convention* on the Settlement of Investment Dispute and Nationals of Other States (ICSID) as well as the enforcement of arbitral awards under the *New York Convention*. [1] As to disputes not covered by the New York Convention, the Philippine courts may, on the grounds of comity and reciprocity, recognize and enforce a non-convention award as a convention award. [2] The Philippines also adheres the procedures laid down by the World Trade Organization (WTO) in settling disputes between members.

With respect to private parties dispute settlement, the following laws are applicable, to wit:

1. *Republic Act No.* 9285—otherwise known as the *Alternative Dispute Resolution Act of* 2004.

2. *Executive Order No.* 1008—otherwise known as the *Construction Industry Arbitration Law.*

3. *Republic Act No.* 876—otherwise known as *The Arbitration Law* (for Domestic Arbitration)

4. *Presidential Decree No.* 442, as amended-otherwise known as the *Labor Code of the Philippines.*

Aside from the agreements and treaties for settling disputes, the Philippines also adhere to the following basic tenets under the *Bilateral*

---

[1] Philippine Foreign Investment Brief, www. chanrobles. com.

[2] Section 43, *R. A.* 9285.

Treatment Treaties①, to wit:

(1) Promotion of investments in either economy by investors of the other economy through the creation of favorable conditions of investments to foster their respective economic developments.

(2) Provision on Most-Favoured-Nation (MFN) Treatment arrangement where respective investors are accorded treatment no less favorable than that accorded to investors of any third state.

(3) Provision on expropriation which ordains that if any investors of either economy suffer losses in the other economy by reason of national e-mergency, revolution, revolt or similar events, the host economy shall accord treatment to that economy no less favorable than that it accords to investments of any third state.

(4) Provision on transfer of investments which guarantees the free transfer of investments and returns held in the territory of one contracting e-

---

① Bilateral Investment Treaties:
a) Philippines and Kingdom of Great Britain and Northern Ireland;
b) Philippines and Kingdom of Netherlands;
c) Philippines and Republic of Italy;
d) Philippines and Socialist Republic of Vietnam;
e) Philippines and Chinese Taipei;
f) Philippines and People's Republic of China;
g) Philippines and Kingdom of Spain;
h) Philippines and Romania;
i) Philippines and Republic of Korea;
j) Philippines and France;
k) Philippines and Australia;
l) Philippines and Czech;
m) Philippines and Thailand;
n) Philippines and Iran;
o) Philippines and Canada;
p) Philippines and Chile;
q) Philippines and Switzerland;
r) Philippines and Germany;
s) The ASEAN Agreement for the Promotion and Protection of Investments.

conomy to the other economy.

(5) Provision on subrogation of rights. [1]

The Philippines encourage foreign investors to be part of its national development by placing their investments. It allows 100% foreign ownership/equity in businesses not included in the Negative List. Its laws and orders are not only regulatory in nature but also provide incentives to select activities to foreign investors. It also adheres to the policy of mutual respect, comity and reciprocity. The Philippine laws also implement the principles on "Liberality of Contracts", "Mutuality of Contracts" and the "Doctrine of Incorporation". And most importantly and which the author is very proud of, Filipinos are good workers, and they have good reputation around the world.

The author is an Assistant State Prosecutor in the National Prosecution Service of the Department of Justice, Philippines. He was one of the participants in the 6th China-ASEAN Legal Training Base held in Chongqing, China, last October-November 2012.

The author would like to extend his thanks and regards to the following:

a) The Officers and Organizers of the China-ASEAN Legal Training;

b) The Officers and Organizers of the China Law Society;

c) The Lawyers, Professors and Students of the SWUPL University;

d) The participants from Myanmar, Laos, Brunei, Indonesia, Cambodia, Thailand, and Vietnam;

e) Jerry Zhu, Li Bin, Sun Chao, Lin Yifan, Chen Zhe, Leo, Luffy, Chang and those student-organizers who sincerely assisted us during the training, and;

f) Atty. Kristina "*Kring*" Zamora.

---

[1] Philippine Foreign Investment Brief, www. chanrobles. com.

菲律宾仲裁制度及其解决国际投资争端的方法

Herbert Calvin P. Abugan*
Karla A. Funtila-Abugan**
司晓玲 译

摘要 菲律宾有一套历史悠久的规制其国际关系的基本法律框架和政策。菲律宾正对其司法系统进行持续改革,尤其是建立和改善其非讼纠纷解决制度,扩大其在国内和国际上的发展。菲律宾对不同国际条约的信守和在各条约下参与不同模式的争端解决表明了其致力于促进国家间,尤其是东盟成员国之间合作的热忱。

关键词 外交关系 对外投资 非讼纠纷解决 仲裁 国际争端解决

一、菲律宾有关国际关系的法律框架

> 在国际法领域,每一条国际法规则都对国家有着法律约束力,因为这是国际法律秩序的意义所在。
>
> ——丹尼斯·劳埃德《法理学》①

菲律宾外交政策的目标是保护菲律宾在处理与外国、区域组织和国际机构之间关系的国家利益。该目标可通过三个历史悠久的途径来实现:一是增强国际安全;二是增进经济外交;三是保护菲律宾在国外的权益。

菲律宾进入国际社会,保护其利益的各项准备依赖于其法律框架所规定的几项协商,包括:

---

* 菲律宾司法部第二检控官。

** 菲律宾最高法院陪审法官办公室 Lucas P. Bersamin 第六法庭律师。

① J. Eduardo Malaya, Maria Antorina Mendoza Oblena, Philippine Treaty Law and Practice, *Integrated Bar of the Philippines Journal*, Vol. 35, No. 1, 2010, p. 1.

(1)菲律宾宪法；

(2)立法工作；

(3)通过条约或行政协定的国际协定；

(4)法理或法庭决定；

(5)总统发布的行政命令；

(6)由不同政府机构颁布的规则和条例。

根据宪法至上主义,菲律宾意识到,在法律体系中宪法是"国家基本的、至高无上的和最高的法律,它被写在每一部成文法和每一条契约之中"①。因此,除非另有证明,每一部法律的实施都具有宪法性。

菲律宾也采纳了国际法中的融合理论。菲律宾1987年宪法第2部分第二条规定:"菲律宾采纳普遍接受的国际法原则作为土地法的一部分,并坚持与所有国家和平、平等、公正、自由、合作及友好的政策。"

1987年宪法为菲律宾加入自由贸易协定提供了四项重要的指引,包括:

(1)菲律宾发展战略的参数

(2)处理对外关系的一般原则

(3)外商参与菲律宾经济活动的宪法性限制

(4)对自由贸易区协商和承诺的制度框架。②

作为菲律宾国家全方面发展的整体框架,1987年宪法要求国家必须促进社会秩序的公正和活力,以确保菲律宾的独立性,通过政策提供充足的社会服务实现贫穷人民的自由,促进全面就业,提高生活标准,改善所有人民的生活质量。③而且,同样也要遵守菲律宾在1935年宪法和1973年宪法中提到的

---

① Barcenas, Lai-Lynn Angelica, *Analysis of Specific Legal and Trade-Related Issues in a Possible PH-EU Economic Partnership*: *The Philippine Constitution*, *Competition Policy*, *Government Procurement*, *Intellectual Property Rights*, *Dispute Settlement and Trade Remedies*, October 10, 2013, p. 13.

② Barcenas, Lai-Lynn Angelica, *Analysis of Specific Legal and Trade-Related Issues in a Possible PH-EU Economic Partnership*: *The Philippine Constitution*, *Competition Policy*, *Government Procurement*, *Intellectual Property Rights*, *Dispute Settlement and Trade Remedies*, October 10, 2013, p. 13.

③ Article Ⅱ, Section 9 of the 1987 *Constitution*.

"社会公正"概念。①

"公正有活力的社会秩序"和"社会正义"这两个概念,反映了国家关注减轻贫困、改善生活质量、鼓励经济活动更能促进国家的包容性增长。②

根据这一基本框架,1987 年宪法对制定经济政策以实现稳定发展目标规定了一套广泛的框架。一方面,第 19 部分第二条采用了民族主义的方法,规定:"国家应当发展由菲律宾有效控制的自立自足的国民经济。"再得,第 20 部分突出了私营部门的作用,从而通过鼓励加大投资的规定促进私营企业的发展。

菲律宾 1987 年宪法第一部分第十二条规定了更多制定经济政策的指导,该条设定了如下国民经济目标:

(1)市场机会、收入和财富更加合理分配;

(2)政府为人民利益而提供的物品和服务总量稳定增长;

(3)重点扩大生产力以提升全体人民,尤其是享受特殊待遇人群的生活水平。③

在对外贸易关系方面,1987 年宪法要求政府:(1)奉行独立的外交政策,首先要考虑国家主权、领土完整、国家利益和国家自决权;(2)在平等互惠的基础上,在利用所有交易形式和安排时,制定满足人民总体利益的贸易政策。④

本着给予菲律宾公民更多优惠待遇的经济政策,1987 年宪法还对外商在菲律宾从事经济活动作出了限制性规定。为了落实这一宪法限制,立法机关

---

① Article Ⅱ, Section 10 of the 1987 *Constitution*; social justice was further reinforced in the 1940 case of Calalang vs. Williams where the Supreme Court clarified that—social justice is neither communism, nor despotism, nor atomism, nor anarchy, but the humanization of laws and the equalization of social and economic forces by the State so that justice in its rational and objectively secular conception may at least be approximated. Social justice means the promotion of the welfare of all the people, the adoption by the Government of measures calculated to ensure economic stability of all the component elements of society, through the maintenance of a proper economic and social equilibrium in the interrelations of the members of the community, constitutionally, through the adoption of measures legally justifiable, or extra-constitutionally, through the exercise of powers underlying the existence of all governments on the time-honored principle of salus populi est supremo lex. (G. R. No. 47800, December 2, 1940)

② *Supra* Note 5, p. 15.

③ *Id.*, p. 16.

④ *Id.*, p. 17.

制定颁布了《第 7042 号共和国法案》(R. A. 7042),作为修正法案的《第 8179号共和国法案》(R. A. 8179)及《1991 年外商投资法》。为鼓励外商投资,《1991 年外商投资法》及随后的法律明确承认外国投资者在菲律宾的各种权利,包括撤回投资、将收入汇至本国和征收豁免(公众使用、出于国家福利或防御的利益和基于公平赔偿的情况除外)的权利。①

根据 1987 年宪法和外商投资法,外商在公司、合伙企业和其他经济体中享有合法权益,法律规定这些公司、合伙企业和其他经济体不能从事那些法律保留的只针对菲律宾公民或者完全由菲律宾公民控制的企业活动。公司允许的最高外资股权份额取决于公司从事的经济活动类型。②

2012 年 10 月 29 日,菲律宾总统颁布了《第 98 号行政命令》(E. O. 98),公布了《第九次定期外商投资负面列表》,③该表反映了在符合现行法律和有关机构建议下某些外国所有权要求的变化。

List A: Foreign Ownership is Limited by Mandate of the Constitution and Specific Laws

Foreign Ownership/ Maximum Foreign Equity	Area/Activity/Industry
No foreign ownership	Mass media except recording
	Practice of all professions (This is limited to Filipino citizens save in cases prescribed by law)
	Retail trade enterprises with paid-up capital of less than US $ 2,500,000
	Cooperatives
	Private security agencies
	Small-scale mining
	Utilization of marine resources in archipelagic waters, territorial sea, and exclusive economic zone as well as small-scale utilization of natural resources in rivers, lakes, bays, and lagoons

---

① *Doing Business in the Philippines* 2009, Quisumbing Torres Law Firm, p. 3.

② *Doing Business in the Philippines* 2009, Quisumbing Torres Law Firm, p. 3.

③ The Ninth Regular Foreign Investment List now provides the following limitations on foreign investment ownership.

续表

Foreign Ownership/ Maximum Foreign Equity	Area/Activity/Industry
No foreign ownership	Ownership, operation and management of cockpits
	Manufacture, repair, stockpiling and/or distribution of nuclear weapons
	Manufacture, repair, stockpiling and/or distribution of biological, chemical and radiological weapons and anti-personnel mines
	Manufacture of firecrackers and other pyrotechnic devices
Up to 20% Foreign Equity	Private radio communications network
Up to 25% Foreign Equity	Private recruitment, whether for local or overseas employee
	Contracts for the construction and repair of locally-funded public works, except: a. Infrastructure/development projects covered in R. A. 7718; and b. Projects which are foreign funded or assisted and required to undergo international competitive bidding
	Contracts for the construction of defense-related structures
Up to 30% Foreign Equity	Advertising
Up to 40% Foreign Equity	Exploration, development, and utilization of natural resources
	Ownership of private lands
	Operation and management of public utilities
	Ownership/establishment and administration of educational institutions
	Culture, production, milling, processing, trading except retailing, of rice and corn and acquiring, by barter, purchase or otherwise, rice and corn and the by-products thereof

续表

Foreign Ownership/ Maximum Foreign Equity	Area/Activity/Industry
Up to 40% Foreign Equity	Contracts for the supply of materials, goods and commodities to government-owned or controlled corporation, company, agency or municipal corporation
	Project proponent and facility operator of a BOT Project requiring a public utilities franchise
	Operation of deep sea commercial fishing vessels
	Adjustment companies
	Ownership of condominium units where the common areas in the condominium project are co-owned by the owners of the separate units or owned by a corporation
Up to 49% Foreign Equity	Lending companies
Up to 60% Foreign Equity	Financing companies regulated by the Securities and Exchange Commission
	Investment houses regulated by the Securities and Exchange Commission

List B: Foreign Ownership is Limited for Reasons of Security, Defense, Risk to Health and Morals and Protectionof Small- and Medium-Scale Enterprises

Foreign Ownership/ Maximum Foreign Equity	Area/Activity/Industry
Up to 40% Foreign Equity	Manufacture, repair, storage and/or distribution of products and/or ingredients requiring Philippine National Police (PNP) clearance: a. Firearms (handguns to shotguns), parts of firearms and ammunition therefore, instruments or implements used or intended to be used in the manufacture of firearms b. Gunpowder c. Dynamite d. Blasting supplies e. Ingredients used in making explosives Telescopic sights, sniper scope and other similar devices

续表

Foreign Ownership/ Maximum Foreign Equity	Area/Activity/Industry
Up to 40% Foreign Equity	Manufacture, repair, storage and/or distribution of products requiring Department of National Defense (DND) clearance: a. Guns and ammunitions for warfare b. Military ordnance and parts thereof c. Gunnery, bombing and fire control systems and components d. Guided missiles/missile systems and components e. Tactical aircraft, parts and components thereof f. Space vehicles and component systems g. Combat vessels and auxiliaries h. Weapons repair and maintenance equipment i. Military communications equipment j. Night vision equipment k. Stimulated coherent radiation devices, components and accessories l. Armament training devices m. Others as may be determined by the Secretary of DND
	Manufacture and distribution of dangerous drugs
	Sauna and steam bathhouses, massage clinics and other like activities regulated by law because of risks posed to public health and morals
	All forms of gambling, except those covered by investment agreements with PAGCOR pursuant to *R. A.* 9487, or the *PAGCOR Charter*
	Domestic market enterprises with paid-in equity capital of less than the equivalent of US $ 200,000
	Domestic market enterprises which involve advance technology or employ at least fifty (50) direct employees with paid-in capital of less than the equivalent of US $ 100,000

Supra Note 12, p. 5.

另一方面,另一部制定实施的法——《反假冒法》,规定了对违反了外资股权限制的自然人、法人的民事和刑事处罚。根据该法,对于以其名义或权益、特许、特权、所有或经营受其控制(而法律特别规定这些权利、特许、特权、所有或经营只能给菲律宾公民或至少有60％资本由菲律宾公民所有的合资组织）的外国人，将：

（1）不得允许利用和享有这些给予不符合法定资质的个人、公司和组织的权利、特许、特权、所有或经营；

（2）任何方式下都不得允许不适格的人介入上述权益、特许、特权、所有或经营的管理和操控，无论是官员、雇主或劳工，无论是否有酬劳（由司法部秘书处特别委任的技术人员除外）。

但是，外国人可以作为公司的董事会或理事会成员，从事部分与其实际和允许股权相符的国有化经济活动。①

菲律宾第一政策也是菲律宾经济的重要支柱。该政策体现在1987年《宪法》第12部分第十二条中，规定国家"促进本国劳工、国产材料和地方产物品的优先使用，并采取措施使其有竞争力"。把菲律宾业界实践的限制和发放作为外国人在菲工作之必需的就业许可，②明显体现了该政策的实施。按照《菲律宾劳动法》，该就业许可仅在无任何菲律宾公民适合、有能力和愿意提供所要求服务时才会发放。③

在自由贸易协定的谈判方面，有权代表国家利益参与协商的政策制定者和官员是由宪法规定的，以确保贸易协定：

（1）促进经济的包容性和持续性增长；

（2）与市场导向经济相符，保护利益相关者，尤其是菲律宾公民，免于遭受不公平竞争和参与不公平活动；

（3）使菲律宾继续独立于外资控制；

（4）尊重保护性战略行业的限制；

（5）促进与菲贸易伙伴的平等互惠。④

综合以上所述的政策、框架和宪法规定，菲律宾已加入下列贸易协定，见表1。

---

① *Supra* Note 12，p. 5.
② *Supra* Note 5，p. 23.
③ *Id.*
④ *Id.*

表1 菲律宾加入自由贸易协定的现状①

现状	区域性的	双边性的
已生效	东盟自由贸易协定(1993) 东盟—中国自由贸易协定(2005) 东盟—韩国自由贸易协定(2006) 东盟—日本关于建立更紧密经贸关系的安排(2008)	日本—菲律宾 EPA(2008)
已签署	东盟—澳大利亚—新西兰关于建立更紧密经贸关系的安排(2009) 东盟—印度自由贸易协定(2009)	

除了加入自由贸易协定,菲律宾还制定了贸易和投资政策来增加其在国际市场上的角色重要性。这些政策包括,见表2。

表2 菲律宾其他贸易和投资政策②

贸易政策	投资政策
内向型进口替代政策和出口鼓励措施法案(1950—1970 年) 关税改革和进口自由化计划(1981—2003 年) 出口发展法(1994 年) 实施信息技术协议(2000 年)	综合投资法典 对外贸易者签证(第 758 号行政命令) 经济特区法(1995 年) 设立出口加工区: ※18 个农业产业经济区 ※187 个信息科技园/中心 ※65 个制造产业经济区 ※2 个医疗旅游公园/中心 ※17 个旅游经济区(截至 2013 年 6 月 30 日)

菲律宾创设的作为关税区域外(保税区)来对待的经济区,开放并吸引了一些外国投资机会,因为这些经济区对投资者给予了激励措施。初期的激励措施采取了如下财政和非财政利益的形式,见表3。

---

① Wignaraja, Ganeshan, Dorothea Lazaro and Genevieve De Guzman, *FTAs and Philippine Business*: *Evidence from Transport*, *Food*, *and Electornic Firms*, ADBI Working Series, January 2010 (No. 185), p.31.

② Wignaraja, Ganeshan, Dorothea Lazaro and Genevieve De Guzman, *FTAs and Philippine Business*: *Evidence from Transport*, *Food*, *and Electornic Firms*, ADBI Working Series, January 2010 (No. 185), p.31.

表 3　经济特区的激励措施①

财政的	非财政的
所得税免税(ITH)—100％免除企业所得税 5％的总收入特别税,并免除所有的国家和地方税 原材料、基础设备、机器和零部件的进口免税 豁免码头费、出口税费 对符合 BIR 和 PEZA 要求的当地采购增值税实行零税率 免除所有地方政府税捐、费用、许可费和税款的缴纳 豁免扩展性预扣税	简化进出口程序 非居民外国人可被 PEZA 登记的经济区企业雇佣从事监管、技术或咨询工作 对下列 PEZA 登记的经济区企业中的非居民外国人给予享有多次入境特权的非移民签证:从事监管、技术或咨询职位的投资者、主管、雇员及其配偶、21 岁以下的未婚子女

对国际协议的协商和承诺是通过菲律宾总统或参议院行使权力来进行的。②司法部也参与进来了,在需要对条约进行解释以确定其合宪性和有效性的案件中充当裁判者。③在这方面,下一部分将对菲律宾司法制度和法律体系中出现的非讼纠纷解决机制之意义做简要说明。

二、菲律宾的非讼纠纷解决机制

菲律宾的法律体系,包括其司法规则,主要是吸收了西方国家,尤其是美国的法律制度,并受到了这些制度的影响。法律争端主要是通过法院解决的,因为法院的主要功能就是保障当事方权利的实现和义务的履行。无论是自然人还是法人,诉诸法院是他们常用的保障自身权利和确保义务履行的救济途径。

然而,由于案件数量激增,每天都有新的争端出现,未决案件的日益增多催生出了一种更迅捷更经济的案件处理新机制。通过"庭外"程序来处理某些案件从而被引进菲律宾的法律体系。通过立法设立机构和机制来帮助法庭处理繁多的案例,同时也为当事方提供了选择性的权益保障途径。

---

① 　www. peza. gov. ph. Visited on November 14, 2013.

② 　Article Ⅶ, Section 21 of the 1987 *Constitution*.

③ 　Article Ⅷ, Section 4(2) of the 1987 *Constitution*.

各种非讼纠纷解决办法诸如仲裁、调解和调停的采取,不仅加速了案件的解决,而且也提高了司法效率和司法有效性。这使得最高法庭在制定议事规则时,优先考虑下列因素:(1)处理所有法院的现有堆积案件;(2)研究未按期处理宪法授权案件的原因并对此加以解决;(3)推广非讼纠纷解决模式。[①]

菲律宾司法制度的背景简介

1987 年宪法规定司法权力属于最高法院,在其之下的法院可依法设立。[②]法院的等级及其各自管辖权由不同的立法规定。根据经修订已于 1983 年 1 月 18 日生效的第 129 号国家法律(也被称为《1980 年司法重组法》)和其他法律,菲律宾的司法系统由以下法院组成:

(1)大城市法院(MeTC),市法院(MTC)、各城市法院(MTCC)、市巡回法院(MCTC)被称为第一级法院或限制管辖权法院。

菲律宾的每个城市都有自己的市法院。如果有两个或两个以上的城市,就称为市巡回法院。作为与其他政治分支的区分,"大城市法院"通常是指在马尼拉的城镇和城市中的市法院。"各城市法院"指的是在马尼拉之外的城市法院。

(2)第二级法院是地区法院(RTC)。在菲律宾,地区法院是有一般司法管辖权的法院。地区法院分别在菲律宾的 13 个地区中建立,数量与法律规定的一致。

(3)第三级是上诉法院(CA)。上诉法院拥有地区法院和其他司法机构的上诉管辖权,由 1 名首席法官和 6 名陪审法官组成,对地区法院和某些准司法机构及委员会的裁决有上诉管辖权。

(4)最高法院是菲律宾最高一级的法院,处于四层法院系统的最高层。它是唯一的由宪法创设并称为终审裁决法院的"宪法性法院"。全国只有一个最高法院,由 1 名首席法官和 14 名陪审法官组成,是所有案件的终裁机构。在审理案件时,由全体法官出庭或者酌情分为 3 人、5 人或 7 人分庭。最高法院严格遵守法院层级政策,除涉及国家利益的案件,不得受理任何直接提交给它的案件。[③]

---

① *The Davide Watch*:Leading the Philippine Judiciary and the Legal Profession Towards the Third Millennium,December 1998.

② Article Ⅷ,Section 1 of the 1987 *Constitution*.

③ Article Ⅷ,Section 1 of the 1987 *Constitution*.

菲律宾非讼纠纷解决制度

在菲律宾,非讼纠纷解决制度并不是新生的争端解决制度。早在1953年7月19日,菲律宾国会就制定颁布了第876号共和国法案(*R.A.* 876),该法案也被称为《仲裁法》。该法案规定了民事纠纷的仲裁程序,对仲裁的采用和仲裁协议的提交进行了授权,并规定了仲裁员的任命。根据该法,协议双方可以按其约定的特别程序对争议提请仲裁,若无相关规定,将补充适用该法案的规定。

然而,尽管实施了第876号共和国法案,诉讼案件的数量仍然日益增加,这使得最高法院和整个国家政府都为此担忧。为解决这一问题,1987年宪法授权最高法院可制定快速处理案件的简易程序规则。①

根据这一宪法规定,最高法院发布了公告、备忘录和行政命令对某些类型的民事案件强制适用非讼纠纷解决机制。《民事诉讼规则》甚至允许诉讼当事人可通过和解和非讼程序来解决纠纷。② 为了更有效地执行这一规定,最高法院在2001年9月16日颁布了第21—2001号行政命令,指定菲律宾司法学会(PHILJA)作为处理诉讼调停案件和其他非讼纠纷的组成机构,并建立了菲律宾调停中心(PMC)。

此外,还采取了诸如下列立法和行政措施来解决这一问题:

(1)根据第7160号共和国法案制定的《1991年地方政府法》,在将纠纷诉诸法院之前,每个巴朗艾(barangay)的一级市(lupon)有权以达成纠纷和解为

---

①   Article Ⅷ, Section 5, paragraph 5 of the 1987 *Constitution*.
②   Rule 18, Section 2 of the Revised Rules of Court.

由集合实际居住在同一城市的当事方,另有规定的除外;①

(2)第 7394 号共和国法案(R. A. 7394),也被称为《1992 年菲律宾消费者法》。该法为消费者规定了仲裁人员,这些人员是由拥有调停、调解、审理、判决一切消费纠纷的最初性和排他性管辖权的卫生部、农业部或贸工部的秘书处任命的政府工作人员;②

(3)第 7942 号共和国法案(R. A. 7942),也被称为《1995 年矿业法》。该法规定了环境与自然资源部每一区域办事处的政府雇佣仲裁员的任命,并规定这些仲裁员对关于矿区、采矿协议或采矿许可、表面业主或占用人、债权持

---

① Section 408 of *R. A.* 7160 provides:

Section 408. Subject Matter for Amicable Settlement; Exception Thereto. The lupon of each barangay shall have authority to bring together the parties actually residing in the same city or municipality for amicable settlement of all disputes except:

(1)Where one party is the government, or any subdivision or instrumentality thereof;

(2)Where one party is a public officer or employee, and the dispute relates to the performance of his official functions;

(3)Offenses punishable by imprisonment exceeding one year or a fine exceeding five thousand pesos (P5,000.00);

(4)Offenses where there is no private offended party;

(5) Where the dispute involves real properties located in different cities or municipalities unless the parties thereto agree to submit their differences to amicable settlement by an appropriate lupon;

(6) Disputes involving parties who actually reside in barangays of different cities or municipalities, except where such barangay units adjoin each other and the parties thereto agree to submit their differences to amicable settlement by an appropriate lupon;

(7) Such other classes of disputes which the President may determine in the interest of Justice or upon the recommendation of the Secretary of Justice.

The court in which non-criminal cases not falling within the authority of the lupon under this Code are filed may, at any time before trial motu proprio refer the case to the lupon concerned for amicable settlement.

② Article 160 of *R. A.* 7394 provides:

Article 160. Consumer Arbitration Officers—the concerned Department Secretaries shall appoint as many qualified consumer arbitration officers as may be necessary for the effective and efficient protection of consumer rights. Provided, however that there shall be not more than ten (10) consumer arbitration officers per province, including the National Capital Region.

有者或特许经营者的纠纷行使最初性和排他性的管辖;①

(4)根据 1985 年 2 月 4 日第 1088 号行政命令创设的菲律宾建造业仲裁委员会(CIAC)。该委员会是为解决日益增多的诉讼案件,包括业内契约索偿的目的而设立的。

(5)《第 8293 号共和国法案》(R. A. 8293),也被称为《1998 年知识产权法》。该法规定:"技术转让协议中应当规定仲裁事项,仲裁规则应当选用《菲律宾仲裁规则》、《菲律宾仲裁法》、《联合国国际贸易法委员会仲裁规则》(UNCITRAL)或《国际商会(ICC)仲裁规则》,仲裁地应当是菲律宾或任何中立国家。"

关于非讼纠纷解决的最近立法是《第 9285 号共和国法案》(R. A. 9285),也被称为《2004 年非讼纠纷解决法》。该法于 2004 年 4 月 14 日由国会颁布,根据该法,菲律宾政府要"积极推进纠纷解决当事人意思自治或当事人自由安排纠纷解决,鼓励并积极促进非讼纠纷解决机制成为迅速、公正、缓解诉讼累积的司法途径"②。

为了实现《非讼纠纷解决法》的目标,非讼纠纷解决办事处(OADR)成立

---

① Section 77 of R. A. 7942 states:

Sec. 77 Panel of Arbitrators. There shall be a panel of arbitrators in the regional office of the Department composed of three (3) members, two (2) of whom must be members of the Philippine Bar in good standing and one licensed mining engineer or a professional in a related field, and duly designated by the Secretary as recommended by the Mines and Geosciences Bureau Director. Those designated as members of the panel shall serve as such in addition to their work in the Department without receiving any additional compensation. As much as practicable, said members shall come from the different bureaus of the Department in the region. The presiding officer shall be on a yearly basis.

The members of the panel shall perform their duties and obligations in hearing and deciding cases until their designation is withdrawn or revoked by the Secretary. Within thirty (30) working days, after the submission of the case by the parties for decision, the panel shall have exclusive and original jurisdiction to hear and decide on the following:

(1) Disputes involving rights to mining areas;

(2) Disputes involving mineral agreements or permits;

(3) Disputes involving surface owners, occupants and claimholders/concessionaires; and

(4) Disputes pending before the Bureau and the Department at the date of the effectivity of this Act.

② R. A. 9285, April 2, 2004.

了。OADR 是司法部(DOJ)的附属代理,在司法部的直接监督下运行,并负有监督国家公私领域非讼纠纷解决的责任。

OADR 的目标是:(1)促进、发展、扩大 ADR 在公私领域的适用;(2)协助监督、研究、评估公私领域 ADR 的适用;(3)向国会提出在国际标准下 ADR 实践的发展、加强和改善之必要法律更改的建议。为实现这些目标,国会也授予 OADR 以非常大的权利和职能。①

三、菲律宾解决国际贸易和投资争端的方法

与国内案件相同,争端解决对维护国家间的和谐与合作是非常重要的。作为诸多国际组织的成员和国际条约的缔约者,菲律宾坚持用不同模式的争端解决方式来解决条约解释时和行使契约权利时发生的冲突。依前最高法院首席法官 Andres R. Narvasa 所言,可对"国家间争端解决机制"做如下定义:

"一种审视国际争端解决的更传统的方式,应当是看第三方介入该争端的程度。若该争端解决仅是双边性的,则该解决方式可被视为协商。若第三方可以严格限制的理由介入,即,使双方坐到一起开始彼此的协商(斡旋);除此

---

① (1) To act as appointing authority of mediators and arbitrators when the parties agree in writing that it shall be empowered to do so; (2) To conduct seminars, symposia, conference and publish proceedings of said activities and relevant materials/information that would promote develop and expand the use of ADR; (3) To establish an ADR library or resource center that will contain laws, rules and regulations, jurisprudence, books, articles and other information about ADR in the Philippines and elsewhere for easy access to the public; (4) To establish training programs for ADR providers/practitioners, both in the public and private sectors; and to undertake periodic and continuing training programs for arbitration and mediation and charge fees on participants. It may do so in conjunction with or in cooperation with the IBP, private ADR organizations, and local and foreign government offices and agencies and international organizations; (5) To certify those who have successfully completed the regular professional training programs provided by the OADR or other ADR provider organizations as approved by the OADR; (6) To charge fees for services rendered such as, among others, for training and certifications of ADR providers; (7) To accept donations, grants and other assistance from local and foreign sources; and (8) To exercise such other powers as may be necessary and proper to carry into effect the provisions of the ADR Act of 2004 (*R. A.* 9285).

之外,第三方可为一方向另一方传递建议,在此种情况下,该方法叫作调停。若第三方被授权为争端解决提供独立的主动性建议,则该方法叫作调解。若第三方被授权可替代性地认定先决事实或引起争端的事实,在此情况下,该第三方是调查委员会。若第三方被授权独立解决争端,要么通过仲裁,要么通过司法程序,这取决于第三方是临时被选中的还是其本身就是解决争端特别指定的制度框架和持续性系统的一部分。在此情况下,第三方可能是独立的仲裁者、仲裁委员会或法院、法庭或法官。"①

因此,菲律宾已认可、利用了下述模式②来解决其管辖权范围内的国际贸易和投资争端,见表 4。

表 4　菲律宾采取的国际争端解决模式

争端类型	争端解决模式
政府间的	WTO 争端解决机制 联合国国际贸易法委员会和 UNCITRAL 模式 菲律宾—日本经济合作协定中的争端解决机制 东盟—中国自由贸易协定中的争端解决机制
政府和私人间的	国际投资争端解决中心(ICSID) 关于承认及执行外国仲裁裁决的公约(纽约公约)
私人间的	R. A. 876 R. A. 9285 E. O. 1008

在 WTO 争端解决机制下,菲律宾在条约项下权利和义务的争端会被提请至贸工部和关税及相关事宜委员会主席处。③ 司法部和律政专员办事处则会各

---

① Dispute Settlement under the Aegis of the World Trade Organization, in Odyssey and Legacy: the Chief Justice Andres R. Narvasa Centennial Lecture Series, at 180 (1999), cited in *Toward the Formulation of a Philippine Position in Resolving Trade and Investment Disputes in APEC* by now Supreme Court Chief Justice Ma. Lourdes P. A. Sereno, PASCN Discussion Paper No. 2001—15, December 2001, pp. 5~6.

② *Toward the Formulation of a Philippine Position in Resolving Trade and Investment Disputes in APEC* by now Supreme Court Chief Justice Ma. Lourdes P. A. Sereno, PASCN Discussion Paper No. 2001—15, December 2001, p. 24; see also Supra Note 5, pp. 65~69.

③ *Supra* Note 5, p. 72.

自代表菲律宾政府。① 迄今为止,菲律宾已是 22 个 WTO 争端案件的当事方,即:5 个案件中的申诉方,6 个案件中的应诉方及 11 个案件中的第三方。②

由于 WTO 争端解决机制是全球性的,其程序和结果对其他国际协议下的争端解决制度产生了巨大的影响,包括东盟—中国自由贸易区(ACFTA)框架协议中的争端解决制度。

鉴于菲律宾是 ACFTA 和 WTO 的签署国和成员国,ACFTA 框架协议中的贸易争端解决可由菲律宾按照 ACFTA 下的争端解决机制或按照 WTO 协定提出。由于其历史悠久,WTO 在争端解决上有充分的法理依据。因此 ACFTA 下的争端解决机制可能不得不依赖于 WTO 或 GATT 下的争端解决机制。在 ACFTA 框架协议下,申诉方可选择一个排他性的法庭,除非当事方已明确约定可用更多的法庭来解决争端。③ 但是,为了避免所选法庭的不确定性,必须适用 ACFTA 框架协议下争端解决机制的排除规则,该规则规定:"一旦根据 ACFTA 或其他已签署条约启动了争端解决程序,申诉方选择的法庭应当排除任何其他类似争端的解决。"④

对仲裁的适用、仲裁庭达成共识的要求是 ACFTA 框架协议中的争端解决机制的特性,是"东盟方式"的反映。因此将它与 WTO 争端解决机制分别开来。⑤

同样值得关注的是,在菲律宾严格遵守《关于承认及执行外国仲裁裁决的公约》时,缔约国不同国籍当事方之间的外国仲裁协议的强制性是由菲律宾管辖的。⑥

---

① *Executive Order No.* 292, otherwise known as the *Administrative Code*, as amended, Book Ⅳ, Title Ⅲ, Chapter 1, Section 1 and Chapter 12, Section 35.

② http://www.wto.org/english/tratop_e/dispu_e/dispu_by_country_e.htm. Visited on November 19,2013.

③ Zhu Weidong, *The Dispute Settlement Mechanism of ASEAN Free Trade Area (AFTA) and Its Implications for SADC*, citing Article 2(6) and (7) of the Agreement on the Dispute Settlement Mechanism, p. 16.

④ Wang Jiangyu, *ASEAN-China Free Trade Agreements: Legal and Institutional Aspects*, citing DSM Agreement, Article 2.6, p. 129. http://www.eastlaw.net/jyworks/wang-acfta0001.pdf. Visited on November 20, 2013.

⑤ See *supra* Note 38, pp. 18~19

⑥ *National Union Fire Insurance Co. of Pittsburg vs. Stolt-Nielsen Philippines, Inc.* G.R. No. 87958, April 26, 1990, 184 SCRA 682.

The Philippine Arbitration System And Its Approach To Resolving International Investment Disputes

Herbert Calvin P. Abugan[①]
Karla A. Funtila-Abugan[②]

Abstract　The Philippines has long-established a fundamental framework and set of policies that govern its international relations. The Philippines' continuing reform in its judicial system, more particularly with regard to the institution and improvement of its alternative dispute resolution system, magnifies development not only in the domestic sphere but in the international level as well. The Philippines' adherence to various international agreements and its participation to the different modes of dispute settlement under each agreement manifest its growing enthusiasm to strengthen efforts of promoting cooperation between and among nations, especially those included in the ASEAN.

Keywords　Foreign Relations; Foreign Investments; Alternative Dispute Resolution; Arbitration; International Dispute Settlement

1. The Philippines' Legal Framework on International Relations

Every rule of international law imposes a legal fetter on national states in the international sphere, for this is the very sense and meaning of an in-

---

　①　Prosecution Attorney II at the Department of Justice of the Philippines.

　②　Court Attorney VI under the Office of Associate Justice Lucas P. Bersamin of the Supreme Court of the Philippines.

ternational legal order.

Dennis Lloyd, *The Idea of Law* [1]

The purpose of Philippine foreign policy is to secure the national interest of Filipinos in dealing with foreign nations, regional organizations and international bodies. This purpose has been done through three long-established pillars: (1) promoting national security; (2) enhancing economic diplomacy; and (3) protecting the rights and welfare of Filipinos overseas.

The Philippines' readiness to enter into international relations, bearing in mind its various interests, are dependent on several negotiating parameters provided by its legal framework, which include the following:

(1) The Philippine Constitution;

(2) Legislative enactments;

(3) International agreements either through treaties or executive agreements;

(4) Jurisprudence or judicial decisions;

(5) Executive orders issued by the President; and

(6) Rules and regulations issued by different government agencies.

The Philippines, under the doctrine of constitutional supremacy, recognizes that in the hierarchy of laws, the Constitution "is the fundamental, paramount and supreme law of the nation, it is deemed written in every statute and contract"[2]. Every law enacted is, therefore, presumed constitutional unless proven otherwise.

The Philippines further adopts the *doctrine of incorporation* with respect to international laws. Article II, Section 2 of the 1987 *Philippine*

---

[1] J. Eduardo Malaya, Maria Antorina Mendoza Oblena, Philippine Treaty Law and Practice, *Integrated Bar of the Philippines Journal*, Vol. 35, No. 1, 2010, p. 1.

[2] Barcenas, Lai-Lynn Angelica, *Analysis of Specific Legal and Trade-Related Issues in a Possible PH-EU Economic Partnership: The Philippine Constitution, Competition Policy, Government Procurement, Intellectual Property Rights, Dispute Settlement and Trade Remedies*, October 10, 2013, p. 13.

Constitution provides that "the Philippines adopts the generally accepted principles of international law as part of the law of the land and adheres to the policy of peace, equality, justice, freedom, cooperation, and amity with all nations".

The 1987 Philippine Constitution sets out four (4) important guidelines for the Philippines in entering into free trade agreements. These are the following:

1. Parameters for Philippine Development Policy;

2. General Principles Governing External Economic Relations;

3. Constitutional Limitations on Foreign Participation in the Philippine Economy; and

4. Institutional Framework for the Negotiations and Commitment to Free Trade Agreements (FTAs). [1]

As a general framework for all aspects of the country's national development, the 1987 Philippine Constitution mandates that the State shall promote a just and dynamic social order that will ensure the independence of the Philippines and freedom of poverty through policies that provide adequate social services, promote full employment, a rising standard of living, and an improved quality of life for all. [2]

---

[1] *Id.*

[2] Article II, Section 9 of the 1987 *Constitution.*

Further, the concept of *social justice*, [1]which was earlier recognized under the 1935 and 1973 Philippine Constitution, must likewise be observed.

These two (2) concepts, *just and dynamic social order* and *social justice*, reflect the concern of the State to alleviate poverty, improve quality of life and encourage economic activity as a means of promoting more inclusive growth for the country. [2]

Following this general framework, the 1987 Philippine Constitution provides a broad framework for economic policy-making to achieve its goal of sustained growth.

Article II, Section 19 thereof adopts a nationalistic approach and mandates that "the State shall develop a self-reliant and independent national economy effectively controlled by Filipinos". Section 20, on the other hand, highlights the role of the private sector and thus promotes private enterprise with provision for incentives to boost investment.

More specific guidance for economic-policy making is provided by Article XII, Section 1 of the 1987 Philippine *Constitution* where it set the goals for the national economy as follows:

(1) More equitable distribution of opportunites, income and wealth;

(2) Sustained increase in the amount of goods and services produced by

---

[1] Article II, Section 10 of the 1987 Constitution; *Social justice* was further reinforced in the 1940 case of *Calalang v. Williams* where the Supreme Court clarified that—social justice is neither communism, nor despotism, nor atomism, nor anarchy, but the humanization of laws and the equalization of social and economic forces by the State so that justice in its rational and objectively secular conception may at least be approximated. Social justice means the promotion of the welfare of all the people, the adoption by the Government of measures calculated to ensure economic stability of all the component elements of society, through the maintenance of a proper economic and social equilibrium in the interrelations of the members of the community, constitutionally, through the adoption of measures legally justifiable, or extra-constitutionally, through the exercise of powers underlying the existence of all governments on the time-honored principle of salus populi est supremo lex. (G. R. No. 47800, December 2, 1940)

[2] *Supra* Note 5, p. 15.

the nation for the benefit of the people; and

(3) Expanding productivity as the key to raising the quality of life for all, especially the underprivileged. ①

In its external trade relations, the 1987 Philippine Constitution directs the government to one, pursue an independent foreign policy, the foremost consideration for which is the State's national sovereignty, territorial integrity, national interest, and its right to self-determination, and two, pursue a trade policy that serves the general welfare of the people while utilizing all forms and arrangements of exchange on the basis of equality and reciprocity. ②

The 1987 Philippine Constitution also imposes certain limitations on foreign participation in the Philippine economy in line with its economic policy to give preferential treatment to Filipino citizens. To implement this constitutional limitations, the legislature enacted *Republic Act No. 7042* (*R. A. 7042*), as amended by *Republic Act No. 8179* (*R. A. 8179*), otherwise known as the *Foreign Investments Act of* 1991. To encourage foreign investments, the Foreign Investments Act and subsequent laws expressly recognize various rights of foreign investors in Philippines, including the rights to repatriation of investments, remittance of earnings, and freedom from expropriation (except for public use or in the interest of national welfare or defense and upon payment of just compensation). ③

Under the 1987 Philippine Constitution and Foreign Investments Act, foreigners may hold interests in corporations, partnerships, and other entities in the Philippines, provided that such corporations, partnerships, and other entities are not engaged in an activity that is reserved by law only to Philippine citizens or to entities that are wholly owned by Philippine citizens. The maximum amount of foreign equity that is allowed in a company depends on the type of activity that the company is engaged in. ④

On October 29, 2012, the President of Philippines issued Executive

---

① *Id.*, p. 16.

② *Id.*, p. 17.

③ *Doing Business in Philippines* 2009, Quisumbing Torres Law Firm, p. 3.

④ *Id.*

Order No. 98 (*E. O.* 98) promulgating the *Ninth Regular Foreign Investment Negative List*,① which reflects changes to certain foreign ownership requirements in compliance with existing laws and upon recommendation of concerned agencies.

List A: Foreign Ownership is Limited by Mandate of the Constitution and Specific Laws

Foreign Ownership/ Maximum Foreign Equity	Area/Activity/Industry
No foreign ownership	Mass media except recording
	Practice of all professions (This is limited to Filipino citizens save in cases prescribed by law)
	Retail trade enterprises with paid-up capital of less than US $ 2,500,000
	Cooperatives
	Private security agencies
	Small-scale mining
	Utilization of marine resources in archipelagic waters, territorial sea, and exclusive economic zone as well as small-scale utilization of natural resources in rivers, lakes, bays, and lagoons
	Ownership, operation and management of cockpits
	Manufacture, repair, stockpiling and/or distribution of nuclear weapons
	Manufacture, repair, stockpiling and/or distribution of biological, chemical and radiological weapons and anti-personnel mines
	Manufacture of firecrackers and other pyrotechnic devices
Up to 20% Foreign Equity	Private radio communications network

① The Ninth Regular Foreign Investment List now provides the following limitations on foreign investment ownership.

续表

Foreign Ownership/ Maximum Foreign Equity	Area/Activity/Industry
Up to 25% Foreign Equity	Private recruitment, whether for local or overseas employme
	Contracts for the construction and repair of locally-funded public works, except: a. Infrastructure/development projects covered in *R. A.* 7718; and b. Projects which are foreign funded or assisted and required to undergo international competitive bidding
	Contracts for the construction of defense-related structures
Up to 30% Foreign Equity	Advertising
Up to 40% Foreign Equity	Exploration, development, and utilization of natural resources
	Ownership of private lands
	Operation and management of public utilities
	Ownership/establishment and administration of educational institutions
	Culture, production, milling, processing, trading except retailing, of rice and corn and acquiring, by barter, purchase or otherwise, rice and corn and the by-products thereof
	Contracts for the supply of materials, goods and commodities to government-owned or controlled corporation, company, agency or municipal corporation
	Project proponent and facility operator of a BOT Project requiring a public utilities franchise
	Operation of deep sea commercial fishing vessels
	Adjustment companies
	Ownership of condominium units where the common areas in the condominium project are co-owned by the owners of the separate units or owned by a corporation

续表

Foreign Ownership/ Maximum Foreign Equity	Area/Activity/Industry
Up to 49% Foreign Equity	Lending companies
Up to 60% Foreign Equity	Financing companies regulated by the Securities and Exchange Commission
	Investment houses regulated by the Securities and Exchange Commission

List B: Foreign Ownership is Limited for Reasons of Security, Defense, Risk to

Health and Morals and Protectionof Small- and Medium-Scale Enterprises

Foreign Ownership/ Maximum Foreign Equity	Area/Activity/Industry
Up to 40% Foreign Equity	Manufacture, repair, storage and/or distribution of products and/or ingredients requiring Philippine National Police (PNP) clearance: a. Firearms (handguns to shotguns), parts of firearms and ammunition therefore, instruments or implements used or intended to be used in the manufacture of firearms b. Gunpowder c. Dynamite d. Blasting supplies e. Ingredients used in making explosives Telescopic sights, sniper scope and other similar devices
	Manufacture, repair, storage and/or distribution of products requiring Department of National Defense (DND) clearance: a. Guns and ammunitions for warfare b. Military ordnance and parts thereof c. Gunnery, bombing and fire control systems and components d. Guided missiles/missile systems and components e. Tactical aircraft, parts and components thereof f. Space vehicles and component systems g. Combat vessels and auxiliaries h. Weapons repair and maintenance equipment i. Military communications equipment j. Night vision equipment k. Stimulated coherent radiation devices, components and accessories l. Armament training devices m. Others as may be determined by the Secretary of DND

117

续表

Foreign Ownership/ Maximum Foreign Equity	Area/Activity/Industry
Up to 40% Foreign Equity	Manufacture and distribution of dangerous drugs
	Sauna and steam bathhouses, massage clinics and other like activities regulated by law because of risks posed to public health and morals
	All forms of gambling, except those covered by investment agreements with PAGCOR pursuant to *R. A.* 9487, or the PAGCOR Charter
	Domestic market enterprises with paid-in equity capital of less than the equivalent of US $ 200,000
	Domestic market enterprises which involve advance technology or employ at least fifty (50) direct employees with paid-in capital of less than the equivalent of US $ 100,000

Supra Note 12, p. 5.

The *Anti-Dummy Law*, on the other hand, is another legislative enactment which imposes civil and criminal penalties on persons, natural or juridical, violating foreign equity limitations. Under the *Anti-Dummy Law*, a person who, having in his name or under his control a right, franchise, privilege, property or business, the exercise or enjoyment of which is expressly reserved by law to Philippine citizens or to corporations or associations where at least 60 percent (60%) of the capital is owned by such citizens, is prohibited from:

(1) permitting or allowing the use, exploitation or enjoyment of such right, franchise, privilege, property or business by a person, corporation or association not possessing the qualifications prescribed by law, or

(2) in any manner permitting or allowing any person not so qualified to intervene in the management, operation, administration or control of such right, franchise, privilege, property or business, whether as an officer, employee, or laborer, with or without remuneration (except technical personnel whose employment may be specifically authorized by the Secretary of Justice).

However, foreign nationals may serve as members of the board or governing body of corporations engaged in partially nationalized activities in a number proportionate to their actual and allowable equity in the company. [1]

The *Filipino First Policy* is also one of the most important pillars of the Philippine economy. This policy is subscribed by Article XII, Section 12 of the 1987 Philippine *Constitution* and mandates the State to "promote the preferential use of Filipino labor, domestic materials and locally produced goods, and adopt measures that help make them competitive". The exercise of this policy is manifested by the limitation on the practice of profession in Philippines and the issuance of an alien employment permit as a requisite to allow a foreigner to work in the Philippines. [2] As provided in the Philippine Labor Code, this permit will only be issued if no Filipino is available, able, willing and competent to perform the services required. [3]

In relation to negotiating free trade agreements, policy-makers and officials having the authority to negotiate in behalf of the State are constitutionally mandated to ensure that the trade agreement:

(1)Promotes inclusive and sustained growth;

(2) Is consistent with market-driven economy that is subject to regulation to protect stakeholders, especially Filipinos, from unfair competition and unfair trade practices;

(3)Maintains Philippine independence from foreign control;

(4)Respects the limit on protected strategic industries; and

(5)Promotes equality and reciprocity with the Philippines' trading partner. [4]

Observing the foregoing policies, framework and constitutional mandate, the Philippines was able to enter into the following free trade agreements with other countries,See Table 1.

---

[1] *Supra* Note 12, p. 5.
[2] *Supra* Note 5, p. 23.
[3] Supra Note 5, p. 23.
[4] Id.

Table 1. Status of Philippines' Free Trade Agreements[①]

Status	Regional	Bilateral
In Effect	ASEAN FTA (1993) ASEAN-PRC FTA (2005) ASEAN-Korea FTA(2006) ASEAN-Japan CEPA(2008)	Japan-Philippines EPA(2008)
Signed	ASEAN-Australia-New Zealand CER (2009) ASEAN-India FTA (2009)	

Aside from entering into free trade agreements, the Philippines also adopted trade and investment policies to improve its role in the international market. These policies include the following, See Table 2.

Table 2. Philippines' Other Trade and Investment Policies[②]

Trade Policies	Investment Policies
1. Inward-looking, import substitution policy and Export Incentives Act (1950s to 1970s) 2. Tariff Reform & Import Liberalization Programs (1981—2003) 3. Export Development Act (1994) 4. Implemented Information Technology Agreement (2000)	1. Omnibus Investment Code 2. Foreign Traders' Visa (E. O. 758) 3. Special Economic Zone Act (1995) 4. Established export processing zones • 18 Agro-Industrial Economic Zones • 187 IT Parks/Centers • 65 Manufacturing Economic Zones • 2 Medical Tourism Parks/Centers • 17 Tourism Economic Zone (As of June 30, 2013)

The Philippines' creation of economic zones, which are treated as outside the customs territory, attracted and opened a number of foreign investment opportunities in the country because of the incentives that these provide to investors. Primary incentives take the form of fiscal and non-

---

① Wignaraja, Ganeshan, Dorothea Lazaro and Genevieve De Guzman, *FTAs and Philippine Business: Evidence from Transport, Food, and Electornic Firms*, ADBI *Working Series*, January 2010 (No. 185), p.31.

② Wignaraja, Ganeshan, Dorothea Lazaro and Genevieve De Guzman, *FTAs and Philippine Business: Evidence from Transport, Food, and Electornic Firms*, ADBI *Working Series*, January 2010 (No. 185), p.3.

fiscal benefits such as the following, See Table 3.

Table 3. Incentives in Special Economic Zones[①]

Fiscal	Non-Fiscal
1. Income Tax Holiday (ITH) —100% exemption from corporate income tax	1. Simplified Import—Export Procedures
2. 5% Special Tax on Gross Income and exemption from all national and local taxes	2. Non-resident Foreign Nationals may be employed by PEZA-registered Economic Zone Enterprises in supervisory, technical or advisory positions
3. Tax and duty free importation of raw materials, capital equipment, machineries and spare parts	
4. Exemption from wharfage dues and export tax, impost or fees	3. Special Non-Immigrant Visa with Multiple Entry Privileges for the following non-resident Foreign Nationals in a PEZA-registered Economic Zone Enterprise:
5. VAT zero-rating of local purchases subject to compliance with BIR and PEZA requirements	
6. Exemption from payment of any and all local government imposts, fees, licenses or taxes	Investor/s, officers, and employees in supervisory, technical or advisory position, and their spouses
7. Exemption from expanded withholding tax	and unmarried children under twenty-one years of age

The negotiations and commitment to an international agreement take place through the powers exercised by the President and the Senate of the Philippines. [②]

The Judiciary also participates in the endeavor by serving as the arbiter in cases requiring the interpretation of an international agreement to determine its constitutionality and validity under Philippine laws. [③] In this regard, the next section will provide a brief description of the Philippine judicial system and the significance of the emergence of an alterative dispute resolution mechanism in the Philippine legal system.

---

① www. peza. gov. ph. Visited on November 14, 2013.

② Article Ⅶ, Section 21 of the 1987 *Constitution*.

③ Article Ⅷ, Section 4(2) of the 1987 *Constitution*.

2. The Philippines' Alternative Dispute Resolution Mechanism

The Philippine legal system, including its judicial rules, were adopted from and influenced mainly by western countries, more particularly the American system.

Legal issues and controversies are resolved primarily through the courts whose primary function is to settle the rights of the parties and enforce legal obligations.

The filing of court action is the common recourse of persons, natural or juridical, seeking remedy to protect their rights and enforce legal obligations due them.

However, because of the fast growing number of cases and disputes being filed everyday, the increasing docket of pending cases compelled the adoption of a new mechanism to resolve cases in a more expeditious and less costly manner. The concept of *outside-the-court* proceeding in resolving certain cases was then introduced in the Philippine judicial system. Legislation established mechanisms and institutions to help de-clog court cases and at the same time gave parties an alternative venue to adjudicate their rights and interests.

The adoption of various modes of alternative dispute resolution—such as arbitration, conciliation and mediation—not only expedited the resolution of cases, but also improved judicial effectiveness and efficiency. As a result thereof, the Supreme Court prioritized the following goals when enacting rules of procedure: (1) dispose of the existing backlog of cases in all courts; (2) study and address the causes of failure to observe the periods to decide cases mandated by the Constitution; and (3) promote alternative modes of dispute resolution. [1]

---

[1]　The Davide Watch: Leading the Philippine Judiciary and the Legal Profession Towards the Third Millennium, December 1998.

Brief Background on the Philippine Judicial System

The 1987 Philippine Constitution provides that judicial power shall be vested in one Supreme Court and such lower courts as may be established by law. [1] The hierarchy of courts and their respective jurisdictions are provided by various legislative enactments. Under Batas Pambansa Blg. 129 (BP 129), otherwise known as the *Judiciary Reorganization Act of* 1980, as a-mended, which took effect on January 18, 1983, and other laws, the Philippine judicial system consists of the following courts:

(1) The Metropolitan Trial Courts (MeTC), the Municipal Trial Courts (MTC), the Municipal Trial Courts in Cities (MTCC), and Municipal Circuit Trial Courts (MCTC) are called the *first level courts* or courts of limited jurisdiction.

Every municipality in the Philippines has its own Municipal Trial Court. If it covers two or more municipalities, it is called Municipal Circuit Trial Court.

Municipal Trial Courts in the towns and cities in the Metropolitan Manila area, as distinguished from the other political subdivisions in the Philippines, are referred to as Metropolitan Trial Courts. On the other hand, Municipal Trial Courts in cities outside the Metropolitan Manila are referred to as Municipal Trial Courts in Cities.

(2) The *second level courts* are the Regional Trial Courts (RTC). In Philippines, RTCs are called courts of general jurisdiction. Regional Trial Courts were established among the thirteen regions in Philippines. There are as many Regional Trial Courts in each region as the law mandates.

(3) Next is the Court of Appeals (CA), an appellate court vested with the jurisdiction over appeals from the RTCs and other judicial agencies. The Court of Appeals is composed of one Presiding Justice and sixty-eight Associate Justices. It is vested with jurisdiction over appeals from the decisions of the Regional Trial Courts and certain quasi-judicial agencies, boards or commissions.

---

[1] Article Ⅷ, Section 1 of the 1987 *Constitution.*

123

(4) The Supreme Court is the highest court in Philippines and is at the apex of this four-tiered judicial hierarchy. It is the only "constitutional court", the sole judicial body created by the Constitution itself and is called the court of last resort. There is only one Supreme Court composed of one Chief Justice and fourteen Associate Justices. It is the final arbiter of any and all judicial issues. When so deciding, it may sit *en banc* or in divisions of three, five or seven members. The Supreme Court observes a policy of strict observance of the hierarchical structure. It will not accept cases, except in cases involving national interest, directly filed to it. [1]

The Philippines' Alternative Dispute Resolution System

Alternative dispute resolution is not a new species of resolving cases and disputes in Philippines. As early as July 19, 1953, the Philippine Congress has enacted *Republic Act No.* 876 (*R. A.* 876) otherwise known as the *Arbitration Law*.

R. A. 876 provided the procedure for arbitration in civil controversies. It authorized the adoption of arbitration and submission agreements and provided for the appointment of arbitrators. Under this law, parties to the contract are allowed to bring their controversy to arbitration under a specific procedure stipulated by them and, in the absence or insufficiency thereof, the provision of *R. A.* 876 will apply suppletorily.

However, despite the adoption of *R. A.* 876, the increasing court dockets alarmed not only the Supreme Court but the whole Philippine government as well.

To address this concern, the enactment of the 1987 Philippine Constitution mandated the Supreme Court to promulgate rules that shall provide *a simplified and inexpensive procedure for the speedy disposition of cases.* [2] In compliance with this constitutional provision, the Supreme Court issued Circulars, Memoranda and Administrative Orders making alternative dispute resolution mandatory in certain types of civil cases.

---

[1] Article VIII, Section 1 of the 1987 *Constitution*.

[2] Article VIII, Section 5, paragraph 5 of the 1987 *Constitution*.

The Rules of Civil Procedure even gave the litigants the opportunity to consider the possibility of an amicable settlement or of submitting the case to alternative modes of dispute resolution. ① To further effectively implement this provision, the Supreme Court promulgated on September 16, 2001 Administrative Order No. 21 − 2001 designating the Philippine Judicial Academy (PHILJA) as its component unit for court-referred, court-related mediation cases and other alternative dispute resolution mechanisms, and establishing the Philippine Mediation Center (PMC) for said purpose.

Legislations and executive issuances were also made to address this growing problem such as, but not limited to, the following:

(1) The *Katarungang Pambarangay Law* under Republic Act No. 7160 (*R. A.* 7160), also known as the *Local Government Code of* 1991. Pursuant to the *Katarungang Pambarangay Law*, the *lupon* of each *barangay* shall have authority to bring together the parties actually residing in the same city or municipality for amicable settlement of all disputes,

---

① Rule 18, Section 2 of the Revised Rules of Court.

except in the cases provided therein, [①] as a condition before filing an action in court;

(2)Republic Act No. 7394 (*R. A. 7394*), or *The Consumer Act of the Philippines of 1992. R. A. 7394* vests consumer arbitrators, who are government employees appointed by either the Secretaries of Health, Agriculture or Trade and Industry, with original and exclusive jurisdiction to mediate, conciliate and hear or adjudicate all consumer complaints; [②]

(3)*Republic Act No. 7942 (R. A. 7942)*, or *The Mining Act of 1995*,

---

① Section 408 of *R. A. 7160* provides:

Section 408. *Subject Matter for Amicable Settlement; Exception Thereto.* The lupon of each barangay shall have authority to bring together the parties actually residing in the same city or municipality for amicable settlement of all disputes except:

(1) Where one party is the government, or any subdivision or instrumentality thereof;

(2) Where one party is a public officer or employee, and the dispute relates to the performance of his official functions;

(3) Offenses punishable by imprisonment exceeding one (1) year or a fine exceeding five thousand pesos (P5,000.00);

(4) Offenses where there is no private offended party;

(5) Where the dispute involves real properties located in different cities or municipalities unless the parties thereto agree to submit their differences to amicable settlement by an appropriate lupon;

(6) Disputes involving parties who actually reside in barangays of different cities or municipalities, except where such barangay units adjoin each other and the parties thereto agree to submit their differences to amicable settlement by an appropriate lupon;

(7) Such other classes of disputes which the President may determine in the interest of Justice or upon the recommendation of the Secretary of Justice.

The court in which non-criminal cases not falling within the authority of the lupon under this Code are filed may, at any time before trial motu propio refer the case to the lupon concerned for amicable settlement.

② Article 160 of *R. A. 7394* provides:

Article 160. Consumer Arbitration Officers—the concerned Department Secretaries shall appoint as many qualified consumer arbitration officers as may be necessary for the effective and efficient protection of consumer rights. Provided, however that there shall be not more than ten (10) consumer arbitration officers per province, including the National Capital Region.

which provides for the appointment of a panel of government-employed arbitrators in every regional office of the Department of Environment and Natural Resources to exercise exclusive and original jurisdiction involving disputes over mining areas, mineral agreements or permits and surface owners or occupants and claimholders or concessionaires;[1]

(4) The Philippine Construction Industry Arbitration Commission (CIAC) was created by Executive Order No. 1008 on February 4, 1985 for the specific purpose of resolving the rising number of litigation cases involving contractual claims within the industry; and

(5)*Republic Act No.* 8293 (*R. A.* 8293), otherwise known as *The Intellectual Property Code of* 1998, which provides that "in the event the technology transfer agreement shall provide for arbitration, the procedure of arbitration of the *Arbitration Law* of the Philippines or the Arbitration Rules of the United Nations Commission on International Trade Law (UNCITRAL) or the Rules of Conciliation and Arbitration of the International Chamber of Commerce (ICC) shall apply and the venue of arbitration shall

---

[1]   Section 77 of *R. A.* 7942 states:

Sec. 77 Panel of Arbitrators. There shall be a panel of arbitrators in the regional office of the Department composed of three (3) members, two (2) of whom must be members of the Philippine Bar in good standing and one licensed mining engineer or a professional in a related field, and duly designated by the Secretary as recommended by the Mines and Geosciences Bureau Director. Those designated as members of the panel shall serve as such in addition to their work in the Department without receiving any additional compensation. As much as practicable, said members shall come from the different bureaus of the Department in the region. The presiding officer shall be on a yearly basis.

The members of the panel shall perform their duties and obligations in hearing and deciding cases until their designation is withdrawn or revoked by the Secretary. Within thirty (30) working days, after the submission of the case by the parties for decision, the panel shall have exclusive and original jurisdiction to hear and decide on the following:

(1) Disputes involving rights to mining areas;

(2) Disputes involving mineral agreements or permits;

(3) Disputes involving surface owners, occupants and claimholders/concessionaires; and

(4) Disputes pending before the Bureau and the Department at the date of the effectivity of this Act.

be the Philippines or any neutral country".

The most recent legislation regarding alternative dispute resolution is *Republic Act No.* 9285 (*R. A.* 9285), otherwise known as the *Alternative Dispute Resolution Act* (*ADR Law*) *of* 2004, which was enacted by the Philippines' 12th Congress on April 4, 2004. Under the ADR Law, the Philippine Government undertakes the policy "to actively promote party autonomy in the resolution of disputes or the freedom of the party to make their own arrangements to resolve their disputes; and, to encourage and actively promote the use of Alternative Dispute Resolution (ADR) as an important means to achieve speedy and impartial justice and declog court dockets"[1].

To realize the objective of the ADR Law, the Office for Alternative Dispute Resolution (OADR) was created. The OADR is an attached agency of the Department of Justice (DOJ), which operates under the direct supervision of the Secretary of Justice, and tasked to oversee the state of both public sector and private sector alternative dispute resolution.

The objectives of the OADR are(1)to promote, develop and expand the use of ADR in the private and public sectors;(2)to assist in the monitoring, studying and evaluating the use of alternative dispute resolution by the public and private sectors; and(3)to recommend Congress needful statutory changes to develop, strengthen and improve alternative dispute resolution practices in accordance with world standards. The Congress also vested the

---

① *R. A.* 9285, April 2, 2004.

OADR with vast powers and functions① in order to implement these objectives.

3. The Philippines' Approach to Resolving International Trade and Investment Disputes

Same as in domestic cases, dispute settlements also play an important factor in maintaining harmony and cooperation among nations. The Philippines, being a member of various international associations and a signatory to a number of international instruments, has adhered to various modes of dispute settlement to resolve conflicts arising from treaty interpretations and enforcement of contractual rights. According to former Supreme Court Chief Justice Andres R. Narvasa, the mechanism of settling disputes between nations may be defined as follows:

> A more traditional way of looking at the settlement of disputes between states would be to examine the degree to which a third party intervenes in the process of settlement. If the process by which settlement is reached purely bilateral, the exercise is characterized as negotiations. A third party may intervene for a strictly limited

---

① (1) To act as appointing authority of mediators and arbitrators when the parties agree in writing that it shall be empowered to do so; (2) To conduct seminars, symposia, conference and publish proceedings of said activities and relevant materials/information that would promote, develop and expand the use of ADR; (3) To establish an ADR library or resource center that will contain laws, rules and regulations, jurisprudence, books, articles and other information about ADR in the Philippines and elsewhere for easy access to the public; (4) To establish training programs for ADR providers/practitioners, both in the public and private sectors; and to undertake periodic and continuing training programs for arbitration and mediation and charge fees on participants. It may do so in conjunction with or in cooperation with the IBP, private ADR organizations, and local and foreign government offices and agencies and international organizations; (5) To certify those who have successfully completed the regular professional training programs provided by the OADR or other ADR provider organizations as approved by the OADR; (6) To charge fees for services rendered such as, among others, for training and certifications of ADR providers; (7) To accept donations, grants and other assistance from local and foreign sources; and (8)To exercise such other powers as may be necessary and proper to carry into effect the provisions of the ADR Act of 2004(R.A. 9285).

purpose, say, to bring the parties to sit together and begin inter se negotiations (good offices). In addition to bringing the parties together, the third party may transmit proposals from one party to another; in this case, the process is called mediation. Should the third party be authorized to initiate motu proprio independent proposals for the settlement of the dispute, the process is called conciliation. The third party could, alternatively, be authorized to determine the antecedent facts, or the facts constituting a dispute; in this case, the third party is known as an inquiry commission. If a third party intervenes because he has been authorized to resolve the dispute on his own, there is either arbitration or judicial settlement, depending on whether the third party is chosen on an ad hoc basis, or is part of an institutionalized framework and standing system that is specifically designed for dispute resolution. The third party in this context may be an individual arbitrator, an arbitral board or tribunal, or a judge or court. ①

The Philippines has, thus, recognized and utilized the following modes② of resolving international trade and investment disputes within its jurisdiction,See Table 4.

Table 4. Modes of International Dispute Settlement Adopted by the Philippines

Classification of Dispute	Mode of Dispute Settlement
Between governments	1. WTO Dispute Settlement Mechanism 2. UN Commission on International Trade Law and UNCITRAL Model 3. Dispute Settlement Mechanism under the Philippines-Japan Economic Partnership Agreement, and 4. Dispute Settlement Mechanism of the ASEAN-China Free Trade Area

---

① Dispute Settlement under the Aegis of the World Trade Organization, in Odyssey and Legacy: the Chief Justice Andres R. Narvasa Centennial Lecture Series, at 180 (1999), cited in Toward the Formulation of a Philippine Position in Resolving Trade and Investment Disputes in APEC by now Supreme Court Chief Justice Ma. Lourdes P. A. Sereno, PASCN Discussion Paper No. 2001−15,December 2001, pp. 5∼6.

② *Toward the Formulation of a Philippine Position in Resolving Trade and Investment Disputes in APEC* by now Supreme Court Chief Justice Ma. Lourdes P. A. Sereno, PASCN Discussion Paper No. 2001−15, December 2001, p. 24; see also *Supra* Note 5, pp. 65∼69.

续表

Classification of Dispute	Mode of Dispute Settlement
Between governments and private parties	1. Convention on the Settlement of Investment Dispute (ICSID), and 2. Convention on the Recognition and Enforcement of Foreign Arbitral Awards (New York Convention)
Between private parties	1. *R. A.* 876 2. *R. A.* 9285, and 3. *E. O.* 1008

Under the WTO Dispute Settlement Mechanism, disputes covering the rights and obligations of the Philippines under the agreement are elevated to the Department of Trade and Industry as the Chair of the Tariff and Related Matters Committee. [1]

The Philippines and its government shall then be represented by the Department of Justice and the Office of the Solicitor General, respectively. [2] To date, the Philippines has already been a party to a WTO Dispute Settlement for a total of 22 cases, to wit: 5 cases as complainant, 6 cases as respondent, and 11 cases as third party. [3]

Considering the global scope of WTO's Dispute Settlement Mechanism, its procedures and output greatly influence the dispute settlement systems under other international agreements, including that provided under the ASEAN-China Free Trade Area (ACFTA) Framework Agreement.

The resolution of trade disputes arising under the ACFTA Framework Agreement may be brought by the Philippines under the Dispute Settlement Mechanism (DSM) of the ACFTA or under the WTO Agreement considering that the Philippines is a signatory and member of the ACFTA and WTO, respectively. The WTO is replete with jurisprudence on dispute

---

[1] *Supra* Note 5, p. 72.

[2] Executive Order No. 292, otherwise known as the *Administrative Code*, as amended, Book Ⅳ, Title Ⅲ, Chapter 1, Section 1 and Chapter 12, Section 35.

[3] http://www. wto. org/english/tratop_e/dispu_e/dispu_by_country_e. htm. Visited on November 19, 2013.

settlement in view of its long history of existence such that dispute settlements brought under the DSM of the ACFTA Framework Agreement may have to rely significantly with those rendered by the WTO/GATT. Under the ACFTA Framework Agreement, the complaining party may select a forum under which the dispute may be resolved to the exclusion of all others, unless the parties expressly agree to the use of more than one forum for the settlement of that particular dispute. ①However, to avoid uncertainty as to which forum to select for resolving the dispute, the *rule of exclusion* under the DSM of the ACFTA Framework Agreement must be applied, which mandates that "once dispute settlement proceedings have been initiated under ACFTA or any other treaty to which the parties concerned are signatories, the forum chosen by the complaining party shall be used to the exclusion of any other for such a dispute"②.

The adoption of arbitration and the requirement of consensus within the arbitral tribunal is a peculiar characteristic of the DSM under ACFTA Framework Agreement, a reflection of the "ASEAN way", and, thus, set it apart from the WTO's Dispute Settlement Mechanism. ③

It is also worthy to note that, with the adherence of the Philippine Senate to the *United Nations Convention on the Recognition and Enforcement of Foreign Arbitral Awards* of 1958, the enforceability of foreign arbitral agreements between parties of different nationalities within a contracting state is recognized in Philippine jurisdiction. ④

---

① Zhu Weidong, *The Dispute Settlement Mechanism of ASEAN Free Trade Area (AFTA) and Its Implications for SADC*, citing Article 2(6) and (7) of the Agreement on the Dispute Settlement Mechanism, p. 16.

② Wang Jiangyu, *ASEAN-China Free Trade Agreements: Legal and Institutional Aspects*, citing DSM Agreement, Article 2. 6, p. 129. *http://www. eastlaw. net/ jyworks/wang-acfta0001. pdf*. Visited on November 20, 2013.

③ See *supra* Note 38, pp. 18~19.

④ *National Union Fire Insurance Co. of Pittsburg vs. Stolt-Nielsen Philippines, Inc.* G. R. No. 87958, April 26, 1990, 184 SCRA 682.

老挝促进外商直接投资的法律政策

Viengphet Sengsongyialorfaichon[*]
黄释谊　译

摘要　外商投资已被公认为是促进国家经济增长,国力持续发展的重要因素。其一个重要的特征是能给东道国带来资本、新技术以及先进的管理经验。与其他资本流动形式相比,外商投资因其长期经营性,对东道国来讲更具有稳定性。在老挝,吸引外商投资是国家长期经济发展计划中的重要部分。因此,本文旨在介绍老挝的吸引外商投资的法律政策以及相关政策对吸引外资的积极作用。

关键词　外商直接投资　法律与政策　老挝经济特区

一、前言

越来越多国家对于外商投资的态度有所转变,并且改革其相关政策以吸引外商投资。因为外商投资可促进本国就业、促进出口和增加税收,先进的外国公司还将淘汰东道国部分落后企业,带来先进的管理经验。由此,各国政府为吸引外资而降低准入壁垒以及开设新部门。越来越多的东道国提供各种优惠政策来吸引外资公司在本地区投资,其中包括财政支持,例如对外国投资者实行免税期或较低的税率;或金融优惠政策,例如向跨国公司提供补贴或优惠贷款;也会采取例如给予市场优先权,建设基础设施甚至垄断权等措施。

老挝人民在老挝革命党的带领下,取得了解放战争的胜利,建立了属于自己国家与人民的政权。1975—1985 年老挝主要实行计划经济,主要的经济政策是恢复战后经济,发展农业与工业,提升人民的生活水平,建设基础设施,让新政权平稳过渡。

---

[*] 万飞,武汉大学博士生、老挝司法部国际合作处副处长。

二、老挝支持外商直接投资的法律政策

1.相关政策

1986 年的革命党第四次全国大会后,老挝政府决定进行名为"新经济机制"的社会主义市场经济改革。

老挝政府希望通过经济改革,对外开放,引进外商投资提高人民生活水平,提高国民教育水平,提升劳动力的技能水平,争取达到 8％ 的 GDP 年均增长率,促进国内经济发展,从而使老挝的社会经济文化都得到长足的进步。

2.老挝吸引外商投资的相关法律政策

为了适应经济形势的变化,老挝政府制定了一系列的法律法规,于 1988 年制定了《外商投资法》,这是老挝第一部促进投资的法律法规。这部法规允许投资者进入三种投资市场:(1)契约性或合作性商业,必须投资老挝国有公司,私营公司或个人;(2)创办合资企业,外国投资者的投资最少应占公司资本的 30％。一般情况下,该类型企业存在的期限不能超过 20 年;(3)纯外资企业,外国投资者的投资份额为公司资本的 30％～100％。该种形式公司存在的期限为 15 年。对于合资公司和纯外资工资,减免税政策只适用于获利后的 2～6 年。主要依据投资规模的大小,出口产品的价值,产品的本土化程度。

老挝政府还通过颁布相关法律法规来进一步保障私人所有权,这也是促进外商投资的一个重要因素。政府通过税收激励政策(如少征收利润税的 2％～5％)来促进外商投资。外资项目如需获得上述减免税政策支持,需满足以下三个条件:(1)70％的产品须出口;(2)超过 70％的原材料从本国获得;须使用先进的技术;致力于克服恶劣的自然与社会经济条件;(3)以低获利率支援国家经济发展,于 1995 年前完成。外商投资法允许外国投资者根据其选择将利润汇往其国家。

1994 年颁布了《促进外商投资与管理》。1994 年颁布的《促进外商投资和管理法》旨在吸引外商投资,在老挝建立起各种所有制经济。其主要规定了老挝允许外商投资的行业领域,外商在老挝投资的具体程序,外国投资者享有老挝法律保护,并鼓励外国投资者与本国商人合作、竞争以促进老挝的社会经济发展。

1997 年,老挝正式成为 ASEAN 的一员。加入承诺,须进一步完善国内法律制度。为了进一步促进国家经济发展,促进国际合作,老挝在 1994 年《促进投资法》的基础上分别制定了《外商投资促进和管理法》和《国内投资促进法

和管理法》。

国际货币基金组织的主席 M. Camdessus 认为透明度是新的国际金融体系中的"金科玉律"。2009 年的《老挝投资促进法》是一部综合类的投资法,主要包括《国内投资促进法》和《外国投资促进法》,以便为国内和外国投资者创造一个"公平的竞争场";投资审批程序进一步简化,如外国投资者的一般性经营活动不再需要投资许可证,按老挝企业法规定的程序进行即可。2009 年投资促进法进一步保护了外国投资者。

3. 老挝经济特区的外商投资政策

自 2003 年到 2011 年,老挝已批准成立了 10 个经济特区。2011 年 11 月,新修订的税法规定,在经济特区内,外国投资者与国内投资者采用统一的一般利润税。新税率为 24%～28%。对不同的行业采取不同的财政支持。

除了企业的税收优惠政策,投资者亦享有税收优惠政策:(1)在下一会计年度,如果从经营活动产生的净利润用于业务扩张,则豁免个人所得税。(2)豁免直接用于生产的进口原料,设备,配件和车辆税收,免征进口税应符合具体规章。(3)豁免一般商品和产品出口关税。由自然资源和天然资源制造的产品出口应符合有关的法规和法律。一切类型的燃料进口无须缴纳关税和税款。(4)如果投资者在缴纳税款后亏损,在接下来的连续三个会计年度,投资者可申报损失。该优惠期结束后,任何剩余的损失,不再从利润中扣除。

三、老挝的投资争端解决机制

如果外国投资者在老挝投资产生纠纷,解决方式有所不同:(1)如合同一方为政府部门,则解决方法依据合同约定或投资国的 BIT 协定;相关程序可适用国际仲裁组织的相关规定。(2)外资企业签订合同后,相关争端根据合同约定的解决方式解决。并采用合同签订地或公司注册地的相关法律。如果是合资企业或外资企业,双方须把争端提交给中央促进和管理投资委员会或投资许可证的签发地的管理部门,争端解决期限为 30 天,如双方依上述程序未能获得圆满解决则双方可把争端提交国家经济争端仲裁机构或采取双方同意的诉讼程序。

老挝已于 2013 年加入 WTO。加入 WTO 有利于改善老挝国内的投资环境,开放国内更多市场,促进竞争、提升贸易量,更有利于吸引外商投资,并且如遇到投资纠纷则可根据 WTO 的贸易规则来解决与其他成员国的贸易纠纷。

Legal policies on Promotion Foreign Direct Investment in Laos PDR

Viengphet Sengsongyialorfaichon*

Abstract：Foreign direct investment has come to be widely recognized over the past decade as a major potential contributor to growth and development. one key feature，It can bring capital，technology，management know-how and access to new markets. In comparison with other forms of capital flows，it is also more stable，with a longer-term commitment to the host economy. In Laos PDR The Foreign Direct Investment is one key issue which Government put on any periods of National Economic Development Plan. This paper aims to examine the Promotion of foreign directed Investment policies，laws and regulations related to encourage FDI in Laos PDR.

Keywords：Foreign direct investment; Law and regulation; Special Economic zone in Laos PDR.

1. Introduction

The attitude towards inward foreign direct investment （FDI） has changed considerably over the last couple of decades，as most countries have liberalised their policies to attract investment from foreign multinational corporations （MNCs）. On the expectation that foreign MNCs will raise

---

* PHD Candidate of Wuhan University，Project Manager and Deputy Head of Law Research and International Cooperation Institute At the Ministry of Justice，Laos DPR.

employment, exports or tax revenue, or that some of the knowledge brought by the foreign companies may spill over to the host country's domestic firms, governments across the world have lowered various entry barriers and opened up new sectors to foreign investment. An increasing number of host governments also provide various forms of investment incentives to encourage foreign-owned companies to invest in their jurisdiction. [1] These include fiscal incentives such as tax holidays and lower taxes for foreign investors, financial incentives such as grants and preferential loans to MNCs, as well as measures such as market preferences, infrastructure and sometimes even monopoly rights. [2]

After the completing with victory of and proclamation The Lao PDR in 2nd December 1975, opening a new era of independence and true national ownership by the Lao and Ethnic People. And the Lao People's Revolutionary Party, from an underground movement in the past, has become in power and undertakes to lead in all areas of the society in Lao PDR. The government started to drafted National Socio-economic Development Plan which leading by Laos Revolutionary Party as the engine of them. During the 1976—1977. It was the first annual plan of the new regime which aimed at recovering the economy after the war, improving the living standard of the people, recovering the agricultural and industrial production allowing people to make their living, and protecting and developing the nation and new regime peacefully.

In the Period of three-year Plans (1978—1980). Laos Government was focus on reconstruct the nation after the war, provide housing for people and permanent locations to make their living, recover the farming land, reconstruct some districts damaged by the war and repair and operate the existing industrial factories.

The First Five-year Plan (1981—1985). It was formulated to translate

---

[1] Report t of United Nations Conference on Trade and Development (UNCTAD) (2001:6—7)

[2] See United Nations Conference on Trade and Development (UNCTAD) and Brewer and Young 1997 for various incentives.

the resolutions of the 3rd Party Congress into practice. They focus to Support the agricultural-forestry production in order to achieve food sufficiency, Repair the existing factories for regular operation and create a number of new industrial facilities and Construct basic infrastructure: Road No. 9, major bridges along Road No. 13 to link all park form the Northern to south and east to west in Laos.

Conclusion that During 1975—1985. is the period of centrally-Planned system. On these period the Government still focus on protecting and developing the nation and new regime peacefully, Leading recovered the national economy after the war for improving the living standard of the people, recovering and support agricultural-forestry, industrial production, Repair the existing factories for regular operation and create a number of new industrial facilities and Construct basic infrastructure.

2. Policies of supporting Foreign direct Investment in the past Two Decades

1. Policies issue

After The 4Th Revolutionary Party Congress in 1986. The Government considered to reform the centrally-planned toward a new growth direction under a socialist-market economy which called " New Economic Mechanism". The Government Designed to implemented the resolutions to be National development Strategy Plan for medium term plan has duration of less than 10 years and cover 5 years[①]. To driving socio-economic develop going to right way and match the Party 's policies. Government sought any ways to encourage foreign investment as a means of facilitating economic development because they hope that foreign investment projects will help to shift the economy from a subsistence economy to a commodity production basis by improving the management skills of the labor force; introducing advanced technology to the manufacturing sector; fostering economic, scientific, and technological cooperation with other countries; Increasing the production of goods for goods export. On the two decades of Transitional to

---

① History of Laos Revolutionary Party, 2010, page 240.

a Market—Oriented System, they defined to build up Main object to operate such as:

1)Create the structures for growth in agriculture forestry, industry and services, Improve and prepare the laws and regulation for the private sector, "*Open door policy for foreign cooperation* ". ① Focus on stabilize the national economy politics and transform the economic structure with multiple sectors under the policy of moving from the subsistence farming and semi-subsistence economic system into a market-oriented economy under the Party-State leadership. Because of most people living in the rural area, limited education and they survive by taken subsistence farming. Most the Local Investors just emerged as infant company which lack experience of development and expansion coordination with Foreign investors.

2)Transform the natural economy to commodity production economy, Continue to improve the infrastructure for socioeconomic development and approval system for foreign economic development and approval system for foreign investment and cooperation, Promote foreign cooperation and foreign investment ②.

3)Creating8 national priority programs was aim to increase the roles and support the capacity of the party in all professional fields, improve and upgrade the management and state laws, enhance unity within the party and the people ensuring the stability and security of the nation, Encourage all economic sectors and people to contribute to the national development and promote savings for the national balance and self-reliance provide social welfare and increase the number of the people participating in the national economy, Promote and expanding cooperation with regional and international community in order to obtain assistance and necessary inputs for the national socioeconomic development. ③

4)As it was the period that the globalization provided both several op-

---

① Political report of the 4ᵗʰ Congress 1986, page 110

② History of Laos Revolutionary Party, 2010, page 277.

③ 8 National priority program to developed.

portunities and challenges because the poverty reduction became the obligation of all countries in the world. hence, Laos PDR has designed for-mulating the National Growth and Poverty Reduction Strategy (NGPES) that became the basis for reducing poverty, supporting the national policy on "Industrialization and Modernization", and helping to achieve Millennium Development Goals (MDGs). Specially, it was designed as "Arrow (progressive) Approach" plan to ensure the successful implementation of the socio-economic development plan until 2020.

5) Transforming the multi-sectoral economy from uneven performance to fast and stable development within the market mechanism guided by the State. It will require the mobilization of all resources including a renewed drive for internal resources to take full advantage of the opportunities. The main focus areas are: promoting economic development, with human development as a key vehicle; increasing competitiveness and utilizing comparative advantages to implement effectively international economic commitments in the framework of the ASEAN and other bilateral and multilateral commitments, including WTO; and strengthening the positive linkages between economic growth and social development, in addressing social issues such as poverty and other social evils, and help keep the socio-political situation stable. The indicators and targets for the Plan coincide with most of those for the Millennium Development Goals (MDGs) and the Brussels Program of Action for the Least Developed Countries (2001—2010). [1]

6) On the Processing to implement the Resolution of the Ninth Party Congress. It is also the means to implement the Socio-Economic Development Strategy until 2020 and transform the country into a modern and industrial society. It is also the necessary thrust to graduate the country from the Least-Developed Country (LDC) status by 2020, and creates op-portunities for strengthened regional and international cooperation. This five

---

[1] The Sixth national Socio-Economic development Plan, Page 4, Available at http://www. unlao. org/Links/Lao/20NSEDP/20VI/20Draft/20Final. pdf.

year plan is the main objectives Seventh National Socio—Economic Development Plan (2011—2015)which it is part of the long term goal of the country to implement its policy of national development, achieve economic growth of at least 8% annually, reduce poverty, achieve the Millennium Development Goals by 2015 and construct basic infrastructure for industrialization and modernization in the times to come. The targets and directions of the Five-Year Social-Economic Development Plan are: 1) Ensure continuation of national economic growth with security, peace and stability. 2) and ensure GDP growth rate of at least 8% annually and GDP per capita to be at least USD 1,700; 3) Achieve the Millennium Development Goals by 2015, and adopt appropriate technology, skills and create favourable conditions for graduating the country from LDC by 2020 ; 4) Ensure the sustainability of development by emphasising economic development with, cultural and social progress, preserving natural resources and protecting the environment and last is Ensure political stability, peace and an orderly society. [1]

2. Investment Promotion Act developed for attractive FDI

As mention in above that Since the proclamation of Lao PDR in the year 1975, the Party and State had focused primarily on the restoration of life of the people, the remedy of damages suffered from the war period, the recovery of the economy of the state and the restoration of national unity. Therefore, the state, socio-economic administration at this first stage is based on the policy of the party and some simple levels of legislations issued by the state such as: decree, orders and others. The adoption of Laws is thus not dominant in the state administration. Since the Lao Revolutionary Party adopted its new policy with certain principles in the year 1986, to date it increasingly requires the Country to administer the State and socio-economic development through the Constitution and Laws, which has become a necessary objective for the Country in order to be able protect and develop the Nation, under the condition of market economic expansion and

---

[1] National Socio—Economic Development Plan (2011—2015), Available At.

international integration.① Therefore, in the end of 1980 decade Laos Government stared to deal with making up laws and amended decrees, regulation etc… and finally the Foreign Investment Act was announced the in 1988。 This act performed as the first regulation for promoting investment in Laos. The Act allows investors enter into three types of investment arrangements such as: The first type of arrangement, contractual or cooperative businesses, entails investment in existing state or private companies, or with Laotian individuals. The second type of arrangement, joint ventures, requires foreigners to invest a minimum of 30 percent of total capital.② In general, terms for either of these arrangements are not to exceed twenty years. The third type of arrangement, private ventures, requires foreigners to invest 30 percent of total capital, up to a maximum of 100 percent. Terms are generally limited to fifteen years. Tax exemptions or reductions for joint ventures and private enterprises are available for two to six years after the first year of profit, depending on the size of the investment, the volume of goods exported as a result of the project, the location of the project, and the sector on which it focuses.

Beside that, Government also announced several new laws and decrees such as law on property rights (1990), Law contractual obligation (1990), law on inheritance (1990), law criminal (1990), law on civil procedures (1990), and law on labor (1991). The main objectives of These laws is to protects the right to private ownership, *is also an important factor in encouraging foreign investment*. They provided the tax incentives—a reduction of 2 to 5 percent in the profit tax—are also used to encourage foreign investment. In order to qualify for the reduction, a foreign investment project has to meet three of the following criteria: the project will export more than 70 percent of the goods it produces; will obtain domestically more than 70 percent of the raw materials it uses; will use advanced technology; will aim to overcome unfavorable natural or socio-economic conditions; will contribute to national economic development

---

① Laos Legal Sector master Plan 2009, page 4.

② Laos Law on Foreign Investment 1994 Art 6.

despite low profit margins; or will be established before 1995. The Foreign Investment Law allows foreign investors to remit profits to the countries of their choice. ①

Prior to 1990, the development and promulgation of laws and other legislation had no legislative procedure for reference thus making the research, development and proposal of laws and other legislations anunsytematic, inconsistent and duplicating process, which in turn largely affects the function of the State's administration. Hence, To driving the law making compliance with Party Policies and math the National Socio-economic Development plan, In 1991 The first constitution was promulgated. it was the milestone for the Lao PDR State to continue development of its complete legal system in a systematic manner. Therefore, the Government and the National Assembly have begun to consider developing legislative procedures for drafting and adapting laws and different levels of legislation step by step commencing from the Notification of the Office of the Prime Minister No. 662/PMO, dated 26/05/1994 on the Improvement of the Procedure and Drafting of Laws. ② hence, In 1994 The Foreign Direct Investment Act was developed to be law called "Law on Foreign Investment Promotion and Management" On the same year government also announced the law on enterprise (1994).

The 1994 FDI law describes the procedure for foreign investment in Laos. It designed to attract capitalist style enterprise and contains liberal provisions for repatriation of profits and the involvement of foreign equity in Lao businesses. It outlines the areas in which foreign investment is encouraged and those areas where foreign investment is not allowed. and the law on enterprise Provided the equality in Business Transactions, allow domestic and foreign investor are equal before the law in business activities, and may compete and cooperate in expanding production forces, [and in] extending their production, business and services. Designed business Sectors

---

①   Sommala Sisombat, International Journal of Business and management 2008.

②   Legal Sector Master Plan 2009, page 5.

for encourages and promotes domestic and foreign persons and organizations to establish enterprises or to participate in business activities in all non-restricted sectors by issuing customs and tax policies, regulations, [and] measures, [and by] providing information, services and other facilities to enterprises to contribute to socio-economic development. ①

In 1997 Laos PDR was completed of negotiated to be ASEAN member. Hence, 1) To improved legal enforcement and establish institutions standard accordance with ASEAN. 2) To encourage all economic sectors contribute to the national development and promote savings for the national balance and self-reliance, Increase the roles and support the capacity of the party in all professional fields, Promote international cooperation and pursue an open door policy with international friend. hence, The 1994 investment promotion law was revised in Second time and Promulgated by the Presidential Decree No. 11/NA on 22 October 2004. And separated into two laws called "(i) Foreign Investment Promotion and Management Law, and (ii) Domestic Investment Promotion and Management Law".

Further, the Foreign investment law sets out new policy incentives including the promoted zone areas. The legislation shortens the investment application procedures and processing time. It has reduced the time in the investment license approval from 60 days to less than 50 days for promoted sectors, 25 working days for promoted sectors with some restrictions, and 45 days for large-scale projects/or projects related to natural resources. ②

Based on the Legal Sector Master Plan (LSMP) guidance to reform Legal System of Laos PDR with goal of "Development of a uniform, coherent, clear, credible and predictable, with quality, just and all people accessible legal framework, in a transparent and participatory manner"③. One hand, To support promoting economic development policy with human development as a key vehicle; increasing competitiveness and utilizing

---

① Law on Enterprise Article 6.

② World Bank(WBG, 2005).

③ Legal Sector master plan was commenced in 2003 and adopted by Government Sep 11. 2009.

comparative advantages to implement effectively international economic commitments in the framework of the ASEAN and other bilateral and multilateral commitments including WTO rule ; and strengthening the positive linkages between economic growth and social development, in addressing social issues such as poverty and other social evils, and help keep the socio-political situation stable. [1] And the other hand, To helping Laos' accession to the World Trade Organization (WTO). The Improving Law on Investment, commercial law tax law, Intellectual Property law and other Law key related to Business issue into conformity with WTO standards[2] is necessary. Therefore, with technical assistance and support from the International Finance Corporation (IFC), the World Bank Groups for law on Investment Promotion revised in third time and changed the Domestic investment law and Foreign Promote investment law in 2004 to be new Investment Promotion Law was promulgated in July 2009, which offers a range of new and improved investment incentives.

3. The transparency Investment Promotion Law 2009

In general, The Law on Investment Promotion is the one of key issue to bring out Government policies related to the Promotion of investment sectors to be protocol details for creation of environment and conditions in various fields for both domestic and foreign investments in order to enable the investors to undertake the business activities M. Camdessus, the Managing Director of the IMF, thinks of transparency as the "golden rule" of the new international financial system. [3]

The Unified Investment Law is a combination of the domestic investment promotion law and the foreign investment promotion law in order to create a "level playing-field" for both domestic and foreign investors. Another major improvement is the further streamlining of investment

---

[1] The Sixth National Socio Economic Development Plan (2006—2010).

[2] American Embassy, 2005, pp. 17~20.

[3] Taken from his speech at the 24the Annual Conference of the International Organization of Securities Commission in Lisbon, on May 25, 1999. Also reported in IMF Survey, June 7, 1999.

approval procedures, i. e. an investment license is no longer needed for foreign investment in general open business activities. Foreign investors can simply register their businesses under the Enterprise law. There are other attractive incentives being offered such as profit tax exemption, exempt land lease or land concession, Exemption of import duties and taxes on raw materials and capital equipment, Exemption of export duty on export products, Additional tax holidays, and reduced tax rates for large scale projects with special concession are available upon negotiation.

The Law on Investment Promotion 2009 was Promote Protection of foreign invest such as 1) Making up a good convenient climate for investors operate business compliance with the laws and regulations for entrance; 2) Defined all principles, regulations and measures relating to the promotion and management of the investments in both domestic and foreign, in order to make them convenient, speedy, correctly and allow them to receive the protection from the State, ensure the rights and interests of the investors as well as of the State and the peoples with the aim of raising the usefulness and roles of the investments in the continual and sustainable growth and expansion of the national economy. Guidance investors operate their business going by legally, transparency and accounting. [1] 3) Providing Investment promotion incentives, Taxation Policies in and Economic Special Economic Zone. [2]

4. Special Economic Zone and Taxation policies

Based on expect outcome of Seventh National Economic plan designed that Ensure political stability, peace and an orderly society, Ensure the sustainability of development by emphasizing economic development with, cultural and social progress, preserving natural resources and protecting the environment, Ensure GDP growth rate of at least 8% annually and GDP per capita to be at least USD 1,700; Achieve the Millennium Development Goals

---

[1] Art 1 of Law on Investment Promotion law 2009.

[2] Article 33 of Law on Investment Promotion law 2009.

by 2015 and taken Laos from the Least-Developed Country (LDC) by the year of 2020. [1]

Relating to the lesson learned of implementation the New Economic mechanism by reform central economic Planning to market-oriented or market economic System more than two decades by the main objectives of Creating structures for growth in agriculture forestry, industry and services, Open door policy for foreign cooperation, Develop education, public health, and upgrade people's livelihoods, Privatize of former state enterprise, improve and prepare the laws and regulation for the private sector are the basic to contribute a rapid national socio-economic development, to integrate Lao economy into the regional and international economies, to promote an economic reform based on market mechanism under the supervision of the state by reflecting our country characteristics via implementation of the " breakthrough approach " of the government using One Stop Service Mechanism namely " Smaller Administration Unit, but Wider Society" or " Special and Specific Economic Zone "

(1)FDI Policies on Special Promotion Zones

A concept of special economic zone development in the Lao P. D. R is recently bring into use; thus, many views are different especially with respect to use of promotion policy, management and administration mechanism of special economic zone development in the Lao P. D. R. The objective of Special and Specific Economic Zone Development is aim for building an industrial foundation moving forward to modernization by transformation of land into capital, using strategic position potentiality as a passing way to integration East-West in order to overcome the least development country. It is two meaning inside them for entrance. 1) it's forms economic development which identified specific locations to attract both domestic and foreign investors by offering tax and duty incentives in order to promote infrastructure development, service, production, skill development and transfer modern technology. 2) It's to contribute into the rapid growth of the economy, regional and international integration,

---

[1] Strategic Direction of the Seventh NSEDP(2011—2015), page 11.

promotion of economic reform based on the market economic principles and characteristic of the country, implementation of progressive Strategy into SEZ development and management in accordance with "Small Administration Unit Wider Society" laying the foundation for gradual industrialization, turning land into capital and optimization of a State strategic location along the east-west economic corridor. Hence, even sin 2003 to end of April 2011, the Lao government has approved 10 Special Economic Zones (SEZs). [1]

Table 4 Approved Special Economic Zone

No	Name	Date of Establishment	Location	Area and land Tenure	Purpose of Investment
1	Savan-Seno Special Economic Zone	2003	Savanakhet province	—Area 954 ha —Land tenure 75 years	—74,000.000 $ US —Trade, service, Industry, processing
2	Boten Beautiful Land Specific Economic Zone	2003	Luangnamtha Province	—Area1,640 Ha —Land tenure 50 years	— 500.000.000 $ US —Service, Trade
3	Golden Triangle Special Economic Zone	2007	Bokeo Province	—Area 3,000 Ha —Land tenure 50 years	—86,600,000 $ US —Service, trade
4	Vientiane Industrial and Trade Area	2009	Vientiane capital	—Area110 ha —Land tenure 75 years	—Trade, service, —Industry processing
5	Saysetha Development Zone	2010	Vientiane capital	—Area 1,000 ha —Land tenure 50 years	—128,000,000 $ US —Trade, service,
6	Phoukhyo Specific Economic ZONE	2010	Khammuane Province	—Area 4,850 ha —Land tenure 99 years	— 708,000,000 $ US —Trade, service, Industry processing, Airport and Logistic

---

[1] Development Strategy for Specialand Specific Economic Zone (SEZ) in the Lao PDR, 2011—2020.

续表

No	Name	Date of Establishment	Location	Area and land Tenure	Purpose of Investment
7	Thatluang Lake Specific Economic Zone	2011	Vientiane Capital	—Area 365 ha —Land tenure 99 years	—1, 600, 000, 000 $ US —Commercial, Industrial, Residential, Institutional
8	Longthanh Specific Economic Zone	2012	Vientiane Capital	—Area 557,75 ha —Land tenure 50 years	—1, 000, 000, 000 $ US —Trade, service,
9	Dongposy Specific Economic Zone	2012	Vientiane Capital	—Area 53,9 ha —Land tenure 50 years	—50,000,000 $ US —Commercial, Industrial, Residential, Institutional
10	Thakhek Specific Economic Zone	2012	Khammuane Province	—Area 1,035 ha —Land tenure 75 years	—80,000,0004US —Trade service, Institutional, Transportation, andect⋯

Example: Savan-Seno Special Economic Zone (SSSEZs)

Savan-SENO Special Economic Zone is the first special economic area established with land tenure 75 years according to the decree of Prime Minister No 148/PM on September 29, 2003. The SSSEZ comprise of 954 Ha separated in 4 zones, situated at tip of 2nd Friendship Bridge and along the Road No 9 in Savannakhet province. Estimate investment funding 74. 000. 000 $ US by Government 100%.

The main objective of establishment of SEZ is to promote the investment for production, trade and services along East-West economic Corridor (EWEC) managed by specific decree of the zone based on the market economic mechanism under the management and inspection of government. Hence, they focus on 4 main Sectors as 1) Service Sector: The service Sectors which approved to conduct activities in SSSEZ are providing in the guidance book are banking, Financial institution and Insurance, tourism promotion service, Hotel resort, restaurant, amusement park, Entertainment center, sport center, office construction for rent, guest house, school and hospital ect… 2) Trade Sectors are duty free shop, duty free border trade, import-export business, exhibition-trade promotion center, Department store, wholesale-retail store. 3) Distribution Logistics service sector are Transportation business, distribution service, warehouse, cool storage and 4) industrial Sector consist electrical wire manufacturing factory, food Processing factory, wood products industry, textile, shoes, bag manufacturing plant and automobile assembly plant and other electronic parts assembly plant [1]…

To support the activities in SSSEZs going by the expect outcome tax inventive is key attractive to invest. hereby, the authority concern to the SSSEZs defined to reduce tax incentive by sector as service sector shall be granted to exemption of profit tax for a period 2~10 years and afterward 8% or 10% corporate profit tax will be applied based on investment capital when the trade sector shall be granted exemption of their profit tax 2~5years afterward 10% corporate tax will be applied and the industrial sector is 5~10 yeas of exemption tax admitted to 8% when corporate profit tax should be applied[2].

From the founder SSSEZs 2003 to present time there are 27 companies with total investment value of 96. 65 million US dollars have been authorized for internal investment and have registered for 156 workers in order to approve investment in the zone. Now, 16 companies have started activity with registration cost of 30. 95 millions UD dollars. The out standing activity is that value added tax collection on import lead from Khammouane province to produce in the zone is succeeded. Authorizing import of vehicle, heavy machinery, engines, and materials for use in development of total of value Three Hundred Thousand US dollars. Land allocation is solved and it allows re-compensate and constructions to 32 families affected by the project

---

① See SSSEZ available at http://www. sncsez. gov. la/index. php/en/savan-seno-sez.

② See SSSEZ available at http://www. sncsez. gov. la/index. php/en/savan-seno-sez

in amount of 137 million kip equal to 64% of total program. [1]

2. Policies on tax andcustom duty for FDI

The reduce Tax and Duty is oneof the government policies in promoting FDI, encourage investment to developed rural area, country side to moving in to central city Step by step. To make a good atmosphere environmental to Investment, Government entitled the Sectors which Promotion of investment through custom duty and tax incentives such as agriculture, industry, handicraft and services. These sectors were charged with making detailed list of activities in three levels based on the priority activities of the Government, the activities related to the eradication of poverty, improvement of living standard of the peoples, construction of infrastructures, development of human resources, creation of job opportunities[2], etc···

1)General Customs and Tax System and Fiscal Incentives

Regular Customs and Tax Systems in the Lao PDR are regular Import duty rates are between 3%~40%, Indirect taxes include Business turnover tax between 5%~10% and excise tax between 5%~90%, when the Direct taxes on Corporate Profit Tax which Existing law on tax providing for Foreign (20%) and Domestic (35%). On November 2011, the law on tax is in the course of revising to unify the general profit tax for foreign and domestic investors. The new tax rate is speculated in the range of 24%~28%. Minimum tax at the rate of 0.1% of total revenue Personal income tax between 0~25% (progressive rate) after revising the law on tax and Fees and service charges.

2)Tax Incentive policies by Sector:

a)The Service Sector shall be granted the exemption of profit tax for a period 2~10 years and afterward 8% or 10% corporate profit tax will be applied based upon investment capital. These sector including Banking, financial Institute and Insurance, tourism Promotion Services, Hotel, resort, restaurant, Amusement park, Entertainment Center, Sport Center,

---

[1] Development Strategy for Special and Specific Economic Zone (SEZ) in the Lao PDR, 2011 — 2020, page 7.

[2] Article 49, Law on Promotion investment law 2009.

Conference Hall，Skill Center，office Construction for rent，Guest house，School and Hospital. etc…

b)Trade Sector shall be granted the exemption of profit tax for period 2～5 years and afterward 10% corporate profit tax will be applied. These Sector are Duty free shop，duty free border trade，Import-export Business，Exhibition-Trade Promotion center，Department store and Wholesale-Retail Store etc …

c)Industrial sector shall be granted the exemption of profit tax 5～10 years and afterward 8% corporate profit tax will be applied. These majors are Electrical Wire Manufacturing factory，Food-Processing Industry，textile，shoes，bag manufacturing plant，Automobile Assembly Plant and other Electric parts Assembly etc…

d) Distribution Logistics Services are Transportation Business，Distribution Service and Warehouse，Cool Storage.

(3)Investment Promotion Incentives

According to the law on the Promotion of Foreign investment，the three promoted zones based on social-economic conditions and geographical locations in the zones are as show in the table Incentive on Corporate Profit Tax.

Table 5　(based on the article 50 and 51 of IP Law 2009)

Zone	Level	Period of Exemption (years)
The zone has the economic and social infrastructures which cannot provide the facilities to the investment and the geographical location is mostly mountainous and remote areas. This zone will receive the highest level of investment promotion.	1	10
	2	6
	3	4
The zone has the economic and social infrastructures which can partly provide the facilities to the investment and the geographic location is not as dangerous as in Zone 1. This Zone will receive a medium level of investment promotion.	1	6
	2	4
	3	2
The Zone has the economic and social infrastructures which can highly facilitate the investment. This Zone will receive a low level of investment promotion.	1	4
	2	2
	3	1

(3)Promotion Incentives

In addition to the corporate tax incentives, investors shall be also entitled to customs duty and tax incentives there are 1) Exemption from profit tax in the next accounting year, if the net profit derived from business activities is used for business expansion; 2) Exemptions from import duties for the importation of raw material, equipment, spare parts and vehicles which are directly used for production. However, exemption of import tax shall comply with specific regulations; 3) Exemption from export duties for exportation of general goods and products. The exportation of natural resources and natural resources-made products shall comply with concerned regulations and laws. The importation of all types of fuel is not exempted from duties and taxes and 4) If an investor suffers losses after completion of tax finalization with the tax office, the investor shall be permitted to carry the losses forward to three consecutive accounting years. After ending of the period, any remaining losses shall not be allow to be deducted from profit. For special economic zones and specific economic zones, the provision of incentive treatment shall be in compliance with the Decree on the Establishment and Activities of respective zone. ①

Specific Promotion Incentives

The investment related to service which were receive addition policy of exemption of profit tax 5 years and exempted land lease or land concession 15 year in zone one and other 10 years in zone Two. These specific Promotion are the construction of hospitals, kindergartens, academic schools, vocational schools, colleges, universities, research centers and public utilities. ②

(4)Type and term of investment

In term for support FDI which defined down in Chapter Ⅱ of Law on Promotion investment, They classified into Three types for investment such as:

①General Business is an investment: General Business is an investment

---

① Article 52 of Law on Promotion investment law 2009.

② Article 54 of Law on Promotion investment law 2009.

in the general business sector including businesses defined in the list of controlled businesses and it is not a concession business. The investment in general business has unlimited term of investment except business of which the term has been determined in separate regulations and laws of relevant sectors. The composition of investment application procedure belong to role of Industrial and commercial issue business license. ①

②Concession Business：The Concession of Business belong to the Ministry of Planning and investment issue Concession license because of these business is refers to investment activities authorized by the Government to utilize ownership and other rights of the Government in conformity with regulations，for the purpose of developing and conducting business operations；these include rights on land concession, minerals, electric power， airlines， telecommunication， insurance and financial institutions. The term of investment in concession depends on the nature，size，investment value；conditions of the concession activities based on concerned regulations and laws but shall not exceed 99 years and may be extended with the approval of the government. ②

③Activities in the development of special economic zones

Activities in the development of special economic zones are investment for the purpose of construction of complete infrastructure and new city development. Activities in the development of specific economic zones are investment for the purpose of construction of infrastructure and development of each zone as required for the specific zones in accordance to actual conditions and laws；including industrial zones，export processing zones，touristic zones，etc.

The organization and activities of special economic zones and specific economic zones(SEZ) are determined in separate regulations. investors who wish to invest in SEZ shall submit the application for the investment to the SEZ.

---

① Article 20 of the investment promotion law 2009.

② Article 28 of the investment promotion law 2009.

The term of investment in the special economic zones and specific economic zones depends on the type, size and conditions of each special economic zone and specific economic zone; it shall not exceed ninety nine (99) years and may be extended on a case by case basis with the approval of the Government, especially in the case where the project has generated maximum benefits to the country, the investor has effectively implemented the signed agreement and has recorded good performance in contributing to local development. [1]

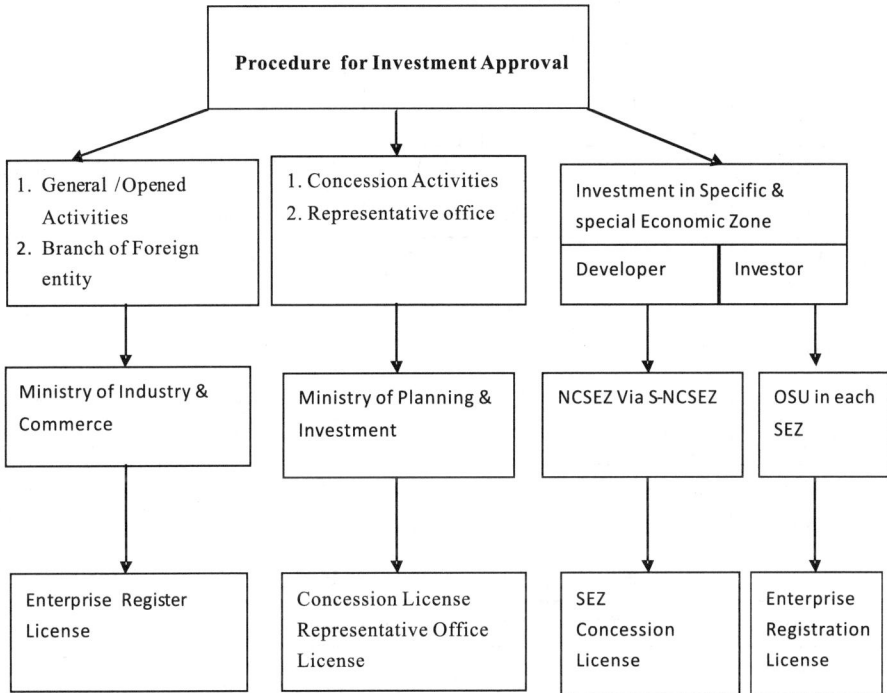

```
                    ┌──────────────────────────────────┐
                    │ Procedure for Investment Approval  │
                    └──────────────────────────────────┘
```

1. General /Opened Activities 2. Branch of Foreign entity	1. Concession Activities 2. Representative office	Investment in Specific & special Economic Zone	
		Developer	Investor
Ministry of Industry & Commerce	Ministry of Planning & Investment	NCSEZ Via S-NCSEZ	OSU in each SEZ
Enterprise Register License	Concession License Representative Office License	SEZ Concession License	Enterprise Registration License

④FDI inflow in to LAOS

Since the economic reform and opening up to the outside, Laos has attracted increasingly large amount of foreign capital. There are mainly three forms of foreign capital inflow: foreign loans, direct foreign investment and other foreign investment Between 1989 and 2012, There are

---

[1]   Article 42 of the Investment promotion law 2009.

more than 2,899 foreign companies registered and operation Business to whole kinds of business Sectors in capital, cities and remote areas in Laos[①] and Promoted to Gross Domestic Product— GDP increase from Zero in 1975 to 1,395 $ US in 2012. [②]

Table 2 Approval Increase The Foreign Investment by Country from 2001—2010.

No	Country	2001		2002—2005		2006—2010		2000—2010 (December)	
		Project	Value of investment (Dollars)	Project	Value of investment (Dollars)	Project	Value of investment (Dollars)	Project	Value of investment (Dollars)
1	Thailand	8	3291000	100	610808244	133	2035524913	241	2649624157
2	China	9	13415000	126	268747809	205	2303453795	340	2585616604
3	Vietnam	6	3412570	56	122077043	149	2037635044	211	21163124657
4	France	6	12608000	31	403746500	31	377729246	68	454083756
5	Korea	15	10374000	51	150956305	76	384002210	142	545332515
6	Japan	1	500000	23	12264583	18	420295780	42	433442363
7	India	0	0	2	330000	4	352477000	6	352807000
8	Australia	2	400332	15	315977196	15	18076000	32	334453528
9	Malaysia	1	1500000	24	82253237	18	67564737	43	151317974
10	Singapore	1	250000	12	41220000	16	71770650	29	113240650
11	Russia	1	300000	5	5050000	8	47738310	24	53088310
12	Switzer-land	1	750000	4	30300000	4	14902452	9	45952452
13	USA	3	3211560	13	12343000		21369326	15	36923886

---

① Approved Foreign Investment by country 2009, Available at http://www. investlaos. gov.-la/show_encontent. php? contID=29.

② Available at http://www. nsc. gov. la.

续表

	Year	2001		2002—2005		2006—2010		2000—2010 (December)	
15	England	—	—	9	1409700	10	32220000	19	33629700
16	Taiwan	1	300000	3	5620000	9	12950000	13	18870000
	17. Sweden, Norway, Poland, Germany, Italy, Peru,Cambodia, Panama,Holland, Myanmar,Island, Israel, Indonesia, Belgium,Sri Lanka,Cuba, Portugal,Turkey, Nepal,Philippine, Berkmarb, Hungary.	9	3784500	19	29310000	32	257473431	60	290567931
Total		64	54097712	583	2146892579	728	8459082394	1387	12266000190

Source: Statistic from which Approved Foreign and Domestic Investment Projects by Sector 210[1].

The adoption FDI policies need to balance with level of Socio-development of Host country,and compliance with any commitments which the host country signed. By the signed BIT with many countries and Multilateral Agreements for supporting the FDI policies. Due to the Priority majors and promote incentive Majors for develop of Government,ever since Laos open door policies there are Some Foreign investors nation invested in Laos and increased (See the table 2 and table 3).

---

[1] Available at http://www.nsc.gov.la/index.php? option=com_eventlist&view=categories&Itemid=138.

Table 3   Approval The Top 10 Foreign Investments by Country from 1989—2012

No	Country	Project	Value (US$ Million)
1	Vietnam	429	4913
2	Thailand	742	4082
3	China	801	3952
4	R. Korea	287	748
5	France	224	490
6	Malaysia	99	430
7	Japan	104	428
8	India	21	161
9	USA	113	150
10	Singapore	79	134
	Total:	2899	15488

Sources: statistic of ministry of Investment and planning2012. [①]

Table 4   Approved Foreign and Domestic Investment Project
By Sector period 01/Jan/2000 to 31December 2012.

No	Sector	Unit	Local share		Foreign share	Value of investment (US$)
			Private	Government		
1	Mining	220	994401366	37319900	3979194920	5010916187
2	Electric Generation	24	228241313	1013539700	3351589328	4393370341
3	Agriculture	880	401146134	6309860	2128333992	2535789986

---

① Available at http://www. investlaos. gov. la/show_encontent. php. contID=29.

续表

| No | Sector | Unit | Local share | | Foreign share | Value of investment (US$) |
			Private	Government		
4	Service	561	398103850	73168573	1787832330	2259104753
5	Industrial & Handicraft	813	592037734	17039361	1309333565	1918410660
6	Construction	112	158971849	11620000	49370380	667962229
7	Hotel and Restaurant	380	237083708	10627857	319494208	567205773
8	Trading	247	88064537	93294	156171924	244329756
9	Banking	18	17320000		223443622	24073622
10	Wood Industry	181	80996472	3053850	151547525	235597847
11	Telecom	14	45156309	5070800	84441786	134668895
12	Public Health	12	11079706		52303030	63382736
13	Consultancies	135	161169439		43482220	59651659
14	Garment	47	5532019		35837530	41369549
15	Education	76	12129739	500000	18356041	30985780
Total:		3720	3286434117	1178343195	13938732402	18403509774

Source: Statistic Department. ①

⑤Dispute Resolution mechanism on the Investment conflict

According to the guidance by the Chapter Ⅷ of the Law on promote investment 2009. And the vision of support foreign promote investment to getting protection for their benefit in case of violation, infringement or the confliction raised related to conducted business between Foreign Enterprise, should noted in two case 1) in case of enterprises having an agreement with

① Available at http://www. investlaos. gov. la/files/rpt _ Invest _ Summary _ Sector1A. pdf .

159

government, resolution shall be based on terms and conditions of the agreement or based on BIT related to investor's nation for example the case of Thai-Lao Lignite (Thailand) Co. , Ltd. ("TLL"), [1]. The procedure of resolution can file to International Arbitration organization to medication. 2) The foreign Investment Enterprise in case of a dispute arises in business operation under the form of business by contract, and the dispute shall be resolved as prescribed in the Contract. it mean that resolution will be resolved by the content which two parties signed in contract, anywhere contract will make up under Law providing and taken register in the local Justice Department which company located. conversely, in case of a dispute in a joint venture enterprise, or 100% foreigner owned investment enterprise, the parties shall proceed for resolution into dispute mediation to Committee for Promotion and Management of Investment (CPMI) at the central or local where investment licenses were issued. The duration for mediation of disputes is within 30 working days. but in case of the two parties not get result in a satisfactory outcome in the first step, the parties may file their complaint to the State Arbitration Agency for Economic Dispute or to judicial process as agreed by the disputing parties[2].

Conclusion: During the twenties years of the Implementation the Laos Revolutionary Party policy on New Economic Mechanism. The FID policy was mentioned in any resolutions of party and FDI also were put down in the each period of designation on National Socio-Economic development plan. the very outstanding of make up a good environment to attracted FDI was the expanded party policies into Law, decrees and regulations for guidance for conduction Business, ever since, started to Operation FDI polices up to Present time Laos government Promulgated more than 90 laws and thousands of decrees. [3] And secondly are Designed National Socio-Economic

---

① Case available at Case 1:10-cv-05256-KMW—DCF Document 50 Filed 08/03/11 Page 8 of 40.

② Article 81 of Law on Investment Promotion. 2009.

③ Legal Sector master plan 2009.

development plan in seven times①.

The policies of attract FDI in the Past. Government Provided whole economic Sectors into Priority Programs, Special Economic Zone and General Economic business, Established Government agencies related their majors Business Sectors in Central to Local areas. Even though FDI policies were successfully launched and implemented in some strategically selected "experimental" Special Economic Zone and then further extended to other parts, cities and Local area. But In general, foreign investors still considered government practices and administration' should be the most important policy category urgently called or improvement for furthering investment promotion because of the restriction of the build up Economic development structure are not enough responding to the demand for developing such as Road, transport delivery, telecommunication, Internet and etc···

In the early of 2013, Laos is already completed to be formal WTO member After nearly 15 years of talks and negotiation With the accession. ② Agreement with WTO membership, Laos membership package contains the market access commitments that Laos is making in goods and services—tariff ceilings on goods, subsidy limits in agriculture, and access to its services markets. For example some commitments as: For goods, Laos is committing "bound" tariffs (effectively maximum rates) that average 18.8% for all products—19.3% on average for agricultural products, and 18.7% for the rest and in services, Laos has made market access commitments in 10 sectors, covering 79 sub-sectors. ③

Other commitments include: Tariffs will be "ordinary customs duties" only, within committed levels, with no additional duties and charges, Agricultural subsidies to be according to Laos' "schedule" of commitments including no export subsidies, WTO rules, such as rules of origin, reshipment inspection, anti-dumping measures, countervailing duty,

---

① Laos national socio-economic development plan 7th.

② See article 23 of law on arbitration 2010.

③ available at http://www.wto.org/english/news_e/news07_e/acc_laos_nov07_e. htm.

safeguards, customs valuation, export measures including prohibitions, subsidies, trade-related investment measures, free zones, laws on transit operations, preferential trade under bilateral, regional and other agreements, to comply with WTO agreements immediately, Technical Barriers to Trade (product standards and labelling) and Sanitary and Phytosanitary Measures (food safety and animal and plant health) agreements fully implemented by 1 January 2015. Intellectual property protection to comply fully with the WTO Trade-Related Aspects of Intellectual Property Rights (TRIPS) Agreement by 31 December 2016, WTO rules on trading rights to apply from the date of becoming a member, with some exceptions for two years, although measures can be applied under WTO agreements on import licensing, technical barriers to trade (product standards and labelling) and sanitary and Phyto-sanitary measures (food safety and animal and plant health), State enterprises to import or export broadly under commercial terms, and to notify their imports and exports to the WTO, Price controls will be consistent with WTO rules on trade in goods, agricultural products and services, Companies and individuals to have the right to legal appeal on government administrative actions covered by WTO rules, including those on trade regulations, subsidies, customs valuation, intellectual property rights and domestic regulation in services, Laos' commitments and WTO rules to be applied throughout the country and enforced by the government without the need for recourse to the courts, Government fees and charges for services will be according to WTO agreements, Taxes and other charges on imports to comply with WTO agreements including national treatment (non-discrimination between imported and domestically produced products), No quantitative restrictions such as licensing, quotas, prohibitions, bans and other restrictions, except if for balance of payments purposes, which would follow WTO rules, Transparency: Laos to submit initial notifications as required within six months. All relevant laws, regulations and other measures will be notified as required by WTO rules and be made public in print and on the Internet. An Official Gazette to be set up within three years. ① Through its commitment to open up many new sectors of potential investment, it is expected that foreign firms will continue to invest in Laos PDR.

The scholar found that Laos promised to abide the WTO's basic principles of non-discrimination, pro-trade, pro-competition and so on. In return, Laos PDR will have the privileges enjoyed by WTO members and will also be able to enjoy the privileges provided to WTO members. These will have significant implications for future FDI inflow in Laos PDR.

On one hand, WTO accession provides incentives for more export-oriented FDI. First of all, the world export market for Laos PDR, as a WTO member, will be larger and more predictable. Quota and restrictive measures against Laos is export will be either eliminated or reduced. In addition, Laos will be able to resolve trade disputes with other member states under WTO's trade dispute settlement mechanism. As a result, FDI in industries where Laos has comparative advantage will grow. On the other hand, opening up of domestic market will attract FDI in industries where market potentials are great. In particular, industries that were originally dominated by relatively inefficient state-owned enterprises, such as telecommunication, banking, and insurance, will see increasing interest from foreign investors, especially from large multinational.

More importantly, WTO membership will serve to encourage Laos to implement further economic reform as well as various legal and institutional restructuring to fulfill its WTO obligations. As a result, there will be important improvement in Lao's business environment for foreign as well as domestic companies.

---

① Available at http://wto. org/english/news_e/news13_e/acc_lao_08jan13_e. htm.

中国—东盟自由贸易区法律框架下的老挝投资仲裁机构与机制

Phongphana Lvangamoth[*]
Chansouk Khahphou[**]
谢镇远　译

　　摘要　在老挝,投资仲裁被看作是在解决民商事纠纷,教导人们严格遵守和实行法律方面最为重要的方法。老挝政府试图通过仲裁解决机制和条约来改善法院系统。在本文中,笔者将讨论适用于几种有关国际贸易和投资的条约纠纷的纠纷解决机制,其中,笔者会特别考察在 WTO 纠纷解决规则及程序的谅解和中国—东盟自由贸易协定下的纠纷解决程序。随着投资者影响力的扩大,以及政府不断推进政策,相关的贸易参与者的利益与纠纷的解决便不能被忽视。为在此种关系中获利,我们须认真考察私人部门与国家将如何在不同的机制中相互作用。

　　关键词　贸易与投资　仲裁解决机制　老挝经济纠纷解决法

一、背景

　　老挝在 19 世纪 70 年代后期建立了法院系统,且自 1989 年开始,包括 1991 年老挝宪法在内的法律生效后,有关商业的问题逐渐出现。老挝政府致力于提高法治水平,依法治国,并在构建公正高效的法律体系中取得了进步。在 1975 年革命后的 10 年,老挝政府并未关注法律官员的发展,因而没有足够的专家,缺乏人力资源,特别是在法律领域中,这成为一个很大的问题。老挝已经历了向市场经济的快速过渡,自 1997 年加入东盟后实现了较为稳定的经

---

　　[*]　老挝最高人民法院刑事法官助理。
　　[**]　老挝最高人民法院司法研究与培训机构技术官员。

济增长。

为应对这些问题,老挝政府力图颁布和修改法律。根据社会和经济变化,政府颁布了关键性的法律及修正案,其中包括 2009 年的《人民法院法》、2012年的《民事诉讼法》、1990 年的《合同法》、1991 年的《宪法》、2004 年的《外国投资促进法》、2005 年的《经济纠纷解决》,以及《企业法》、《新预算法》、《商业银行法》、《增值税法》以及其他法律。而为构建和完善老挝的法律及法院体系,最重要的因素是法律的稳定性和可预见性。法院须具备良好的法院程序、管理体系以及调节程序,来保证其公正及透明性。因此,为迎接来自全球化的挑战,法院须具备良好的诉讼程序、审判程序、有关解决冲突的更好方法以及法院管理。

为保证国家建设的可预见性,诸如法治、良好的管理以及消除贫困对于加强人民法院特别是在民商事初审方面的能力建设而言是必需的。另外,加强能力建设也是吸引在老挝从事商业活动的国内及外国投资者的基础。民事诉讼法从 11 年前开始实施,并于 2012 年进行了修改。作为社会与经济增长、现代科技发展的结果,为保证老挝法院体系与东盟国家间的整体性,法院应该去解决逐渐增多的纠纷,同时从事相关法律工作的官员,如检察官、法官、警察、律师、法律执行机构的官员和公众应该去发现什么是有利于完善民事诉讼法的。因此,为了适应政治和经济领域发生的变化以及人民的需求,一些实质条款有所改变。此外,它还决定着有关诉讼参与者权利义务、司法管辖权、法院调解、一审程序、地区法院和上诉法院的原则和方法。为与国家政策及经济社会发展相一致,应使诉讼高效、全面、完整和客观,以保证在符合事实、法律和公正的基础上解决民事纠纷、商事纠纷、家庭纠纷和青少年纠纷,保护国际和集体的财产权以及机构、企业和公民的合法权益和利益,增强对立法的利用,消除与防止对法律的破坏,教育公民严格守法用法。

私营部门的发展以及吸引国外直接投资对于老挝人民民主共和国政府而言是较优先的事项。最近由立法机关批准的新投资促进法为本地及外国投资者提供了平台,包括获取土地,取消本地成分投资的要求以及透明度。尽管不足的基础设施建设仍是一个关键的挑战,投资者们依然能感受到政府在改善商业环境,入世后在多边贸易体系中的整体性和开放性以及提供相对稳定的政治环境方面所做的努力。目前大部分投资主要是集中于水电和采矿业,这两个部分占了在老挝外商直接投资总额的近四分之三。但投往农业、旅游业以及其他服务产业的投资也日益增多,并且新的投资促进法也吸引着更多的投资投往这些部门。

随着1986年新的经济机制的引入,老挝人民民主共和国以更加开放的姿态面对世界,并不断改善其商业环境来方便投资。

在诸如企业法、商业银行法和投资促进法等最近修订的法律中引入了惠及投资者并促进其事业的条款,这表明了老挝解决问题的决心。特别是2009年的投资促进法,统合了国内与外国投资者,从而为双方提供商业所要求的流动性、标准化、协调性以及程序和鼓励机制。而对外国投资者而言,最大的利益是可以购买土地,而在之前这项权利只属于本国企业。

政府通过努力,实现了这些管理和制度的改善,同时也得到了来自国际捐助者以及双边和超区域伙伴的支持,来改善这里的基础设施服务和人力资源状况。

老挝人民民主共和国拥有丰富的矿产资源,包括铜、金、银、锌、锡、重晶石、石膏、煤和蓝宝石。虽到目前为止,只有30%的领域得到了开发,但预期矿业活动将在不久的未来得到进一步发展,现已有650处被确认有矿。

由于在水力发电方面具有潜能,老挝希望能够成为东南亚的蓄电池,并预期这在大量和长期的外国投资的不断投入下,能于不久的将来实现。在这个部门的投资在未来五年内能达到52亿,这占了平均每年的国民生产总值的14%,并预期在25年内能获得大约20亿的收入。

投资者所面临的困难

尽管一个国家在贸易的许多方面取得了大的进步,但都不可避免的仍会在某些投资者所关心的关键领域中仍然存在问题。在老挝进行商业活动,最常见的限制是不足的技术,高花费的基础设施服务以及持续滋生的腐败的管理瓶颈。

老挝投资的挑战

老挝拥有大量未开发的自然资源和丰富的文化遗产,政府在法律及管理中的大规模改革使得其有关基础物质建设及处理技术不足的计划和项目在符合国际社会预期的同时,沿着正确的方向进行。并且,其入世申请和与东盟间更好的整合性积极有效地使得老挝能投入更多力量来进行改革,为此,在老挝投资也面临着如下挑战:

(1)承诺改革并使得商业监管环境合理化;

(2)东盟成员的经济自由化;

(3)提供便利的通道进入东南亚和中国的动态市场;

(4)在水电、采矿及旅游业的实质投资机会。

一个关键的挑战是如何去保证法律和规则如预想的那样被尊重和实行。如有关起草法令的速度,保证不同法律间的一致性。此外,尽管现在的营业登记和投资法发生了很大的变化,这些存在的制度与行政瓶颈显然还是不利于投资者。而关于投资者也是如此,如不足的物质基础设施和国家技术。

贸易与投资

减少贸易壁垒已成为老挝在东盟地区的最有成效的政策。与东盟国家间的贸易占了老挝69%的出口和55%的进口,这可能促进未来几年来自东盟国家的外商直接投资。再加上加入了大西洋自由贸易区,老挝已经和18个国家签署了双边贸易协定,并在36个国家获得了优惠关税制度地位。作为大西洋自由贸易区共同的优惠关税承诺的一部分,老挝减少了超过98%的关税,幅度在0到5%之间。原材料和必需品关税减少了5%,而供进一步加工以及供外资私营部门项目使用的原材料进口关税则被免除了。但课征奢侈品与加工木材和汽车的进口税依然保持在一个较高的水平。成品不征收出口税,而木材和其他非加工自然产品要课征出口税。

二、老挝的仲裁解决机制

中华人民共和国政府和老挝人民民主共和国政府希望在互相尊重主权,平等互利原则的基础上,鼓励、保护双方间的投资,并为之创造有利条件,以促进双方经济的进一步合作。在老挝,仲裁与调解是解决经济纠纷的首选办法,也是用以避免诉讼程序的积极方法。《经济纠纷解决法》No.02/NA(2005年5月19日)264,于2005年5月25日由总统颁布,制定了有关国内外实体与政府机构间经济纠纷解决的原则、规则和程序。

老挝于1998年9月15日加入了承认及执行外国仲裁裁决公约,即1958年纽约公约。然而老挝从未被要求过执行外国仲裁裁决。老挝同时也是联合国国际贸易法委员会(UNCITL)的成员。为实现在老挝人民革命党第九次代表大会的决议中所要求的四个突破方法,特别需要法律官员在案例考察和人力资源发展上取得突破。因此,经济纠纷解决法将经济纠纷规定为发生在国内和国外的政府和私人之间的产品和商业运营纠纷。该法律并未区分定居与半定居的区别。如果一个合同存在于这样的实体之间,那么根据《合同法》No.41/PO(1990年7月27日)34条,当事双方必须尽力根据合同规定去解决经济纠纷。在这一纠纷不能以这种方式解决时,那么在向法院提起诉讼前,各方必须先向国内或国际调解/仲裁机构寻求解决。外国投资者若不能按照他们的合同友好地解决纠纷,则须按《外国投资促进法》No. 11/NA(2004年10月22日)的要求向许可其投资的促进与管理投资委员会(CPMI)提起初步投诉。如果CPMI无法调解该纠纷,当事双方才可以向老挝经济纠纷解决办公室(OEDR)或经济纠纷解决单位(UEDR)或被双方都认可的仲裁机构提交仲裁。

在实践中,许多在老挝运营的以及与老挝公司开展业务的外国实体会在他们的合同中加入一项条款来规定在需要仲裁时相关的程序、规则和机构。由于老挝仲裁体系的不可靠和低效,这样的条款中通常会选择外国仲裁机构,并加入UNICTRAL仲裁规则。当双方不能就仲裁机构达成一致时,他们需要向OEDR或UEDR提交纠纷。当收到一个由双方同意的申诉时,OEDR或UEDR会决定其是否符合老挝法律和规则中关于经济纠纷解决的标准,如果该申诉被接受,那么当事双方则会被要求讨论和决定是通过调解还是仲裁来解决他们的经济纠纷。

一个作为调解或是仲裁并由OEDR来处理的纠纷必须是一个经济纠纷,并且从未被提交到人民法院。当事双方必须就向OEDR提出的申请中关于纠纷的实质内容达成一致。在仲裁程序中,必须遵守以下规则:调解员或仲裁员应公正地履行其职责;当事双方须享有平等的权利;所有相关人员必须履行保密义务;须使用老挝语(如果存在不懂老挝语的人,可有翻译人员参加)。除了这些要求外,当事人有选择仲裁规则和程序的自由。根据2012年《民事诉讼法(修正案)》第194条,诉讼当事人有权要求人民法院审查还未被执行的由OEDR或UEDR所作出的调解解决方案或仲裁裁决。人民法院必须在接到请求后的三十日内作出终审判决。人民法院会评估仲裁程序和仲裁裁决是否符合老挝关于经济纠纷解决的法律和规则中的规定以及是否有利于稳定、和平和社会秩序。如果程序合法、裁决未与任何老挝法律冲突,人民法院则会确认OEDR或者UEDR的决定,并使裁决具有强制执行力。如果人民法院确认一个仲裁裁决是错误的,或者人民法院的决定与OEDR的仲裁裁决不一致,则诉讼当事人是没有权利上诉的。如果一个仲裁裁决违背了老挝的法律与规则,则不会得到人民法院的确认,那么,仲裁裁决的当事人可以选择将纠纷重新提交OEDR或UEDR,或者向法院起诉请求判决。

在老挝解决商事纠纷主要有以下途径:协商、调解、仲裁和诉讼。对相关当事人而言,协商一般是其首要的选择,因为协商的花费最低,并且也是解决纠纷的最为友好的方式。调解,尤其是在司法程序中,易被接受并受支持,因为这种方式能有效保证相关当事人之间的合作关系。而相比诉讼而言,更多的当事人倾向于仲裁,因为它节约时间,程序简便。诉讼被认为是解决纠纷的最后手段。在老挝,和中国的当事人一样,外国当事人享有在法院提起诉讼的平等权利。

经济纠纷解决

基于美挝双边贸易协定,老挝鼓励用仲裁的方式来解决商事交易纠纷,并承诺不禁止商事交易的当事人以任何形式的仲裁或者根据在该仲裁中适用的法律达成协议。自1998年老挝加入承认及执行外国仲裁裁决公约(纽约公约)以来,老挝承诺在境内有效地承认及执行仲裁决议。老挝加入世界贸易组织后,更加强化了以仲裁这种首选方式快速地解决经济纠纷。

《经济纠纷解决法》(2010)允许经济纠纷的当事人选择任何形式的纠纷解决路径:

(1)双方当事人达成和解;

(2)由调解或者仲裁作出决议;

(3)法院诉讼。

而村民调解小组在教育和调解中都扮演了重要角色,特别是对那些争议较小不具有很高价值的民事案件,如家庭内部纠纷、动物所有权纠纷、通行权纠纷和其他不需要法院开庭审理的纠纷。在老挝,调解已经成为民事法律程序中的一部分,因为民事案件未经村民调解小组调解法院不会受理。老挝在法庭内和法庭外都适用调解。村民调解小组(VMU)设立于每个乡镇,并受司法部的监督管理。

村民调解小组由村长、妇女代表、青年代表和村里德高望重者组成。村民调解小组在协调诉讼当事人,避免引起社会纠纷方面扮演着重要的角色。"并且,在调解之前,诉讼当事人之一必须向村民调解小组报告或请求。"村民调解小组试图在没有胁迫的情况下达成和解。

如果诉讼当事人不能达成和解,当事人可以直接到法院立案或者将该纠纷提交至该地区的司法所,接受教育,达成和解,并再次在当事人间进行调解。"法律规定较小的纠纷必须经过调解,并且诉讼当事人也可将影响较大的纠纷提交至村民调解小组进行调解。"在未来,老挝政府计划修改民事诉讼法,并在现行规定的基础上起草商事程序法以保护公民和投资者的合法权益。调解是民事诉讼的一种纠纷解决方式。因为调解可以取代民事诉讼的所有程序,调解不仅适用于庭外的村民调解和经济纠纷解决办公室,而且法院也可在开庭中进行调解。①

一审民事法庭倾向于将更多的诉讼进行调解,这源于一审法院的作用主要在于法制教育和对当事人进行调解。一审民事法庭可以在两个阶段进行调解:法庭调查阶段和法庭听证阶段。负责任的法官可能在任何阶段都鼓励当事人达成和解。当事人达成和解后,一审法院必须在调解之日起五日内将协议结果记录在案,和解协议与法院判决具有同等约束效力。如果当事人双方没有达成和解,一审法院根据案件事实、证据和相关法律按照民事诉讼程序进行审理。原告不能基于已经结案的案件提起新的诉求。一审民事法院无权审理当事人已经达成和解的案件。

法院对案件的审查和判决是民事法律程序中非常重要的一步。该步骤包括对证据的审查和评估,确定案件的客观事实,告知当事人的权利和义务,依照案件事实和相关法律送达判决,判决过程是为了确认庭前交付的证据和事实并重新审查诉讼参加人提交的证据和证言。法庭听证必须公开,除非该案件涉及安全或机密事项或者该案件的公开将会对社会道德产生影响。

开庭前,法院书记员应做好庭前准备,宣布法庭纪律,核实当事人到庭情况,并且有必要召开一个庭前会议,查看是否有充足的证据,案件是否应当开庭,哪些人应当到庭,哪个法官审判。列好诉讼参加人的名字给书记员以传唤这些诉讼参加人。在开庭时,主审法官在庭审中扮演主要角色,控制庭审进程,要求当事人向合议庭出示证据。审判庭首先要求原告简洁地陈述主张,然后是被告简洁地陈述答辩,接下来是证人和个人陈述。当事人可以在审判期间向审判庭提交新的证据。

审判庭设立法庭辩论阶段以供当事人解释和澄清他们提交的证据来证明案件事实。审判庭允许当事人公正合理地辩论,专注于解决纠纷以得到更多的有效的证据直到当事人没有新的证据向审判庭提交。审判庭将在法庭辩论结束后重估证据,如果没有充足的证据以作出决定,审判庭将会请求公诉人在法官的监督下就案件给出意见。审判庭必须结束辩论并且宣布暂时休庭,在封闭的房间进行合议。如果有必要搜集新证据,审判庭可以宣布延期审理。

---

① 《经济纠纷解决法》(2012)第2条经济纠纷及其解决方案和第43条调解者和投资者。

作出判决

审判庭成员必须基于庭审结果和案件档案的所有证据独立地作出决定。审判庭成员将会在每个成员作出决定后一起合议以作出最后的判决。审判庭成员各自的决议并不相同但是必须基于多数表决达成最终的决议。然而,与最终决议意见相左的审判庭成员有权在合议庭笔录上表达自己的观点,合议庭笔录将会保存在案件档案中供上级法院参考。审判庭在回到法庭宣布判决之前将会花费一些时间起草最后的决议。当事人必须站在审判庭前听取宣告判决,主审法官指派审判庭的一名成员负责清晰地宣布判决并告知当事人有权对此判决提起上诉。当审判庭不能在开庭日宣布判决时,可以在开庭之日起七天内延期宣判。然后主审法官将会把判决送至打印室打印,如果没有错误,法官、书记员在判决书上签名并盖章。如果诉讼参加人对判决不满可以向上级法院逐步上诉。

三、结论

商事纠纷解决机制在保护老挝投资者合法权益方面扮演了非常重要的角色。现在,商业贸易逐渐增加,不仅包括国内贸易,还包括涉及国际条约的国际贸易,违反商务合同,侵犯知识产权等等问题。这些所有的纠纷不再是以前那种简单的问题,已经发展成了更加复杂的问题,这些问题需要专业的知识和技能才能解决。法官不可避免地必须不断充实完善自己以解决社会中这些更为复杂的纠纷问题。国内或者国外个人之间的利益冲突导致了经济纠纷,这些纠纷可能是因违背契约或者在生产经营过程中产生的。经济纠纷解决是一种通过人民法院之外的调解或者仲裁的利益纠纷解决方式。[①] 世界上的许多国家拥有自己的法律制度,这种法律制度对于管理国家具有非常重要的作用。因此,每个国家修改自己法律制度以适应国家标准。每个国家必须注重人力资源的发展,特别是东盟国家在加强同中国的经济、贸易和投资合作方面扮演着重要的角色。在未来,农业、能源、矿产资源和旅游将会成为中国同老挝的重要合作点。笔者相信亚洲地区在世界经济发展和贸易方面将发挥更为重要的作用。东盟成员国将会互相支持。老挝未来经济发展的挑战在于为全球化

---

① 《经济纠纷解决法》(2012)第 2 条经济纠纷及其解决方案。

挑战提供更为稳固的合作基础。"合作促进和平、人权和可持续发展,并且对于应对气候变化也是至关重要的。我们有责任去维护和平,为共同繁荣发展作出努力。"

Investment Arbitration Institution and Mechanism in Laos under the Legal Framework of China-ASEAN Free Trade Area

Phongphana Lvangamoth*
Chansouk Khahphou**

Abstract　Investment arbitration settlement in Lao PDR is regarded as the most important court in solving civil and commercial dispute and educats the ethnic group people to strictly respect and implement the law. The government of Lao PDR has endeavored to improve the court system by arbitration settlement mechanism and treaties. In this paper, I will discuss the dispute settlement mechanism available in different types of treaty's disputes relating to international trade and investment, specially, I will examine dispute settlement processes under WTO's understanding on rules and procedures governing the settlement of disputes and the China-ASEAN free trade agreement. With investors becoming more influential and state increasingly pushing the policies and interests, the benefits of all players involved in trade and dispute settlement cannot be neglected. In order to benefit from such a relationship, we need to carefully examine how the private sector and the state may interact through different mechanisms.

Keywords　trade and inustment; Arbitration settlement Mechanism Resolution of Economic Pisputes; Laos PRD

---

*　Judge Assistant, Criminal member under the People's Supreme Court.

**　Technical Officer, the Judical Research and Training Institute Under the People's Supreme Court.

173

1. Background

After the establishment of the court system in the late 1970s and adoption of laws from 1989, including the constitution of the Lao PDR in 1991, the commercial problems gradually appeared in the Lao PDR. The government of Lao PDR is committed to promoting the rule of law and governs the country by the rule of law, and has made progress towards developing a just and effective legal system. Lao government did not focus on the development of legal officials for the decade after the revolution in 1975; it has not enough experts, and lacks of human resources, particularly in the field of law which has become a great problem. Laos has been rapidly proceeding with the transition to market economy and has accomplished relatively stable economic growth since Laos joined ASEAN in 1997.

In order to cope with these issues, the Lao government has tried to enact and revise laws, according to social and economic changes, and therefore the key laws were enacted including the amended the law on *people's Court in* 2009, *Civil Procedure Code in* 2012, *Contract Law in* 1990, *Lao Constitution in* 1991, *Foreign Investment Promotion Law in* 2004, *Resolution of Economic Dispute in* 2005, *the Enterprise Law*, *the New Budget Law*, *the Commercial Bank Law*, *the Value-Added Tax Law* and other laws. Therefore, building and improving the legal and court system is necessary for Lao PDR. So the legal stability and foreseeability are the very important elements. Courts are required to good proceeding, better process at the court, manage court system and great way deal with mediation processes, so that courts can ensure the justice and transparency. Therefore, good procedure, judgments, qualified process, better way to settle conciliation processes and court managements are requested and challenged issues in the globalization's inspiration.

In order to guaranty foreseeability on developing the country such as rule of law, good governance and poverty eradication are necessary to strengthen capacity building of the people's courts, particularly in the first instance on the civil and commercial procedure. Moreover, strengthen

capacity building is a basic condition necessary to attract domestic and
foreign investors those who do businesses in Laos. The Law on Civil
Procedure was implemented 11 years ago and it was amended in 2012 as the
result of social and economic growth, modern technology. The court system
of Laos integrates with Court system of ASEAN member countries, the
increasing civil disputes, the number of civil cases request the court to solve
disputes increased day by day and also the sections, officials related to work
in the field of law, for example, the Office of the Public Prosecutor, the
people's courts, police officers, Lao Bar Association, the Law Implementing
Agencies and public to see that it is necessary to improve Law on Civil
Procedure, so it was changed some substantial articles to fit for the new
changing of political, economic regime and the present demand of people.
Furthermore, it still determines the principles and measures pertaining to
the rights and obligations of participants in proceedings, jurisdiction of
judicial tribunals, mediation in the courts and the method of case
proceedings in the court of first instance, regional court, and the court of
cassation in line with the government's policy and guideline and national
socio-economic development of country, making the proceedings in the court
effective, comprehensive, complete and objective in order to ensure solving
civil disputes, commercial disputes, family disputes and juvenile disputes in
a manner consistent with the reality, laws and justice, to protect the
property rights of the State and collectives, and the legitimate rights and
interests of organizations, enterprises and citizens; enhancing the use of legislation; eliminating and preventing the violation of laws; and educating the
citizenry to strictly respect and implement the laws.

In particular, private sector development and the attraction of foreign
direct investment are on the Lao People's Democratic Republic
Government's top priorities. The new law on investment promotion,
recently approved by the legislature, levels the playing field for local and
foreign investors, including the access to land, eliminates local content-
related investment requirements and transparency, as well as inadequate
basic infrastructure, remain among the key challenges, investors appreciate
the government's efforts in improving the business environment, its

opening-up and greater integration into the multilateral trading system with accession to the World Trade Organization in sight, and the country's relatively stable political environment. The majority of investments is currently concentrated in hydropower and mining, with close to three quarters of total FDI into the Lao People's Democratic Republic directed to these two sectors. Increasingly, however, investments are also pouring into agro-business, tourism and other services industries and will likely increase with the attractive incentive packages provided in the new law on investment promotion. ①

With the introduction of the new economic mechanism in 1986, the Lao People's Democratic Republic has opened itself to the rest of the world and has consistently embarked on improving its business environment to make the country more investor-friendly. The inclusion of provision that favour investors and facilitate their business undertakings in the more recently revised laws such as the enterprise law, the law on commercial banks, and the law on investment promotion is a demonstration of the country's resolve to put its house in order. In particular, the 2009 law on investment promotion, which merges the laws on domestic and foreign investors as it provides the streaming, standardization and harmonization of business requirements, procedures and incentives for both foreign and domestic investors. Of utmost interest to foreign investors is the possibility to purchase land, a right that in the past was afforded only to local businesses.

These regulatory and institutional improvements are complemented by the government's efforts, with support from international donors and bilateral and super regional partners, at improving and modernizing the country's basic infrastructure service and human resources. The Lao People's Democratic Republic's rich mineral resources includes copper, gold, silver, zinc, tin, barite, gypsum, coal and sapphires. With only 30 percent of its territory explored so far, activity An investment guideline of Lao PDR 2010. in the mining sector is expected to rise in the near future,

---

① An investment guideline of Lao PDR 2010.

with at least 650 locations identified to have metal ores.

With its potential in hydropower generation, the Lao people's democratic republic's aspiration to be the battery of south-east Asia could well see realization in the near future with large and long-term foreign investment continually pouring in this sector. It alone could reach $ 5. 2 billion over the next five years, averaging the equivalent of around 14 percent of gross domestic product a year, it is expected to raise around $ 2 billion in revenue over a 25 year period.

Difficulties Facing Investors

A country in transition, although making big stride in many respects, would unavoidably be still wanting in some areas of key concern for investors. The most often cited constraints when it comes to doing business in the Lao People's Democratic Republic include skills shortage, inadequate (or sometimes non-existent) and high-cost basic infrastructure services, and persistent administrative bottlenecks which breed corrupt practices.

The Challenges of Investment in Lao PDR

Lao PDR is location its largely untapped natural resource and rich cultural heritage, the government has steady strides in reforming its laws and regulations to make them consistent with the expectations of the international community and its plans and projects with respect to improving the basic physical infrastructures and addressing the issue of skills shortage, are step in the right direction. Likewise, its bid for WTO member and its greater integration into the ASEAN are very constructive and are effective driving forces to push the country to enact much clamored reform, therefore, the challenges of investment in Laos as following:

(1)Commitment to reforming and rationalizing the business regulatory environment;

(2)Economic liberalization of the ASEAN membership;

(3)Providing a convenient access to the dynamic market of south-east Asia and China;

(4) Substantial yet to-be explored investment opportunities in hydropower, mining, and tourism.

A key challenge is how to ensure that the letter of laws and regulations are respected and implemented as envisioned. There are concerns raised with respect to the pace of drafting implementing decrees to give effect to laws, as well as ensuring coherence of these different laws. Moreover, despite the very ambitious changes in current business registration and investment laws, these remain institutional and administrative bottlenecks which are clearly welcoming of investors. Additional concerns for investors, and rightly so, are the inadequacy of (and by extension, costly) physical infrastructure, together with inadequate country skills.

Trade and Investment

Reduction of trade barriers has been one of the Lao People's Democratic Republic's most effective policies into the ASEAN region. ASEAN countries account for more than 69 percent of the Lao People's Democratic Republic's total exports and 55 percent of its imports. This is likely to boost FDI from ASEAN countries in the coming years. In addition to being part of AFTA, the country has signed bilateral trade agreements with 18 countries and been granted generalized system of preferences status in 36 countries. It is likewise at the final stages of its accession process to the WTO. As part of its AFTA-common effective preferential tariff commitment, the country has reduced more than 98 percent of its tariff to between 0 and 5 percent. Raw materials and essential consumer goods benefit from 5 percent tariffs. Raw materials imported for further processing or for foreign-financed private sector projects are exempt from tariffs. However, import duties remain high on luxury products and processed wood and cars. Finished goods may be freely exported. However, timber and other non-processed natural products are subject to export duties.

2. Arbitration Settlement Mechanism in Laos

The Government of the People's Republic of China and the Government of the Lao People's Democratic Republic (hereinafter refer to as contracting states), desire to encourage, protect and create favorable conditions for investment by investors of one contracting state in the territory of the other contracting state based on the principles of mutual respect for sovereignty, equality and mutual benefit and for the purpose of the development of economic cooperation between both states[1]. In the Lao PDR, arbitration and mediation are the preferred methods for solving economic disputes and are actively encouraged throughout the laws and regulations of the country as a means of avoiding court proceedings. The *Law on Resolution of Economic Disputes* No. 02/NA (19 May 2005)264, which was promulgated by the President on 25 May 2005, set out the principles, regulations and processes for the resolution of economic disputes involving domestic and foreign entities and government organizations[2].

The Lao PDR became a party to the new york convention of 1958 on the recognition and enforcement of foreign arbitral awards on 15 September 1998. Laos has, however, never been asked to enforce a foreign arbitral award. Laos is also a member of the United Nations Convention on International Trade Law (UNCITL). In order to reach the four breakthrough approaches that determined in the resolution of the 9th Congress of Lao People's Revolutionary Party, particularly the court officials must implement breakthrough in term of case consideration and human resources development. Therefore, The Law on Resolution of Economic Disputes defines economic disputes as those relating to production and business operations occurring between both domestic and foreign organizations and individuals. The law does not differentiate between parties domiciled or half-domiciled in the country. If a contract exists between such entities, then in accordance with Article 34 of the *Law on Contract* No. 41/PO (27 July 1990) the parties must first endeavor to resolve the economic dispute according to the terms of that contract. In the event that the dispute cannot be resolved in this manner then the parties must use a domestic or international mediation/arbitration institution before resorting to court proceedings. Foreign investors who are unable to resolve their dispute

---

[1]   The governments of the two countries signed an agreement on establishing the Laos-China cooperation committee on economics, trade and techniques on June 11, 1996.

[2]   *Resolution of Economic Disputes* No. 02/NA (19 May 2005)264.

amicably in accordance with their contract are required under the *Law on Promotion of Foreign Investment* No. 11/NA (22 October 2004) to file an initial complaint with the Committee for Promotion and Management of Investment (CPMI) where their investment license was issued. If the CPMI is unable to mediate the dispute, then the parties can submit their complaint for arbitration to the Lao Office of Economic Dispute Resolution (OEDR) or the Unit of Economic Dispute Resolution (UEDR), or a foreign arbitration institution agreed by both parties①.

In practice, many foreign entities operating in Laos or conducting business with Lao companies will incorporate a clause into their contracts that defines the process, rules and institution they wish to use in case arbitration is necessary. Due to the often unreliable and inefficient character of Lao's arbitration systems, such clauses will often include a referral to a foreign arbitration institution and incorporate the UNICTRAL arbitration rules. In the event that the parties cannot agree on an arbitration institution, they will need to submit their dispute to the OEDR or the UEDR. Upon receiving a petition agreed by both parties, the OEDR or UEDR will decide whether it meets the criteria for economic dispute resolution under the laws and regulations of the Lao PDR. If the petition is accepted, the parties will then be invited to discuss and decide whether they wish to use mediation or arbitration to resolve their economic dispute.

For a dispute to be considered by the OEDR for mediation or arbitration, it must be an economic dispute, which is not and has never been resorted to the People's Court. The parties must also agree upon the substance of the dispute in their petition to the OEDR. During the arbitration proceedings the following rules must also be followed: mediators or arbitrators shall be impartial in the performance of their duties, the parties shall have equal rights, confidentiality will be maintained by all affected persons and the Lao language shall be used (a translator can attend the arbitration for those persons who do not have sufficient knowledge of the

---

① *New York Convention of* 1958.

language). Apart from these requirements, parties have the freedom to select the rules and procedures to be followed during the arbitration. Under Article 194 of the amendment of *Civil Procedure Law* 2012, litigants have the right to request the People's Court to review a mediation settlement or arbitration award of the OEDR or UEDR, provided the award has not yet been implemented by the parties. Upon receipt of the parties' request, the People's Court must issue a final judgment not later than thirty (30) days from the date of receipt of the request[1]. The People's Court will assess whether the procedure of the proceedings and the arbitral award were in compliance with the laws and regulations of the Lao PDR on economic dispute resolution and those on stability, peace and social order. If the proceedings were legitimately held and the award did not conflict with any Lao laws, the People's Court will confirm the decision of the OEDR or UEDR, and the award will become enforceable. The litigants will have no right to appeal this decision, unless the People's Court has confirmed a wrong arbitral award or if the decision of the People's Court is inconsistent with the OEDR arbitral award. The People's Court will not confirm an arbitral award if they believe it was given in violation of Lao laws and regulations. The parties to the arbitral award can then either request the OEDR or UEDR to re-examine the dispute, or file a claim in the People's Court for adjudication.

Basically there are the ways to resolve a commercial dispute in Laos: negotiation, mediation, arbitration and litigation. Negotiation is normally the first choice of parties concerned because it is the least expensive and most friendly approach to resolve a dispute. Mediation is also welcomed and encouraged especially during the judicial procedure, and it can effectively preserve the cooperation relationship of the parties involved. Compared with litigation, arbitration is a preference for most parties mainly because it is not that time consuming and the procedure is relatively simple. Litigation is regarded as a final way to resolve a dispute. In Laos, foreign parties have

---

[1] Civil procedure code 2012, Article 194 mediation between the litigants and Article 195 mediation in court.

equal rights to bring action in courts as Chinese parties. The PRC law contains no political method of dispute resolution.

Economic Dispute Resolution

Based on the US-Lao Bilateral Trade Agreement, the Lao PDR encourages the use of arbitration for the settlement of disputes arising out of commercial transactions, and has committed not to prohibit parties to a commercial transaction from agreeing upon any form of arbitration, or on the law to be applied in such arbitration. Since 1998, the Lao PDR, which is a party to the New York Convention on Foreign Arbitral Awards, has committed itself to ensure the effective recognition and enforcement of arbitral awards on its territory. The accession of Lao PDR to the World Trade Organization has reinforced the need for development of arbitration as the preferred way to swiftly settle economic disputes. The Law on the Resolution of Economic Disputes (2010) allows the parties to an economic dispute to select any form of dispute resolution:

(1)Conciliation made by the parties;

(2)Resolution made by mediation or arbitration; or

(3)Litigation in courts.

As regards to the village mediation unite, it play an important role in education and mediation, especially the civil cases related to small disputes or disputes which are not of high value such as family disputes, disputes related to the possession of animals, rights of way, the land use right and other disputes in order to avoid handling by court. In Lao PDR, the mediation has become a part of civil proceedings because the court will not accept civil cases without mediation in the village mediation units. The Lao PDR has used mediation in both outside and inside the court.

The village mediation units (VMU) were established in each village under supervision of the Ministry of Justice. The village mediation unit is composed of chief of village, representatives from women, youth, and respected people in the village. The village mediation unit plays very important role to reconcile the litigants in order to avoid making problems in the society. "However, before conciliation one of the litigants in a suit must report or request to village mediation unit." The village mediation unit tries reaching a settlement without any coercion if the litigants cannot reach a set-tlement, the litigants can file the case directly to the court or bring the disputes to the justice office of district to educate, encourage reconciliation, and mediate between the litigants again. "The small disputes as provided in the law must conduct mediation, however a dispute involves a high value, the litigants can also bring the dispute to the process of mediation in the village mediation unit. " In the future, Lao PDR government has planned to improve the civil procedure code and create the commercial procedure law for the present requirement, protecting the legitimate benefits and rights of the peoples and investors.

Conciliation is an extra step in the civil proceeding. Because the conciliation may take the place of all steps, the conciliation not only made in outside as the village level and the Economic Dispute Resolution Office, but court can conciliate the parties as well[①].

Taking one more the lawsuit into conciliation in the civil court of the first instance due to the main role of first instance court is to educate and mediate the parties' dispute. Conciliation of the civil court in the first instance can be made in two periods: during investigation and hearing in the courtroom. The responsible judges may encourage parties to settle the case at any time. When the litigants reach a settlement, the court of first instance must make a record of the result of settlement within five days from the date of the mediation, which has the same biding effect as a court decision or final judgment. If the parties cannot settle the case, the court of the first instance undertakes civil proceeding based on information, evidence and law. The plaintiff has no right to file a new petition when the case that has been settled. The civil court of the first instance has no power to consider the case that the parties have already settled.

Examination and judgment of the case by the court is an important step in civil proceedings. This stage involves the examination and evaluation of

---

① *The Resolution of Economic Dispute* 2012, Article 2 economic dispute and their resolution and Article 43 mediators and investors.

evidence, determination of the actual facts of the case, notification of the litigants' rights and obligations, delivery of judgment in accordance with the true facts of the case and the laws. The trial process is made in order to reconfirm what has been offered previously and in order to re-examine the evidence and opinions of those who attend the trial. The hearing in court room must be public, except for cases related to security or confidential matters or the case will affect social morality.

Before the trial, the court clerk prepares the courtroom by ready courtroom's regulations, and verifying the attendance of parties involved and also a panel is necessary to consider whether there is sufficient evidence and whether the case is ready for trial and person who will participate in the trial, which judge will list the name of participants and give to the court clerk to summons those persons to participate in the trial. In the trial session, the presiding judge takes the leading role to control the trial, asks the litigants to present the evidence to the panel. The panel asks the plaintiff to present briefly about his or her claim, and then asks the defendant to present briefly about his or her counterclaim, and followed by the witnesses and individual involved. The litigants can present additional evidence to the tribunal during the opening trial.

The tribunal opens debate session for the litigants to explain and clarify their evidence in order to find fact. The panel allows the litigants to debate impartially, reasonably, and focus on the conflict resolution to get more sufficient evidence until the litigants do not have any evidence to present to the panel. The tribunal will evaluate the evidence after completing a debate, if there is enough evidence to make decision, the panel will request the public prosecutor to make the statement related to the case under his or her supervision. The court must close the debate and declare a temporary recess of the trial in order to make a decision in private room. The panel can declare an adjournment of trial if it is necessary to collect new evidence.

Making and Pronouncing Decision

The members of the tribunal must make the decision independently base on the result of trial and all evidences in the case file. The members of panel will share their own decisions together after each member made a decision in

order to have one final decision. The decisions of the members of penal are
not the same but the final decision must be reached based on the majority
votes. However, the members of the panel who disagree with the final
decision have the right to express an opinion in writing and be kept in the
case file for the higher court to consider.

The panel spends some time to draft the final decision before coming
back to the court room to pronounce a decision. The litigants must stand in
front of the panel to hear the pronouncement of a decision, the presiding
judge assigns a member of the panel to take the role to read the decision
clearly and inform the litigants the right to appeal the decision. In case of
the panel cannot pronounce the decision at the day of trial, it may be
adjourned to another day not exceeding seven(7) days. Then presiding judge
will send it to the type writer for typing, if have no mistake, judges, clerk
sign and apply the stamp on it. If the parties not satisfy with the judgment,
they can appeal to the higher court step by step.

3. Conclusion

Commercial dispute settlement plays a significant role in protecting the
legitimate benefits and rights of investors in Lao PDR. Nowadays, the
business transitions are increased more and more, it's not only domestic
business, but also international trade with international treaties, breach of
commercial contract, and violation of intellectual property ... etc which all of
that disputes is not simply problems as before but such conflict has
developed itself to be super complex which need special knowledge and skill
to deal with. Therefore, it's indispensable that judges must develop
themselves in order to overcome such super complex disputes which occurred
in society. Economic disputes are conflict of interest between individuals
whether domestic or foreign that may arise from the breach of a contract or
(from a dispute related to) production or business operations. Economic
dispute resolution is the resolution of a dispute related to interests by

mediation or arbitration conducted outside the People's Court[①]. Therefore, Many countries in the world will have the legal system by themselves, and the legal system is very important for governing the country. So, each country will improve and develop the legal system to reach international standard. But, each country must focus to human resources development. Especially, ASEAN countries play a significant role in boosting cooperation in the terms of economy, trade and investment between china and ASEAN including Laos. In the future, the sector of agriculture, energy, mineral resources and tourism will be the important point of china and Laos cooperation. I believe Asian community is becoming more important in the world, in terms of economic development and trade. ASEAN members will support each other. The challenges for future economic development in my country is stressed that the solid relationship provides the foundation for stronger cooperation amidst global challenges. "Cooperation to promote peace, human rights, sustainable development and climate change is essential. We have a historical responsibility to safeguard peace and work together for prosperity and growth. "

---

① *Law on the Resolution of Economic Disputes* 2012, Article 2 economic disputes and their resolution.

缅甸仲裁法研究
及中国经验

Zhang Xiaojun[*]
Yin Yin Han[**]
Sun Nanxiang[***]
魏彬彬　译

摘要　正如实践中展现的,在国家中投资仲裁和商事仲裁机构对于吸引全球范围内的外国商业和投资十分重要。在缅甸经济改革期间,大量的商事法律和规则被修改。缅甸正在起草一部新的仲裁法。毫无疑问,中国的经验在一定程度上是有价值的。缅甸仲裁法和中国仲裁法存在差异,但是它们的立法意图是一致的,即为国际贸易和外国投资推进一种公正的氛围。

关键词　商事仲裁　缅甸 1944 年仲裁法　缅甸仲裁法(草案和协议)
中国仲裁法　纽约公约

一、简介

缅甸是东盟的成员国,东盟是 1992 年发起的自由贸易区。自贸区旨在东盟国家中消除关税壁垒,此举的关键在共同优惠的关税体制,即到 2010 年或 2015 年关税逐步减到 0~5％。缅甸也是东盟服务框架协议的签约国,这个协议旨在加强东盟地区服务供给者的合作,减少服务贸易限制,逐步使服务贸易自由化。此外,缅甸也是东盟投资区域框架协议的成员,此协议旨在至 2010年 1 月 1 日把东盟地区建成竞争投资区域,同时至 2020 年促进建成一个自由投资环境和投资自由流动区域。为了促进经济发展,争端解决机制和仲裁是

---

[*]　张晓君,西南政法大学国际法学院院长,教授。
[**]　Yin Yin Han,缅甸最高法院研究中心主任。
[***]　孙南翔,西南政法大学博士研究生。

重要的事实。

在改革开放的政策实施后,市场经济在中国建立起来。从20世纪80年代开始,中国经济飞速发展,这主要归功于外国直接投资和国际贸易的发展。在投资和贸易发展的同时,中国积极参加国际经济事务。因此,在缅甸经济改革期间,中国的经验在某种程度上是有价值的。故而本文陈述了缅甸的仲裁以及缅甸仲裁法和中国仲裁法关于国际商事仲裁的比较研究。

根据《布莱克法律词典》,仲裁是指一种争端解决的过程,即中立的第三方在听取双方当事人的要求后作出裁决。仲裁是自愿的,争议双方选择有权力作出具有约束力的裁决的仲裁员。缅甸商事仲裁的定义与中国的不同。在缅甸,不仅私人实体之间可以适用商事仲裁,政府与私人实体之间也可以适用。因此,为了描述缅甸商事仲裁,本文相继研究各个种类的争端解决。

二、缅甸投资仲裁机制

缅甸投资协议如下:

同中国(2002年批准)

同印度(2009年批准)

同老挝(2003年签署,尚未批准)

同菲律宾(1998年批准)

同泰国(2008年签署,尚未批准)

同越南(2000年签署,尚未批准)

东盟综合投资协议

东盟

缅甸投资委员会在2013年已经准许超过100项外国投资,包括啤酒商和香烟制造商。从1月到12月19日,缅甸投资委员会准许118项外国投资和合资企业在国内运营。其中包括国际大牌如英美的烟草公司来制造和分销香烟等等。其他的商业有汽车制造、家具制造、竹纤生产、汽车维修、食品生产、IT服务、制药和装饰屋顶制造。在2013年,一些制造业已经被准许。截至2013年11月末,在缅甸的外国投资超过440亿美元,而且中国、泰国的投资者最多。

1944年缅甸仲裁法没有国际投资仲裁案例和国际商事仲裁案例是在英语环境下进行的公开记录。非常少的国际投资仲裁案例和国际商事仲裁案例在缅甸实施。这可能反映了缅甸1988年之前减少同外国的经济关系的经济政策。从 1988 年开始,缅甸开始采用市场经济体系,外国投资者、国内企业和政府开始在缅甸投资。2013 年 9 月,在缅甸签订的外国投资额达到 5345 万美元,并把自 1988 年以来的总数提至 442 亿美元。

从 1988 年到 2013 年,只有 Myanmar Yaung Chi Oo Trading PTE Ltd. v. Government of the Union of Myanmar 这一个投资商事仲裁案件。在这个案件当中,1993 年 11 月 29 日,MFI 与缅甸国家工业部门之间达成合资企业协议。此协议创造一个合资公司,即 Myanmar Yaung Chi Oo Company Ltd. ,这是为了联合投资符合缅甸外国投资法的规定。MFI 捐助机器和其他物品,Mandalay. MYCO 在 3 年内贡献资金和技能等等,这都是为了运营啤酒厂和促进产品分发。MFI 占 55% 股份,MYCO 占 45%。除非提前终结条款,这个协议的期限是 5 年。关于解释和适用合资协议的争端,可以依据缅甸 1944 年仲裁法案提交仲裁。

1994 年 10 月 1 日,MYCO 的运营已经获得相关许可。这存在巨大的成功:啤酒厂的产量剧增,MYCO 收益颇丰。在通过合资企业协议时,缅甸还不是东盟的成员国。1997 年,缅甸被公认为东盟成员。随后,缅甸在东盟的工作中作出了突出贡献。

1997 年的后半年,合资企业协议当事人之间的关系出现大量问题。原告声称在 1997 年 12 月 17 日被告派武装人员接管了曼德勒啤酒厂。法院一致判决:

(1)关于目前的请求没有裁判权;

(2)各方当事人应当承担自己的花费,并均等承担法院和秘书处的费用。当原告和被告签订协议时,缅甸还不是东盟的成员国。缅甸没有加入许多东盟的协议,包括 1987 东盟协议。因此从法律上讲,法院没有裁判权。

投资争端是存在于外国投资者和国家之间的,因此 BITs 或者多边投资协议对投资争端的解决有重要作用。现在,缅甸在 2013 年 7 月 15 日签署了纽约公约。2012 年的《涉外投资法》的第 43 条鼓励将仲裁作为争端解决机制。因此,如果外国投资者与国家产生争端且同意仲裁,那么可以选择缅甸仲裁法。

三、缅甸商事仲裁机制

商事仲裁适用于合同当事方的争端,且争端主要涉及 BOT、JV、PSC、顾问协议、建筑合同、贷款协议、供给协议和 MOA 的协议。

缅甸规制仲裁的法律主要有两个:关于缅甸国内仲裁的 1944 年仲裁法和关于外国仲裁事项的仲裁法。没有国际商事仲裁案件适用了 1944 年缅甸仲裁法的公开记录。从 1944 年至 2013 年,共有 26 件缅甸国内商事仲裁案件。

依据《仲裁法》第 30 条,仲裁员的裁决被提交给高院一审裁决。高级法院一审裁决撤销了仲裁员的裁决,因此上诉人上诉到高院。依据 1944 年《仲裁法》第 30 条,只有以下情形才能撤销裁决:

(1)仲裁员或裁判人使仲裁或自身行为不当;

(2)根据第 35 条,在法院签发废除仲裁或仲裁程序的命令后作出的裁决无效;

(3)裁决被不正确地得出或者是无效的。这个案件不能依据仲裁法第 30 条来适用第二或第三种情形。高院没有得出不正当行为被承认有效由于仲裁员对于这个案件完全没有发言机会。基于这些原因,高院撤销高院原方并承认仲裁员的裁决。

四、外国仲裁裁决在缅甸的强制执行

1939 年仲裁法适用于所有关于服从不同签约国司法权的当事方之间的商业事务的仲裁协议。然而,缅甸已经制定关于强制执行仲裁的互惠条款,并且在缅甸公报上已印有正式通知。如此,依据 1939 年法案外国仲裁不能被强制执行。

(1)外国仲裁裁决的强制执行

外国裁决可被强制执行,如果:

①它是依据法律下有效的仲裁协议作出的;

②它是协议中提供的或者当事人同意组成的仲裁庭作出的;

③符合法律规定仲裁程序的;

④在作出国视为终审的;

⑤它涉及一个在缅甸法下被合法提交仲裁的事项;

⑥它不违反缅甸法的公共政策。

如果法院解决的案件满足以下条件,强制执行可以被拒绝:

①该裁决已经被作出国废除;

②当事人反对强制执行裁决,没有注意到在充足时间内使他呈现案件的仲裁,或者当事人无法律上的行为能力;

③裁决没有解决所有相关问题或者超出仲裁协议范围。

（2）国内仲裁裁决的强制执行

当裁决被仲裁员作出,它只能通过法院的力量来生效。在缅甸,民事法院获得了使仲裁裁决像法院裁决一样执行的授权。

通常有两种方式可以通过国内裁决或者申请获得判决或法院命令的强制执行。当判决债务人的财产在缅甸以外,裁决的强制执行必然需要相关外国法院的法律援助。在 RUMFCCI 下,商法和仲裁委员会形成了,它是半官方性组织,专门解决当地成员和外国投资者之间产生的商事争端。

《缅甸公司法》中规定的仲裁条款:

（1）公司可以通过书面协议提交仲裁,与仲裁法关于现在或将来与其他公司的争端相一致;

（2）公司可能代表仲裁员的权力来解决事项或者决定任何事能被合法地解决或者公司自己决定或者主管人和管理机构;

（3）仲裁法的条款应当适用于支持此法案的公司和个人间的所有仲裁。

五、缅甸仲裁法和中国仲裁法的比较与差异

（1）适用性

缅甸仲裁法同时适用于缅甸发生的国内或国际仲裁,而中国仲裁法明确规定只有合同争端、自然人、法人和其他组织间的财产利益争端可能被仲裁。

（2）仲裁庭的组成

缅甸仲裁法没有明确要求仲裁庭仲裁员的数量。这种情形与中国不同,依据中国的仲裁法,仲裁庭必须由一或三个仲裁员组成。

（3）仲裁庭的形成

在缅甸,仲裁组织局限于临时仲裁,而中国把机构仲裁视为仲裁的主要形式。为了使仲裁成为解决争端的有效方式,包括涉外仲裁委员会的仲裁委员会已经在中国建立。

（4）法院干预

缅甸仲裁法规定大量法院参与,比如仲裁员的任命、仲裁协议的强制执行、法院对于法律问题的意见。而中国仲裁法尽力限制法院参与。在中国仲裁法中,所有可能出现的法院参与的例子都被列出来。

此外,在缅甸,法院更多的是干预仲裁庭。与其不同,中国的仲裁裁决仅会被法院撤销或驳回其强制执行的申请。

六、结论

从历史的角度看，仲裁被视为平等主体间的正义。但是，随着仲裁裁决明确规定各当事人的权利和义务，法律和规章应当规定仲裁实体和程序上的要件。此外，为了防止区分外国仲裁裁决，一些国际仲裁协定已经在全世界范围内生效。

自1987年，中国就是纽约公约的缔约国。而缅甸仅刚刚在2013年7月15日成为缔约国。毫无疑问，这值得喝彩，这是落实缅甸发生的商事争端能够被公正有效解决的正确一步。

从全球来看，公共和私人争端的解决适用于不同的诉讼程序。如果争议的当事人包含政府或国家的性质，那么国家豁免条款应当被考虑进来，同时强制执行公共争端的裁决比私人的更加复杂。因为，最好在理论和实践领域区分公共争端和私人争端。

缅甸的外国投资已经被缅甸司法系统的透明度和公正问题消极地影响了。当缅甸同意加入纽约公约，在缅甸投资的外国公司就可以运用中立的仲裁机构。更明确地说，本质上外国的主要关注点是对仲裁裁决有效性的怀疑和法院对仲裁的干涉。

根据中国的经验，特别是中国国际经济贸易仲裁委员会的成功，表明了在缅甸建立常设的仲裁机构可以增加仲裁裁决的透明度和有效性。常设的仲裁机构可以提供仲裁员名册和持续监管仲裁员，这样可以提高仲裁裁决的合理性和公正性。另一方面，减少法院干涉可以提高仲裁员的独立性和裁决的公正性。

综上所述，中国和缅甸的仲裁法，尽管存在一些不同之处，但是公正和平地解决商事争端的立法意图是一致的。在缅甸，对外国投资者而言，目前颁布的外国投资法允许争端解决与相关协议中规定的争端解决机制一致。此外，缅甸正在起草一部新的仲裁法，将在不久之后适用。通过研究，仲裁法的发展仍然有空间，同时，伴随着市场经济的发展，缅甸仲裁体系将愈发完善。

Commercial Arbitration in Myanmar and China's Experience

Zhang Xiaojun[*]
Yin Yin Han[**]
Sun Nanxiang[***]

Abstract   As the experience showed, the investment arbitration and commercial arbitration institutions in countries are definitely vital to attract the foreign trade and investment globally. During the period of economic reform in Myanmar, a number of commercial laws and regulations have been under modification. A new arbitration law in Myanmar is drafting, doubtlessly, China's experience could be valuable to some degree. There exist differences between Myanmar arbitration act and PRC arbitration law; however, the legislative intent is totally the same, namely, to boost a fair and peaceful atmosphere for international trade and foreign investment.

Keywords   Commercial Arbitration; The Arbitration Act of 1944, Myanmar; The Arbitration (Protocol and Convention) Act, Myanmar; PRC Arbitration Law; New York Convention

[*]   Zhang Xiaojun, Dr. & Prof. of Law, the Dean of International Law School in Southwest University of Political Science and Law.

[**]   Yin Yin Han, the research Director of the Union of Myanmar Supreme.

[***]   Sun Nanxiang, PHD Candidate of International Law in Southwest University of Political Science and Law.

193

1. Introduction

Myanmar is a member of the ASEAN which was a free trade area (AFTA) initiated in 1992. AFTA seeks to eliminate tariff barriers among ASEAN countries, and the key to this is the Common Effective Preferential Tariff (CEPT) Scheme, under which tariffs are gradually reduced to 0~5% by 2010 or 2015. Myanmar is also a signatory to the ASEAN Framework Agreement on Services (AFAS) which is aiming at strengthening the cooperation among service suppliers in the ASEAN region, reducing restrictions to trade in services, and progressively liberalizing trade in services among ASEAN counties. In addition, Myanmar is also a party to the Framework Agreement on the ASEAN Investment Area (AIA) which is aiming at establishing the ASEAN region as a competitive investment area by 1 January 2010, as well as facilitating a liberal and transparent investment environment and free flow of investments in the region by 2020. To get economic development, dispute settlement mechanism and arbitration are important.

After the implement of Open and Reform Policy, the market-oriented economy in China is established. From 1980s, china' economy boosts, which is mainly due to increasing of the direct foreign investment and international trade. As the development of trade and investment, China government takes active part in international economic affairs. Therefore, during the period of economic reform in Myanmar, China's experience could be valuable to some extent. Therefore in this paper, it is stated arbitration in Myanmar and comparative study with Myanmar arbitration laws and the PRC arbitration laws on international commercial arbitration.

According to *Black Law Dictionary*, arbitration means a process of dispute resolution in which a neutral third party (arbitrator) renders a decision after hearing at which both parties have an opportunity to be heard. Where arbitration is voluntary, the disputing parties select the arbitrator *who has the power to render a binding decision.* [1] It is better to be stated here, the definition of commercial arbitration in Myanmar is distinguished from that in China. In Myanmar, not only the disputes between private entities can be applied to commercial arbitration, but also the disputes between government and private entities. Therefore, to depict the commercial arbitration in Myanmar, this article would focus on both types of dispute settlement sequentially.

2. Commercial Arbitration on Investment in Myanmar

To sum up, Myanmar investment treaties are stated as follows:
- with China (ratified 2002)
- with India (ratified 2009)
- with Laos (signed 2003, not ratified)
- with Philippines (ratified 1998)
- with Thailand (signed 2008, not ratified)
- with Vietnam (signed 2000, not ratified)
- ASEAN Comprehensive Investment Agreement
- ASEAN

Myanmar Investment Commission (MIC) has granted permission for more than 100 foreign investment businesses in 2013, including beer and cigarette makers. For the period of January to December 19, MIC granted permission for 118 foreign investment businesses and joint ventures to operate in the country. Some of them include international big names such as British American Tobacco for cigarette manufacturing and distribution, Myanmar Carlsberg for beer manufacturing and distribution, APB Alliance Brewery Company and Beer Chang International Limited for beverage manufacturing and distribution. Other businesses are auto manufacturing, home appliances making, bamboo fiber production, auto servicing, consumer foods production, IT services, medicines making and decorated roof manu-

---

[1] *Black Law Dictionary.*

facturing. Several manufacturing businesses have been allowed to operate in 2013. The foreign investment in Myanmar exceeded US $ 44 billion by the end of November 2013, and China, Thailand topped the list of largest investors in the country for 2013. [①]

There is no public record of any international investment arbitration cases and international commercial arbitration cases have been conducted under the English based, Myanmar Arbitration Act 1944. There are very few international investment arbitration cases and international commercial arbitration cases conducted in Myanmar. This probably reflects the economic policy of Myanmar prior to 1988 of minimizing economic relations with foreign countries. Since 1988, Myanmar has adopted market oriented economic system and the foreign investors and domestic entrepreneurs or governments have been making investment in Myanmar. Contracted foreign investment in Myanmar amounted to 53.45 million U. S. dollars in September, 2013, bringing the total to over 44.21 billion US dollars at the end of the month since 1988. [②]

From 1988 to 2013, it is only one investment commercial arbitration case which is Myanmar Yaung Chi Oo Trading PTE Ltd. v. Government of the Union of Myanmar (ASEAN I. D Case No. ARB/01/1). In this case, On 29 November 1993, a Joint Venture Agreement was concluded between MFI and the State Industrial Organization of Myanmar, of the one part, and YCO, of the other part. The Agreement provided for the creation of a joint venture company, Myanmar Yaung Chi Oo Company Ltd. (hereafter "MYCO"), "for the purpose of joint investment under the Union of Myanmar Foreign Investment Law". MFI was to contribute machinery and other items and the use of the land comprising the Beer Factory, Mandalay. MYCO was to contribute specified amounts of capital within three(3) years, as well as expertise, marketing, provision of foreign raw materials, etc. , for the purposes of operating the brewery and promoting and distributing its

---

① Sources from Myanmar Investment Commission.

② Sources from the Central Statistical Organization.

products. Ownership shares were allocated 55% to MFI, 45% to MYCO. Unless earlier terminated for causes, the term of the agreement was five years, with provision for renewal for a further five year term with the approval of the Myanmar Foreign Investment Commission (hereafter "FIC"). The Parties were to apply to the competent authorities of the Government of the Union of Myanmar for a grant to MYCO of the right to manufacture and distribute beer and soft drinks, in Myanmar and abroad, for an initial term of five years. The issue of a permit under the Union of Myanmar Foreign Investment Law and Procedures was a condition precedent to the entry into force of the Agreement and the incorporation of the joint venture company. The joint venture agreement was subject to the law and jurisdiction of the Union of Myanmar. For disputes concerning the interpretation and application of the joint venture agreement, arbitration was available in Yangon pursuant to the Arbitration Act 1944 of Myanmar.

After the relevant permissions and approvals having been obtained, on 1 October 1994 MYCO began to operate. These were, according to the Claimant, highly successful; the output of the Mandalay Beer Factory increased greatly and MYCO made significant profits. At the time of the conclusion of the Joint Venture Agreement, Myanmar was not a member of ASEAN. In 1997, Myanmar applied for ASEAN membership and was admitted. Pursuant to the protocol of admission, on 23 July 1997 Myanmar acceded to a number of existing ASEAN treaties, including the 1987 ASEAN Agreement and the Jakarta Protocol of 12 September 1996 (the 1996 Protocol). Subsequently Myanmar has played a full part in the work of ASEAN. In particular, it became a party to the Framework Agreement for the ASEAN Investment Area of 7 October 1998 (the 1998 Framework Agreement), which came into force for all ASEAN member states on 21 June 1999.

By the latter part of 1997, a number of problems had occurred in the relationship between the parties to the Joint Venture Agreement. Briefly, the claimant alleged that on or about 17 December 1997 the respondent sent armed servants or agents to take over the Mandalay Brewery. Although control of the Mandalay Brewery was subsequently returned to the investor on or about 12 January 1998, the interim seizure by the respondent was said to have resulted in production stoppages and loss in profits. Following this alleged first armed seizure, the claimant further alleged that on or about 11 November 1998, the respondent sent around 60 armed servants or agents forcibly to take over control and management of the Mandalay Brewery. In its view, the subsequent domestic court proceedings were merely an attempt to legitimize the earlier expropriation of the claimant's interests in the joint venture. The respondent's conduct was that, the claimant alleged, in breach of substantive provisions of the 1987 Agreement, in particular Articles Ⅲ, Ⅳ and Ⅵ.

The claimant requested the tribunal to prescribe certain provisional measures. The tribunal set time limits for the claimant to submit in writing its application for provisional measures (21 January 2002), and for the respondent to reply (4 February 2002). The claimant submitted an application for provisional measures within this time limit. The respondent objected to this application, both on the grounds that the tribunal lacked jurisdiction and as to the substance of the measures sought. In particular the respondent argued that the tribunal had no jurisdiction to interfere, and in any event should refrain from interfering, in pending liquidation and other legal proceedings in myanmar. The tribunal unanimously rejected the claimant's application for provisional measures. As to the further procedure, the tribunal decided to join the issue of its jurisdiction to the merits of the dispute, and set time-limits for the parties within which to submit their respective written pleadings on the merits of the case. The tribunal unanimously decides:

(1) That it has no jurisdiction in respect of the present claim;

(2) That each party shall bear its own costs, and shall bear equally the fees, costs and expenses of the tribunal and the secretariat. ① When claimant and respondent made the contract, Myanmar was not a member of ASEAN. Myanmar didn't accede to a number of existing ASEAN treaties, including

---

① ASEAN I. D case No. 68.

the 1987 ASEAN Agreement. In the legal nature, therefore tribunal had no jurisdiction.

Investment disputes are between foreign investors and the State. Therefore, BITs or multilateral investment treaties play an important role to settle investment disputes. Now, Myanmar signed New York Convention on 15th July 2013. Section 43, subsection (b) of the *Foreign Investment Law 2012* encourages arbitration as a disputes settlement mechanism. Therefore, if there is a dispute between foreign investors and the State and they agree to arbitrate, they can choose the Myanmar arbitration law.

3. **Commercial Arbitration On Private Practice In Myanmar**

Commercial arbitration is used for disputes between parties to contracts. Various kinds of contracts are build, operate and transfer agreements (BOT), joint venture agreements (JV), production sharing contracts (PSC), consultancy agreements, construction contract, loan agreement, supply agreement and memorandum of agreement (MOA).

There are two main laws in Myanmar relating to arbitration, namely the Arbitration Act 1944, which relates to local arbitration within Myanmar and the Arbitration (Protocol and Convention) Act, which relates to foreign arbitral awards. According to the Myanmar Export/Import Rules and Regulations issued by the Ministry of Commerce, entrepreneurs having trade disputes with foreign companies can only resolve the disputes in accordance with the Arbitration Act 1944, thus requiring contracts to be under Myanmar arbitration.

There is no public record of any international commercial arbitration cases having been conducted under Myanmar Arbitration Act 1944. From 1944 to 2013, there had been 26 domestic commercial arbitration cases conducted in Myanmar. In Burma Indo-Ceylon Rice Corporation Limited (appellant) v. the State Agricultural Marketing Board (respondent) case, by an agreement dated the 29th January 1947 between the Governor of Burma and the appellant the Burma Indo-Ceylon Rice Corporation Limited, the appellant the Burma Indo-Ceylon Rice Corporation acted as agent of the governor of Burma and of the Agricultural Projects Board who were the predecessors of the respondent State Agricultural Marketing Board, for purchasing rice and rice products on the terms as set out in the said agreement. On the 25th April while the appellant was acting as the agent of the respondent for buying rice in zone two, they were held up by dacoits and the sum of two lakhs of rupees was taken away by those dacoits.

A report was promptly made to police and to the appellants' head office and to the Agricultural Project Board. Some of the dacoits were arrested, tried and convicted, among those convicted was an employee of the Tharrawaddy Treasury, who sent a message to the dacoits on the day of incident that two lakhs of rupees had been drawn from the Treasury. A dispute then arose between the appellant and the respondent over the loss of this sum of two lakhs of rupees by dacoits. The parties then referred the matter to arbitration by an agreement dated the 6th January 1951. The appellant nominated Mr. P. K. Basu as its arbitrator, and the respondent nominated Mr. K. W. Foster as its arbitrator. The only matter referred to the arbitrator was whether the loss of Rs. 200,000 should be borne by the Burma Indo-Ceylon Rice Corporation or by the State Agricultural Marketing Board. On this issue, the two arbitrators could not come to a unanimous decision and the result was that the matter was referred to an umpire as provided in the agreement for arbitration.

The arbitrators appointed U Paing, Barrister-at-Law to be the umpire. U Paing, by his award dated the 25th June 1953, decided that the loss of Rs. 2 lakhs by dacoity was not due to the negligence on the part of the appellant but that it was due to information conveyed to the dacoits by an employee of the Tharrawaddy Treasury and that loss should be borne by the State Agricultural Marketing Board.

The award of the umpire was filed on the original side of the High Court under Section 30 of the *Arbitration Act*. The original side of the High Court set aside the award made by the umpire. So appellant put this appeal case to the High Court. Under Section 30 of the *Arbitration Act*, 1944, an award cannot be set aside except on one or more of the following grounds, namely:

(1) That an arbitrator or umpire has misconducted himself or the proceedings;

(2) That an award has been made after the issue of an order by the Court superseding the arbitration or arbitration proceedings, which have become invalid under Section 35;

(3) That an award has been improperly procured or is otherwise invalid. In this case, it couldn't fall the second or third ground under Section 30 of *Arbitration Act*. The High Court didn't see any irregularity had been committed by the umpire in his conduct which amounted to no hearing of the case at all. For the reasons, the High Court set aside the original side of the High Court and confirmed the award of the umpire in its entirety with costs throughout. [1]

4. Enforcement of Arbitral Awards in Myanmar

The Arbitration (Protocol and Convention) Act 1939 formed as a domestic legal promulgation of two international instruments namely, the Protocol on Arbitration Clauses, 1928 known as the Geneva Protocol and Convention on the execution of Foreign Arbitral Awards 1927. The Arbitration (Protocol and Convention) Act 1939 provides for enforcement of foreign awards in Myanmar made either by action or in the same manner as a domestic award is formed. These treaties have had an important effect upon uniformity in the recognition and enforcement of foreign awards among their signatories. [2] They are the important sources of law Myanmar regarding international commercial arbitration.

The Arbitration (Protocol and Convention) Act 1939 applies to all arbitration agreements in relation to commercial matters between the parties subject to the jurisdiction of different signatory countries, irrespective of the

---

[1] 1958 *Burma Law Report* (H. C.) p. 68.

[2] Section 4(1) of the Arbitration (Protocol and Convention) Act.

place of arbitration.[1] However, reciprocal provisions regarding enforcement of arbitral awards have been made for each such country by Myanmar and that there has been formal notification thereof published in Myanmar's official Gazette.[2] Thus, foreign arbitral awards can't be enforced under 1939 Act.

(1)Enforcement of Foreign Arbitral Award

A foreign award may be enforceable if:

①it has been made pursuance of an agreement for arbitration which was valid under the law by which it was governed;

②it has been made by the tribunal provided for in the agreement or constituted in manner agreed upon by the parties;

③it has been made in conformity with the law governing the arbitration procedure;

④it becomes final in the country in which it was made;

⑤it has been in respect of a matter which may lawfully be referred to arbitration under the law of Myanmar; and

⑥it is not contrary to the public policy of the law of Myanmar.[3]

Enforcement can be refused if the court dealing with the case is satisfied that:

①the award has been annulled in the country in which it was made; or

②the party against whom it is south to enforce the award was not given notice of the arbitration proceedings in sufficient time to enable him to present his case or was under some legal incapacity and was not properly represent, or

③the award does not deal with all the questions referred or contains decisions or matters beyond the scope of the agreement for arbitration.

---

① Alec Christic & Suzanne Smith, *Foreign Direct Investment in Myanmar* 1997, p. 255.

② James Finch and *Saw Soe Phone Myint*, Arbitration in Myanmar, *International Arbitration Journal*, Vol. 14(4), 1997, p. 101 and Section 2 of the Arbitration(Protocol and Convention) Act 1939.

③ Section 7 of the *Arbitration(Protocol and Convention) Act* 1939.

(2) Enforcement of Domestic Arbitral Awards

When an award has been made by arbitrators/umpire, it can only be implemented through the powers of the Civil Court. In Myanmar, the Civil Court is given the power to enforce the award like a judgment decree passed by a Civil Court.

There are usually two ways in which judgments or court order of enforcement can be obtained by a domestic award or by application made by decree holder. ① Such a decree can be enforced by one or more of the parties in accordance with the Code of Civil Procedure, Order 21. If a decree is for the payment of the money, the court may, on the oral application of the decree holder at the time of the granting of the decree, order immediate execution thereof by the arrest of the judgment debtor. ②

Where the property of the judgment-debtor is located outside Myanmar, award enforcement inevitably requires judicial assistance from the relevant foreign court. The foreign court will be entrusted by Myanmar court to execute against the property of the judgment-debtor. This judicial assistance is normally based on the international agreements that Myanmar has signed. Both a Myanmar court and foreign court may mandate each other to pursue certain legal actions on each other's behalf. ③

In the case of *Agriculture and Food Product* Trading Corporation (Myanmar) vs. Ennitra Co. Ltd. (Hong Kong), the award couldn't be enforced. In Myanmar, a foreign company (Hong Kong) and *Agricultural and Food Products* Trading Corporation (Myanmar) entered into the agreements to build vessels, providing corporations to arbitration clauses under the Myanmar Arbitration Act 1944. The tribunal delivered an award in favor of the Trading Corporation. The foreign company filed an appeal at the Supreme Court but was rejected. The foreign company had no assets in Myanmar to enforce the award. The foreign company built the vessels in

---

① Section 5 (1) of the *Arbitration(Protocol and Convention) Act* 1939.

② *Code of Civil Procedure*, Order 21, Rule 11(1).

③ Dr. Tin May Tun, A Comparative Approach of the Arbitration Act in Myanmar *Journal of Office of the Attorney General*, Vol. 2, December, 2013, p. 162.

Singapore and could not confer the vessels within the time-limits of the a-greement. At that time, there was no bilateral or multilateral treaty between the government of Myanmar and Singapore or Hong Kong regarding the enforcement of arbitral awards. Myanmar's efforts to enforce the award in the foreign country failed. ①

Under the Republic of the Union of Myanmar Federation of Chamber of Commerce and Industry (RUMFCCI), Commercial Laws and Arbitration Committee were formed and it is a quasi-official organization, to solve the commercial disputes arising between the members from local and foreign investors. From 2011 to 2013, this Committee decided 27 local disputes and no foreign disputes. ② Committee is a non-governmental organization (NGO). The members of the Committee are business person elected by the federation members. The RUMFCCI is the member of Paris-based International Chamber of Commerce (ICC) and ASEAN Chamber of Commerce and Industry (ASEAN-CCI). It also maintains close cooperation with other chamber promoting bilateral trades and investment opportunities for mutual benefits in the international commercial field.

The arbitration provisions in the *Myanmar Companies Act* state:

(1) A company may by written agreement refer to arbitration, in accordance with the Arbitration Act on existing or future differences between itself and any other company or person.

(2) Companies, parties to the arbitration, may delegate to the arbitrator power to settle any term or to determine any matter capable of being lawfully settled or determined by the companies themselves, or by their directors or other managing body.

(3) The provisions of the Arbitration Act shall apply to all arbitrations between companies and persons in pursuance of this Act. ③

---

① Agricultural and Food Product Trading Corporation (Myanmar) v. Ennitra Co. Ltd(Hong Kong) 1981, Civil Regular Suit No. 118 of Yangon Division Court 1982, 1st Appellate Suit No. 29 of the Supreme Court.

② Sources from RUMFCCI.

③ *Myanmar Companies Act*, Sec 152, 153, 153-A, 153-B, p. 304, 305, 306.

5. Key Differences Between Myanmar Arbitration Act and Prc Arbitration Law

The Arbitration Law of the People's Republic of China (PRC Arbitration law), which was adopted at the 9th session of the Standing Committee of the Eighth National People's Congress on August 31, 1994, is hereby promulgated and shall come into force on September 1, 1995. As with the rapid development of Chinese economy, PRC Arbitration Law plays a vital role in settling economic disputes, particularly the private disputes with foreign investors. The key differences between the two neighboring countries would be described as follow:

(1) Applicability

Myanmar Arbitration Act is applicable to both domestic and international arbitrations seated in Myanmar, ① including the commercial arbitrations and investment arbitrations between Myanmar government and private investors. However, PRC Arbitration Law stipulates expressly that only contractual disputes and other disputes over rights and interests in property between citizens, legal persons and other organizations that are equal subjects may be arbitrated. ② At the same time, foreign-related arbitration rules may be formulated by the China Chamber of International Commerce in accordance with PRC Arbitration Law and the relevant provisions of the Civil Procedure Law in China. ③

(2) The Composition of Arbitration Tribunal

Myanmar Arbitration Act does not require exactly the quantity of arbitrators in one tribunal. ④ Therefore, it is common to have two arbitrators in tribunal if the parties disputed agree with this. If an arbitration agreement provides for the appointment of more arbitrators than

---

①   Section 46, 47 of the Myanmar *Arbitration Act* 1944.

②   Article 2 of PRC *Arbitration Law*.

③   Article 72 of PRC *Arbitration Law*.

④   Section 4, 5, 8, 9, 10 of the Myanmar *Arbitration Act* 1944.

three, the Article 10 of Myanmar Arbitration Act states that the award of the majority prevails. The situation is quite different in China; the arbitration tribunal should be composed of either three arbitrators or one arbitrator, according to PRC Arbitration Law. [1]

(3) The Formation of Arbitral Tribunal

In Myanmar, the organization of arbitration is limited to *ad hoc* arbitration. However, PRC Arbitration Law regards institutional arbitration as the key formation of arbitration. In order to function the arbitration as an efficient method to settle the disputes, the arbitration commissions, a foreign-related arbitration commission included, who are required to appoint arbitrators and offer the arbitrators' list, were established in China. [2] The parties to the disputes select the arbitration commission through the agreement. [3]

(4) Court Intervention

Myanmar Arbitration Act provides for extensive court involvements such as appointment of arbitrators, enforcement of arbitration agreements and court opinion on the questions of law. Under 1944 Arbitration Act, there are certain functions of courts in arbitration:

①Court can assist in the composition of the arbitral tribunals, [4]

②If arbitrators commit irregularity or misconduct, court can intervene appropriately, [5]

③If there has been submission to arbitration by the parties before the commencement of legal proceeding, If a party to an arbitration agreement commences legal proceeding in any court against the other party, in respect of any matter agree to refer to arbitration, the other party may apply to court to stay proceeding, at any time after appearance and before delivering

---

[1]   Article 20 of PRC *Arbitration Law*.

[2]   Article 11,12,13,14,15 of PRC *Arbitration Law*.

[3]   Article 6 of PRC *Arbitration Law*.

[4]   Section 8 of the Myanmar *Arbitration Act* 1944.

[5]   Section 30 of the Myanmar *Arbitration Act* 1944.

any pleadings or taking any other step in the proceeding, [1]

④High Court can make rules consistent with the Act. [2]

PRC Arbitration Law seeks to restrict court involvement as much as possible. According to PRC Arbitration Law, all instances of possible court involvement could be listed as below:

①The people's court can set aside an arbitration award, or disallow its enforcement in accordance with the law, [3]

②A party can apply to the people's court for a ruling, for the reason of challenging the validity of the arbitration agreement. [4]The counts have the ability to determine validity of arbitration agreement;

③ A party can submit his application to the people's court for preservation of the evidence, under circumstances where the evidence may be destroyed or lost or difficult to obtain at a later time. [5]

Furthermore, the court has more intervention on arbitral tribunals in Myanmar. When it regards to making tribunal awards, firstly, tribunal has power to seek opinion of court on the questions of law in Myanmar. In Section 13 of Myanmar *Arbitration Act*, tribunal's power to seek opinion of court on questions of law is available[6] but there is no such power in PRC Arbitration Law. And then, according to Section 15 of Myanmar Arbitration Act, court has power to correct or modify awards. [7]Differently, Chinese tribunal awards could only be either set aside or disallowed its enforcement by the courts. [8]

---

[1] Section 34, 35 of the Myanmar *Arbitration Act* 1944.

[2] Section 44 of the Myanmar *Arbitration Act* 1944.

[3] Article 58, 63 of PRC *Arbitration Law*.

[4] Article 20 of PRC *Arbitration Law*.

[5] Article 46 of PRC *Arbitration Law*.

[6] Section 41 of the Myanmar *Arbitration Act* 1944.

[7] Section 15 of the Myanmar *Arbitration Act* 1944.

[8] Article 30 of PRC *Arbitration Law*.

6. Conclusion

Historically, arbitration was regarded as justice among peers. [①] However, as arbitral awards state expressly the rights and duties of each party, essentially, laws and regulations should stipulate the substantial and procedural elements of arbitration. Furthermore, in order to prevent from discriminating against foreign arbitral awards, some international arbitration conventions, taking Convention on the Recognition and Enforcement of Foreign Arbitral Awards 1958 (the New York Convention) for instance, have been brought into force all around the world.

China is a signatory to the New York Convention since 1987, while Myanmar has just already become a signatory on 15th July 2013. Without doubts, after entering the convection above, it is therefore to be applauded and it is a step in the right direction in putting in place by which the resolution of commercial disputes arising in Myanmar can be dealt with fairly and efficiently. Definitely, China's experience in recognizing and enforcing foreign and domestic arbitration awards could be valuable to Myanmar to some extent, particularly in the respects of how to make efficient and enforceable arbitrative awards.

Globally, the settlement of public and private disputes is subjected to different proceeding. In the NAFTA case Corporation v. United States of America, the United States argued that the investment case at hand "was to be distinguished from a typical commercial arbitration on the basis that a State was the Respondent, the issues had to be decided in accordance with the treaty and the principles of public international law and a decision on the dispute could have a significant effect extending beyond the two Disputing

---

[①] Jacques Werner, The Trade Explosion and Some Likely Effects on International Arbitration, *Journal of International Arbitration*, Vol. 5, 1997, pp. 10~11.

Parties"①. Additionally, if the parties disputes involve the government or the state's property, the state immunity rules should be considered, and it is more complicated to enforce the awards of public disputes than those of private ones. Therefore, it is better to distinguish with public disputes and private ones in theoretical and practical fields, which could gain efficiency in arbitration in Myanmar in return.

Foreign investment in Myanmar has been adversely affected by concerns about the transparency and impartiality of Myanmar's judicial system. When Myanmar accedes to the New York Convention, foreign entities investing in Myanmar can use a neutral arbitration center such as Singapore or Hong Kong to resolve contractual disputes and enforce a favorable arbitration award obtained outside Myanmar against assets of the opposing party located within Myanmar. More specifically, the main concerns for foreign in essence are the doubts of accountability in arbitration tribunals and court intervention towards arbitration.

Compared with experience in China, especially the success of China International Economic and Trade Arbitration Commission, it is suggested to build the institutional arbitration in Myanmar, which can increase the transparency and accountability of arbitration tribunals, the issue of procedure in particular. The institutional arbitrative body can introduce the requirements of arbitrators and supervise the arbitrators continually, in order to enhance the reasonableness and fairness of arbitral awards. On the other hand, reducing the court intervention would enhance the independence of arbitrators and the impartiality of awards, which is required by international arbitration conventions, as well as expected by the parties to disputes.

In conclusion, after scrutiny in arbitration law between China and Myanmar, though some differences appeared, the legislative intent, of settling the commercial disputes fairly and peacefully, is the same. In Myanmar, for foreign investors, the recently promulgated Foreign

---

① Stephan Wilske, Martin Raible, Lars Markert, International Investment Treaty Arbitration and International Commercial Arbitration—Conceptual Difference or Only a "Status Thing"? 1 Contemp. Asia Arb. J. 213,2008,pp. 213~220.

Investment Law allows for settlement of disputes in accordance with the dispute settlement mechanism as stipulated in the relevant agreement [Section 43 (b) (ii)]. ① Moreover, a new Arbitration Law in Myanmar is drafting and it is processed to be used in the very near future. Room for advancement of arbitration is also made through studies and research and as the market-oriented economy develops each day, Myanmar arbitration system is following closely in its weak.

---

① Section 43(b) (ii) of the *Foreign Investment Law*.

中国—东盟自贸区法律框架下缅甸投资仲裁机构与机制研究

Khin Khin Phyu* & Win Khin Moe Sint**
李杨 译

2002 年 11 月 4 日,中国与东盟十国在柬埔寨首都金边共同签署《中国—东盟全面经济合作框架协议》,提出在 2010 年前建立自由贸易区的设想。2010 年 1 月 1 日贸易区正式全面启动。中国—东盟自由贸易区是世界上人口最多的自由贸易区,也是全球第三大自由贸易区。

中国与东盟自贸区的全面经济合作提出了中国与东盟加强和增进各缔约方之间的经济、贸易和投资合作;促进货物和服务贸易,逐步实现货物和服务贸易自由化,并创造透明、自由和便利的投资机制;为各缔约方之间更紧密的经济合作开辟新领域等全面经济合作的目标。

《中国—东盟自由贸易区投资协议》旨在通过下列途径,促进东盟与中国之间投资流动,建立自由、便利、透明和竞争的投资体制:

(a)逐步实现东盟与中国的投资体制自由化;

(b)为一缔约方的投资者在另一缔约方境内投资创造有利条件;

(c)促进一缔约方和在其境内投资的投资者之间的互利合作;

(d)鼓励和促进缔约方之间的投资流动和缔约方之间投资相关事务的合作;

(e)提高投资规则的透明度以促进缔约方之间投资流动;

(f)为中国和乐盟之间的投资提供保护。

《中国与东盟全面经济合作框架协议》的目标是:

---

* 缅甸联邦总检察长办公室的助理署长。

** 缅甸联邦最高法院参事。

(a)加强和增进各缔约方之间的经济、贸易和投资合作；

(b)促进货物和服务贸易,逐步实现货物和服务贸易自由化,并创造透明、自由和便利的投资机制；

(c)为各缔约方之间更紧密的经济合作开辟新领域,制定适当的措施；

(d)为东盟新成员国更有效地参与经济一体化提供便利,缩小各缔约方发展水平的差距。

在中国—东盟自由贸易区内,来自缔约方的投资者采用合资经营形式。当分歧和纠纷出现时,调解中心将以不损害商事关系和贸易关系的方式协助解决纠纷。

合同缔约方同意将全部或任何可能出现的与该合同有关的商业事务或其他事务提交仲裁解决。因此,缔约方之间的争端解决机制尤为重要。

众所周知,任何商业合同都有争端解决条款。该条款在纠纷产生时对于解决争端具有重要作用。本文将探讨缅甸争端解决的相关的法律。

1944年缅甸仲裁法颁布于1944年3月1日。该法是缅甸的主要仲裁程序法律,其主要原则来自于1950年英国仲裁法案,与其他普通法国家的法律相似。该法案涉及仲裁员的任命、仲裁庭免职监管、在民事法庭的强制执行、上诉等等。民事诉讼及以下相关情况可称为仲裁：

(a)不能出庭；

(b)可能没有在庭上询问证人的情况；

(c)可能不是由法院作出最后裁决的情况。

根据该法案,它有如下三个方面：

(1)没有法院介入的仲裁；

(2)有法庭干预但是没有未决诉讼的仲裁；

(3)仲裁诉讼。

以下是该法案程序的具体介绍：

1. 没有法院介入的仲裁

必须有仲裁协议才能提交仲裁。

(1)仲裁协议里的条款

第3节 仲裁协议,除非有明确规定,应该被认为包含第一计划表里的相关条款,使其得以适用。本法规第三节里暗含了仲裁协议的条件。

(2)仲裁协议的暗含条件(第一计划表)

1.除非明确规定,否则只有一名仲裁员。

2.如果有偶数位仲裁员,那么自弃任期的最晚一个月之内应再指定一名仲裁人。

3.仲裁裁决应在进入程序后的 4 个月内或者法庭所允许的合理期限内作出。

4.如果仲裁员没有在相应期限内作出裁决或者传达给缔约方仲裁协议或者以书面形式提示裁判员,那么仲裁人应立即介入,代替仲裁员。

5.仲裁人的仲裁裁决应在进入程序后的 2 个月内或者法庭所允许的合理期限内作出。

6.缔约方或者相关当事人应该遵守相关法律的规定,将相关争议提交仲裁,并呈交仲裁员或仲裁人进行仲裁所需要的相关材料。

7.仲裁裁决是最后裁决,并对当事人产生效力。

8.裁决产生的相关费用应有仲裁员或者仲裁人判定。

(3)法庭任命仲裁员或仲裁人的权利

第 8 节规定

"(1)在如下情况下

(a)仲裁协议规定当事人同意可以指定一名或多名仲裁员,那么当出现异议时,当事人不得重新指定;

(b)如果仲裁员或者仲裁人拒绝裁决,不能裁决,或者死亡,并且仲裁协议没有标明这个空缺不能弥补,那么就应该弥补;

(c)当当事方或者仲裁员没有被要求指定仲裁人或者没有任命仲裁人,那么任何一方都可以以书面提示的方式重新任命仲裁员或者弥补空缺。

(2)在该书面提示发出的 15 个工作日内,那么法院可以,在一方当事人提出申请或者告知另一方的情况下,任命仲裁员或者仲裁人。如果当事方均同意,那么新任命的仲裁员或者仲裁人拥有相同的权利作出裁决。"

(4)当事方任命新仲裁员,以及在某些特定情况下任命一名仲裁员的情况

第 9 节　仲裁协议约定,除非另有明确规定,那么应有两名仲裁员,一方当事人指明一名仲裁员。

(a)如果一名仲裁员拒绝裁决,不能裁决,或者死亡,那么指定他的当事人可以重新指定一名仲裁员。

(b)如果一方当事人没有指定新的仲裁员,在另一方当事人提出书面通知之后的 15 日内,可以指定另一方指定的仲裁员为单独的仲裁员,该仲裁员的裁决对双方当事人均有法律效力。

(5)任命三名以上仲裁员的条款

第 10 节规定:

(1)当仲裁协议规定需要 3 名以上仲裁员的时候,双方当事人各指定一名仲裁员,第三名由双方指定的仲裁员指定。如果第三名是指定的仲裁员的话,那么该协议有效。

(2)当仲裁协议规定需要指定三名仲裁员时,而不是如(1)所规定,除非仲裁协议另有规定,那么应采用大多数裁决。

(3)当仲裁协议规定需要指定三名以上仲裁员时,除非仲裁协议另有规定,应采用大多数裁决。或者,如果仲裁员的裁决出现平局,那么应以仲裁人的裁决为准。

(6)仲裁员权利

第 13 节规定,除非仲裁协议另有规定,仲裁员或者仲裁人权利如下:

(a)要求当事方或者证人宣誓;

(b)针对涉及的法律表明观点,或者全部或部分地表明裁决;

(c)作出有条件的或者具有可替代性的裁决;

(d)更正由于意外或者疏忽造成的错误裁决;

(e)回应当事方的书面质询。

(7)在特定环境下法院取消仲裁员或者仲裁人资格的权利

(1)如果仲裁员或者仲裁人不合理地遵守仲裁程序或者作出裁决,那么法院可以取消仲裁员或者仲裁人资格;

(2)仲裁员或者仲裁人有不当行为的;

(3)仲裁员或者仲裁人被取消资格后丧失获取酬劳的权利;

(4)本节中所指"程序"包括需要仲裁人的情况。

(8)仲裁员被取消资格后法院的权利

第 12 节规定:

(1)当被取消资格的仲裁人或者一名或者更多仲裁员(不包括全部)还未进入仲裁程序时,法院可以基于当事方的申请或者仲裁协议重新指定。

(2)经法院许可,仲裁员或者仲裁人资格被取消后,或者已经进入仲裁程序的仲裁员资格被取消后,法院可以基于任何一方当事人的申请以及仲裁协议:

(a)指定一名仲裁员单独行使权利;或者

(b)宣布仲裁协议效力终止。

(3)新任命的仲裁员或者仲裁人拥有与之间的仲裁员或者仲裁人相同的权利,并需根据仲裁协议作出裁决。

(9)裁决

第 14 节

（1）仲裁员或者仲裁人作出裁决后,应在仲裁裁决上签名并提示当事方签名,给付仲裁费用等;

（2）经任何一方当事人申请或者法院要求,仲裁员或者仲裁人应将相关材料提交给法院,法院应提醒当事方将裁决归档;

（3）当仲裁员或者仲裁人据 13 节（b）款提出特殊情况,法院在提醒当事方或者听取其意见之后,应据此发表建议,该建议应该成为裁决的一部分。

（10）法院修改裁决的权利

第 16 节　法院在以下情况下可以修改或者更正裁决:

（1）仲裁裁决涉及未提交仲裁的事项,该事项部分的裁决可以与其他事项分开并且不影响剩余部分的效力;

（2）裁决形式上有瑕疵,或者在不影响裁决效力的情况下包含一些可以被更改的明显错误;

（3）裁决错误是由于书记员错误或者疏忽造成的。

（11）撤销裁决的权利

①在如下情况时,法院可以随时撤销裁决或者要求仲裁员或者仲裁人重新审查:

（a）提交仲裁的事项未被裁决或者对未提交仲裁的事项作出裁决并且该事项不能在不影响仲裁效力的情况下被单独分开;

（b）仲裁裁决模糊不清导致无法执行;

（c）仲裁裁决显失合法性。

②当根据第（1）款撤销裁决时,法院应该给予合理期让仲裁员或者仲裁人提交意见。法院可以根据情况延长该期限。

③根据第（1）款被撤销的裁决不具有法律效力。

（12）仲裁裁决的宣判

第 17 节　当没有合理事项足以让法院宣布撤销裁决或者重新审议时,那么法院应该宣布该裁决,并且该裁决具有终局效力,不得上诉,除非超出裁决权限。

2.在没有诉讼的情况下法院介入的仲裁

（1）申请提交法院仲裁协议

①在争议事项进入诉讼程序之前,或者其他不同情况出现时,当事方之间可以达成仲裁协议,将争议事项提交法院仲裁;

②该申请应该是以书面形式存在并被编号、注册,是当事方之间的诉讼,

相关当事方为原被告；

③这样的申请一旦作出，法院应该告知剩下的所有当事方，要求他们在指定时间内提出相反意见；

④当相关当事人不足以证明相反意见，法院应该安排相关议程，让当事方指定仲裁员；

⑤在此之后的仲裁程序应该按照本法令严格执行。

3. 仲裁诉讼

(11)诉讼当事人可申请参考仲裁

第21节　当诉讼双方一致认为争议事项可以提交仲裁时，他们可以在法院作出裁决前书面申请法院仲裁。

第22节　仲裁员应该由当事人双方指定。

第23节

①法院应告知仲裁员需要解决的事项，并给予合理期限让其作出裁决。

②当争议事项被提交仲裁之后，法院不得超越本法案规定的权限，用诉讼方式解决该争议事项。

9.3.2　提交仲裁的部分当事人

第24节　当仅有部分当事人选择按照第21节的方式将争议事项提交仲裁时，法院在认为合适的情况下，可以将其转为仲裁(在该事项可以与其他事项分开的情况下)，但是剩下的事项仍然继续诉讼。作出的仲裁裁决仅仅对选择参与仲裁的当事方具有约束力。

(3)适用于本章的仲裁条款

第25节 本法案的其他条文，只要具有适用性，都适用于本章规定。

假设在8、9、11、12节提及的任何情况下，法院可以弥补空缺或者指定仲裁员，作出替代仲裁的决定，开始诉讼程序，或者根据第19节作出替代仲裁的决定，法院应该继续诉讼。

第19节规定在裁决无效的情况下法院可以宣布代替诉讼，仲裁协议效力终止。

正如之前所提及，当事方可以选择在诉讼开始前或者开始后仲裁。如果同意提交仲裁，仲裁员就有全部权利仲裁并且仲裁裁决对当事方均产生约束力。但是法院可以根据第30节宣布仲裁裁决作废。

(4)宣布裁决作废的情况

第30节仲裁裁决只有在以下情况下可以宣布作废：

(1)仲裁员或者仲裁人有不当行为或者程序不公；

（2）在法院替代仲裁程序之后作出的裁决,后者根据第 35 节在仲裁程序已经无效的情况下作出的裁决;

（3）通过不正当方式获得的仲裁裁决以及其他使得仲裁裁决无效的情况。

（5）1927 年缅甸与日内瓦公约

1944 年仲裁法的第一计划表规定了仲裁协议的暗含条件。这个计划表是仲裁协议的必备条件。除了 1944 年仲裁法,还有 1939 年仲裁公约,它源自于 1937 年印度法案(六)。该法案使得仲裁条款的公约(1923 年维也纳协定)在国内生效。同样的,执行外国仲裁裁决的公约在该法案的第二计划表里生效。1923 年维也纳议定书与该公约一起,统称为 1927 年维也纳公约。

（6）缅甸 2012 年《外商投资法》

提及争端解决,缅甸 2012 年外商投资法第 43 节规定:

因投资争端产生的任何争议,

①应当以友善的方式解决;

②如若不能根据上述方式解决,那么应该:

（a）如果没有在相关协议里规定争端解决机制,遵守、按照缅甸的现有法律解决;

（b）按照相关协议里规定的争端解决机制解决。

联合国国际贸易委员会规则现在同样适用于外商投资合同。国会批准加入纽约公约以及联合国国际贸易委员会仲裁规则。2013 年 4 月 16 日,外事部履行了加入纽约公约的义务,该公约生效于 2013 年 7 月 15 日。因此,在外商投资以及商事合同领域,缅甸执行上述公约。

联合国国际贸易委员会规则

联合国国际贸易委员会是由联合国创建,致力于通过制定统一惯例以及程序,创制标准法律文本与规则来协调及统一国际贸易法。联合国国际贸易委员会仲裁规则涵盖了仲裁程序里的所有程序来解决国际贸易争端。联合国国际贸易委员会仲裁规则的主要规定如下:

（a）合同里仲裁条款的范本;

（b）任命仲裁员的程序;

（c）仲裁程序;

（d）仲裁裁决的文本形式、生效以及执行。

联合国国际贸易委员会仲裁规则还被用于规范一系列程序:

（a）没有仲裁机构的相关商事当事人之间的争端;

（b）国家与外商投资者之间的投资争端仲裁;

（c）国与国之间的争端。

纽约公约以及缅甸实践

外商投资法规定争端应该按照相关协议里规定的争端解决方式解决。然而,由于缅甸并不是纽约公约的缔约方,外商投资者或者商事主体的惯常利益很难得到保障。例如,国外仲裁裁决具有终局效力,并应得到国内的承认与执行很难实现。

因此,基于外商投资法,纽约公约不应该仅仅适用于外商投资,而可以扩展适用至所有商事主体。

缅甸是 1927 年日内瓦公约的缔约方,该法仍然对缔约国之案件具有效力。唯有国家之间签订纽约公约之后,该法才被纽约公约取代。

值得注意的是,1944 年缅甸仲裁法紧急规定了国内仲裁而没有规定对国外仲裁的承认与执行。因此,该法正在不断修订中。显而易见的,它可以为投资者创造一个更好的投资环境,完善缅甸仲裁机制,从而使其与国际化水平保持一致。

总而言之,签订纽约公约,实施联合国国际贸易委员会仲裁规则,颁布2012 年外商投资法,2012 年外币监管法,2013 年中央银行法,致力于起草新的仲裁法案,是在中国—东盟自贸区的法律框架内缅甸探索仲裁机制完善的有利尝试。

中国与东盟同意升级中国—东盟自贸区,解决领土争端。中国与东盟国家均将考虑相关情况,加强协商与合作,增强多方谅解与信任,以友好协商的方式解决争端,为区域发展与繁荣创造一个和平和稳定的环境。

Investment Arbitration Institution and Mechanism in Myanmar under the Legal Framework of China-ASEAN Free Trade Area

Khin Khin Phyu[*] & Win Khin Moe Sint[**]

Presentation by Ms. Khin Khin Phyu, Assistant Director of the Union Attorney General's Office of Myanmar and Ms. Win Khin Moe Sint, Staff Officer, Supreme Court of the Union.

China-ASEAN Free Trade Area is a free trade area among the ten member states of the Association of Southeast Asian Nations (ASEAN) and People's Republic of China. The framework agreement was signed on 4 November 2002 in Phnom Penh, Cambodia, with the intent on establishing a free trade area among the eleven nations by 2010. The free trade area came into effect on 1 January 2010. The CAFTA is the largest free trade area in terms of population and third largest terms of nominal.

China-ASEAN Free Trade Area on comprehensive economic cooperation between China and ASEAN proposed between the parties to strengthen and enhance the economic, trade and investment cooperation ; promote trade in goods and services, gradually realize the goods and liberalization of trade in services investment mechanism, and create a transparent, free and convenient environment, to open up new area of comprehensive economic cooperation as the closer economic cooperation between all the parties of the

---

[*] Assistant Director of Attorneg General Office, Myanmar.

[**] Counsellor of Supreme Court, Myanmar.

219

target.

The objectives of agreement on investment of the *Framework Agreement on Comprehensive Economic Cooperation* between the Association of the Southeast ASEAN Nations and the People's Republic of China are to promote investment flows and to create a liberal, facilitative, transparent and competitive investment regime in ASEAN and China through the following:

(a) Progressively liberalizing the investment regimes of ASEAN and China;

(b) Creating favorable conditions for the investment by the investors of a party in the territory of party;

(c) Promoting the cooperation between a party and the investor who has investment in the territory of that party on mutually beneficial basis;

(d) Encouraging and promoting the flows of investment among the parties and cooperation among the parties on investment-related matters;

(e) Improving the transparency of investment rules conducive to increased investment flows among the parties; and

(f) Providing for the protection of investment in ASEAN and China.

And also the objectives of the *Framework Agreement on Comprehensive Economic Cooperation* between the Association of Southeast Asian Nations and the People's Republic of China are

(a) strengthening and enhancing economic, trade and investment cooperation between the parties;

(b) progressively liberalizing and promoting trade in goods and services as well as create a transparent, liberal and facilitative investment regime;

(c) exploring new areas and developing appropriate measures for closer economic cooperation between the parties; and

(d) facilitate the more effective economic integration of the newer ASEAN member states and bridging the development gap among the parties.

Investors from the CAFTA countries make joint venture parties in CAFTA region. Where differences in opinion and disputes arise, the mediation center will help resolve disputes without damaging business relationships and trade ties.

The contracting parties to a contract agree to submit to arbitration all or any difference that may arise in connection with such contract relating to commercial matters or to any other matter capable of settlement by arbitration. So settlement of dispute between contracting parties is very important.

As corporate lawyers know, all commercial contracts have a settlement of dispute clause. The clause serves the contracts as a modus vivendi which is mode of settlement when disputes arise. In this paper, I shall present the laws that concern the modus vivendi of dispute resolution in Myanmar.

The Myanmar Arbitration Act, 1944 was promulgated on 1st March, 1944 as Myanmar Act IV, 1944 which is applied domestically. It is the main procedural. law for arbitration in Myanmar. This law is based on the principles that are found in the English Arbitration Act of 1950. Though it is promulgated in 1944, we find the principles the same as the English Act. The Arbitration Act, 1944 is designed as an Act similar to those in other common law countries. The appointment of arbitrators, the supervision by the court for their removal, the award, the enforcement of award in the civil court, appeal from an award are all mentioned in this Act. Civil suits and relevant cases may be referred to arbitration, which need the following grounds:

(a) The case may not be before the court;

(b) The case may be no examination of witnesses after the court;

(c) The case may be no final decision by the court.

It has three proceedings according to the Arbitration Act:

(i) Arbitration without intervention of a court;

(ii) Arbitration with intervention of a court where there is no suit pending;

(iii) Arbitration in suit.

Now I would like to mention the proceeding of this Act.

1. Arbitration without Intervention of a Court.

If the arbitration proceeding is referred into arbitration it needs to enter into an arbitration agreement.

(1) Provision Implied in Arbitration Agreement

Section 3. An arbitration agreement, unless a different intention is expressed therein, shall be deemed to include the provisions set out in the First Schedule in so far as they are applicable to the reference. The conditions of the agreement are implied at the First Schedule of this act according to the Section 3.

(2)Implied Conditions of Arbitration Agreement(The First Schedule)

1. Unless otherwise expressly provided, the reference shall be a sole arbitrator.

2. If the reference is to an even number of arbitrators, the arbitrators shall appoint an umpire not later than one month from the latest date of their respective appointment.

3. The arbitrators shall make their award within four months after entering into the reference or after having been called upon to act by notice in writing from any party to the arbitration agreement or within such extended time as the court may allow.

4. If the arbitrators have allowed their time to expire without making an award or have delivered to any party to the arbitration agreement or to the umpire a notice in writing stating that they cannot agree, the umpire shall forthwith enter into the reference in lieu of the arbitrators.

5. The umpire shall make his award within two months of entering into the reference or within such extended time as the court may allow.

6. The parties to the reference and all persons claiming under them shall, subject to the provisions of any law for the time being in force, submit to be examined by the arbitrators or umpire on oath or affirmation in relation to the matters in difference, and shall, subject as aforesaid, produce before the arbitrators or umpire all books, deeds, papers, accounts, writings and documents within their possession or power respectively, which may be required or called for, and do all other things which during the proceedings on the reference, the arbitrators or umpire may require.

7. The award shall be final and binding on the parties and persons claiming under them respectively.

8. The costs of the reference and award shall be in the discretion of the arbitrators or umpire, who may direct to, and by, whom, and in what

manner, such costs or any part thereof shall be paid, and may tax or settle the amount of costs to be so paid or any part thereof and may award costs to be paid as between legal practitioner and client.

(3)Power of Court to appoint Arbitrators or Umpire

Section 8 provides that:

(1) In any of the following cases—

(a) Where an arbitration agreement provides that the reference shall be to one or more arbitrators to be appointed by consent of the parties, and all the parties do not, after differences have arisen, concur in the appointments; or

(b) If any appointed arbitrator or umpire neglects or refuses to act, or is incapable of acting, or dies, and the arbitration agreement does not show that it was intended that the vacancy should not be supplied, and the parties or the arbitrators, as the case maybe, do not supply the vacancy; or

(c) Where the parties or the arbitrators are required to appoint an umpire and not appoint him, any party may serve the other parties or the arbitrators, as the case may be, with a written notice to concur in the appointment or appointments or in supplying the vacancy.

(2) If the appointment is not made within fifteen clear days after the services of the said notice, the court may, on the application of the party who gave the notice and after giving the other parties an opportunity of being heard, appoint an arbitrator or arbitrators or umpire, as the case may be, who shall have like power to act in the reference and make an award as if he or they had been appointed by the consent of all parties.

(4)Power to Party to Appoint New Arbitrators or, in Certain Cases, a Sole Arbitrator

Section 9. Where an arbitration agreement provides that a reference shall be to two arbitrators, one to be appointed by each party, then, unless, a different intention is expressed in the agreement,—

(a) If either of the appointed arbitrators neglects or refuse to act, or is incapable of acting, or dies, the party who appointed him may appoint a new arbitrator in his place;

(b) If one party fails to appoint an arbitrator, either originally or by way of substitution as aforesaid, for fifteen clear days after the service by the other party of a notice in writing to make the appointment, such other party having appointed his arbitrator before giving the notice, the party who has appointed an arbitrator may appoint that arbitrator to act as sole arbitrator in the reference, and his award shall be binding on both parties as if he had been appointed by consent; Provided that the Court may set aside any appointment as sole arbitrator made under clause (b) and either, on sufficient cause being shown, allow further time to the defaulting party to appoint an arbitrator or pass such other order as it thinks fit.

Explanation

The fact an arbitrator or umpire, after a request by either party enter on and proceed with the reference, does not within one month comply with the request may constitute a neglect or refusal to act within the meaning of Section 8 and this section.

(5)Provisions as to Appointment of Three or More Arbitrators

Section 10 provides that:

(1) Where an arbitrator agreement provides that a reference shall be to three arbitrators, one to be appointed by each party and the third by the two appointed by each party and third by the two appointed arbitrators, the agreement shall have effect as if it provided for the appointment of an umpire, and not for the appointment of a third arbitrator, by the two arbitrators appointed by the parties.

(2) Where an arbitration agreement provides that a reference shall be to three arbitrators to be appointed otherwise than as mentioned in sub-section (1), the award of the majority shall, unless the, arbitration agreement otherwise provides, prevails.

(3) Where an arbitration agreement provides for the appointment of more arbitrators than three, the award of majority, or if the arbitrators are equally divided in their opinions, the award of the umpire shall, unless the arbitration agreement otherwise provides, prevails.

(6)Power of Arbitrator

Section 13 provides that the arbitrators or umpire shall, unless, a different intention is expressed in the agreement, have power to:

(a) Administer oath to the parties and witnesses appearing;

(b) State a special case for the opinion of the court on any question of law involved, or state the award, wholly or in part, in the form of a special case of such questions for the opinion of the court;

(c) Make the award conditional or in the alternative;

(d) Correct in an award that any clerical mistake or error arising from any accident slip or omission;

(e) Administer to any party to the arbitration such interrogatories as may, in the opinion of the arbitrators or umpire, be necessary.

(7) Power to Court to Remove Arbitrators or Umpire in Certain Circumstances

Section 11 provides that:

(1) The court may, the application of any party to a reference, remove an arbitrator or umpire who fails to use all reasonable dispatch in entering on and proceeding with the reference and making an award;

(2) The court may remove an arbitrator or umpire who has misconducted himself or the proceedings;

(3) Where an arbitrator or umpire is removed under this section, he shall not be entitled to receive any remuneration in respect of his services;

(4) For the purpose of this section the expression "proceeding with the reference" includes, in a case where reference to the umpire becomes necessary, giving notice of that fact to the parties and to the umpire.

(8) Power of Court Where Arbitrator is Removed or His Authority Revoked

Section 12 provides that:

(1) Where the court removes an umpire who has not entered on the reference or one or more arbitrators (not all the arbitrators), the court may, on the application of any party, to the arbitration agreement, appoint persons to fill the vacancies.

(2) Where the authority of an arbitrator or arbitrators or umpire is revoked by leave of the court, or where the court removes an umpire who has entered on the reference or a sole arbitrator or all the arbitrators, the Court may, on the application of any party to the arbitration agreement, ei-

ther:

(a) Appoint a person to act as sole arbitrator in the place of the person or persons displaced; or

(b) Order that the arbitration agreement shall cease to have effect with respect to the difference referred.

(3) A person appointed under this section as an arbitrator or umpire shall have the like power to act in the reference and to make an award as if he had been appointed in accordance with the arbitration agreement.

(9)Making Award

Award to be signed and filed.

Section 14.

(1) When the arbitrators or umpire have made their award, they shall sign it and shall give notice in writing to the parties of the making and signing thereof and of the amount of fees and charges payable in respect of the arbitration and award;

(2) The arbitrator or umpire shall, at the request of any party to the arbitration agreement or any person claiming under such party or if so directed by the court, and upon payment of the fees and charges due in respect of the arbitration and award and of the costs and charges of filing the award, cases the award or a signed copy of it, together with any deposition and document which may have been taken and proved before them, to be filed in court, and the court shall thereupon give notice to the parties of the filing of the award;

(3) Where the arbitrators or umpire state a special case under clause (b) of Section 13, the court, after giving notice to the parties and hearing them, shall pronounce its opinion thereon and such shall be added to, shall form part of the award.

(10)Power of Court to Modify Award

Section 15.

The Court by order modify or correct an award:

(a) Where it appears that a part of the award is upon a matter not referred to arbitration and such part can be separated from the other part and does not affect the decision on the matter referred; or

(b) Where the award is imperfect in form, or contains any obvious error which can be amended without affecting such decision; or

(c) Where the award contains a clerical mistake or an error arising from an accidental slip or omission.

(11)Power to Remit Award

Section 16.

(1) The court may from time to time remit the award or any matter referred to arbitration to the arbitrators or umpire for reconsideration upon such terms as it thinks fit:

(a) Where the award has left undetermined any of the matters referred to arbitration, or where it determines any matter not referred to arbitration and such matter cannot be separated without affecting the determination of the matters referred; or

(b) Where the award is so indefinite as to be incapable of execution; or

(c) Where an objection to the legality of the award is apparent upon the face of it.

(2) Where an award is remitted under sub-section (1) the Court shall fix time within which the arbitrators or umpire shall submit their decision to court; Provided that any time so fixed may be extended by subsequent order of the court.

(3) An award remitted under sub-section (1) shall become void on the failure of the arbitration or umpire to reconsider it and submit their decision within the time fixed.

(12)Judgment in Terms of Award

Section 17.

Where the court sees no cause to remit the award or any of the matters referred to arbitration for reconsideration or to set aside the award, the court shall, after the time for making an application to set aside the award has expired, or such application having been made, after refusing it, proceed to pronounce judgment according to the award, and upon the judgment so pronounced a decree shall follow, and no appeal shall lie from such decree except on the ground that it is in excess of, or not otherwise in accordance with the award.

2. Arbitration with Intervention of a Court Where There Is No

Suit Pending

(1)Application to File in Court Arbitration Agreement

Section 20

(a) Where any person has entered into an arbitration agreement before the institution of any suit with respect to the subject matter of the agreement or any part of it, and where a difference has arisen to which the agreement applies, they or any of them, instead of proceeding under Chapter Ⅱ, may apply to a Court having jurisdiction in the matter to which the agreement relates that the agreement be filed in court;

(b) The application shall be in writing and shall be numbered and registered as a suit between one or more of the parties interested or claiming to be interested as plaintiff or plaintiffs and the remainder as defendant or defendants, if the application has been presented by all the parties, or if otherwise, between the applicant as plaintiff and the other parties as defendants;

(c) On such application being made the court shall direct notice thereof to be given to all parties to the agreement other than the applicants, requiring them to show cause within the time specified in the notice why the agreement should not be filed;

(d) Where no sufficient cause is shown, the court shall order the arrangement to be filed, and shall make an order of reference to the arbitrator appointed by the parties, whether in the agreement or otherwise, or, where the parties cannot agree upon an arbitrator, to an arbitrator appointed by the Court;

(e) Thereafter the arbitration shall proceed in accordance with, and shall be governed by, the other provisions of this Act so far as they can be made applicable.

3. Arbitration in Suits

(1)Parties to Suit May Apply for Order of Reference

Section 21. Where in any suit all the parties interested agree that any matter in difference between them in the suit shall be referred to arbitration, they may at any time before judgment is pronounced apply in writing to the court for an order of reference.

Section 22. The arbitrator shall be appointed in such manner as may be agreed upon between the parties.

Section 23.

(a) The court shall, by order, refer to the arbitrator the matter in difference which he is required to determine, and shall in order specify such time as it thinks reasonable for the making of the awards;

(b) Where a matter is referred to arbitration, the court shall not, save in the manner and to the extent provided in this Act, deal with such matter in the suit.

(2)Reference to Arbitration by Some of the Parties

Section 24. Where only some of the parties to a suit apply to have the matters in difference between them referred to arbitration in accordance with, and in the manner provided by, Section 21, the court may, if it thinks fit, so refer such matters to arbitration (provided that the same can be separated from the rest of the subject matter of the suit) in the manner provided in the section, but the suit shall continue so far as it relates to the parties who have not joined in the said application and to matter not contained in the reference as if no such application had been made, and an award made in pursuance of such a reference shall be binding only on the parties who have joined in the application.

(3)Provisions Applicable to Arbitrations under this Chapter

Section 25. The other provisions of this Act shall, so far as they can be made applicable, apply to arbitrations under this Chapter.

Provided that the court may, in any of the circumstances mentioned in Sections 8, 9, 11 and 12, instead of filing up the vacancies or making the appointments, make an order superseding the arbitration and proceed with the suit, and where the court makes an order superseding the arbitration under Section 19,it shall proceed with the suit.

Section 19 provides that where an award has become void under subsection e (3) of the Section 16 or has been set aside, the court may by order supersede the reference and shall thereupon order that the arbitration agreement shall cease to have effect with respect to the difference referred.

Above the mentioned, the parties may refer their disputes to the arbitration either before the suit or after the suit. If they agree to refer to arbitration, the arbitrators have full power and their decisions bind on both parties in the case. But the court may set aside the decision of arbitration in accordance with the Section 30.

(4)Grounds for Setting Aside Award

Section 30. An award shall not be set aside except on one or more of the following grounds, namely:

(a) That an arbitrator or umpire has misconducted himself or the proceedings;

(b) That an award has been made after the issue of an order by the court superseding the arbitration or after arbitration proceedings have become invalid under Section 35;

(c) That an award has been improperly procured or is otherwise invalid.

(5)Myanmar and Geneva Convention 1927

In the First Schedule of the Arbitration Act, 1944, there are implied conditions of arbitration agreement. This Schedule is deemed to be part of the agreement between parties for arbitration. At this moment, the Arbitration Act 1944 is under review. Besides the Arbitrations Act of 1944, we also have the Arbitration (Protocol & Convention) Act of 1939. Its origin is the India Act Ⅵ of 1937. This Act gives the domestic legal effect to the Protocol on arbitration clauses (The Geneva Protocol of 1923). In the same way, the Convention on the Execution of Foreign Arbitral Awards has been given the legal effect in the Second Schedule of this Act. The Protocol, as we all know is called the Geneva Protocol, 1923 and the Convention is known as Geneva Convention of 1927.

(6)Foreign Investment Law 2012 of Myanmar

As regards dispute settlements, Section 43 of the *Foreign Investment Law* 2012 provides as follows:

If any dispute arises in respect of the investment business.

(a) Dispute arisen between persons of dispute shall be settled amicably.

(b) If such dispute cannot be settled under sub-section (a):

(i) It shall be complied and carried out in accord with the existing laws of the Union if the dispute settlement mechanism is not stipulated in the relevant agreement;

(ii) It shall be complied and carried out in accord with the dispute settlement mechanism if it is stipulated in the relevant agreement.

It is to be noted that the UNCITRAL Rules (United Nations Commission on International Trade Arbitration Rules) are now used for contracts with foreign investors. The Parliament (we call Pyidaungsu Hluttaw) approved to accede the New York Convention and UNCITRAL Rules of Arbitration. On 16th April 2013, the Ministry of Foreign Affairs deposited the instrument of accession for the New York Convention and this Convention came into force on 15th July 2013. As such, Myanmar is now practicing the UNCITRAL Arbitration Rules and the New York Convention in the area of commercial contracts including foreign parties.

United Nations Commission on International Trade Arbitration Rules (UNCITRAL Rules).

UNCITRAL or the United Nations Commission on International Trade Law was established by the United Nations to harmonize and unify laws around the world related to international business and trade. It does this in part by promoting uniform practices and procedures and by creating model laws and rules, such as the UNCITRAL Rules. The UNCITRAL Arbitration Rules are set of procedural rules covering all aspects of the arbitration process, which parties may agree to in part or in whole in order to help resolve the international disputes. The UNCITRAL Arbitration Rules provides, among other things:

(i) A model arbitration clause for contracts;

(ii) Procedure for the appointment of arbitrators;

(iii) Procedures for the conduct of arbitration proceedings; and

(iv) Requirements about the form, effect and interpretation of an arbitration award.

And then the UNCITRAL Arbitration Rules have been used to govern a broad range of procedures, including:

Dispute between private commercial parties where no arbitral institution is involved (*ad hoc* arbitration);

231

Dispute between states and foreign investors (investment arbitration);

Dispute between two countries (State-to-State) dispute.

The UNCITRAL Rules provide users from around the world with a procedural framework for arbitration proceeding that is not necessarily tied to a specific arbitral institution and that may provide greater flexibility.

New York Convention and Myanmar

The Foreign Investment Law provides that disputes will be settled in accordance with the dispute resolution mechanism stipulated in the relevant agreement. However, for as long as Myanmar is not a party to the New York Convention, a foreign investor or commercial party is not guaranteed the usual benefits of (foreign) arbitration i. e. that a foreign arbitral award is final and binding and will be recognized and enforced by the enforcement state save in very limited grounds.

In this respect, the New York Convention would also expand the benefits of arbitration to all commercial parties and not simply foreign investors as contemplated under the Foreign Investment Law.

Myanmar is a state party to the Geneva Convention on the Execution of Foreign Arbitral Awards 1927 (Geneva Convention 1927). This precursor to the New York Convention is still in force between two state parties and is not superseded by the New York Convention until such time both state parties have signed up to the New York Convention (see Article VII, clause 2 of the New York Convention). However, any foreign arbitral award that has been recognized and enforced in Myanmar under the Geneva Convention 1927.

It is to be noted that Myanmar's Arbitration Act 1944 only provides for domestic arbitration and does not provide a framework for the recognition and enforcement of foreign arbitral awards. So that the Arbitration Act, 1944 endeavored to be revised. It is apparent that it will create a better environment for investors and reform the Myanmar arbitration infrastructure to keep up with the international standards obtaining confidence from investors.

In conclusion, entering into the New York Convention, practicing the UNCITRAL Arbitration Rules, enacting the new Foreign Investment Law

2012, the Foreign Currency Supervision Law 2012, the Central Bank Law 2013 and endeavoring to draft the new Arbitration Act are mechanism in Myanmar under the legal framework of China-ASEAN Free Trade Area.

China-ASEAN agreed to upgrade the China-ASEAN Free Trade Area and solve territorial dispute. Between People's Republic of China and ASEAN countries is necessary to take the general situation into consideration, strengthening consultation and coordination, enhancing mutual understanding and trust, properly handling the dispute through friendly consultation, as well as creating a peaceful and stable environment for regional development and prosperity.

作为替代性争端解决方式的仲裁——以印度尼西亚为视角

Marcellino Gonzales S.[*]
Makmur Mukhtar Supu[**]
凌波　译

一、仲裁概述

(一)定义

英文"Arbitration"一词源自拉丁文的"the arbitrare"或荷兰语的"arbitrage"，其意思是依据自由裁量来解决某项事情的权力，其所指的是以自由裁量为基础，争议各方通过将争端提交其选择或任命的仲裁员或相关人士，并遵循仲裁裁决的方式来解决争端。仲裁员所作出的裁决，通常也适用法官在审判过程中所创立的判例法。

依据布莱克法律大词典对"仲裁"的定义，仲裁是指依靠争端各方共同认可的一个或一个以上的第三方作出有约束力的裁决来解决争端的方法。或者说，在一些争端事项中，争端各方约定遵循其所选出的人士所作出的裁决来解决纠纷的一种安排，其不同于通过司法途径解决纠纷，能避免繁杂的程式，不当的迟延，昂贵的费用以及司法程序其他的一些烦扰。

同时，依据印度尼西亚(以下简称"印尼")法学家 Sudargo Gautama 的说法，仲裁是通过比普通程序更好的方式来解决争端的方法。此外，依据1999年颁布的印尼第30号法律第一条第1款，仲裁是争端各方依据书面仲裁协议，在国家司法机关以外解决民事争端的一种方式。

---

[*]　印度尼西亚，东努沙登加拉 Lembata 岛区法院，法官。
[**]　印度尼西亚，苏拉威西望加锡区地方法院，法官。

此外,在该法的第一条第 8 款关于仲裁和替代性争端解决方式的规定,有如下表述:仲裁机构是由争议各方选择的,对特定争端作出裁决的机构。该机构也可对在该争端中未提起的特定法律关系提供约束性意见。

在仲裁中,争端各方同意通过将争议提交中立的第三方裁决。争端各方选择其各自的仲裁员,授权其对所涉纠纷作出裁决。该裁决是终局性的、有约束力的,同时也是一个有胜负之分的解决方法。

仲裁协议基本上可以分为两类,也即:

(1)争端各方在纠纷发生前达成的书面协议中包含的仲裁条款;或

(2)在纠纷发生后有争端各方达成的独立的仲裁协议。

在印尼《仲裁法》颁布之前,有关仲裁的法律,在印尼《民事诉讼程序法》的第 615 条至第 651 条有相关规定。此外,在印尼 2009 年颁布的第 40 号法律第 58 条关于"司法权力"的规定中,也提及允许当事人通过协议的方式,采用法庭之外的方法解决争端。印尼前高级法院法官 Yahya Harahap. SH. 博士指出,在 1999 年第 30 号法律颁布之前,仲裁这种争议解决方式就已在印尼得到法律认可。HIR 法的第 377 条为当事人依其意愿将争端通过司法程序以外的方式解决提供了可能性和合法性。

参考所有关于仲裁的定义,它们有很多相似之处,如:

(1)仲裁是争端各方同意将纠纷交由经授权的第三人裁决的协议,是非司法程序纠纷解决方式;

(2)该协议应是有关私人权利的,特别是贸易、商业以及金融等事项;

(3)仲裁裁决应该是终局的和有约束力的。

(一)印尼的仲裁体系

1.印尼的有关仲裁的法律规定

在印尼,有如下法律规范对通过仲裁解决国内或国际纠纷作出了相关规定:

1981 年第 34 号总统法令(批准 1958 年《纽约公约》)

该法令旨在批准《纽约公约》在印尼的适用,将《纽约公约》纳入国内法体系。

1968 年第 5 号法律(批准《关于解决国家和其他国家国民投资争端公约》)

该法律旨在批准《关于解决国家和其他国家国民投资争端公约》在印尼的适用。

印尼高级法院 1990 年第 1 号规则(承认和执行外国仲裁裁决)

该规则旨在实施上述 1981 年第 34 号总统法令,使外国仲裁裁决能在印尼得到承认和执行。

1999 年第 30 号法律(仲裁和替代性纠纷解决方式)

该法律旨在适应印尼国内尤其是在商业团体中日益增长的希望通过司法程序以外的替代性方式解决纠纷的趋势。该仲裁法于 1999 年 8 月 12 日颁布,在此之前,有关仲裁程序的规定依据 Rv.法的第 615 条至第 651 条。该法并没有参照联合国国际贸易法委员会颁布的示范法,也没对国内和国际仲裁作出区分。

2.印尼对仲裁范围的规定

1999 年第 30 号法律对仲裁范围的规定涉及各类民事案件。商业、劳动以及当事方能控制的有关私人权利的所有纠纷皆可通过仲裁解决。包括与公共利益无关的私人权利,如离婚、收养、继承等。此外,该法也规定了除仲裁外的其他替代性争端解决方式,如协商、调解、斡旋以及依据程序规则和 BANI 规则提供意见等当事各方协商一致的方式。

3.印尼的仲裁机构

印尼的仲裁机构并没有在立法中明确规定,而是由政府承认的社会机构设立,印尼现有的仲裁机构有:

(1)BANI(印尼国家仲裁委员会)

印尼国家仲裁委员会(BANI)是一个能提供与仲裁、调解、约束性意见和其他争端解决方式相关的一系列服务的仲裁机构。BANI 是在三名知名律师,已故的 Soebekti 博士、Haryono Tjitroebono 先生和 Priyatna Abdurrasyid 博士的倡议下,于 1977 年设立,成立之初得到了印尼商业和产业部的支持。其总部位于雅加达,在印尼的一些主要城市都设有办事处,如泗水、万隆、坤甸、登巴萨、棉兰、巴邻旁和巴淡岛。

为了实现其作为一个仲裁机构完整的中立性和独立性,BANI 制定了其自身的仲裁规则和程序,包括仲裁机构作出裁决的时间范围。这些规则适用于在印尼进行的国内和国际仲裁。当前,BANI 拥有超过一百位具有不同专业背景的仲裁员,其中 30% 是外籍仲裁员。

在印尼,上述有关仲裁和替代性纠纷解决机制的 1990 年第 30 号法律的颁布,进一步促进了人们对通过仲裁来解决纠纷的兴趣。这也是和在经济全球化的背景下,商业实体希望通过司法程序以外的方法来解决纠纷的选择相一致的。除了迅速、高效等优点外,仲裁还能依据双赢的原则来解决纠纷,同时无上诉和撤销判决等繁杂程序。此外,仲裁的优点还在于其裁决是终局性的和有约束力的,同时由于仲裁程序和裁决结果都不公开,它还兼具保密性的优点。基于互惠原则,涉及外国企业的外国仲裁裁决能在印尼得到执行,印尼作出的涉外仲裁也同样能在其他国家得到执行。

BANI 通过对贸易、产业和金融的各个部门发生的纠纷开展仲裁或应用其他替代性争端解决方式参与印尼的法律实施进程,所涉及的部门有诸如公司、保险、金融机构、航空、通信、煤矿、海运和空运、制造业、知识产权、许可、特许权、建筑、海事纠纷、环境纠纷、遥感等其他任何法律法规和国际实践允许的事项。

①BANI 通过仲裁或其他替代性解决方式(如依据 BANI 程序规则或当事人选择的其他规则进行的协商、调解、斡旋和提供约束性意见)提供服务;

②在履行法律和维护公正上,BANI 实行自我管理,独立运作;

③为印尼对有关仲裁和其他替代性争端解决方式的研究和教学计划提供支持。

印尼国家仲裁委员会(BANI)是印尼政府设立的,旨在为与贸易、产业和金融的各个部门有关的纠纷提供仲裁或其他替代性争端解决方式,这些部门可能涉及诸如公司、保险、金融机构、航空、通信、煤矿、海运和空运、制造业、知识产权、许可、特许权、建筑、海事纠纷、环境纠纷、遥感等其他任何法律法规和国际习惯允许的事项。该机构在履行法律和维护公正上实行自我管理,独立运作。地区法院无权审理当事人约定提交仲裁的纠纷。

仲裁是一种当事人善意排除地方法院的管辖,通过替代性解决方式解决民事纠纷或协调不同意见的方法。

为了与其他国家和地区在商业领域的仲裁开展合作,促进本国国际仲裁和其他替代性争端解决方式的水平提高,BANI 与下述仲裁机构签订了合作协议:

①日本商事仲裁协会(JCAA);

②荷兰仲裁协会(NAI);

③大韩商事仲裁院(KCAB);

④澳洲国际商事仲裁协会(ACICA);

⑤菲律宾纠纷解决中心(PDRCI);

⑥中国香港国际商事仲裁中心(HKIAC);

⑦国际商事仲裁和替代性纠纷解决方式基金会(SICA-FICA)。

(2)BAPMI(印度尼西亚货币市场仲裁委员会)

BAPMI 由行业自律组织共同创办,如雅加达证券交易所、泗水证券交易所、印尼结算和担保公司、印尼中央证券登记处以及资本市场上的其他组织,旨在为与资本市场有关的纠纷提供司法程序以外的争端解决途径。

BAPMI 解决与资本市场有关的纠纷。其设立目的是为印尼资本市场主体提供一个不同于法庭的争端解决模式,以便他们能够更快,更容易,花费更少地解决资本市场纠纷,并且该纠纷解决方式还是终局性的和有约束力的。BAPMI 能为印尼本国或国际的资本市场参与者提供服务,无论他们的交易是发生在印尼还是印尼以外的地方。最重要的是当事方之间有将他们的纠纷提交 BAPMI 解决的协议。

在 BAPMI 框架下,争端各方可以选择以下三种途径解决他们的纠纷:

①约束性意见

约束性意见是在争端各方要求下,由 BAPMI 提供,旨在为当事方的有模糊的协议条款提供确定的解释。因为如果对一个协议条款有不同的解释,将会导致新的纠纷。

BAPMI 的约束性意见会在审议开始后最迟 30 个工作日内作出,该意见是书面的,且由 BAPMI 主席签署。审议通过邮件进行,而非通过召开会议。

依争端各方请求作出的 BAPMI 约束性意见是终局性的和有约束力的,因此争端各方都不能抵制和否认。约束性意见在作出后的 30 天内生效。

②调解

BAPAMI 调解是当事各方在一个中立的第三方帮助下,通过协商解决争端。这位独立调解方被称为会议推动者,其作用是使争端各方明白争端的前景,他们所处的位置以及对方的利益所在,并帮助他们寻求完满的解决办法。调解的目的是通过平和的方式解决纠纷。

调解通常在一个由 BAPMI 指定的或由争端各方共同决定的地点闭门进行,整个过程通常持续 14 个工作日。

③仲裁

BAPMI 仲裁是争端各方授权中立的第三方(也即仲裁员)来审理争议事项并作出裁决的争端解决方式。仲裁员作出的任何决定对争端各方而言都是终局性的和有约束力的。

仲裁审理时间最长会持续到独任仲裁员或仲裁庭选出以后的第 180 天。仲裁员可以在申请方和被申请方的同意下延长审理时间。

(3)伊斯兰国家仲裁机构(BASYARNAS)

BASYARNAS(由 SK MUI No. Kep-09/MUI/XII/2003 于 2003 年 12 月

24 日创立)是一个致力于依据伊斯兰法律体系解决贸易纠纷的仲裁机构。BASYARNAS 此前被称为印尼伊斯兰教仲裁机构(BAMUI).

二、仲裁机构:BANI

BANI 作为印尼的一个仲裁机构,其制定了自身的仲裁程序规则(BANI 规则)。然而,争端各方可以选择临时仲裁或机构仲裁,并遵循他们共同选择的仲裁规则。争端各方也可以协议变更 BANI 规则的某些规定,只要这种变更不违反法律的强制性规定或 BANI 的政策。

(一)对仲裁员和仲裁裁决的监管

依据 BANI 规则第 11 条,如果仲裁员在事实上或法律上未尽职责,BANI 主席有权启动质询或更换仲裁员的程序。依据 BANI 规则第 11 条和印尼仲裁法第 22 和 23 条,争端任何一方有权在对仲裁员的公正性和独立性有合理怀疑的情况下,要求质询或更换仲裁员。

印尼仲裁法为撤销仲裁(无论国内或是国际仲裁)裁决提供一个机制,只要所涉裁决:

有违公序良俗;

在仲裁过程中采纳了错误的文件或有重要文件被一方当事人隐藏;

一方当事人提供了错误的证据。

(二)设立仲裁庭

依据 BANI 规则第 6 条第 1 款,开启仲裁程序,需要申请人注册并提交仲裁申请书。在申请仲裁时,申请人可以任命一位仲裁员或交由 BANI 主席任命。BANI 在收到申请人的仲裁申请书后,会将申请人的陈述及时发送给被申请人,然而这一过程并无时间限制。依据 BANI 规则第 8 条第 3 款,被申请人收到仲裁申请书后的 30 天内,应向 BANI 作出回复。在回复中,被申请人可以任命一名仲裁员或交由 BANI 主席任命。如果被申请人没有任命其仲裁员,BANI 主席可以任命仲裁员。

若存在法定原因,这个时间可以延长。依据第 8 条第 4 款,此类延长最大限度是 14 天。依据第 8 条第 3 款,如果在被通知或要求后的 14 天内,争端任何一方未能提名或任命仲裁员,BANI 主席有权代表该方任命一位仲裁员。

总之,仲裁庭能在申请人提交申请书后的 44 天内设立。

（三）一方当事人拒绝参加仲裁程序

依据印尼仲裁法第13条，如果没有关于仲裁员提名任命的协议，地区法院主席必须依自由裁量权任命一名仲裁员。

争端任何一方违反共同选择的仲裁规则或阻碍仲裁顺利开展时，仲裁庭有权对其施予制裁。

若仲裁申请方在首席仲裁员召集争端各方的14天内未参与仲裁程序，该申请将被撤销。

若仲裁被申请方在首席仲裁员召集争端各方后未参与仲裁程序，仲裁庭有权在被申请方缺席的情况下继续仲裁程序。除非申请人的主张缺乏合理依据，否则仲裁裁决将会支持申请人的主张。

依据仲裁法第3条，地区法院无权管辖当事人约定通过仲裁解决的纠纷。依据仲裁法第11条，已签订仲裁协议的当事人也无权再通过地区法院解决纠纷。

（四）仲裁的临时措施

依据印尼仲裁法，当地法院无权采取临时措施阻止仲裁裁决的作出。依据 BANI 仲裁规则，在仲裁过程中，仲裁庭为了仲裁的顺利开展，有权采取其认为适当的临时措施，如费用担保、货物保存、易腐坏物品的出售等。

（五）对指定的仲裁员提出异议的权利

1. 印尼仲裁法

印尼仲裁法规定了当有证据表明仲裁员缺乏独立性时，争端各方皆可对指定的仲裁员提出异议。争端任何一方若发现仲裁员存在以下情形，皆可对该指定的仲裁员提出异议：

与一方当事人存在亲属、金钱或工作上的联系；

年龄在35岁以下；

在仲裁裁决上存在利益关系；

在其行业的从业经验不足15年。

2. BANI 规则

依据 BANI 规则第11条，争端当事方若对仲裁员的公正性和独立性存在合理怀疑，其有权对该指定的仲裁员提出异议。若争端当事一方要提出异议，其需要在得知仲裁员身份后的14天内向 BANI 提出书面申请，并附上载有异议依据的相关文件。

或者,若申请异议的当事方在仲裁员被任命后,得知异议的相关证据,其需在 14 天内递交申请。若异议申请未被仲裁员或另一方当事人接受,那么 BANI 的仲裁庭对异议申请作出审查,若仲裁庭认定异议有效,则通过与此前同样的方式重新任命一名仲裁员;若仲裁庭认定异议无效,则允许被异议的仲裁员继续履行其职责。

依据 BANI 规则第 12 条第 2 款,若仲裁员与争端各方有利益冲突,那么他们有义务辞任;否则,在没有被异议的情况下,任何仲裁员不得辞任。

如果独任仲裁员被替换了,那么此前的程序无效,仲裁程序将重新开始。如果仲裁庭由三位仲裁员组成,首席仲裁员被替换,若仲裁庭其他成员认为有必要,举证程序要重新开始。然而,若仲裁庭中的非首席仲裁员被替换,替换程序可以简化,并且不需要重复此前的程序,除非有极端情况发生。

(六)在印尼执行仲裁裁决

依据 1981 年第 34 号总统法令,理论上,外国仲裁裁决在印尼是可以被执行的。但这个法令并未为仲裁的执行规定相应的程序,只是承认了 1958 年《纽约公约》在印尼的效力。因此,那时许多外国仲裁裁决并未能在印尼得到执行。

然而,自高级法院 1990 年第 1 号规则颁布以后,外国仲裁裁决便可在印尼得到执行。依据该规则第 3 条,外国仲裁裁决要想在印尼得到执行,需要满足以下条件:

该仲裁裁决是在一个与印尼签订双边协议的国家作出的。印尼加入了关于承认和执行外国仲裁裁决的国际公约。印尼基于互惠承认和执行的外国仲裁裁决需要符合印尼法律的相关规定,并属于贸易法的管辖范围;

仲裁裁决没有违反公共秩序;

雅加达地区法院院长签署了执行令(授权行为)。印尼仲裁法第 66 条复述了此要求。此外,若印尼是一项国际仲裁的争端一方,该项仲裁裁决只有在得到印尼高级法院签署的执行命令后才能得到执行。(其后委托给雅加达地区法院)依据 1990 年第 1 号法律第 5 条第 4 款,需要递交给雅加达地区法院的文件包括:

经认证的仲裁裁决原件;

仲裁裁决的翻译原件;

经认证的仲裁协议;

仲裁协议的翻译原件;

仲裁裁决作出国的外交代表出具的,证明该国和印尼有双边关系的文件。同时,该国也是关于承认和执行外国仲裁裁决国际公约的签署国。

(七)仲裁费用

仲裁费用由独任仲裁员或仲裁庭决定。依据印尼仲裁法第76条,仲裁费用包含:

仲裁员的聘用费用;

仲裁员的出行费用和其他杂费;

证人或专家证人的费用;

行政费用。

实践中,仲裁费用包含仲裁员的酬金和其他花费,包括交通费和住宿费;开庭费用,如会议室的租用费和起草文件的费用;法律顾问、证人、专家证人的酬金,交通费和运输费;仲裁机构和秘书的费用,包括注册和行政费用。依据一般规则,费用将由败诉方承担。然而,如果申诉方只是赢得一部分裁决,那么仲裁费用将由当事双方平均负担。

三、印度尼西亚仲裁

(一)当今印尼仲裁法

1999年第30号有关仲裁和替代性纠纷解决方式的法律对承认和执行外国仲裁裁决作了相关规定。该法第六章第65至69条规定了上述事项。这些有关承认和执行外国仲裁裁决的法律条文基本上与1958年纽约公约的规定相一致。

1999年第30号法律第65条规定了负责承认和执行外国仲裁的机构是雅加达地区法院。

此外,该法第66条规定了以下事项:一项外国仲裁裁决能在印尼的领土范围内得到承认和执行,只要其满足以下条件:

该项仲裁裁决是由与印尼在有关承认和执行外国仲裁裁决的方面签订双边或多边协议的国家的仲裁员或仲裁庭作出的;

该项仲裁裁决的内容在贸易法的范围之内;

该项仲裁裁决不违反公共秩序;

该项仲裁裁决得到了雅加达地区法院院长的执行令；

以印尼为争端一方的国际仲裁裁决需要得到印尼高级法院的执行令，并随后委托雅加达地区法院。

此外，第 67 条规定了外国仲裁裁决在该裁决通过仲裁员或其代理人提交雅加达地区法院后，对承认和执行该项裁决的申请生效。

尽管相比于在对承认和执行外国仲裁缺乏相关规定的时期（1999 年第 30 号法律颁布前），印尼在 1999 年第 30 号法律对承认和执行外国仲裁裁决作出了较为明确规定，印尼依然在这方面饱受国际社会的诟病。

国际社会认为印尼依然是一个"仲裁不友好国家"，外国仲裁裁决在印尼很难得到执行。基于这样的预期，在 Karahabodas 一案中，赢得仲裁一方寻求在拥有 Pertamina（印尼国有仲裁公司）财产的其他国家申请执行仲裁裁决也就不难理解了。

国际社会最常提及的是印尼法院往往以一项裁决违反公共政策或公共秩序为由拒绝承认和执行外国仲裁裁决。众所周知，尽管公共政策也是由规则、法律以及一国国家利益组成的，但在印尼，要做得准确适用这些标准却非易事，国际社会把这种情况看作是印尼法律的不确定性。

有趣的是，1999 年第 30 号法律只规定了公共政策作为拒绝承认和执行外国仲裁裁决的理由，然而《纽约公约》第 5 条却规定了一系列其他可以作为拒绝承认和执行外国仲裁裁决的理由，这些理由大多与仲裁程序的正当性相关。尽管上述 1999 年第 30 号法律并未对这些理由作出规定，但印尼法院也应遵循上述规定，因为印尼是《纽约公约》的缔约国。

一项外国仲裁裁决在印尼被批准执行后，依然面临着很多问题，可能基于各种原因出现抵制仲裁裁决执行的情况。1999 年第 30 号法律第 1 条第 9 点明确规定了，外国仲裁是由在印尼管辖权范围以外的仲裁机构或仲裁员作出的或由仲裁机构依印尼法律作出的，会被认为是外国仲裁的裁决。

在印尼管辖权范围内作出的仲裁裁决不是外国裁决。

1958 年《纽约公约》适用于因自然人或法人间之争议而产生且在申请承认及执行地所在国以外之国家领土内作出的仲裁裁决。

《纽约公约》同样适用于对于仲裁裁决经申请承认及执行地所在国认为非国内裁决的仲裁裁决。

1999 年第 30 号法律只规范了外国仲裁裁决在印尼的承认与执行，并未对外国仲裁程序作出规范。简单地说，在印尼领土内作出的仲裁裁决是国内仲裁。印尼的国内仲裁的执行程序与外国仲裁程序在印尼的执行有很多不同之处以及时间段。

《联合国国际贸易法委员会国际商事仲裁示范法》第 1 条很清楚地规定了何为国际仲裁。也即如果:

(1)仲裁协议的各方当事人在缔结协议时,其营业地点位于不同国家;或

(2)下列地点之一位于各方当事人营业地点所在国以外:仲裁协议中确定的或根据仲裁协议而确定的仲裁地点;履行商事关系的大部分义务的任何地点或与争议事项关系最密切的地点;或各方当事人明确同意,仲裁协议的标的与一个以上的国家有关。

换言之,由印尼仲裁机构[印尼国家仲裁委员会(BANI)]所作出的包含外国因素的裁决,也应被认定为外国仲裁裁决。(1999 年第 30 号法律第 59 条,第 4 条,第 5 条)。从《纽约公约》的角度来看,此类裁决应该被认定为外国仲裁裁决,因此能在属于《纽约公约》的其他缔约国得到承认和执行。

此外,实践中可能会遇到这样一个问题,也即外国仲裁机构,如 ICC 在印尼作出仲裁裁决,此类仲裁能否被认为是印尼的国内仲裁。

上述问题之所以出现是因为印尼不像其他国家(包括新加坡),印尼的有关外国仲裁的规定并没有参照《联合国国际贸易法委员会国际商事仲裁示范法》。印尼仲裁立法中还有其特点,这反映在其他条款中,如为了公正和彰显对上帝的信仰,在审判和裁决中必须包含有 Irah-Irah。这在其他国家看来是很难理解的。

为了符合仲裁这一争端解决方式在国际上公认的特征,并使得印尼的立法与其他有助于解决国际争端的国家的法律规定保持和谐关系,印尼有关仲裁的立法,尤其是 1990 年第 30 号法律,需要对其进行修订,使得其条款和国际社会的通行做法相一致,包括《联合国国际贸易法委员会国际商事仲裁示范法》。

此外,印尼地区法院的法官和相关利益方也应该充分了解仲裁的含义和本质,这种司法程序以外的争端解决方式具有实用性、非对抗性、高效性和有效性。

四、总结

综上所述,印尼的仲裁法需要完善,同时也应从整体上参考借鉴《联合国国际贸易法委员会国际商事仲裁示范法》,以期能颁布与相关国际公约相协调的新仲裁法,并删除,例如为了公正和彰显对上帝的信仰,在审判和裁

决中必须包含有的 Irah-Irah 等内容。这样就能使得印尼的仲裁裁决遵循国际规则。

　　印尼地区法院的法官需要了解仲裁的含义和本质，这种司法程序以外的争端解决方式具有实用性、非对抗性、高效性和有效性。

Arbitration as an Alternative Dispute Resolution in Indonesia

Marcellino Gonzales S. *
Makmur Mukhtar Supu **

1. Brief View of Arbitration

(1)Definition

Arbitration is derived from *the arbitrare* (Latin) or *arbitrage* (Netherland), which means the power to get things done according to discretion, it means that dispute resolution by an arbitrator or a person on the basis of discretion and the parties will submit to or obey the verdict given by arbitrators that they select or appoint. Decisions of the arbitrators usually continue to apply the law as made by the judge in court. [1]

According to the Black's Law Dictionary, it also gives the definition about Arbitration as a method of dispute resolution involving one or more neutral third parties who are usually agreed to by the disputing parties and whose decision is binding, or Arbitration is an arrangement for taking an abiding by the judgement of selected persons in some disputed matter, instead of carrying it to establish tribunals of justice, and is intended to

* Judge, District Court of Lembata Island, East Nusa Tenggara, Indonesia
** Judge, District Court of Makassar, South Sulawesi, Indonesia

[1] Gunawan Widjaja and Ahmad Yani, *Arbitration Law Business Law Series*, Jakarta: PT. Raja Grafindo Persada, 2000, p. 3.

avoid the formalities, the delay, the expense and vexation of ordinary litigation.

Also according to Sudargo Gautama, the Law Scientist in Indonesia said that Arbitration is a method of dispute resolution considered much better than another dispute through ordinary channels. ①While according to Article 1 (1) of Law No. 30 Year 1999, Arbitration is the way settlement of civil disputes outside the public court based on the abitrate agreement made in writing by the parties. ②

Furthermore, in Article 1 point (8) of Law Number 30 Year 1999 on Arbitration and Alternative Dispute Resolution, stated: " Arbitration Institute is a body chosen by the disputing parties to make a decision on the particular dispute, the agency can also provide opinion binding on a particular legal relationship in dispute has not been raised. "

Arbitration (arbitration) in which the parties agreed to settle the dispute to a neutral party. In arbitration, the parties choose their own party who act as judge and arbiter of law applicable. ③Essentially a private judge so as to have the competence to make decisions on a dispute, the decision is final and binding, as well as an win-loss solution.

Basically arbitration can be either in two (2) forms, namely:

a. Arbitration clause contained in a written agreement made by the parties before the dispute arises (*factum de compromitendo*); or

b. A separate arbitration agreement made by the parties after the dispute arises (*Deed of compromise*).

Before the Arbitration Act applies, the provisions regarding arbitration

---

① Sudargo Gautama, *Arbitrase Dagang International*, Bandung: Alumni, 1979, p. 1.

② Also see the Article 59 paragraph (1) of the *Constitution Act* No. 48 of 2009, arbitration is a way of settling a civil dispute out of court based on the arbitration agreement made in writing by the parties to the dispute, the type of law the court stated, in contrast to Act No. 30 of 1999, it kind of general court.

③ Khotibul Umam, *Penyelesaian Sengketa Di Luar Pengadilan*, Yogyakarta: Pustaka Yustisia, 2010, p. 12.

set in Article 615 to Article 651 Reglement Civil Procedure (Rv). In addition, Article 58 of Law No. 48 Year 2009 on Judicial Power mentions that the out of court settlement through procedures agreed upon by the parties to be allowed. Former Supreme Court Justice Prof. Yahya Harahap, S. H. , asserted that the existence of the arbitration before the Law No. 30 Year1999, the starting point of Article 377 or Article 705 R. Bg/HIR, the provisions of Article 377 HIR have provided the possibility and permissibility for the parties dispute to bring and resolve cases arising outside the lines court if they so desire. Settlement and the decision can be they fully submit to the arbitrator who is commonly known by the name ar-bitrate.

Refer to all the definitions about Abitration, there were a lot of similarities, such as:

a. Aggrement between the parties to solve the cases by using the persons or a few persons outside the parties, and give them right to make a settlement dispute outside the court;

b. The agreement should be the private rights, especially trading, industry, and finance issues;

c. The award of arbitration should be the final and binding decisions.

2. Arbitration in Indonesia

1)Arbitration Regulation in Indonesia

There are several regulations can be used to resolve the national or international problems through arbitration, that are related to the enactment of the law of arbitration in Indonesia, namely:

• Presidential Decree No. 34/1981 (Ratification *New York Convention* 1958)

This rule was made with the aim of regulating the application of *New York Convention* itself, in order to be implemented into national legislation.

• Law No. 5/1968 (Approval for *Convention on the Settlement of Investment Disputes between States and Nationals of other States*)

This rule was made with the aim of regulating the application of *Convention on the Settlement of Investment Disputes between States and*

Nationals of other States itself, in order to be implemented into Indonesia.

　• Supreme Court Rules No. 1/1990 (recognition and implementation foreign arbitral decision)

This regulation is made for the purpose of implementing regulations of Presidential Decree No. 34/1981, so the arbitration awards from outside the country could be implemented in Indonesia.

　• Law No. 30/1999 (arbitration and alternative dispute resolution)

The Law was made to fulfill the Indonesian needs about carrying out the provisions of the arbitration, which is increasingly popular in the business community especially to look for alternative dispute resolution, outside the court. The Arbitration Law was enacted on 12 August 1999. Previously, arbitration proceedings in Indonesia were based on Article. 615—651 Rv. The law does not follow the UNCITRAL model law, nor does it distinguish between domestic and international arbitrations, except for the purpose of enforcement.

　2) The Scope of Arbitration in Indonesia

The scope of arbitration in Law 30/1999 which covers all types of civil cases. cases can be completed in arbitration disputes in the fields of business, labor, throughout the dispute concerning personal rights that can be fully controlled by the parties. As for the personal rights that are rights which are not related to the enforcement of public interest, such as divorce, adoption, inheritance, etc. It also provides services for the implementation of dispute resolution through arbitration or other forms of alternative dispute resolution, such as negotiation, mediation, binding conciliation and giving opinion in accordance with the rules of procedure or rules BANI other procedures agreed upon by the parties hereto.

　3) The Arbitration Bodies in Indonesia

Arbitration bodies in Indonesia are not specifically regulated in the legislation, but established by the institutions of society recognized by the government, and the current arbitration bodies in Indonesia today are:

1. BANI (the Indonesian National Board of Arbitration):[①]

Indonesian National Board of Arbitration (BANI) is an arbitral institution, providing a range of services in relation to arbitration, mediation, binding opinion and other forms of dispute resolution. BANI was established in 1977 on initiative of three prominent lawyers, namely the late Prof. Soebekti and Mr. Haryono Tjitrosoebono and Prof Dr. Priyatna Abdurrasyid. With initial support of Indonesia Chamber of Commerce and Industry. The Center is located in Jakarta with offices in some Indonesia major cities including Surabaya, Bandung, Pontianak, Denpasar, Medan, Palembang and Batam.

Committed to complete neutrality and independence in its role as an arbitral institution, BANI has developed its own rules and procedures for arbitrations, including the time frame in which arbitral tribunal has to render award. Such rule is used in both domestic and international arbitration taking place in Indonesia. Presently, BANI has more than 100 arbitrators with various professional backgrounds, about thirty percent are foreign nationals.

In Indonesia, interest to settle dispute through arbitration began to grow with the promulgation of Law number 30 Year1999 on arbitration and alternative dispute resolution (Arbitration Law). The growing interest has been consistent with the globalization in which the out of court settlement has become the choice of business entities to resolve their disputes. Besides its speedy, efficient and final characteristics, arbitration uses the principle of win-win solution and directs as no appeals and cassation. Other benefits of arbitration award are that the award final and binding, besides has confidentiality characteristics, in which the proceeding and the award are not published. Based on reciprocal principle, the foreign award that involves foreign company may be executed in Indonesia; also the Indonesian arbitration award involving foreign company may be executed in overseas.

a. To participate in the law enforcement process in Indonesia through

---

① www. bani-arb. org/21st November 2013.

the application of arbitration and alternative dispute resolution for resolving disputes in the various sectors of trade, industry and finance, such as concerning corporate matters, insurance, financial institution matters, aviation, telecommunication, mining, sea and air transportation, manufacturing, intellectual property rights, licensing, franchise, construction, shipping/maritime issues, environmental issues, remote sensing and others within the scope as set forth by laws and regulations and international practices.

b. To provide services for the dispute settlement through arbitration or other forms of alternative dispute resolution, such as negotiation, mediation, conciliation and binding opinion in accordance with the Rules of Procedures of BANI or other rules as opted by the parties concerned.

c. To act autonomously and independently in regard of upholding law and justice.

d. To carry out studies and research and trading/education programs pertaining to arbitration and alternative dispute resolution.

Indonesian National Board of Arbitration or BANI is a body set up by the Indonesian government to law enforcement in Indonesia in the settlement of disputes or differences of opinion that occur in various sectors of trade, industry and finance, arbitration and other forms of alternative dispute resolution, among others in other areas corporate, insurance, financial institutions, manufacturing, intellectual property rights, licensing, franchising, construction, shipping / maritime, environmental, remote sensing, and others within the scope of the regulations and international customs. The agency is acting autonomously and independently in law enforcement and justice. district court has no authority to adjudicate the parties' dispute that has been bound in the arbitration agreement.

Dispute resolution through arbitration is a way to resolve civil disputes or differences of opinion between the parties through alternative dispute resolution that is based on good faith to the exclusion of settlement of litigation in the district court.

In order to develop an international arbitration and other forms of alternative dispute resolution in commercial field among entrepreneurs in the countries concerned, the BANI has entered into cooperation agreements with various institutions in these countries, among others, by:[1]

a. The Japan Commercial Arbitration Association (JCAA);

b. The Netherlands Arbitration Institute (NAI);

c. The Korean Commercial Arbitration Board (KCAB);

d. Australian Center for International Commercial Arbitration (ACICA);

e. The Dispute Resolution Center Philippines Inc. (PDRCI);

f. China Hong Kong International Arbitration Center(HKIAC);

g. The Foundation for International Commercial Arbitration and Alternative Dispute Resolution (SICA-FICA)

2. BAPMI (the Indonesian Capital Market Arbitration Board)[2]

Established by the Self Regulatory Organizations (SROs) the Jakarta Stock Exchange (JSX), the Surabaya Stock Exchange (SSX), PT Indonesian Clearing and Guarantee Corporation (KPEI), and PT Indonesian Central Securities Depository (KSEI) as well as associations in the Indonesian capital market environment to be a civil dispute resolution in the areas of capital markets through outside court resolution mechanisms.

BAPMI handles disputes relating to the capital market sector. The main objective of establishing BAPMI is to provide an alternative dispute resolution forum from the courts for all capital market players in Indonesia. The intention is to allow them to settle their capital market disputes through a faster, easier, less expensive mechanism, with final and binding settlement. BAPMI is available to both domestic and foreign capital market participants, whether their transactions take place in Indonesia or abroad. The most important factor is for there to be mutual agreement between the parties that their dispute will be settled through BAPMI.

In the BAPMI, the disputing parties may choose 3 alternative means of dispute resolution, namely through:

---

① *Ibid.*

② www. bapmi. org/en/index. php; 20th November 2013.

a. Binding opinion

"Opinions binding" BAPMI is the opinion given by BAPMI at the request of the parties regarding the interpretation of a vague provision in the agreement between the parties that did not happen again differences of interpretation that can open any further dispute.

BAPMI binding will give an opinion in writing and signed by the chairman BAPMI at the latest within 30 working days after the commencement of the examination, which is sent by registered mail, rather than in a meeting forum.

Binding opinion given by BAPMI is final and binding to the parties who requested it and, therefore, may not be filed resistance or denial. Binding opinion must be exercised within 30 days from the issuance, and any action contrary to a binding treaty violation.

b. Mediation

BAPMI mediation is a way of solving problems through negotiations between the parties to the dispute with the help of a neutral third party and independent mediator is called the meeting facilitator helping each side understand the perspectives, positions and interests of other parties in relation to the problems faced and together to find solutions. The purpose of mediation is to achieve peace between the problematic parties.

The mediation process will last for 14 working days in a meeting (hearing) held at the place specified by BAPMI or other place agreed upon by the parties and is closed to the public.

c. Arbitration

BAPMI arbitration is the settlement of disputes by way of handing authority to a neutral third party and independent-called the arbitrator to examine and adjudicate at the first and last. Any decision by the arbitrator shall be final and binding upon the parties and can not be appealed.

Examination of the arbitration process will be the longest 180 days since the sole arbitrator / arbitral tribunal is formed. Arbitrator may extend the time period with the consent of the applicant and the respondent.

d. The Shariah National Arbitration Body (BASYARNAS)

BASYARNAS (established by SK MUI No. Kep-09/MUI/XII/2003, 24

December 2003) is an arbitration body dedicated to resolving disputes on transactions which apply an economic Shariah law structure. BASYARNAS was formerly known as the Indonesian Muamalat Arbitration Body (BAM-UI).

2. BANI AS Arbitration Institution

BANI as arbitration institution in Indonesia has published its rules of arbitral procedure (the BANI rules). However, parties may choose *ad hoc* or institutional arbitration, subject to such rules as they may agree. It is also open to the parties to agree modifications in writing to the BANI rules, provided that any such modifications do not contradict mandatory provisions of law or the policies of BANI.

(1)Supervision Arbitrators and Their Awards

The chairman of BANI has the authority to commence proceedings to challenge and replace an arbitrator, if an arbitrator fails to perform his duties, on a *de jure* or *de facto* basis (the BANI rules, Article 11). Both Article 11 of the BANI rules and Articles 22 and 23 of the Indonesian Arbitration Law allow any of the parties to challenge and replace any of the arbitrators if there are justifiable doubts as to the arbitrator's impartiality or independence.

The Indonesian Arbitration Law also provides a mechanism by which an arbitration award may be annulled (both for domestic arbitration awards and foreign arbitration awards) on the basis that:
- It contravenes decency and public order;
- False documents have been used as evidence in the arbitration or an important document has been concealed by a party to the arbitration;
- A party has given false evidence.

(2)A Tribunal Set Up

Under the BANI rules, an arbitration commences with the registration and filing of the petition for arbitration by the party initiating recourse to arbitration (Article 6. 1). In the petition for arbitration, the claimant may nominate an arbitrator or leave the appointment to the BANI chairman. Upon receiving the claim from the claimant, BANI delivers the statement of claim to the respondent as soon as possible. However, there is no time limit for delivering the claim to the respondent.

Within a period of not longer than 30 days after receiving the petition for arbitration, the respondent must submit its reply. In the reply, the respondent may nominate an arbitrator or leave the appointment to the BANI chairman (Article 8. 3). If, in the reply, the respondent does not nominate its arbitrator, then the BANI chairman may appoint the arbitrator.

An extension of this period may be granted if there are legitimate reasons. The maximum period of any such extension is 14 days (Article 8. 4). If either party fails to nominate or appoint an arbitrator within the relevant time limits, within not more than 14 days from a notice or request to do so, the chairman shall be authorised to make the appointment on behalf of that party (Article 8. 3).

In summary, a tribunal could be set up within 44 days from the date of the claim submission.

(3)One Party Refuses to Participate in the Process

If there is no agreement on the nomination of an arbitrator, the chairman of the district court must appoint an arbitrator at the chair's discretion (Indonesian Arbitration Law, Article 13).

The arbitration tribunal has the power to impose sanctions on any party which fails to comply with a rule it makes or otherwise engages in conduct which impedes the smooth adjudication of the dispute.

If an applicant fails to attend the arbitral proceedings 14 days after a summons from the presiding arbitrator, the claim will be deemed void and the arbitral proceedings shall be considered a fresh.

If a respondent fails to attend the arbitral tribunal after a summons from the presiding arbitrator, the panel of arbitrators will continue the arbitration proceedings without the respondent, and the arbitration award will be rendered in favour of the applicant's claim, unless the claim is considered to be without any reasonable grounds.

The district court has no jurisdiction to try disputes between parties bound by an arbitration agreement（Article 3）. Further parties to an arbitration agreement are not entitled to seek resolution of the dispute through the district court（Article 11）.

（4）Interim Measures of Arbitration

Under the Indonesian Arbitration Law, the local Indonesian courts do not have the power to grant interim relief pending the outcome of an arbitration. The BANI rules provide the tribunal with the power to make some interim awards or decisions which deem appropriate to regulate the proceedings, including security attachments（such as security for costs, deposit of goods with the parties and the sale of perishable goods）.

Equally, the parties to the arbitration agreement can agree that such interim measures are to be available.

（5）Right to Challenge the Appointment of an Arbitrator

①Under the Indonesian Arbitration Law

Article 22 of the Indonesian Arbitration Law provides for challenges to arbitrators where evidence of a lack of independence is put forward. A party may also file a challenge against an arbitrator where the arbitrator:

Has a family, financial or working relationship with one party or proxy

Is under the age of 35;

Has an interest in the arbitration award;

Does not have at least 15 years' experience in their field.

②Under the BANI rules

An arbitrator may be challenged if circumstances exist that give rise to justifiable doubts as to the arbitrator's impartiality or independence（Article 11 of the BANI rules）. A party wishing to make such challenge must notify BANI in writing within 14 days from the time it is advised of the identity of the arbitrator, attaching documentation establishing the basis for the challenge.

Alternatively, if the information which forms the basis of the challenge becomes known to the challenging party after the arbitrator's appointment, any challenge must be submitted within 14 days after the challenging party becomes aware of the grounds of the challenge, If the challenge is not accepted by the arbitrator or the other side, the challenge will be reviewed by a panel from BANI. The panel will either, if they believe that the challenge is valid, provide for the appointment of another arbitrator in the same manner as the challenged one or, if they consider that the challenge is not valid, they will then allow the arbitrator to continue their duties.

If an arbitrator has a conflict of interest with the case or the parties, he is obliged to resign (Article 12. 2); otherwise, no arbitrator can resign unless challenged.

If a sole arbitrator is replaced, any earlier proceedings must be repeated. If the tribunal comprises three members and the chairman is replaced, witness testimony must be repeated if deemed necessary by the other members of the tribunal. However, if an arbitrator other than the chairman is replaced, then the replacement will·be briefed and there will be no repetition of previous hearings, except in extraordinary circumstances.

(6)Enforcing an Arbitration Award in Indonesia

A foreign arbitration award is in theory enforceable in Indonesia under Presidential Decree No. 34/1981. However, this decree does not set out a procedure for enforcement, as it only deals with the acceptance of the New York Convention 1958 in Indonesia. As a result, many foreign arbitration awards could not previously be enforced in Indonesia.

However, the enforcement of foreign arbitral awards is now possible [following the publication of Supreme Court Regulation No. 1/1990 (SC No. 1/1990)]. To enforce a foreign arbitration award, the following requirements (SC No. 1/1990, Article 3) must be met:

a. The award was made by an arbitrator or arbitration council in a country which has bilateral relations with, and has been bound collectively with, Indonesia in an international convention on the recognition and execution of international arbitration awards, based upon reciprocity the international arbitration award is limited to a decision which, according to the provision in Indonesian laws, falls under the scope of trade law

b. The arbitration decision does not contravene public order

c. An *exequator* is received from the Central Jakarta District Court chairman (authorising action). Article 66 of the Indonesian Arbitration Law restates the requirements set out above. In addition, it contains a requirement that an international arbitration concerning the State of the Republic of Indonesia as a party to the dispute may only be executed after securing an execution order from the Supreme Court of the Republic of Indonesia (later delegated to the Central Jakarta District Court). The documents to be submitted to the Central Jakarta District Court are as follows (SC No. 1/1990, Article 5.4):

(i)Original authenticated award;

(ii)Original translation of the award;

(iii)Original agreement which was the basis of arbitral agreement (authenticated);

(iv)Original translation of the agreement according to Indonesian law;

(v)Documentation from a diplomatic representative in the country in which the award was made stating they have a bilateral relationship with Indonesia and are also bound collectively in a convention on the recognition and enforcement of foreign arbitration awards.

(7)Cost of Arbitration

The arbitration costs are decided by the arbitrator or panel of arbitrators. Under Article 76 of the Indonesian Arbitration Law these may consist of arbitrator(s)' fees; travel expenses and miscellaneous costs of the arbitrator (s); cost of witnesses or expert witnesses needed in the examination of disputes; and administrative costs.

In practice, arbitration costs cover an honorarium and the costs of the arbitrators, including transportation and accommodation; the courts' costs, including room rental and transcript drafting; an honorarium for the legal consultant and witnesses and expert witnesses' expenses, including transportation and accommodation costs; the costs of the institution and secretariat, including registration and administration costs. As a general rule, costs are recoverable from the losing party. However, if the claimant is only partially successful, the arbitration fees are charged equally to the parties.

3. Implementedarbitration in Indonesia

(1)The Arbitration Law in Indonesia Nowadays

The provisions concerning the implementation (execution) of foreign arbitral decisions (International) in Indonesia contained in Law No. 30 Year 1999 on arbitration and alternative dispute resolution. The rules contained in Chapter Ⅵ of Chapter 65 to Chapter 69. These provisions are essentially in line with the provisions on recognition and enforcement of foreign arbitral awards (internationally) as set out in the New York Convention 1958.

Article 65 of Law No. 30 Year 1999 stipulates that the authorities address the issue of recognition of the implementation of international arbitral awards is the Central Jakarta District Court.

Furthermore Article 66 regulates the following matters: an international arbitral award recognized and can only be implemented in the territory of the Republic of Indonesia, if it meets the following requirements:

International arbitration award rendered by the arbitrator or the arbitral tribunal in a country with Indonesia tied to agreements, both bilateral and multilateral, concerning the recognition and implementation of international arbitral awards.

International arbitral award referred to paragraph(a) limited ruling that under trade law.

International arbitral award referred to in a letter can only be implemented in Indonesia is limited to decisions that are not contrary to public order.

International arbitration decision can be implemented in Indonesia after obtaining execution of Chairman Central Jakarta District Court, and international arbitral award referred to in paragraph (a) concerning the Republic of Indonesia as one of the parties to the dispute, can only be implemented after obtaining an execution of the Supreme Court of the Republic of Indonesia, which subsequently delegated to the Central Jakarta District Court.

Furthermore Article 67 stipulates that the application for enforcement of an international arbitration conducted after the verdict was submitted and registered by the arbitrators or their proxies to the Central Jakarta District Court clerk.

Although there has been considerable setting clear and firm on the implementation of foreign arbitral awards(international) in Law 30 Year 1999, compared with the period when the absence of clear regulation on the matter (i. e. before the Law. 30 Year 1999), Indonesia is often drawn criticism from the international community regarding the enforcement of international arbitration.

The general impression in the international community that Indonesia is still "an arbitration unfriendly country", which is difficult to be able to implement the decision of the international arbitration. Due to anticipating such things, it is no surprise that the winning Karahabodas case as an international arbitration case filed execution of international arbitral awards in other countries where there is a wealth of Pertamina(Government Petrol Company).

The main issue that is often raised by the international community that the Indonesian courts are reluctant to enforce the arbitral award or refuse enforcement of foreign arbitral awards (international) on the grounds that the verdict is contrary to public policy or public order. As is known, though public policy is formulated as rules and laws principal joints and the national interests of a nation, in this case Indonesia, but in a concrete application of these criteria are not always clear, so the situation is thus seen by the international community as a legal uncertainty.

It is interesting to note that the Law No. 30 Year 1999 only includes public policy as a reason for the rejection of foreign arbitral awards (international), whereas the New York Convention in Article 5 also includes a number of other provisions which may constitute grounds for rejection of foreign arbitral awards (international), which concerns matters diligence related to batch-process of law can be questioned, although other provisions are not included in the legislation Indonesia (Law No. 30 Year 1999) is an Indonesian court judge is not bound by such provisions, while Indonesia is a member of the New York Convention.

If the execution had been obtained and still leaves many problems in the field, in case of resistance to the execution of the concerned for any reason. As is known, the execution of the procedure according to the law of civil procedure conducted in accordance with the process of examination of the case in court which means it can last for a long time. Of course, such circumstances give rise to a feeling of uncertainty in the law of the parties concerned.

Another problem also ambiguous in the law of arbitration in Indonesia is about the notion of international arbitration itself. As is known, Article 1 point 9 of Law No. 30 Year 1999 to formulate an international arbitration decision is a decision handed down by arbitration institution or individual arbitrator outside the jurisdiction of the Republic of Indonesia or the decision of an arbitration institution or individual arbitrator in accordance with the laws of the Republic of Indonesia is considered as an international arbitration verdict.

With the formula as such can be interpreted that the awards have been handed down within the jurisdiction of the Indonesia is not a foreign award (international), or domestic arbitral awards (national).

This is an issue given that the New York Convention in 1958 in relation to the issue of recognition and enforcement of arbitral awards concerning arbitration is imposed in a different country than the country in which recognition is requested and practices regarding physical or legal disputes arose between them to the dispute.

It is also stressed that the New York Convention also applies to the decision by the State in which the judgment is recognized and enforceable arbitral awards are not considered as domestic.

As is known, Law 30 Year 1999 only regulates the recognition and enforcement of arbitration International in Indonesia, but it is not set at all about international arbitration process in Indonesia. Easily interpret that any arbitration held and ruled on in the territory of Indonesia is the domestic arbitration (national). As is known regarding the enforcement of arbitration held in Indonesia and execution of foreign arbitral awards (international) there are differences in the procedures and the registration period, and so on.

While the UNCITRAL Model Law in Article 1 made clear that arbitration is international if:

a. The parties to the arbitration agreement at the time of making the agreement concerned, have accrued to businesses in different countries;

b. Arbitration place, place of execution of the contract or where the object of the dispute is located in a different country from the seat of business of the parties to the dispute or if the parties expressly agree that the matters relating to the arbitration agreement in question involve more than one country.

In other words, the arbitration practice in Indonesia too (among others in the Indonesian National Arbitration Board/BANI) held an arbitration involving foreign elements (different stakeholders nationality/country), where the court is concerned arbitration award handed down in accordance with the legal provisions apply to the arbitration proceeding in Indonesia (Article 59 and Article 4 and Article 5 of Law No. 30 Year 1999). However, when seen from the perspective of the New York Convention, the decision can be regarded as a decision of an international arbitration, so the execution can be carried out in other countries that are the members of New York Convention.

Another fact that also occurs and can cause problems is if a foreign arbitration institutions (international), for example, the ICC and also hold a session or drop decision in Indonesia. Question may arise whether the agency arbitration decision by an Indonesian court considered a domestic arbitral award with all its consequences concerning the implementation of the procedure.

Cases like this happen yet how long this interval, which until now cause protracted problem.

Problem as stated above occurs because unlike other countries in general (including Singapore), Indonesian legislation concerning foreign arbitration (international) did not anticipate the UNCITRAL Model Law provisions. So that arbitration legislation Indonesian national is considered too, which is reflected among other things in the provisions regarding the use of Indonesian in the trial and the verdict must include Irah-Irah "for the sake of justice and the belief in God Almighty". It's difficult to be understood by outsiders.

To conform with international and universal nature of arbitration as a dispute resolution concepts and in order to harmonize legislation Indonesia with other countries that appeared to have more favorable conditions for the settlement of disputes of international law, should legislation Indonesian arbitration, in this Law 30 Year 1999, to be reviewed to conform with the provisions in force in the international community, including the UNCITRAL Model Law.

Besides, it is expected that the district court judges Indonesia as well as all the interested parties fully understand the meaning and essence of arbitration because the concept of dispute resolution outside of court that is practical, non-confrontational, efficient and effective.

4. Conclusion

According to all description above, some matters are concluded:

The arbitration law in Indonesia needs to be improved and It also needs to adapt the UNCITRAL Model Law as a whole, to produce the new arbitration law that is consistent with the convention of the international world, and removing the national characteristic such as Irah-Irah "for the sake of justice and the belief in God Almighty", so that can make the award of arbitration in Indonesia follow the International rules.

The Indonesia district court judges must understand the meaning and essence of arbitration so the concept of dispute resolution outside of court that can be more practical, non-confrontational, efficient and effective to enforce in Indonesia.

中国—东盟自贸区法律框架下新加坡的投资仲裁机构和机制

Li Xinyang[*]

范芸　译

摘要　新加坡作为东盟成员也是中国—东盟自贸区的缔约国。然而东盟没有普通法和法律体系。新加坡有着普通法传统,有鉴于此,可通过将已有经验运用到把新加坡建成国际仲裁中心的尝试中来并应对中国—东盟自贸区面临的挑战。

关键词　东盟　法律框架　新加坡争端解决　新加坡法律体系

引　言

中国对东盟的建议及随后 2001 年东盟自由贸易区的建立对中国—东盟关系的发展具有里程碑的作用。

在 2001 年东盟—中国的首脑峰会上,当时中国的朱镕基总理提议十年内建立中国—东盟自由贸易区。此外,中国提出在双方实现互惠前的 5 年,向东盟国家开放一些关键领域。

中国也将会对东盟的一些欠发达国家的货物给予特殊优惠关税待遇,例如柬埔寨、老挝和缅甸。在几轮磋商和正式会谈后,东盟接受了这个提议。中国—东盟自由贸易区于 2010 年 1 月 1 日正式生效。

作为继欧盟和北美自贸区的第三大自贸区,中国—东盟自由贸易区将会对东南亚的贸易和发展带来重要意义。

东盟将允许 90% 的货物——也就是中国与东盟国家大约 7000 项的贸易

---

*　新加坡钟庭辉律师事务所律师,中国—东盟法律研究中心研究员。

实行零关税。同时,到 2015 年,其他"高度敏感"商品的关税将会削减至不超过 50％,包括中国的卫生纸、印度尼西亚的爆米花和泰国的滑雪板。

在 1995 年到 2008 年期间,中国与东盟之间的双边贸易增加了十倍之多。自 2001 年中国加入 WTO 并开启与东盟的会谈时,贸易的增加更为迅速。到 2008 年,中国成为东盟国家的第三大贸易伙伴,东盟也成为中国的第四大贸易伙伴。

此后,中国与东盟着力于进一步加强其正式的双边关系,在 2002 年 11 月的第八次东盟峰会的框架协议上,设定 2010 年建立中国—东盟自由贸易区,根据该协议,早期计划于 2004 年 1 月实施;2004 年 11 月完成货物关税谈判,并在 2005 年 7 月实施,服务贸易协定在 2007 年 1 月签署,投资协定于 2009 年 8 月签署。

此外,中国与东盟的双边投资也有所增加,尽管这只是双方总额的一小部分,在统一的区域经济下,东盟国家的外来投资也有望进一步增加。

东盟的法律框架

东盟缺乏一个完善的法律结构,即一个有效的争端解决机制,这也是阻碍中国—东盟自贸区发展的重要原因。因此,中国—东盟自贸区的成功发展一定程度上取决于法律体制的建设。

东盟各国不同的法律文化下,中国—东盟自由贸易区能否成功也是一个值得考虑的问题。

传统上,东盟国家内部的决策和立法被称为"东盟方式"。它是东盟的一项特色:它是用于表述东盟独特的达成共识方式的术语。这种"东盟方式"是由这一地区的历史和文化发展而来的,它源自马来西亚语"musjawarah"和"mufukat"。"Musjawarah"是指通过磋商和讨论的一系列决策过程,"mufukat"是指通过这种决策过程达到统一的决定。

因此,"东盟方式"是塑造区域组织的各个方面的基础,不仅是通过协商一致进行的会议,还包括通过这种方式达成的谈判和协议。事实上,大多数东盟国家的文件体现了这种"软法"。因此,协议上大多不包括具有法律约束力的条款,而是由一系列非常宽泛的原则构成。

由于自贸协定的稳定性需求,东盟国家可能更加倾向于法律制度化。

从 1967 年的曼谷宣言开始,东盟就把自身设定为非法律性的。该宣言也仅仅是一个政治性的声明,并不需要批准。正如现任东盟秘书长所称,"成立东盟的目的是明确的:成员国希望东盟只是一个宽松的、最小制度化的政治联盟,并且不存在法律特性或者宪法框架"。

1976年,即东盟建立后的第9年,成员国声明建立东盟秘书处,东盟开始进行更加全面的法律构建。在建立东盟秘书处之前,东盟之间的协调必须要经过各成员国的秘书处才能达成。1993年东盟秘书处重新组建。

争端解决机制的不完善妨碍了东盟通过法律途径对经济尤其是自由贸易的规制。东盟成立后的近十年,东盟国家从来没有讨论过建立区域争端解决机制的问题。

东盟计划出台后的几年,东盟国家表示他们没有准备好接受这样的法律协议,因为他们还不能像一个联盟那样运作。

新加坡的法律视角

新加坡是世界上最开放的投资地之一,外国投资者在此建立任何形式的商业实体几乎是没有限制的。

新加坡对国内和外国建立私人有限合伙企业的法律规制是相同的。新加坡的政策规定要区分国外人才的雇佣并限制国外投资者对本国土地的所有权,因此,除了就业和土地财产的购买(例如附着在土地上的房屋)之外,新加坡对于在国内设立、合并企业及投资经营是没有限制的。

新加坡对在本国设立和营运商事企业的法律包括商事登记法(第32章)以及公司法(第50章)。这些法律中所有条款对本国和外国投资者的规定都是相同的。

无论本国人还是外国人都有资格成为董事、股东或者投资者。公司中不存在对外国股份的限制,同时本国股东和外国股东也没有法定的比例要求。

调　　解

新加坡政府鼓励当事人在向法院提起诉讼前进行调解。新加坡正式的或制度性的调解建立于20世纪90年代。在此期间新加坡建立了法院调解中心(后更名为初级争端解决中心,在初级法院)、新加坡调解中心(SMC),社区调解中心等机构和法庭。换句话说,从基层社会到政府和商业组织,调解实践于社会的各方面,并迎合了本国不同种族和社会背景的人群。调解节约了时间和成本,并且保证了隐密性。

与仲裁不同,除了在《社区调解中心法令》第49A章中有所规定外,针对调解没有专门的立法。当事方的合同中有调解条款时,可以适用合同的一般法律原则。国内普遍认同的观点是调解条款并不排除法院的管辖。

调解作为争端解决的一种形式,至 2013 年 3 月 31 日,已有 2127 个案件提交到新加坡调解中心,其中 74％的争端得到很好的解决。自其成立以来,共有约 30 亿新元的争端在新加坡调解中心得到调解,最高一次金额达到2.09亿新元。

仲 裁

与调解类似,仲裁在新加坡的相关领域是一个新的名词。只有在 20 世纪 90 年代通过的仲裁法(第 10 章)及在 1986 年加入的承认与执行国际仲裁的纽约公约并在作为新加坡仲裁法基石的国际仲裁法(第 143A 章)中有所体现。在新加坡作出的裁决,不论是对国内还是国外,都有约束力和执行力。尤其需要指出的是,对方如果是纽约公约的缔约方,在新加坡进行的裁决可以在这一缔约方执行。

正如调解那样,在过去的 20 年中,仲裁成为争端解决方式中大多数人的选择,以至于 2010 年,新加坡被国际仲裁调查杂志评为亚洲区域仲裁的龙头。

仲裁中专业的裁判者和组织确保了仲裁程序的和谐、有效和专业,这一优点使其受到众多机构的拥护。

新加坡国际仲裁中心(SIAC)以及新加坡海事仲裁院是两个非制度化的机构并以他们自身的仲裁员和规则促进了仲裁的发展。新加坡国际仲裁中心还提供培训及资格认证。SIAC 和麦士威议事厅(亚洲组建的首个综合国际争端解决机构)提供最先进的听审设备和综合服务,在 2012 年 SIAC 的年度报道中,SIAC 处理了 235 项案件,比上一年度增加了 25％,同年的争端解决金额也达到 1536 万新元至最高 15 亿——是上一年度的 2 倍。

为了进一步发展新加坡作为国际仲裁领先的地位并提高实务工作者的知识和技能,在 2012 年末,新加坡国立大学国际法中心和法律学院设立了新加坡国际仲裁学院。

新加坡是一个拥有普通法系的国家,法律体系也具有公平、公正和效率的美誉。近期,新加坡也在积极促进仲裁调解和其他可替代争端解决形式的发展。随之在 02-01 麦士威路 32 号建立了新加坡国际仲裁中心,麦士威议事厅,邮政编码 069115。新加坡也积极通过管理推动有关法律的发展:包括与争端解决有关的法律、仲裁的管理,以及新加坡作为仲裁裁决者的管理。

在国际仲裁中心的选择上,新加坡越来越重要。

随着贸易与商业的联系日益紧密,在亚洲,尤其是东盟国家,商业争端领域急需迅速可靠的争端解决机制。新加坡是一个很好的选择,理由如下:

（1）新加坡在国际仲裁中适用联合国国际贸易法委员会（UNCITRAL）的示范法。UNCITRAL 由联合国在 1966 年设立，其目的在于促进国际贸易法的协调。UNCITRAL 在各贸易国之间寻求指导国际仲裁的一系列有共性的规则，最终达成了示范法并于 1985 年 6 月正式被联合国采纳。示范法适用于广义的"国际商事仲裁"，示范法有以下几部分：(a)总则；(b)仲裁协议；(c)仲裁的组成；(d)仲裁庭的管辖权；(e)仲裁程序的进行；(f)裁决的作出和程序的终止；(g)对裁决的追诉；(h)裁决的承认与执行。示范法规定：(a)当事人在仲裁的各方面可以意思自治，若双方没有达成一致就受默认程序（default procedures）约束；(b)当事方和仲裁员在国际商事仲裁程序中不适用国内法的权利（第 19 条）；(c)对法院管辖的限制：(ⅰ)仲裁协议没有对仲裁员的选择达成一致，(ⅱ)双方反对仲裁员的审理结果，(ⅲ)更换的仲裁员不能或不愿意进行裁决，(ⅳ)当事人对仲裁裁决上诉时，法院可以对实行仲裁管辖权的首要问题作出决定；(ⅴ)协助调查取证；(ⅵ)严格控制法院对仲裁裁决的撤销（第 6 条、第 27 条及第 34 条）。实际效果是新加坡的仲裁法律环境在一个法治的环境中并最小程度的减少司法的干预。

（2）新加坡为保证仲裁顺畅有效的进行，提供了完善的配套设施。1991 年 6 月，SIAC 成立，它是一个非营利性组织。根据仲裁规则双方当事人可协商一致决定适用的仲裁规则，但大多数人都选择了 SIAC 的规则作为适用的法律。SIAC 的宗旨是提供以下便利：(1)为国际和国内的商事法律争议提供仲裁和调解服务；(2)促进仲裁和调解在解决商事法律争议中的广泛应用；(3)培养一批熟知国际商事仲裁法律和实务的仲裁员和专家。SIAC 可以应当事人或仲裁庭的要求，为当事人提供一系列的支持和行政服务，包括解决仲裁员的费用，为庭审提供食宿，安排仲裁庭和当事人代表的会议日期，以及为诉状、文件和往来通信进行登记。SIAC 也会协助当事人承认与执行在纽约公约的成员国进行的裁决。

（3）新加坡是东盟成员国公认的具有裁判中立性和地理位置优越性的国家。这一点可以通过 SIAC 自成立以来的受案数量反应出来，SIAC 的受案数量由 1992 年的 7 件到 1995 年的 37 件到 1997 年的 43 件再到 1999 年的 66 件。

综上，新加坡在实践中运用了相关的国际公约，如纽约公约和联合国国际贸易法委员会示范法，为了使国际仲裁在新加坡更好地开展，新加坡国内也提供了许多支持，因此，无论是法律上还是商业上，新加坡都是解决贸易争端的首选之地。

新加坡的仲裁机构

1. 麦士威议事厅（Maxwell Chambers）

麦士威议事厅是世界上首个国际综合争端调解中心，作为国际顶尖的替代性争端解决机构，它拥有最先进的听审设备。麦士威议事厅坐落于前海关大楼，那里是新加坡商业中心的核心地带，是一座翻新成庄严的新古典主义外观的四层建筑。

麦士威议事厅有 23 间特殊设计的审判室和候审室，最大的一间可容纳 140 人。

2. 新加坡国际仲裁中心（SIAC）

公正、公平的规则与程序，效率及竞争力是 SIAC 成功的关键因素。

SIAC 的案件管理职能受到仲裁法院的监督，仲裁法院中不乏在国际上很知名的仲裁员。SIAC 的企业管理和其他职能受董事会的监督，该董事会是由法律界及商业界高级成员组成。

随着国际上对多样化争端解决的呼声越来越高，包括比利时、加拿大、中国、印度、韩国、马来西亚、新加坡及英国，SIAC 致力于全面了解当事方的需求以更好地为他们服务。

作为一个仲裁机构，SIAC 承诺完全公平、透明地审理案件。具体而言，双方在对仲裁员的选择上未达成一致时，SIAC 将帮助当事人选定仲裁员；对仲裁有关的经济和其他相关的事务进行管理；促进仲裁顺利进行。

SIAC 履行这些职责是根据其制定的仲裁规则和指导方针，这些规则和指导方针在其出版的实务纪要中也有所体现。SIAC 旨在促进对案件的审理能力达到最佳水平。

SIAC 有一支由超过 380 名独立的国际仲裁员组成的专家组，这些仲裁员来自 32 个不同的司法管辖区，具有丰富的经验以及深厚的理论和实践基础。其中 204 位专家来自亚洲。

SIAC 有良好的裁决执行记录。SIAC 的裁决在许多国家都得到成功执行，包括澳大利亚、中国、印度、印度尼西亚、英国、美国、越南及其他纽约公约成员。

2012 年 SIAC 受理了 235 个案件，比 2011 年增加了 25%，达到了一个历史新高，目前 SIAC 处理并有效执行了 550 多个案件。

准据法

新加坡的仲裁主要依据仲裁法(第10章)(AA)和国际仲裁法(第143A号法令)(IAA)。具体而言,AA适用于国内仲裁,IAA适用于国际仲裁。

这一区分非常重要,其决定了仲裁适用哪一个法律(仲裁实践中如果当事人在仲裁合同中约定了与上述法律不同的准据法,应当遵从当事人的约定,否则应当按照上述所区分的法律予以适用)。这是因为在不同的仲裁规则下,仲裁的程序也会有所不同。本文并不对两种规则做过多探讨。根据本文的写作目的,我们可以明显看出IAA是以联合国国际贸易法委员会商事仲裁示范法为蓝本,而AA则是以英国仲裁法为蓝本,它的管辖范围比IAA的管辖范围更小。根据在具体仲裁过程中的争议点,两种规则的适用具有明显的不同,这对仲裁的进行及其结果都是至关重要的。

IAA适用于国际仲裁,根据IAA的规定,满足以下条件之一的就被视为具有国际性:

(1)仲裁协议中至少一方当事人的营业地不在新加坡;

(2)根据仲裁协议,仲裁地不在各方当事人营业地所在国;

(3)履行商事关系大部分义务的地点不在各方当事人营业地所在国;

(4)与争议事项关系最密切的地点不在各方当事人营业地所在国;

(5)各方当事人明确约定仲裁协议的标的与一个以上的国家有关。

不同于IAA,AA对是否适用于特定的仲裁没有提供任何指导方针和规则。根据新加坡法律,AA适用于所有的仲裁,除非案件是属于IAA的管辖范围。换句话说,新加坡国内的仲裁默认使用AA。如果各当事方的营业地都在新加坡,并且商事关系义务履行也都在新加坡,那么这样的案件显然是适用AA的。

IAA允许当事方排除IAA中所提出的仲裁规则,如果当事方在仲裁协议中约定,争议发生时不采用IAA或者示范法的第二部分中的有关规定,IAA或者示范法的第二部分中的有关规定就不适用于这一争端。但IAA规则允许当事人协商一致,将IAA适用于国内的仲裁案件中。

当事人不能通过这样的方式排除AA的适用。AA的仲裁规则被视为隐含在仲裁协议中,当事人如果明确表明不适用AA规则,他们才可以不适用AA的相关规则。

本国的裁决在新加坡的执行

在新加坡作出的裁决,无论是有关国内还是国际的裁决,都具有约束力和执行力。为了确保在新加坡作出的裁决得到执行,应当采取以下步骤:

(1)当事人首先必须向新加坡最高法院提出申请执行许可;

(2)执行的申请必需送达对方当事人(即"债权人"),对方当事人有 14 天的时间进行异议;

(3)如果债务人对执行的申请持异议,裁决必须在此异议得到听审并最终确定后才能得以执行。

外国裁决在新加坡的执行

纽约公约成员国的裁决。

新加坡在 1958 年 8 月 21 日加入纽约公约(以下称"公约"),随后以立法形式将公约大部分条款加入 IAA 的第 3 部分。作为公约的成员方,新加坡有义务承认与执行其他成员国的裁决。

这样的外国仲裁需要通过单独诉讼或者将其作为仲裁员在新加坡作出的裁决以同样的方式予以执行。根据 IAA 29(2)条的规定,在新加坡的任何法律程序中,当事任何一方可以此作为答辩、抵消或作为其他依据。

为了使公约的成员国的裁决得到更好的执行,需要执行以下步骤:

(1)向新加坡最高法院高等法庭提出申请执行许可。根据《时效法》第 163 章规定申请必须在裁决后的 6 年内作出。

(2)当事人必需提交仲裁协议和正式认证的裁决原件和复印件。若原件不是英文,当事人应当翻译成经认证的英文版本。此外,当事人应当写明申请人和被执行人的姓名、惯常或最后为人所知的居住地或营业地。

法院只能根据 IAA 第 31 条第 2 款和第 4 款拒绝对外国裁决的执行,对执行申请进行聆讯的法院不能对案件的本身内容进行重新审理。

在出现紧急情况时,法院允许债权人申请单方许可令并送达债务人。

当事方如果想要在新加坡进行仲裁,最好是先确认对方所在国是否是公约的缔约国,如果答案是肯定的,在新加坡作出裁决就可以在对方国家得到执行。

联邦国家的裁决

新加坡作为英联邦的成员国之一,根据《互相执行联邦国家法院判决法案》（RECJA）（第264章），新加坡对英国及英国其他地区作出的裁决予以承认和执行，此外与新加坡签有互惠协议的也可予以承认与执行。该联邦国家共有54名成员，RECJA列出其中有互惠安排的9个国家。

在这些联邦国家进行的裁决，在RECJA下是可以得到执行的，该法案在定义"裁决"时包含了通过仲裁进行的裁决。然而，RECJA规定了在联邦国家进行的仲裁执行必须与其本国法院作出的判决时的执行方式相同。

相比而言，根据RECJA规则下申请执行比依据纽约公约要求更高。例如在RECJA规则下申请执行的注册必须在12个月内完成，而在纽约公约规则下可在6年内完成。

此外，法院对于审理并允许仲裁执行仅仅在法院认为合理方便时进行，这涉及法院的自由裁量权。

从实际角度来看，随着加入纽约公约的国家越来越多，在RECJA规则下的裁决执行变得不那么重要了。RECJA对于未加入公约的国家来说还是具有一定的相关性，例如巴基斯坦和文莱。

在没有涉外因素的争端中，选择仲裁或诉讼几乎没有差别，这需要根据具体案件的情况和当地法院的程序和声誉来定。当事人要使得争端得到有效解决，国内法院和仲裁机构都是很好的选择。

然而，在涉及大型商业实体的国际争端中，仲裁会是一个更好的选择。仲裁具有自身的优势，例如灵活性、程序的非公开性，可以选择一个仲裁机构对具体交易中的所有争端进行仲裁，裁决的可执行性也很强。然而仲裁的缺点是费用高及耗时长。

在选择仲裁时，当事方要确定是提交到常设仲裁机构还是专门的仲裁机构。如果选择了专门仲裁机构仲裁，当事人要再次选择是从头起草准据法的程序规则还是适用现有的规则，例如联合国国际贸易法委员会商事仲裁规则。

中国近期案件的裁决

新加坡最高法院最近首次执行了中国大陆的司法裁决，这被认为是新加坡裁决的里程碑。

原告捷安特轻合金科技有限公司（昆山）（GLMT）向新加坡法院提出根据在中国作出的裁决，执行被告在新加坡的财产。新加坡法院在仔细考量下，决定执行原告的申请。

本案是对2010年11月6日由中国江苏苏州中级人民法院作出的判决进行承认与执行。该案中原告向被告雅柯斯私人有限公司（新加坡雅柯斯）购买了两台电机组,被告违反了双方的协议,具体体现为:(1)该发电机并不是全新的;(2)该发电机并非原产于英国;(3)不能正常使用。该案在中国的诉讼中被告一个是新加坡雅柯斯公司,另一个是上海亚提思机电设备有限公司(上海亚提思),该公司当时是新加坡雅柯斯公司在中国的分销商。

我们注意到根据新加坡《互惠执行外国判决法》(第 265 章 2001 年修订)中国并不是其中的互惠国。为了使中国的裁决在新加坡得到执行,原告必须在新加坡针对新加坡当事人提起新的诉讼,或者在新加坡法院在原有的诉求上提起新的诉讼程序。

这是首次中国的裁决在新加坡得到执行。这意味着新加坡本国投资者在中国进行投资,一旦发生争端,中国法院作出的裁决在新加坡是可以执行的。

新加坡司法机关从普通法出发的新路径对中国裁决的执行将会帮助新加坡在仲裁和争端解决方面获得良好的声誉。由此应当关注的法律意见有:(1)新加坡公司如何在中国进行自己的业务;(2)在中国法院参加诉讼的法律程序。新加坡的这一做法对其公司开展海外业务有广泛的影响,不仅仅是在中国。它将表明新加坡公司作为外国诉讼一方当事人时,外国的司法判决也能在新加坡得到承认与执行,有鉴于此,从而新加坡公司可以决定是否要参与到这样的诉讼中去。

结　　论

新加坡是一个普通法系国家,拥有完整的法律框架,并且采用了大量国际通行的实践做法,因此新加坡更适合作为东盟仲裁中心以便更好地解决东盟国家面临的挑战。

Investment Arbitration Institution and Mechanism in Singapore under the Legal Framework of China-ASEAN Free Trade Area

Li Xinyang*

Abstract   Singapore a member of ASEAN is a signatory of China-ASEAN Free Trade Area. However ASEAN does not have common laws and legal system. Singapore which has a common law tradition has its unique experience in trying to establish itself as an international arbitration center and to meet the challenges of China ASEAN Free Trade Area.

Keywords   ASEAN; Legal Framework; Singapore Dispute Resolution; Singapore Legal System

Introduction

China's proposal to ASEAN countries and the subsequent establishment of a free trade area (FTA) between them in 2001 masked an important milestone in the development of China-ASEAN relations.

At the ASEAN-China summit in November 2001 the then Chinese Premier Zhu Rongji made the proposal for the formation of a China-ASEAN FTA(CAFTA) in ten years. China offered to open its own market in some key sectors to the ASEAN countries five years before they reciprocate.

It would also grant special preferential tariff treatment for some goods

---

　　* Singaporean, Advocate, Soliufar and arbitrator in Chung Ting Fai & Co. Researcher of China-ASEAN Legal Research Center.

from these less developed ASEAN states i. e. Cambodia, Laos and Myanmar. ASEAN accepted this proposal after several rounds of consultations and formal talks. The China ASEAN Free Trade Area came into effect on 1 January 2010.

As the world's third largest free trade area after the European Union and North America FTA, CAFTA will have significant trade and development implication for Southeast Asia.

CAFTA will allow 90% of all goods—that is, around 7,000 items traded between China and ASEAN countries—to be zero-tariff. Meanwhile, by 2015, duties on other "highly sensitive" commodities will be cut to no more than 50%, which would include toilet paper in China, popcorn in Indonesia and snowboard boots in Thailand.

Between 1995 and 2008 bilateral trade between China and ASEAN increased more than ten fold. The growth has been especially rapid since 2001 when China joined the WTO and CAFTA talks were initiated. By 2008 China became ASEAN's third largest trading partner and ASEAN China's fourth largest.

Since then, China and ASEAN have proceeded to further strengthen their formal bilateral ties. The framework agreement at the Eighth ASEAN Summit in November 2002 set 2010 as the year for establishing the China-ASEAN FTA (CAFTA). Under the accord the Early Harvest Program was implemented on 1 January 2004; tariff negotiations for trade in goods were completed in November 2004 and implemented in July 2005. In January 2007, an Agreement on Trade in Services was signed and the Investment A-greement was signed in August 2009.

Bilateral investment between China and ASEAN also increased, although it constitutes only a small portion of the two region's tote (FP) inflow. Inward investment to CAFTA from outside the region is expected to rise further with a harmonized regional economy.

Legal Framework of Asean

One of the greatest impediments to CAFTA's long-term success is

ASEAN's lack of a sufficient legal structure, namely a capable dispute resolution mechanism. Hence, the success of this groundbreaking free trade area may depend on whether ASEAN as an organization undergoes the legal reform necessary for the implementation of CAFTA.

The question often posed is whether CAFTA will succeed despite ASEAN's diverse legal culture.

Traditionally, decision-making and law-making within ASEAN is conducted through what is known as the "ASEAN way". The ASEAN way is ASEAN's trademark: a phrase that is used to describe ASEAN's unique consensus approach. The ASEAN way is steeped in the history and culture of the region. It is derived from the Malaysian concepts of "musjawarah" and "mufukat". "Musjawarah" refers to the process of decision-making through consultation and discussion, while "mufukat" refers to the unanimous decision that is achieved through musjawarah.

Thus, the ASEAN way is fundamental in shaping every aspect of this regional organization. Not only are meetings conducted through the consensus approach, but the resulting negotiations and agreements reflect this consensus style. Indeed, most ASEAN documents reflect this kind of "soft" law. Consequently, agreements generally do not contain many legally-binding provisions but rather consist of a set of very broad principles.

Thus, while ASEAN has been able to survive without significant legal institutionalization, ASEAN must undergo legal reform for CAFTA to succeed.

The ASEAN states may become more inclined to embrace legal institutionalization not only because it is necessary for the sustainability of free trade agreements.

Beginning with the Bangkok Declaration, 1967, ASEAN was predetermined to be non-legalistic. The Declaration itself was only a political statement that required no ratification. As the current ASEAN Secretary-General has described, "[t]he intention was clear: the Founding Fathers wanted ASEAN to be just a loosely-organized political association with minimum institutionalization, and without legal personality or constitutional framework".

ASEAN made its first overtures towards developing a more comprehensive legal framework in 1976, nine years after it was founded, when the ASEAN member states established the ASEAN Secretariat. Prior to the ASEAN Secretariat, all coordination among ASEAN states had to occur through the secretariats based in each member country. In 1993, the ASEAN Secretariat was again restructured.

One of the major limitations preventing ASEAN from using a legalistic approach for economic regulation, specifically free trade regulation, is ASEAN's underdeveloped dispute settlement mechanism. ASEAN never even discussed the possibility of a regional dispute settlement mechanism until nearly ten years after the organization was founded.

In the few years since the CAFTA plan was unveiled, the ASEAN states have indicated that they may not be ready for such a legal agreement because of their continued inability to function as a unit.

Singapore's Legal Perspective

Singapore is one of the most investor friendly territory in the world. There is little or no barriers to any foreigners trying to set up any form of business entity in the republic.

The laws governing the establishment of private limited and partnership is the same for locals as well as foreigners. Apart from employment status and the purchase of landed property i. e. houses attached to land where there are policies that prevent the indiscriminate employment of foreign talents and also to limit the foreign ownership of land, there are no legal obstacles for foreigners to set, to incorporate, to invest and to run businesses in Singapore.

The legislation that governs the establishment of and operation of business vehicles in Singapore includes the Registration of Business Act (Cap. 32) as well as the Companies Act (Cap. 50). In the provisions of both of these Acts there is no provision that makes a distinction between locals and foreigners.

Anybody, local or foreign can be a director, a shareholder or an investor. There is no limitation on foreign shareholding in a company, no stipulated ratio of local shareholders to foreign shareholders.

Mediation

The Singapore Government has actively encouraged prospective litigants to engage in mediation before turning to the courts. Formal or institutionalised mediation was established in the 1990s with the setting up of the Court Mediation Center, renamed the Primary Dispute Resolution Center, in the Subordinate Courts, the Singapore Mediation Center(SMC), the Community Mediation Centers and other agencies and tribunals. In other words, mediation is practised in the various sectors of society catering to the diverse ethnic and social backgrounds of Singaporeans, from the grassroots community to government and business. Mediation saves time and money and guarantees confidentiality.

Unlike arbitration, there is no legislation dealing specifically with mediation with the exception of the Community Mediation Centers Act (Cap. 49A). The common law principles of contract come into play when adjudicating mediation clauses in contracts where they are provided for. The general view is that the existence of a mediation clause does not preclude the jurisdiction of the courts.

As an illustration of the acceptance of mediation as a form of dispute resolution, as at 31 March 2013, 2127 matters were referred to SMC, with 74% of disputes successfully settled. Since its inception, about S $ 3 billion worth of disputes have been mediated at the SMC, the highest quantum being S $ 209 million.

Arbitration

Like mediation, arbitration is a fairly new concept in the Singapore context, only taking root in the 1990s with the passing of the Arbitration Act (Cap. 10) and International Arbitration Act (Cap. 143A) after the country acceded to the New York Convention on the Recognition and

Enforcement of Foreign Arbitral Awards in 1986, the cornerstone of
Singapore arbitration law. Awards made in Singapore, either in respect of a
domestic or international arbitration, are binding and enforceable. In
particular, if a counterparty is from a NY Convention country, an award
obtained in Singapore against that counterparty is enforceable in the latter's
country.

Like mediation, for the past 20 years, arbitration has gained traction as
a popular method to resolve disputes, so much so that in 2010, Singapore
was named the regional leader in Asia for seat of arbitration by International
Arbitration Survey.

Arbitration is well-supported by various institutions, expert arbiters
and infrastructures to ensure that the arbitration process is seamless,
efficient and professional. The Singapore International Arbitration Center
(SIAC) and the Singapore Chamber of Maritime Arbitration are two local
non-institutional organizations that promote arbitration with their own panel
of arbitrators and rules. The SIAC also provides training and certification.
The SIAC, together with Maxwell Chambers, Asia's first integrated dispute
resolution complex, offer state of the art hearing facilities and
comprehensive services to support the conduct of arbitration. In the 2012
SIAC annual report, the SIAC handled 235 cases, a 25% jump from the
previous year, and the average disputed amount for the same year was $15.
36 million— $1.5 billion being the highest—twice the amount from the year
before.

To further develop Singapore's position as a leading international
arbitration player, the Singapore International Arbitration Academy was set
up at the tail end of 2012 by the Center for International Law and the
Faculty of Law, National University of Singapore, to develop practitioners'
arbitration knowledge and skills.

Singapore is a country with a common law legal system. It has the
reputation of being a just, fair and efficient legal system. In recent cases
Singapore is also actively promoting arbitration mediation and other forms of
alternative dispute resolution. With the establishment of the Singapore International Arbitration Center at 32 Maxwell Road 02-01, Maxwell

Chambers, Singapore 069115. Singapore actively promotes Singapore law in governing law, arbitration as a form of dispute resolution and Singapore as the arbiter for arbitration.

Singapore is fast gaining in importance as a choice of the seat of an arbitrator.

The increasing reliance of trade and business involving at least one Asian and in particular an ASEAN country has led to a growing need for the speedy and reliable resolution of commercial dispute in the region. Singapore is now recognized as an excellent seat with the region for the resolution of these disputes for the following reasons:

Singapore has adopted the UNCITRAL Model Law to apply to international arbitrations. UNCITRAL was established by the United Nations in 1966, its purpose being the harmonization of international trade law. UNCITRAL sought the adoption, by trading nations, of a common series of rules for the conduct of international arbitrations and, to this end, agreed to a Model Law which was officially adopted by the United Nations in June 1985. It applies to "international commercial arbitrations" which are widely defined in the Model Law and sets out: (a) the basic requirements; (b) the form of the arbitration agreement; (c) the composition of the arbitration tribunal; (d) the jurisdiction of the tribunal; (e) procedural rules; (f) the award; and (g) recognition and enforcement of the award. It provides for: (a) party autonomy in respect of all aspects of the arbitration, subject to default procedures where no agreement has been reached by the parties; (b) the right of the parties and the arbitrators not to apply the domestic law of the forum to the procedural aspects of the arbitration (Article 19); and (c) the limited role for local courts, whose functions are restricted to: (i) the appointment of arbitrators in default of agreement, (ii) the hearing of challenges to arbitrators, (iii) the replacement of arbitrators unable or unwilling to act, (vi) the determination of preliminary issues as to the jurisdiction of the arbitrators on appeal from their decision on the point, (v) assistance with obtaining evidence, and (vi) the setting aside of awards on narrow grounds (Articles 6, 27 and 34). The practical effect is that arbitrations in Singapore are conducted in a legal environment that minimizes judicial interference.

2. Singapore has supported facilities to assist the smooth and efficient running of arbitrations. In July 1991, the Singapore International Arbitration Center(SIAC), a non profit-making organization, was set up. The SIAC administers most of its cases are under its own rules of arbitration although it is able to administer arbitrations under any other rules agreed to by the parties. The SIAC aims to provide facilities for: (a) international and domestic commercial arbitration and conciliation; (b) promoting arbitration and conciliation as alternatives to litigation for the settlement of commercial disputes; and (c) developing a pool of arbitrators and experts in the law and practice of international arbitration and conciliation. The SIAC provides support and administrative services which include settling fees of arbitrators, providing accommodation for hearings, arranging dates for meetings between the tribunal and parties' representatives and acting as a registry of pleadings, documents and correspondence. The SIAC will also assist parties in arranging the recognition and enforcement of awards in countries which are party to the New York Convention.

3. Singapore is widely recognized by parties trading in the region as a place for conducting arbitrations that is both neutral and geographically convenient in relation to the parties to the dispute. This is reflected in the growing number of cases the SIAC has received since it was first set up, with the number of cases referred to it annually increasing from 7 (in 1992) to 37 (in 1995) and 43 (in 1997) to 67 (in 1999).

In short, as well as having implemented the appropriate international conventions, such as the New York Convention, and adopting the UNCITRAL Model Law, Singapore has taken steps to ensure practical support for international arbitrations conducted here, with the result that it is regarded, both legally and commercially, as a preferred forum for resolving trade disputes.

Singapore Arbitration Institutions

1. Maxwell Chambers

Maxwell Chambers is the world's first integrated dispute resolution complex, housing both best-of-class hearing facilities as well as top international Alternative Dispute Resolution (ADR) institutions. Centrally positioned in the heart of Singapore's business district, Maxwell Chambers is located in the former Customs House, a refurbished four-storey conservation building with a stately neo-classical *fa. ade*.

Maxwell Chambers has 23 custom-designed hearing rooms and preparation rooms, with the largest room able to accommodate some 140 people. Maxwell Chambers offers:

2. Singapore International Arbitration Center(SIAC)

Integrity, fair rules and procedures, efficiency and competence are key to SIAC's success.

SIAC's case management functions are overseen by a Court of Arbitration that comprises luminaries in the international arbitration arena. SIAC's corporate management and other functions are overseen by a Board of Directors comprising of senior members of the legal and business communities.

With an international case management team hailing from different jurisdictions including Belgium, Canada, China, India, Korea, Malaysia, Singapore and the UK who have specialized experience and knowledge of the region, SIAC is devoted to serving all its users with a complete understanding of their needs.

As an institution administering arbitration, SIAC is committed to complete impartiality and transparency in all that it does for parties. Broadly, it helps parties in appointment of arbitrators when they cannot agree on an appointment; management of the financial and other practical aspects of arbitration; and facilitation of the smooth progress of arbitration.

SIAC carries out these responsibilities according to its published rules of arbitration and guidelines as contained in practical notes published from time to time. SIAC seeks to promote the highest standard of conduct and delivery in all arbitrations conducted under its auspices.

The SIAC has an international panel of over 380 independent arbitrators with a spread of expertise, depth of knowledge and experience from over 32 different jurisdictions. 204 of those experts are based in the Asian region.

The SIAC has a proven track record in enforcement of awards. SIAC Awards have been enforced by courts in Australia, China, India, Indonesia, the UK, USA and Vietnam amongst other New York Convention countries.

The SIAC received a record new case load of 235 cases in 2012 up by 25% from the new case filings in 2011 and currently handles an active case load of over 550 cases.

The Governing Law

The Arbitration Act (Cap. 10) (AA) and the International Arbitration Act (Cap. 143A) (IAA) are the two relevant statutes which govern the conduct of arbitration in Singapore. Broadly speaking, the AA applies to domestic arbitrations, and the IAA applies to international arbitrations.

This distinction is an important one, as which Act applied will determine the rules by which the arbitration will be conducted (unless the arbitration agreement itself stipulates a set of rules different from that imposed under either Act, in which case, it is the contractually agreed rules that apply). This is because each Act applies a different arbitration regime that will govern the arbitration proceedings. This article will not discuss the differences between the two regimes of arbitration. For the purposes of this article, it is sufficient to note that the regime adopted by the IAA is the UN-CITRAL Model Law on Commercial Arbitration (the Model Law), while the AA is modelled after the English Arbitration Act and its regime is generally not as extensive or as comprehensive as that of the IAA. These two regimes have some significant differences which, depending on the issues that arise during any specific arbitration, can be critical to its conduct and result.

The IAA governs international arbitrations, and under the IAA, whether any particular arbitration is to be regarded as international will depend on whether it meets any one of the following criteria:

At least one of the parties to the arbitration agreement has its place of business in a country other than Singapore;

The place of arbitration, as determined pursuant to the arbitration agreement, is in a country which is neither party's place of business;

The country, in which a substantial part of the obligations of the commercial relationship is to be performed, is a country which is neither party's place of business;

The country, in which the subject matter of the dispute is most closely connected is a country which is neither party's place of business; or

The parties have expressly agreed that the subject matter of the arbitration agreement relates to more than one country.

Unlike the IAA, the AA does not provide any guidelines or rules as to whether it applies to a particular arbitration. It applies to all arbitrations that come under Singapore law, unless that arbitration is one that comes under the ambit of the IAA. In other words, it is, in a sense, the default law applicable to an arbitration that comes under Singapore law. An arbitration in Singapore where the parties both have their place of business in Singapore and the obligations under the commercial relationship are to be performed in Singapore is the quintessential example of an arbitration coming within the ambit of the AA, and which will thus be subject to its arbitration regime.

The IAA does allow parties to "opt out" of the arbitration regime which it provides, by stating that if parties to an arbitration agreement have agreed that any dispute that has arisen or may arise between them is to be settled or resolved otherwise than in accordance with Part II of the IAA or the Model Law, Part II and the Model Law will not apply in relation to the settlement or resolution of the dispute. Conversely, the IAA allows parties in a domestic arbitration to "opt in" to the IAA regime by stipulating that the IAA shall apply.

Parties cannot "opt out" of the AA as such. The arbitration rules stipulated by the AA are regarded as being implied into an arbitration agreement and where parties expressly provide for their own rules to govern the proceedings of an arbitration, these will apply in place of the implied rules stipulated by the AA.

Enforcement of Local Awards in Singapore

Awards made in Singapore, either in respect of a domestic or international arbitration are binding and enforceable. In order to enforce an arbitration award made in Singapore by way of execution proceedings, the following steps must be taken:

An *ex parte* application must be made to the High Court for leave to enforce the award;

The order must be served on the opposing party (the "debtor") who has 14 days to make an application to set aside the order of court;

If an application to set aside the order is made by the debtor, the award shall not be enforced until the application is heard and finally disposed of.

Enforcement of Foreign Arbitral Awards in Singapore

Awards from New York Convention countries

Singapore acceded to the New York Convention of 1958 (the "Convention") on 21 August 1986 and subsequently re-enacted most of its provisions in Part Ⅲ of the IAA. By acceding to this Convention, Singapore is bound to recognize awards made in any other country which is a signatory to the Convention.

Such foreign awards may be enforced by way of a separate action or in the same manner as an award of an arbitrator made in Singapore. Under Section 29(2) of the *IAA*, parties may also rely on such an award as a defence, set off or otherwise in any legal proceedings in Singapore.

In order to enforce a foreign award made in any of the Convention countries, the following steps must be taken:

An application must be made to the High Court for leave. Section 6 of the *Limitation Act* (Cap. 163) states that this application must be made within six years after the award was made.

An affidavit must be filed to exhibit the arbitration agreement and the duly authenticated original award or a copy thereof. If the award is not in English, a certified translation of it in English must be provided as well. Additionally, the affidavit must state the name and usual or last known place of abode or business of the applicant and the person against whom enforcement is sought.

The court hearing the application for enforcement of the foreign award cannot review the case on its merits and can only refuse to grant leave to enforce the award on the grounds stated in Section 31(2) and 31(4) of the IAA.

The court hearing the application will grant leave on an *ex parte* basis only in urgent cases, in which event the order must be served on the debtor forthwith.

For parties seeking to arbitrate in Singapore, it may be of comfort to know that if the counterparty is from a Convention country, any award obtained in Singapore against the counterparty should conversely be enforceable in its country.

Commonwealth Awards

Singapore is a member of the Commonwealth of Nations and, under the *Reciprocal Enforcement of Commonwealth Judgments Act* (the "RECJA") (Cap. 264), recognizes judgments made in the United Kingdom, as well as jurisdictions that are part of the Commonwealth and which Singapore has reciprocal arrangements with for the recognition and enforcement of judgments. The Act lists the countries with which such arrangements exist, and of the 54 countries that are members of the Commonwealth, nine have been listed.

An arbitration award from each of these countries is, generally speaking, enforceable in Singapore under the RECJA, as the Act defines a "judgment" for its purposes as including an award in proceedings on an arbi-

tration. However, the RECJA does stipulate that this is provided the award
has become enforceable in that country in the same manner as a judgment
given in its courts.

It bears noting that a party wishing to enforce an award under the
RECJA has a more onerous procedure to adhere to as compared to the Convention. For instance, the registration of the judgment to aid enforcement
must be done within 12 months as compared to the six-year limitation under
the Convention.

Furthermore, the court hearing the application to register the award
will allow registration of the award only where it is just and convenient to do
so. This involves an exercise of discretion on the part of the court.

From a practical point of view, as a result of the extensive ratification of
the Convention, the procedure relating to enforcement of judgments under
the RECJA has become less important. The RECJA, however, would still
be relevant for non-Convention countries such as Pakistan and Brunei Darussalam.

In disputes where no international element is involved, the debate
whether to arbitrate or litigate may be finely balanced, depending on the circumstances of each case and the reputation and procedures of the local
courts. Parties who are looking for a binding decision on a dispute will
usually have an effective choice between a national court and domestic arbitration.

However, it is advisable that in international disputes involving large
commercial bodies, arbitration may be preferable. The advantages of
arbitration such as flexibility, privacy of proceedings, ability to choose an
arbitration tribunal to hear all disputes arising from a particular transaction
and wide enforceability of award are likely to suit large multinational
entities; while drawbacks such as higher cost and longer period of resolution
are less likely to be vital considerations.

In choosing to arbitrate, parties will have a choice whether to pursue an
institutional arbitration or an *ad hoc* one. If an *ad hoc* arbitration is chosen,
there is again a choice of whether to specifically draft the procedural rules
governing the arbitration from scratch or to adopt an existing set of rules

like the UNCITRAL Rules.

Recent Case of Judgment From PRC

The Singapore High Court has recently made a landmark ruling in what is believed to be the first instance of a Singapore court enforcing a judgment from the People's Republic of China (PRC).

The plaintiff, Giant Light Metal Technology (Kunshan) Co. Ltd (GLMT), sought to enforce an award from the PRC in a Singapore court against a Singapore-based company. Upon considering the circumstances, the court decided to allow GLMT's application.

This case concerns the recognition and enforcement of a judgment obtained from the Suzhou Intermediate Court, Jiangsu Province, in the People's Republic of China (the PRC Court) dated 16 December 2010 (the PRC Judgment). The PRC Judgment relates to a claim by GLMT that two generator sets purchased from the defendant, Aksa Far East Pte. Ltd. (Aksa Singapore), contrary to the agreement between the parties, (a) were not brand new; (b) did not originate from England, UK; and (c) were incapable of use. The claim before the PRC Court was against Aksa Singapore, as well as Shanghai Yates Genset Co. Ltd. (Shanghai Yates) which was a sub-distributor of Aksa Singapore in China at the relevant time.

It bears noting that judgments from the People's Republic of China are not registrable under the *Reciprocal Enforcement of Foreign Judgments Act* (Cap. 265, 2001 Revised Edition) for enforcement in Singapore. A claimant would have to file a fresh claim against a Singapore-based entity before the Singapore court for recovery of the Chinese judgment sum or commence fresh proceedings before the Singapore Court on the claim.

This is the first time a PRC judgment has been recognized and enforced in Singapore after a full trial. It means that investors who do business with Singapore counterparts who conduct business in China have the comfort of knowing that a judgment from the Chinese courts can be enforced here.

The author's submission is that Singapore judiciary preparedness to enforce a judgment from China is a fresh approach that Singapore is departing from its common law bias and would help build its reputation as an arbitral and dispute resolution in Singapore. It highlights the importance of taking proper legal advice as to (a)how Singapore companies structure their business in China and (b)their participation in legal proceedings before the Chinese courts. This judgment may even have wider implications for companies doing business overseas as well, not just in China. It would clarify the position on the applicable test to apply in determining whether a Singapore company can be said to have maintained a presence in an overseas jurisdiction for the purposes of recognition and enforcement of a judgment emanating out of the overseas jurisdiction.

Conclusion

Singapore being a common law country with a comprehensive legal framework and heavily adapted internationally accepted practices has advantages as a suitable lex arbiter for arbitration proceedings to meet the challenges of CAFTA.

Bibliography

［1］ Sheng Lijun, *China-ASEAN Free Trade Area: Origin, Developments and Strategic Motivations*, ISEAS Working Paper: International Politics & Security Issues Series No. 1, 2003.

［2］ Alyssa B. Greenwald, The ASEAN-China Free Rrade Area (ACFTA): A Legal Response to China's Economic Rise? *Duke Journal of Comparative and International Law*, 2006.

［3］ Sarah Y. Tong & Catherine Chong, *China-ASEAN Free Trade Area in 2010: A Regional Perspective*, East Asian Institute Background Brief No. 519.

越南商事仲裁法概述

Nguyen Phuoc Bao Tri [*]

陈希 译

摘要 本文提供给读者一个与中越协议相一致的越南商事仲裁法概述，该商事仲裁法旨在在争端解决过程中完善仲裁机制以保护投资者。

关键词 商事仲裁法 投资 中国—东盟自由贸易区 越南国际仲裁中心 外国裁决

中国—东盟自由贸易协定法律框架

2002年，东盟国家与中华人民共和国高层代表在柬埔寨金边签署了《全面经济合作框架协议》。该框架协议在加强各方之间的交易关系方面是基本的法律基础和结构。协定建立的中国—东盟自由贸易区（CAFTA）将为下一个10年做准备。

中国—东盟自由贸易区对各成员承诺的特定目标可简短地罗列如下：

1. 巩固和加强缔约国之间的经济合作、贸易和投资；

2. 逐步实现自由化，鼓励货物与服务贸易，并建立透明的、自由和便利的投资机制；

3. 扩大新的领域，发展恰当的措施以加强成员之间的经济合作；

4. 为经济一体化创造便利条件，对东盟新成员更加有效，并缩小成员间经济发展的差距。

在这份框架协议的基础上，东盟国家与中国在2004年11月协商签订了附关税减让表的货物贸易协定，以在2010年建立一个货物贸易自由区。对于包括柬埔寨、老挝、缅甸和越南在内的东盟新成员，这些国家和中国同意在对

---

* 中国法学会 中国—东盟法律研究中心研究员。

自贸区的承诺上放慢脚步,相应的,越南将在 2015 年开放其市场。

除了蓬勃发展的中国—东盟新区域经济,仲裁体系也应当作为争端解决的基本手段在协定中予以考虑。由于速度和成本的优势,投资者认为仲裁是解决法律争端的更好的办法,也是大量争端解决的更优路径。就越南仲裁体系而言,中国和越南在 1998 年签订了民刑事项的法律互助协定。尤其是,过去 20 年越南法律制度改革所取得的进步:门户开放(Doi Moi)政策的发展吸引了更多的外国投资,并形成了一个在透明的法律机制下保护外国投资者权利的法律体系。

越南在投资方面的国际义务

越南在逐渐改变自身投资法律和管理体系的同时,越南政府旨在推进国际义务一体化以对投资提供更好的发展与保护。越南已经成为多个双边和多边投资协定的成员,这些协定也已成为越南发展和保护外国投资的国内法律框架的一个部分。

在中国—东盟自由贸易区法律框架建立之前,越南和中国已经签订了上述协定,其中第二条规定了对投资的法律保护:

1. 成员方公民在其他成员方领土内享有与该成员方公民同样的个人与财产权的法律保护,并有权提起或者参与诉讼。

2. 本条第一段所规定的同样适用于作为适合当事人参与司法程序的在任意一个成员方境内依据其国内法成立的法人和其他机构。

相应的,中国和越南投资者可将争端提交法庭或者其他有权的机构,如仲裁庭。因此,协定第一条规定了判决和仲裁裁决应在成员方境内被承认的范围。由此,仲裁在中国和越南逐渐成为在争端解决方面更为流行的方式,这也使两国的仲裁中心得以发展。

在越南法律体系下外国投资争端仲裁的法律认可

越南规制外国投资最基本最重要的法律是越南投资法。第十二条规定了争端解决的方式:

1. 与在越南投资活动相关的纠纷将根据法律的规定,通过协商、和解、仲裁或诉讼解决。

2. 国内投资者之间或国内投资者与越南国家管理机构之间发生的与在越

南领土上的投资活动相关的纠纷，将通过越南仲裁或者诉讼解决。

3.一方是外国投资者或外资企业或外国投资者之间发生的纠纷，可通过下述机构或者组织之一解决：

(1)越南法院；

(2)越南仲裁；

(3)外国仲裁；

(4)国际仲裁；

(5)由纠纷各方协商成立的仲裁。

4.国外投资者与越南国家管理机关之间发生的与在越南领土上的投资活动相关的纠纷，可通过越南仲裁或越南法院解决，除非国家管理机关与外国投资者之间签订的合同或越南作为成员的国际条约中另有规定。

对于外国法的查明，越南仲裁机构与外国仲裁机构和法庭审判一起作为解决纠纷的手段。因此，外国投资者对于在当地仲裁或者在外国仲裁有自由裁量权。

除了以上条款，越南国民大会在 2010 年通过了新的商业仲裁法，并于 2011 年 1 月 1 日生效。通过仲裁中心解决商业纠纷相比将纠纷提交法院来说，更快也更加有效。

越南国际仲裁中心

根据越南社会主义共和国总理 1993 年 4 月 28 日发布的第 204 号决议，越南国际仲裁中心在越南工商业联合会建立。决议以合并外国贸易仲裁委员会(1963 年建立)和海事仲裁委员会(1964 年建立)为基础。越南国际仲裁中心对于由商业活动引起的纠纷有管辖权。作为仲裁管理机构，越南国际仲裁中心旨在为成员提供公平与透明。

在越南国际仲裁中心网站上，成员可获得越南国际仲裁中心的仲裁规则，规则适用于所有由商业活动引起的纠纷的解决：

1.成员同意选择越南国际仲裁中心以及(或者)其仲裁规则来解决纠纷；

2.成员同意选择越南国际仲裁中心来解决纠纷，但不适用其任何仲裁规则。

对于有涉外因素的纠纷，成员可自由选择仲裁过程中适用的语言。若没有任何协议选择语言，则适用越南语。成员可要求中心提供翻译，但费用自付。

要理解越南的仲裁体系,下面将简单介绍越南法律体系以了解保护外国投资的仲裁管理法。

越南法律体系的基本框架

越南法律体系以共产主义法律理论和法国民法为基础。换句话说,越南法律体系与大陆法系相似,根据国民大会颁布的法具有成文法的层级结构:

第二条　法律文本体系

1.宪法,国民大会颁布的法律和条例。

2.国民大会常务委员会的条例和决议。

3.国家总统的命令和决定。

4.政府的法令。

5.总理的决定。

6.最高人民法院法官委员会的决议以及终审法院首席法官的通告。

7.最高人民检察院检察长的通告。

8.部委一级机构的部长或负责人的通告。

9.国家审计长的决定。

10.国民大会常务委员会或政府和社会政治组织的中心办公室联合决议。

11.最高人民法院首席大法官和最高人民检察院检察长的联合通告,部长或部委一级机构和最高人民法院首席大法官,最高人民检察院检察长联合通告;部委一级机构的部长或者负责人的联合通告。

12.人民议会和人民委员会的法律文件。

对于以上条款,商业仲裁法为法律的最高层级,规定了商业仲裁的管辖权,仲裁的形式,仲裁机构和仲裁员,仲裁规则和程序,成员在仲裁程序中的权利、义务和责任,仲裁活动中的法院判决,在越南的涉外仲裁的组织和操作,以及仲裁裁决的执行。

越南商业仲裁法的一般条款

商业仲裁法的主要特点如下:

仲裁员的任命

包括外国国籍的仲裁员都可以被任命为仲裁员并且加入仲裁中心小组,只要满足以下标准:

第二十条　仲裁员的标准

1.满足以下所有标准的可成为仲裁员:

a.具有民法规定的完全民事行为能力;

b.具有大学学位以及至少五年的专业领域工作经验;

c.特定情形下,拥有高度专业资质和大量实践经验的专家,即使不满足本款 b 项,也可成为仲裁员。

2.满足第一款所有条件但具有以下任何一项情形的将不可成为仲裁员:

a.现任法官,检察官,调查、执法人员和人民法院、人民检察院、调查机关或判决执法机构的公务员;

b.被控告者,被告,服刑人员或曾经服刑但犯罪记录尚未免除的人。

3.仲裁中心可以规定比本条第一款更严的仲裁员标准。

法律的选择

在越南仲裁决定了纠纷是否属于"涉外的"或者"本国的"。在越南民法中,涉外因素存在于:

至少一方为外国;

至少一方为越南国籍的海外机构;

设立或者变更的基础是外国法或者由外国引起或者其中涉及的财产在国外。

因此,可适用于纠纷解决的商事仲裁法清晰地规定了:

第十四条 争端解决适用的法律

1.不具有涉外因素的纠纷,仲裁委员会应适用越南争端解决法。

2.具有涉外因素的纠纷,仲裁委员会应当适用由当事方选择的法律。当事方没有协议选择的,仲裁委员会应当决定适用其认为最恰当的法律。

3.如果越南法律或者当事方选择的法律对所争议事项没有具体规定,仲裁委员会可以适用国际争端解决惯例,只要该惯例或者适用该惯例不会损害越南法的基本原则。

语　　言

对于不具有涉外因素的纠纷,仲裁程序中所用的语言为越南语。除非至少争议一方为外国投资企业,争议一方不能使用越南语的,可以用翻译。

对于具有涉外因素的纠纷或者至少一方为外国投资企业的,当事方应当达成仲裁所适用的语言协议。如果没有这样的协议,仲裁委员会应当决定使用何种语言。

临时救济

商事仲裁法规定,外国仲裁机构的分支机构可在越南设立,由此提高竞争力并为仲裁者提供更多选择。但是,目前在越南没有外国仲裁机构。

对商事仲裁法的反思

商事仲裁法对于将越南经济融入国际经济具有重要意义。越南法学界认为商事仲裁法提升了商事仲裁的竞争力。其他法律也允许通过仲裁来解决纠纷以避免与其他法律的冲突。如投资法就可以规定允许仲裁解决与投资有关的投资者之间的纠纷。

商事仲裁法采用国际惯例以尊重成员方选择仲裁作为纠纷解决的手段的协定。商事仲裁法第十六条规定的仲裁条款与 1985 年 6 月 21 日美国国际贸易法委员会通过的国际商事仲裁示范法具有相同的形式。

在旧法中,如果仲裁协议中没有确定或者没有清晰地确定特定的争端解决仲裁机构,并且当事方也没有达成额外的协议,那么该仲裁协议将被视为无效。新的商事仲裁法获得了巨大进步,允许案件申诉方选择合适的仲裁机构。这使得不足够明确的仲裁协议仍然有效。

此外,法庭对推动仲裁活动起到很大作用。新法在法院支持仲裁活动方面规定得更加具体了:仲裁员的任命、临时仲裁庭的建立、与无效仲裁协议有关的诉求作出决定的仲裁员的变更、对不可执行的仲裁裁决的解决、对与仲裁庭权力范围有关的诉求的解决、对适用禁令救济作出决定以及对仲裁裁决的撤销作出决定。

通过对新法的简单回顾,越南国际仲裁中心逐渐成为外国投资者仲裁机构的选择之一。在过去的十年里,越南仲裁员和法院在涉及外国公司和越南合伙人的交易案件上并不受欢迎。律师通常建议选择新加坡国际仲裁中心或国际商会仲裁,因为他们对合同买卖中的争端解决条款最为熟悉。然而,新的商事仲裁法将使得越南国际仲裁中心对在外国投资者与本国企业之间的纠纷中在越南境内的外国资产的保护起到重要作用。

越南承认和执行外国仲裁裁决的一般原则

中国和越南分别在 1987 年和 1995 年成为纽约公约的成员。因此,根据公约第三条,适合的越南职权机构应当在当事一方就越南现行法律要求的特定条件和规定请求承认和执行时执行中国仲裁裁决。

具体的程序如下:

1.提交仲裁裁决承认和执行申请书;

2.执行国适合职权机构对该仲裁裁决承认和执行的决定；

3.适合执行人员或者判决执行机构对仲裁裁决的执行。

当然,公约也规定了,不是所有有效的外国仲裁裁决都会被承认和执行。公约第五条规定了职权机关拒绝承认和执行外国仲裁裁决的原因。如果一方能够提出以下证据,则职权机关可能拒绝承认和执行外国仲裁裁决:

1.仲裁协议当事方在所适用法律下为无行为能力人,或者根据当事方所适用的法律,该仲裁协议无效;

2.仲裁裁决被诉方没有给出适当的仲裁员任命指示,或者在仲裁过程中没能出席;

3.仲裁裁决裁定了非仲裁协议书中的内容,或者仲裁裁决包含了仲裁协议书范围以外的事项的裁决。

4.仲裁机构的组成或者仲裁程序不符合当事方的协议,或者该协议不符合仲裁所在地的法律;

5.裁决未在当事方之间产生约束力,或者根据该裁决所作出的适用的法律已被当地适合机关中止或暂停。

而执行国适合职权机关唯一的自由裁量权即可以决定:

1.该争议主要事项依据执行国法律不能通过仲裁解决纠纷;

2.该仲裁裁决的执行会有悖于执行国的公共政策。

根据越南法,自越南加入纽约公约,国民大会通过民事诉讼法已将公约视为国内法用以规范外国仲裁裁决被越南的承认和执行。

外国仲裁裁决在越南承认和执行的程序和条件

根据越南法的规定,负责承认和执行裁决的适合机关有以下几个:

1.司法部

2.人民法院

3.民事判决执法当局

如前所述,依据法律,越南当局无权暂停裁决,只有决定是否承认或执行的权利。并且,承认和执行的程序不应损害纽约公约的规定,可按照如下方式:

1.向司法局提交承认与执行外国仲裁裁决的申请,随附符合民事诉讼法

第三百六十四条所规定的信息^①,包括第三百六十五条规定的附件^②;

2.申请书提交后 7 天内,司法局应当将文件移交越南人民法院(民事诉讼法第三百六十六条^③)。法院的权限应当根据民事诉讼法第三十四条和第三十五条确定。依据这些规定,适格人民法院应当由以下条件决定:

(1)第三十四条规定管辖法院应当是省级人民法院。

----

① 第三百六十四条 认可和批准在越南执行外国仲裁决定的申请书

1.认可和批准在越南执行外国仲裁决定的申请书必须送达越南司法部且必须包括下列主要内容:

(1)执行人、执行人在越南的合法代理人的姓名、居住地址或工作地址,如果执行人是机关组织的则必须有该机关组织的详细名称和主要办事处地址;

(2)被执行人的姓名、居住地址或工作地址,如果被执行人是机关、组织的则必须有该机关、组织的详细名称和主要工作单位地址;如果被执行人是在越南没有居住地或工作地的个人,或者被执行人是在越南没有办事处的机关组织,则在申请书中要详细注明有财产的地点和在越南执行外国仲裁决定相关的各类财产;

(3)执行人的申请。

2. 如果申请书是用外文书写的,则必须附带经过公证、证实是合法的越南语译文。

② 第三百六十五条 申请书附带的证件、资料

1.申请书附带的证件和资料是越南已经缔结或参加的国际条约规定的证件、资料。如果国际条约没有规定或没有相关的国际条约,申请书则须附带外国仲裁决定的合法复印件;各方依照相关国家的法律规定可以审理的仲裁方式对审理可能或已经发生的争执的仲裁协议的合法复印件。

仲裁协议可以是已经签订的合同中的条款或争执发生后各方签订的单独的仲裁协议。

2.如果申请书和附带的证件、资料是用外文写的,则须带经过公证、证实是合法的越南语译文。

③ 第三百六十六条 将卷宗送达法院

1.从收到申请书以及附带的证件和资料之日算起的 7 日内,司法部依照本法第三十四条、第三十五条的规定将卷宗送达给有审理权的法院。

2.如果司法部将卷宗送达给法院后又收到外国职能机关的通知称正在审核撤销或已经撤销、停止执行外国仲裁决定,司法部要立即以文书形式向法院通报。

(2)第三十五条第二款(e)项①规定省级人民法院或者集中管理城市的人民法院对此类案件具有管辖权。

(3)自收到司法部移送文件之日起的 3 个工作日内,法院应当接受案件并通知法院已收到裁决承认与执行的申请。

(4)自接受案件之日起两个月内,或最长可延长两个月,法院应当裁决:

(a)暂时中止处理申请;

(b)中止处理申请;

(c)会议研究该申请。

(5)如果法院决定举行会议研究该申请,则该会议应当在作出举行会议的决定之日起 20 日内举行。

(6)会议上,法院应当组成一个由三名法官组成的委员会,共同决定是否对申请的仲裁裁决予以承认和执行。

如果对申请的仲裁裁决是否予以承认和执行的决定没有提出申诉或异议,那么决定一经作出即生效。因此请求承认外国仲裁裁决的当事方有权要求该仲裁裁决在越南得到执行。

---

① 第三十四条　省、中央直辖市人民法院的权限

1.省、中央直辖市人民法院(下列统称为"省级人民法院")具有依照审程序理下列案件的权限:

(1)本法第二十五条、第二十七条、第二十九条、第三十一条规定的关于民事、婚姻与家庭、经营、商贸、劳动方面的纠纷,本法第三十三条第 1 款规定的属于县级人民法院审理权限的纠纷除外;

(2)本法第二十六条、第二十八条、第三十条、第三十二条规定的关于民事、婚姻与家庭、经营、商贸、劳动方面的申请,本法第三十三条第 2 款规定的属于县级人民法院审理权限的申请除外;

(3)本法第三十三条第 3 款规定的纠纷申请。

2. 如果省级人民法院亲自提审,省级人民法院具有依照一审程序审理本法第三十三条规定的属于县级人民法院审理权限内的民事案件的权限。

第三十五条　属地法院的权限

… …

3.法院按照属地审理民事案件的权限明确如下:

(5)如果递交起诉状的是个人或递交起诉状的人在当地有工作单位,如果递交起诉状的是机关、组织,递交起诉状的人居住地、工作地当地法院具有审理申请不承认外国法院审理的民事、婚姻与家庭、经营、商贸、劳动判决书或裁定书而且申请越南法院不予执行的权限;

根据法律的规定,人民法院应当决定是否承认和执行仲裁裁决。如果一个仲裁裁决在越南得到承认并可以执行,那么法院判决应当由民事判决执法当局依照民事判决执行法执行。

依据《民事判决执行法》第二条第一款(d)项①的规定,已被承认并可以执行的裁决应当由民事判决执法当局执行。

依据《民事判决执行法》第三十五条第二款(c)项②的规定,裁决应由法院承认和执行。执行裁决的民事判决执法当局应当是适合的民事判决执法部门。

依据2009年7月13日政府通过的第58号法令(No. 58/2009/ND-CP)第三十三条,民事判决执法机构应当保留申请方支付的用于裁决执行的费用的3%。③

依据《民事判决执行法》第三十条的规定,④判决债权人自承认与执行仲裁裁决决定作出之日起五年内,有权要求民事判决执法机构执行该裁决。截

---

① 第二条

(d)已被承认并允许越南法院在越南执行的外国法院的民事判决和裁决,以及外国仲裁裁决……

② 第三十五条 判决执行的权限

……

2.省级民事判决执行机构有权执行以下判决和裁决:

c.外国法院的判决和裁决、越南法院承认并可以执行的外国仲裁裁决;

③ 第三十三条

1.每一次的执行费用是实际数额或者价值资产的3%,但不超过2亿越南盾。

如果法院没有宣布资产的价值或者做类似的声明,则该价值不再适用因为在收取该笔费用时,变化已经超过了市场价格的20%。费用收取机构应当对资产进行评估以确定适当的执行费用。评估的费用应当由民事判决执法机构从保留的执行费用中支取。

④ 第三十条 限制请求判决强制执行章程

1.从判决或裁定生效五年内,判决的债权人或者债务人可以请求有资格的民事判决执行机关签发判决强制执行决定。如果判决或裁定的义务履行有时间限制,五年的期限可以从义务到期时起算。

如果判决或裁定规定分期履行,五年的期限适用于每个期间并且从义务到期时起算。

2.如果法律规定的判决强制执行推迟或延期,则推迟或延期的期限不算入请求判决强制执行期间,除非判决的债权人允许债务人推迟或延期判决的强制执行。

3.如果判决强制执行的请求者可以证明由于客观阻碍或不可抗力不能在规定的期间内提出请求,则客观阻碍或不可抗力存在的期间不算入请求判决执行的限制当中。

止日期过后的执行申请将不被受理。

在越南执行外国仲裁裁决的实践

依据法律的规定,裁决在越南得到承认和执行后,具体的执行过程与其他越南境内法院的判决和决定执行过程类似。

依据《民事判决执行法》第四十四条第二款和第四十五条第一款的规定①,判决或者仲裁裁决的债务人可以在一个月内向债权人支付债务。如果债务人通过一些方式试图延迟支付或者不支付其债务,那么该支付期可延长最多五个月。

总　　结

越南认为通过更优的仲裁立法以鼓励外国投资和成为国际商事仲裁地是必要的。新的商事仲裁法给予了外国投资者在解决与当地企业纠纷方面更多的信心。尤其是新的商事仲裁法与国际协议和公约(纽约公约)相符,这使得越南和中国步入了又一个十年的合作期。强大的法律框架协议巩固了中国—东盟自由贸易区下中国和东盟的一体化。

---

① 第四十四条

……

2. 在判决执行决定发布之日起或者收到判决债权人检定要求之日起10日内,执行者应当进行检定。除非执行适用紧急措施的决定,检定不得延迟。

检定必须书面备份,随附街道人口四分之一的负责人、人民委员会主席、市镇一级警察局长或者进行检定的机构或组织负责人的检定证书。检定记录必须完整反映检定结果。

第四十五条

1. 判决的自愿执行期限为判决债权人收到执行决定之日或者被适当通知之日起15日。

An Overview of Law on Commercial Arbitration in Vietnam

Nguyen Phuoc Bao Tri *

Abstract   This paper provides an overview of law on commercial arbitration in Vietnam in conjunction with agrement in which Vietnam and China entered into in order to protect investors by promoting the arbitral mechanism in resolving the dispute.

Keywords: Law on Commercial Arbitration; Investment; CAFTA; VIAC; Foreign Award.

Legal Framework of China-ASEAN Free Trade Agreement

In 2002, ASEAN countries and People's Republic of China by their high representatives entered into the Framework Agreement on Comprehensive Economic Cooperation in Phnom Penh, Cambodia. This Framework Agreement is the fundamental legal foundation and structure to strengthen the relationship in trading among parties. As the result, the establishment of Chian-ASEAN Free Trade Area (CAFTA) was designed for the next period of 10 years.

CAFTA can be in short listed out with certain objectives for the direction of parties on schedule of commitments as follows:

To consolidate and strengthen the economic cooperation, trade and investment between the signatory countries;

---

* Researcher of China-ASEAN Legal Research Center.

To gradually liberalize and encourage trade in goods and services as well as create a transparent investment regimes, liberal and facilitated;

To expand the new fields and develop appropriate measures in order to promote economic cooperation between parties; and

To create convenient conditions for the economic integration to be more effective in respect of new member of ASEAN and narrowing gap of economic development between parties.

On the basis of the Framework Agreement, the ASEAN countries and China have negotiated and signed the agreement on trade in goods in November 2004 with the schedule of tariff reduction to establish a free trade area of goods in 2010. In respect of new member of ASEAN including Cambodia, Laos, Myanmar and Vietnam, these countries and China agreed on the slower route in the commitment of CAFTA; accordingly, Vietnam will open its market in 2015.

Beside the emerging new regional economy of ASEAN and China, the arbitral system should be considered parallelly for an agreement as the foundational instrument for CAFTA in settling any dispute arises between parties. As the better means for investors to resolve legal disputes due to speed and cost, the arbitration remains a superior venue to resolve the vast majority of legal disputes. From the perspective of Vietnam's arbitral system, China and Vietnam signed an agreement on mutual legal assistance on civil and criminal issues in 1998 (the "Agreement"). Especially, the progress of reforming legal system of Vietnam in the past 20 years after the promotion of Doi Moi (Open Door) Policy has led to the greater foreign investment and a legal system ensuring the right of foreign investor to be protected under a transparent legal mechanism.

Vietnam's International Obligation on Investment

With Vietnam's gradually change in its own legal and regulatory system on foreign investment, Vietnamese Government is moving toward to the integration of international obligation in order to provide better promotion and protection of investments. Vietnam has already become a party of several bilateral and multilateral investment agreements. And these agreements form an integral part of the country's legal framework for the promotion and protection of foreign investment in Vietnam.

Before the establishment of the legal framework of CAFTA, Vietnam and China already signed Agreement as mentioned above in which Article 2 provides the legal protection stated as follows:

"1. Citizens of the Contracting Party shall enjoy in the territory of the other Contracting Party for the legal protection of personal and property rights as citizens of the other Contracting Party and have the right contacting and performing actions, proceedings before the courts and other competent authorities of civil and criminal the other Contracting Party in accordance with the conditions of the other Contracting Party for its citizens.

2. The provisions of paragraph 1 of this Article shall also apply to legal persons and other organizations that can participate in judicial proceeding as the concerned person is established in the territory of either Contracting Party under the provisions of the law of that country. "

Accordingly, Chinese and Vietnamese investors can bring the dispute to not only the court but also other competent authorities such as arbitral court. Therefore, Article 1 of this Agreement provides the scope that the judgments and arbitral awards shall be recognized in either Contracting Parties' territory. As the result, arbitration in China and Vietnam gradually becomes more popular in settling the disputes which have lead to the development of arbitral center in both countries.

Legal Recognition of Arbitration of Foreign Investment Disputes in Vietnamese Legal System

The basic and most important law regulating foreign investment in Vietnam is the Law on Investment in Vietnam. Its Article 12 provides the resolution for legal dispute as follows:

"Article 12 Dispute Resolution

1. Any dispute relating to investment activities in Vietnam shall be resolved through negotiation and conciliation, or shall be referred to

arbitration or to a court in accordance with law.

2. Any dispute as between domestic investors or as between a domestic investor and a State administrative body of Vietnam relating to investment activities in the territory of Vietnam shall be resolved at a Vietnamese court or arbitration body.

3. Any dispute to which one disputing party is a foreign investor or an enterprise with foreign owned capital, or any dispute as between foreign investors shall be resolved by one of the following tribunals and organizations:

(a) A Vietnamese court;

(b) A Vietnamese arbitration body;

(c) A foreign arbitration body;

(d) An international arbitration body;

(dd) An arbitration tribunal established in accordance with the agreement of the disputing parties.

4. Any dispute between a foreign investor and a State administrative body of Vietnam relating to investment activities in the territory of Vietnam shall be resolved by a Vietnamese court or arbitration body, unless otherwise provided in a contract signed between a representative of a competent State body of Vietnam with the foreign investor or in an international treaty of which the Socialist Republic of Vietnam is a member. "

In light of the legal statement of Foreign Law, Vietnamese arbitration bodies and foreign arbitration bodies are suggested as instruments together with the legal proceeding at court to settle the dispute. Therefore, the foreign investors are in their discretion to resolve dispute either by local arbitration or foreign arbitration in accordance with parties' contractual consensus.

Beside the above provisions, the National Assembly of Vietnam in 2010 approved new Commercial Arbitration Law which took effect from January 1, 2011. Resolving commercial disputes via an arbitration center is a faster and more effective way of addressing disputes rather than taking the matter to court where it risks being delayed.

Vietnam International Arbitration Center

The Vietnam International Arbitration Center at the Vietnam Chamber of Commerce and Industry (the "VIAC") was established under the Decision No. 204/TTg dated 28 April 1993 issued by the Prime Minister of the Socialist Republic of Vietnam on the basis of merging the Foreign Trade Arbitration Committee (established 1963) and the Maritime Arbitration Committee (established 1964). The VIAC has jurisdiction over disputes arising from commercial activities among businesses. As an institution administering arbitration, VIAC is committed to complete impartiality and transparency in all that it does for parties.

On VIAC's website, parties can access to the rules of arbitration of the Vietnam International Arbitration Center at the Vietnam Chamber of Commerce and Industry that shall apply to resolution of all disputes arising from commercial activities, where:

The parties agree to choose the Vietnam International Arbitration Center and/or its rules of arbitration to resolve the dispute; or

The parties agree to choose the Vietnam International Arbitration Center to resolve the dispute, but fail to choose any other rules of arbitration.

As for arbitration of a dispute involving a foreign element, the parties are free to agree on the language to be used in the arbitral proceedings. In the absence of any agreement by the parties to that effect, the language shall be Vietnamese. The parties may require the Center to provide interpreter and shall pay fees thereof.

To understand the arbitral system in Vietnam, the Vietnamese legal system should be briefly discussed in order to look at the governing laws of arbitration having effect on the protection of foreign investment.

Basic Structure of Vietnam Legal System

Vietnamese legal system is based on the communist legal theory and

French civil law. In other words, Vietnamese legal system is similar to the continental legal system with the hierarchy of legal documents and complies with law on the promulgation of legal documents of the National Assembly as follows:

"Article 2. System of Legal Documents

1. Constitution, laws and resolutions of the National Assembly.

2. Ordinances and resolutions of the Standing Committee of the National Assembly.

3. Orders and decisions of the State President.

4. Decrees of the Government.

5. Decisions of the Prime Minister.

6. Resolutions of the Justices Council of the Supreme Peoples Court and circulars of the Chief Justice of the Supreme Peoples Court.

7. Circulars of the President of the Supreme Peoples Procuracy.

8. Circulars of Ministers or Heads of Ministry-equivalent Agencies.

9. Decisions of the State Auditor General.

10. Joint resolutions of the Standing Committee of the National Assembly or the Government and the central offices of socio-political organizations.

11. Joint circulars of the Chief Justice of the Supreme Peoples Court and the President of the Supreme Peoples Procuracy; those of Ministers or Heads of Ministry-equivalent Agencies and the Chief Justice of the Supreme Peoples Court, the President of the Supreme Peoples Procuracy; those of Ministers or Heads of Ministry-equivalent Agencies.

12. Legal documents of Peoples Councils and Peoples Committees. "

Regarding the above provision, the Law on Commercial Arbitration is the highest level of law which provides for the jurisdiction of commercial arbitration, forms of arbitration, arbitration institutions and arbitrators; arbitration orders and procedures; rights, obligations and responsibilities of parties in arbitral proceedings; courts' jurisdiction over arbitral activities; organization and operation of foreign arbitrations in Vietnam, and enforcement of arbitral awards.

General provisions of Law on Commercial Arbitration in Vietnam

The main features of the Commercial Arbitration Law should be noticed as follows:

Appointment of arbitrators

Arbitrators including foreign nationals are able to be appointed by parties as arbitrators and may be admitted to the panels of arbitration centers as long as the following criteria to be fulfilled:

"Article 20. Criteria of Arbitrators

1. A person who satisfies all the following criteria may act as a arbitrator:

(a) Having the full civil act capacity under the Civil Code;

(b) Possessing a university degree and having at least 5 years work experience in the trained discipline;

(c) In special cases, an expert who has high professional qualifications and much practical experience, though not satisfying the requirement specified at Point b of this Clause, may also be selected as arbitrator.

2. Persons who satisfy all the conditions specified in Clause 1 of this Article but fall into either of the following cases may not act as arbitrators:

a/ Incumbent judges, procurators, investigators, enforcement officers or civil servants of peoples courts, peoples procuracies, investigative agencies or judgment enforcement agencies;

b/ The accused, defendants, persons serving criminal sentences or having served the sentences but having their criminal records not yet remitted.

3. Arbitration centers may set criteria for their arbitrators which are higher than those specified in Clause 1 of this Article."

Choice of law

Arbitration in Vietnam determines the factor of the dispute whether it falls under "foreign related" or "domestic". Under the Vietnam Civil Code, a foreign element exits where:

At least one of the parties is foreign;

At least one of the parties is a Vietnamese national residing overseas; or

The basis for establishment or modification of the relationship is the law of a foreign country or such basis arose in a foreign country or the assets involved in the relationship are located overseas.

Therefore, the applicable laws for the dispute settlement under Law on Commercial Arbitration clearly indicate that:

"Article 14. Applicable Laws for Dispute Settlement

1. For a dispute involving no foreign element, the arbitration council shall apply Vietnamese law for settling the dispute.

2. For a dispute involving foreign elements, the arbitration council shall apply the law selected by the parties. If the parties have no agreement on the applicable law, the arbitration council shall decide to apply a law it sees the most appropriate.

3. When the Vietnamese law or law selected by the parties contains no specific provisions concerning the dispute, the arbitration council may apply international practices for settling the dispute, provided such application or consequence of such application does not contravene the fundamental principles of Vietnamese law. "

Language

For disputes involving no foreign element, the language to be used in arbitral proceedings is Vietnamese, except disputes to which at least one party is a foreign-invested enterprise. When a disputing party cannot use Vietnamese, it may use an interpreter.

For disputes involving foreign elements or disputes to which at least one party is a foreign-invested enterprise, the parties shall reach agreement on the language to be used in arbitral proceedings. If they have no such agreement, the arbitration council shall decide on the language to be used in arbitral proceedings.

Interim Relief

Under the Commercial Arbitration Law, branches of foreign arbitral institutions can be established in Vietnam, thus increasing competitions and the choice for users. However, there are no foreign arbitral institution in Vietnam at the present.

Reflection on the law on commercial arbitration

The Commercial Arbitration Law is seen as important for Vietnam's e-conomic integration into the international community. The legal professional community in Vietnam reflects that the law enlarges the commercial arbitration's competence. Also, other laws are left to be opened to regulate dispute settlement by arbitration to avoid conflict from other laws. For instance the law on investment may have provisions to allow arbitration settlement for disputes between investors that are related to investment.

The Commercial Arbitration Law adopted international practices to respect the agreement between the parties in choosing arbitration as the instrument to settle the dispute. The abitration clauses agreed by parties governed under Article 16 of the Commercial Arbitration Law have the same form as the Model Law on International Commercial Arbitration approved by the United Nations Commission on International Trade Law (UNCITRAL) on June 21, 1985.

Under the old ordinance, if the statement of arbitration agreement fails to specify or specifies unclearly the exact competent arbitration institution to settle the dispute, and later the parties reached no additional agreement, the agreement on arbitration shall be deemed to be invalid. This new law on commercial arbitration makes a considerable improvement and allows for the plaintiff, in that case, having the right to select a competent arbitration institution. This shall cause the agreement on arbitration to remain viable even it is not sufficiently specific.

Furthermore, the court plays bigger role in supporting arbitration activities. The new law covers more specifics on the court's supporting activities during the course of the appointment of an arbitrator, establishment of an *ad hoc* arbitration tribunal, replacement of an arbitrator making decisions on the claims related to invalid arbitration agreements, settlement of unenforceable arbitral awards, settlement of claims related to the power of an arbitral tribunal, making decisions on application of injunctive relief, and making decisions on revocation of arbitral awards.

Pertaining to the brief reflection of new law on commercial arbitration, the trend of VIAC has become more as foreign investors' selection of arbitral institution. In the last 10 years, Vietnamese arbitrators and courts are not favoured in transaction involving foreign companies and Vietnamese partners when dispute arises. Singapore International Arbitration Center (SIAC) or ICC Arbitration is usually adviced to be chosen by lawyers as they are most familiar with the dispute settlement clause in contractual transactions. However, new law on commercial arbitration with its new international arbitral adoption has reasons to expect that VIAC will be important for the protection of foreign assets located in Vietnam in disputes between foreign investors and local enterprises.

General principles for recognition and enforcement of foreign arbitral awards in Vietnam

Both China and Vietnam have been members of the New York Convention(NYC) since 1987 and 1995, respectively. Hence, pursuant to Article 3 of the Convention, the competent Vietnamese authorities shall be responsible for enforcing Chinese arbitral awards in cases where a party to such award lodges a petition requesting it to be recognized and enforced in Vietnam under specific conditions and regulations of the current applicable laws of Vietnam.

Specifically, such proceedings shall take place under the following steps:

Submission of an application to recognize and enforce the arbitral award;

Issuance of a decision by the competent authorities in the enforcing country to recognize and enforce such arbitral award;

Enforcement of such arbitral award by the competent bailiff or judgment enforcement body.

Also, as stated in the Convention, not all valid arbitral awards in a foreign country shall be recognized and enforced in the enforcing country. Article 5 of the NYC provides a list of reasons that may compel the competent authorities to decline the recognition and enforcement of a foreign arbitral award, if the party in which the arbitral award is granted against a respondent (in this case, the debtor) can provide proof of the following:

The parties to the arbitration agreement under applicable law are under an incapacity, or the said arbitration agreement is not valid under the law to which the parties have subjected to it;

The arbitral award debtor was not given proper notice of the appointment of the arbitrator, of the arbitration proceedings, or was otherwise unable to present their case;

The arbitral award deals with a difference not contemplated by or not falling within the terms of the submission to arbitration, or the arbitral award contains decisions on matters beyond the scope of the submission to arbitration;

The composition of the arbitral authority or the arbitral procedure was not in accordance with the agreement of the parties, or such agreement was not in accordance with the law of the country where arbitration took place; or

The award has not yet become binding on the parties, or has been set aside or suspended by a competent authority of the country in which, or under the law of which, that award was made.

Alternatively, at sole discretion of the competent authorities in the enforcing country, such authorities may decide that:

The subject matter of such differences is not capable of settlement by arbitration under the law of the enforcing country; or

The recognition or enforcement of the arbitral award would be contrary to the public policy of the enforcing country.

As a matter of laws of Vietnam, since its accession to the NYC, the National Assembly has nationalized the Convention by the Civil Procedure Code to provide regulations in recognizing and enforcing foreign arbitral awards in Vietnam.

Procedures and conditions for recognizing and enforcing the Arbitral Awards in Vietnam

Pursuant to the Vietnamese laws, the competent authorities of Vietnam in charge of the recognition and enforcement of the award are as follows:

The Ministry of Justice (the "MOJ");

The people's courts; and

The civil judgment enforcement authorities (the "CJE").

As stated, in accordance with the law, the authorities of Vietnam do not have the right to set aside the award, but only the right to decide whether it can be recognized or enforced, or otherwise issue a decision to the contrary. In light of this, the procedure for recognizing and enforcing the award in Vietnam shall not object to or contravene the NYC, and may be set forth in the following manners:

(1) Petitions for recognition and enforcement in Vietnam of foreign arbitral awards must submit an application to the MOJ with the information complying with the regulations as stated in Article 364 of the Civil Procedure Code①, including the attachment pursuant to Article 365② therein;

---

① Article 364. Petitions for recognition and enforcement in Vietnam of foreign arbitral awards.

1. Petitions for recognition and enforcement in Vietnam of foreign arbitral awards must be sent to the Vietnamese Ministry of Justice and contain the following principal details:

a) The judgment creditors' full names and addresses of their residence places or work places or their lawful representatives in Vietnam.

If the judgment creditors are agencies or organizations, their full names and head-office addresses must be fully inscribed.

b) The judgment debtors' full names and addresses of their residence places or work places; if the judgment debtors are agencies or organizations, their full names and head-office addresses must be inscribed; in cases where the judgment debtors being individuals have no residence places or work places in Vietnam or the judgment debtors being agencies or organizations have no head-offices in Vietnam, the petitions must be clearly inscribed with the addresses of the places where exist properties and assorted assets related to the enforcement in Vietnam of the foreign arbitral awards.

c) Requests of the judgment creditors.

② Article 365. Papers, documents accompanying petitions.

1. Accompanied with petitions shall be papers and documents prescribed in international treaties which Vietnam has signed or acceded to. In the cases where the international treaties do not prescribe them or such papers and documents are not available, the petitions must be accompanied by valid copies of the foreign arbitral awards and valid copies of the arbitral agreement among the parties on the resolution of their disputes which may arise or have arisen through arbitration procedures, provided that the laws of the relevant countries stipulate that they can be resolved through such procedures.

The arbitral agreement may be the arbitration terms provided for in the contract, or a separate agreement on arbitration, which has been concluded by the concerned parties after the disputes arise.

2. If the papers and/or documents accompanying the petitions are in foreign languages, their lawfully notarized or authenticated Vietnamese versions must also be sent.

2. Petitions in foreign languages must be accompanied by their Vietnamese versions lawfully notarized or authenticated.

(ii) Seven (7) days from the date of the submission, MOJ shall transfer the documents to the people's court of Vietnam (Article 366 of the Civil Procedure Code ①). The competence of the court shall be defined in accordance with regulations of Articles 34 and 35 of the Civil Procedure Code. Under these regulations, the competent people's court shall be determined by the following conditions:

• Article 34 indicates that the court to be in charge in the matter shall be the people's court at the provincial level; and

---

① Article 366. Transferring dossiers to courts.

1. Within seven days as from the date of receiving the petitions as well as accompanying papers and documents, the Ministry of Justice shall transfer the dossiers to competent courts as stipulated in Articles 34 and 35 of this Code.

2. In cases where the Ministry of Justice has already transferred the dossiers to competent courts but later receives notices from competent foreign agencies saying that they are considering the cancellation of, or have already cancelled or suspended the foreign arbitral awards, the Ministry of Justice shall immediately notify the courts thereof in writing.

• Article 35. 2 (e)^① determines that the jurisdiction of the people's court of provinces

or centrally-run cities shall be in charged of handling the case (the "Court").

(iii) Within three (3) working days from the date of receiving the documents from the MOJ, the court shall accept the case and notify that the court is reviewing the application for the recognition and enforcement of the award;

(iv) From the date of the acceptance of the case, within two(2) months and upon a maximum extension of another two(2) months, the court shall issue a decision to:

(a) Temporarily suspend settling the application;

---

① Article 34. Jurisdiction of the people's courts of provinces or centrally-run cities.

1. The people's courts of provinces or centrally-run cities shall have the jurisdiction to settle the following cases and matters according to first-instance procedures:

a) Civil, marriage and family-related, business, trade or labor disputes prescribed in Articles 25, 27, 29 and 31 of this Code, except for disputes falling under the jurisdiction of the district-level people's courts as provided for in Clause 1, Article 33 of this Code;

b) Civil, marriage and family-related, business, trade or labor requests prescribed in Articles 26, 28, 30 and 32 of this Code, except for requests falling under the jurisdiction of the district-level people's courts as prescribed in Clause 2, Article 33 of this Code;

c) Disputes and requests prescribed in Clause 3, Article 33 of this Code.

2. The provincial-level people's courts shall according to first-instance procedures have the jurisdiction to resolve civil cases and matters falling under the jurisdiction of the district-level people's courts as provided for in Article 33 of this Code, which are taken up by provincial-level people's courts for settlement.

Article 35. Territorial jurisdiction of courts

......

2. Territorial jurisdiction of courts to settle civil matters shall be determined as follows:

e) The courts of the areas where the request senders reside or work, if they are individuals, or where the request senders are headquartered, if they are agencies or organizations, shall have the jurisdiction to settle requests not to recognize foreign courts' civil, marriage and family, business, trade or labor judgments or decisions, which are not required to be enforced in Vietnam.

(b) Suspend settlement of the application; or

(c) Open a meeting to examine the application.

(v) In the case where the court issues a decision to bring the application to a meeting for examination, the meeting is required to take place within 20 days from the date of issuing such decision.

(vi) At the meeting, the court shall be comprised of a commission of three judges, who shall jointly make a decision with respect to the recognition and enforcement of the award.

In the event that the decision to recognize and enforce the foreign award is not appealed or protested, then it shall come into effect from the date of its issuance. Hence, party requested to recognize the arbitral foreign award has the right to request for the enforcement of the award in Vietnam.

Pursuant to the law, the people's court shall be responsible in deciding whether to recognize and enforce the award. In the case that the award is recognizable and enforceable in Vietnam, the execution of the court's decision shall be carried out by the Civil Judgment Enforcement authorities governed by the *CJE Law*.

Pursuant to Article 2.1 (d) of the CJE Law,[1] the award that has been recognized and enforced by the court shall be executed by the Civil Judgment Enforcement Authorities.

In accordance with Article 35.2(c) of the *CJE Law*,[2] the Award shall be recognized and is enforceable by the Court. The competent civil judgment enforcement authorities that shall execute the award will be the competent

---

[1]   Article 2.

d/ Foreign courts' civil judgments and rulings, and foreign arbitral awards, which have been recognized and permitted for enforcement in Vietnam by Vietnamese courts.

[2]   Article 35.2. Competence to enforce judgments

......

2. Provincial-level civil judgment enforcement agencies are competent to enforce the following judgments and rulings:

c/ Judgments and rulings of foreign courts, awards of foreign arbitrations recognized by Vietnamese courts for enforcement in Vietnam.

Civil Judgment Enforcement Department.

Pursuant to Article 33 Decree No. 58/2009/ND-CP passed by the Government dated 13 July 2009, the CJE shall withhold 3% (three percent) over the amount paid by applicant in relation to executing the Award. [①]

Please also note that pursuant to Article 30 of the CJE Law,[②] judgment creditor has five years, from the date of the issuance of the decision to recognize and enforce the award in Vietnam, to request the CJE to execute the award. After this deadline, judgment creditor's application to the CJE

[①] Article 33. Fee scheme, procedures for collecting and submitting, managing and using enforcement fee

1. Enforcement fee is 3% (three percent) of the actual amount or asset value but does not exceed 200 million Vietnam Dong per application for the judgment enforcement.

In the event that the court does not declare the value of the assets or does declare as such, such value is no longer appropriate because the change exceeds 20% in comparison to the market price at the time of collecting the fee. The fee collecting authority shall evaluate the asset to identify the appropriate enforcement fee to be submitted to the judgment creditor. The fee for such evaluation shall be borne by the civil judgment enforcement agency from the reserved enforcement fee.

[②] 8 Article 30. Statute of limitations for requesting judgment enforcement

1. Within 5 years after a judgment or ruling takes legal effect, the judgment creditor and judgment debtor may request a competent civil judgment enforcement agency to issue a judgment enforcement decision.

In case a time limit for fulfilling an obligation is set in the judgment or ruling, the 5-year statute of limitations will be counted from the date the obligation is due.

For judgments and rulings subject to periodical enforcement, the 5-year statute of limitations will apply to each period and be counted from the date the obligation is due.

2. In case of postponement or suspension of judgment enforcement under this Law, the postponement or suspension duration will not be counted into the statute of limitations for requesting judgment enforcement, unless judgment creditors agree to allow judgment debtors to postpone the judgment enforcement.

3. In case the judgment enforcement requesters can prove that he/she is unable to request judgment enforcement within the time limit due to an objective obstacle or a force majeure circumstance, the duration when these objective obstacles or force majeure circumstance exists will not be counted into the statute of limitations for requesting judgment enforcement.

will not be accepted.

Practice in Executing a Foreign Award in Vietnam

As a matter of law, after the award has been recognized and enforced in Vietnam, the execution process for the CJE shall be similar to processes used for other judgments and decisions of the court in Vietnam.

Pursuant to Article 44. 2 and 45. 1 of CJE Law,[1] the judgment or arbitral award debtor is required to voluntarily pay its debts to the creditor within one month. In the event that the debtor tries to delay or void their payment obligations through some means, this time period may be prolonged by up to five (5) months.

Conclusion

Vietnam found that it is necessary to adopt favourable arbitral legislation to encourage foreign investment and to compete as a place for international commercial arbitration. With the new law on commercial arbitration, it gives the foreign investment more confidence in resolving the dispute between foreign investors and local enterprises if there is a case.

---

[1] Article 44. Verification of judgment conditions execution

......

2. Within 10 days after issuing judgment enforcement decisions at their own will or receiving judgment creditors' requests for verification, enforcers shall conduct verification. In case of implementation of decisions on application of provisional urgent measures, verification must be conducted without delay.

The verification must be recorded in writing with the certification of the head of the street population quarter, People's Committee President, commune-level police chief or the head of the agency or organization which has conducted verification. A verification record must fully show verification results.

Article 45. Time limit for voluntary execution of judgments

1. The time limit for voluntary execution of a judgment is 15 days after the judgment debtor receives, or is properly notified of, the judgment of the enforcement decision.

Particularly, Law on commercial arbitration is in conjunction with agreement and international convention(i. e. New York Convention) leading Vietnam and China into the new decade of cooperation in which this is the strong legal framework to underline the integration of China and ASEAN regarding China-ASEAN Free Trade Area.

中国—东盟自由贸易区法律框架下的泰国投资仲裁机构和机制

Ornjira Nithichayanon[*] & Vera Mungsuwan[**]

汪智芳　译

摘要　同许多国家一样,泰国一直鼓励使用替代性纠纷解决(ADR)方式,以便于各方在将其案件提交法院审理之前解决争端。相比于正常的法院诉讼,ADR程序更容易且更方便。并且其被证明是成功的,因为其可以为双方当事人提供更为有利的结果。仲裁作为替代性纠纷解决方式之一在泰国被广泛应用。

关键词　投资仲裁机构和机制　中国—东盟自由贸易区　泰国

泰国位于东南亚的中心,这一点使得其真正地处该地区的心脏地带。该地理位置使得泰国更易进入该地区有活力的市场。这些市场包括泰国本身拥有的6.7亿人的国内消费市场,这一点使泰国成为无论对其本国投资者还是外国投资者而言都是最有吸引力的投资地区之一。

在东盟成员国和中国之间的《全面经济合作框架协议之货物贸易协定》生效之前,泰国已对来自中国和东盟成员国的进口产品的关税税率进行了削减。大部分产品可以自由进口到泰国,同样的,泰国的产品也可以自由出口到中国和所有成员国。这极大地扩大了各成员方国家的贸易和投资规模。

多年来,在《中国—东盟自由贸易区框架协定》的运作下市场扩大和市场准入更加自由,这一点以及政府政策都促进了贸易和投资,在泰国的国内外投

---

[*]　泰国中央知识产权与国际贸易法庭,判例发展与国际事务处,外事关系官员。

[**]　泰国中央知识产权与国际贸易法庭,诉讼处,民事判例整编办公室法律官员。

319

资人数迅速增加。随之而来的投资矛盾和纠纷的数量也在不断增加。

如前所述,本文主要侧重于中国—东盟自由贸易区的法律框架下的泰国投资仲裁机构与机制。本文由两部分组成。第一部分是关于中国—东盟自由贸易区的法律框架下的投资仲裁机构与机制。第二部分将侧重于仲裁解决争端、投资争端仲裁机构及泰国的投资仲裁法律制度。

(一)中国—东盟自由贸易区的法律框架下的投资仲裁机构与机制

东南亚国家联盟和中国之间于 2005 年 1 月 1 日生效的《争端解决机制协议》提供了中国—东盟自由贸易区法律框架下的仲裁机制。本协议详细规定了协商、调解、调停和仲裁等争端解决方式的程序与机制。

第 6 条至第 12 条就仲裁程序与机制规定了以下事项:仲裁员的任命、仲裁庭的组成、仲裁庭的职能、仲裁庭的程序、第三方、程序的中止和终止,最后是建议和裁决的执行。

(二)泰国的投资争端的仲裁解决与仲裁机构及投资仲裁法律制度

在泰国,仲裁主要受仲裁法 2545(2002)的规制。该法大部分遵循了联合国国际贸易法委员会(联合国国际贸易法委员会法)仲裁示范法的标准。仲裁法赋予了仲裁庭广泛的权力以及限定了法院干预仲裁程序的范围。此外,仲裁法申明将依泰国的法律体系执行仲裁裁决和仲裁程序。

在泰国,规制仲裁的另一法律是民事诉讼法。有关仲裁的法律条款为第210 条到 222 条。

泰国有两种类型的仲裁。第一种被称为"法院之内的仲裁",而第二种被称为"法庭之外的仲裁"。

泰国民事诉讼法规定了"法庭之内的仲裁"。该类型的仲裁将由原待审案件的法庭进行。当事人可以约定向一个或多个仲裁员提交争议的所有或部分问题。泰国民事诉讼法规定了选任仲裁员、费用、法院为执行目的而进行的授权等。此外,法院还可以传召证人、管理宣誓或者要求当事方提供文件。

泰国仲裁法 B.E. 2545(2002)规定了"法庭之外的仲裁"。该法规定了达成有效仲裁协议的条件、仲裁程序、文件即信息的传达和交换、程序的中止和终止、适用于仲裁裁决的规则以及仲裁裁决的执行。

不过,上述全部是国内仲裁裁决的强制执行程序。泰国法院还允许执行外国仲裁裁决。根据仲裁法,裁决对双方均有约束力而不论其管辖为何。如果裁决是在泰国作出的,该裁决将由管辖法院执行。但是,如果裁决是由外国法院作出的,泰国法院将只执行依据泰国加入的条约、公约或国际协定而作出的裁决,并只限于泰国同意受这些条约、公约或国际协定约束的程度。因此,由于泰国是 1927 年日内瓦公约和 1958 年纽约关于承认和执行外国仲裁裁决的公约的缔约方,完全或主要在外国作出的仲裁裁决和当事方均为非泰国国籍的仍可由泰国法院根据这些公约执行。

外国仲裁裁决执行的程序与国内仲裁裁决的是一样的,也是由泰国仲裁法规范。然而,为了执行 1927 年日内瓦公约和 1958 年纽约关于承认及执行外国仲裁裁决的公约,该裁决还必须满足这些公约的要求。

除此之外,《仲裁法》第 16 条规定了法院可以为了保护双方当事人的利益而在仲裁程序之前或其中采取临时措施。

泰国有两个主要的国内仲裁机构。第一个是泰国替代性纠纷解决办公室(TAI),其由司法局管理。TAI 是泰国主要的仲裁机构,其作用是促进仲裁程序。TAI 通过在必要时协助选择仲裁员、提供进行仲裁所需的物质和人力资源、提供规范仲裁程序的 TAI 仲裁及调解规则的方式来履行其职能。第二个仲裁服务机构由泰国贸易委员会和泰国国际商会组成。贸易委员会拥有一套规范仲裁程序的仲裁规则。泰国国际商会适用位于巴黎的国际商会颁布的规则。

这两个由不同的顾问委员会监督的仲裁机构都备受尊敬,并且配备了标准的仲裁规则,而且拥有合格的可选任的仲裁员名单。各方可提名外部专业人士为仲裁员。行政费用和仲裁费用都通过这两个仲裁机构收取,且这些费用比许多国际仲裁机构要少得多。

上面提到的只是对泰国仲裁法律制度的简要介绍。它可以适用于任何类型的争议,包括投资争议。

Investment Arbitration Institution and Mechanism in Thailand under the Legal Framework of China-ASEAN Free Trade Area

Ornjira Nithichayanon* & Vera Mungsuwan**

Abstract   Same as in many countries, Thailand has encouraged the use of Alternative Dispute Resolution (ADR) in order to settle the dispute before the parties submitting their cases to be tried by the court. ADR process is much easier and more convenient than normal litigation in court, and has proved to be successful as it could provide the favorable outcomes for both parties. Arbitration is one of the alternative dispute resolution widely used in Thailand.

Keywords   Investment Arbitration Institution and Mechanism; China-ASEAN FTA; Thailand

As Thailand located in the center of Southeast Asia, Thailand is truly at the heart of the region with easy access to the region's dynamic markets, including its own domestic consumer market of 67 million people, making Thailand one of the most attractive investment locations not only to Thai investors but to foreigners as well.

---

*   Court of Intellectual Property and International Trade, Tailand, department of case development and International Affairs, officer of International Relations.
**   Court of Intellectual Property and International Trade, Tailand, department of Suit, officer of Civil Case Reorgnization.

The country's investment policies focus on liberalization and encourage
free trade as a means of improving competitiveness and promoting
sustainable economic growth. Thailand is a party to bilateral, multilateral
and regional investment treaties with various countries, especially with the
member states of the Association of Southeast Asian Nations: Brunei
Darussalam, the Kingdom of Cambodia, the Republic of Indonesia, the Lao
People's Democratic Republic (Lao PDR), Malaysia, the Union of
Myanmar, the Republic of the Philippines, the Republic of Singapore and
the Socialist Republic of Vietnam. The first free trade agreement that
Thailand engaged is the ASEAN Free Trade Area in B. E. 2535 (1992).

In November 2001, Thailand attended the China-ASEAN Summit held
in Bandar Seri Begawan, Brunei Darussalam and has made a decision with
ASEAN member states and the People's Republic of China to adopt a
Framework Agreement on Comprehensive Economic Cooperation between
the Association of Southeast Asian Nations and The People's Republic of
China to establish an China-ASEAN Free Trade Area (China-ASEAN FTA)
within ten years with a desire to strengthen the close economic and trade
relations among the contracting parties. The following year, the Framework
Agreement on Comprehensive Economic Cooperation between ASEAN and
the People's Republic of China has been signed in Phnom Penh, the
Kingdom of Cambodia on the 4th November 2002 which entered into force
on the 1st July 2003. The framework agreement covers economic
Cooperation in every aspect, including trade in goods under the Agreement
on Trade in Goods of the China-ASEAN FTA which entered into force in
January 2005, trade in services under the Agreement on Trade in Services
which entered into effect in July 2007, investment under the Agreement on
Investment which signed in August 2009, and also the dispute settlement
procedures and mechanism under the Agreement on Dispute Settlement
Mechanism entered into force in January 2005[1], which is the main issue this

---

① Chinese. data. sources:. http://fta. mofcom. gov. cn/topic/chinaasean. shtml,
visited. in. November. 2013.

paper will concentrate on.

Prior to the entry into force of the Agreement on Trades in Goods of the Framework Agreement on Comprehensive Economic Cooperation between ASEAN member states and the People's Republic of China, Thailand has reduced the tariff rates on products imported from China and ASEAN member states. Most of the products can be imported to Thailand freely, and likewise, can be exported freely to China and all member states, which result in the expansion of trade and investment within the parties' countries. [1]

Due to the expansion and free access to the market under the Framework of China- ASEAN Free Trade Area along with the Government's policies to promote trade and investment, the number of domestic and foreign investors in Thailand has increased speedily over the years. As a consequence of that, the number of investment conflicts and disputes has also increased.

As stated earlier, this paper mainly focuses on investment arbitration institution and mechanism in Thailand under the legal framework of China-ASEAN Free Trade Area. The paper is divided into two parts. The first part will be about investment arbitration institution and mechanism under the legal framework of China-ASEAN Free Trade Area. The second part will focus on arbitration settlement and arbitration institution of investment dispute and investment arbitration legal system in thailand.

1. Investment Arbitration Institution and Mechanism under The Legal Framework of China-ASEAN Free Trade Area

Arbitration mechanism under the legal framework of China-ASEAN Free Trade Area provided in the Agreement on Dispute Settlement Mechanism between the Association of South east Asian Nations and the

---

[1] Thai. data. sources:. http://www. dft. go. th/Default. aspx? tabid = 161&ctl =. DetailUserContent&·mid=683&. contentID=306, visited. in. November. 2013.

People's Republic of China, which entered into force on the 1th January 2005. This Agreement gives detail on the procedures and mechanism of formal dispute settlement by means of consultation, conciliation, mediation and arbitration.

Arbitration procedures and mechanism can be found in Article 6 to Article 12 regarding the following issues: the appointment of arbitral tribunals, the composition of arbitral tribunals, the functions of arbitral tribunals, the proceedings of arbitral tribunals, third parties, suspension and termination of the proceedings, and lastly the implementation of the recommendations and rulings of the arbitral tribunal.

According to the Article 6, the appointment of arbitral tribunals shall be done if the consultations referred to in Article 4 fail to settle a dispute within 60 days after the date of receipt of the request for consultations or within 20 days after such date in case of urgency. The complaining party may make a written request to the party complained against to appoint an arbitral tribunal.

Under Article 7, the arbitral tribunal shall have three members unless otherwise provided in this Agreement or the parties to the dispute agree. The complaining party shall appoint an arbitrator to the arbitral tribunal within 20 days of the receipt of the request for appointment of the arbitral tribunal under Article 6 and the party complained against shall appoint an arbitrator to the arbitral tribunal within 30 days of its receipt of the request for appointment of the arbitral tribunal under Article 6. Once the complaining party and the party complained against have appointed their respective arbitrators, the parties concerned shall endeavour to agree on an additional arbitrator who shall serve as chair. Article 7 also specified the qualification of a member or chair of the arbitral tribunal. As stated in paragraph 6, any person appointed as a member or chair of arbitral tribunal shall have expertise or experience in law, international trade, other matters covered by the Framework Agreement or the resolution of disputes arising under international trade agreements, and shall be chosen strictly on the basis of objectivity, reliability, sound judgment and independence. Additionally, the chair shall not be a national of any party to a dispute and shall not have his or her usual place of residence in the territory of, nor be employed by, any party to a dispute.

Under Article 8, the function of an arbitral tribunal is to make an objective assessment of the dispute before it, including an examination of the facts of the case and the applicability of and conformity with the Framework Agreement. As for the decision, an arbitral tribunal shall take its decisions by consensus; provided that where an arbitral tribunal is unable to reach consensus, it may take its decision by majority opinion. The decision of the arbitral tribunal shall be final and binding on the parties to the dispute.

Article 9 prescribes the proceedings of arbitral tribunals. It is required that an arbitral tribunal shall meet in closed session. The parties to the dispute shall be present at the meetings only when invited by the arbitral tribunal to appear before it. Regarding the venue for the substantive meetings of the arbitral tribunal, it shall be decided by mutual agreement between the parties to the dispute. The deliberations of an arbitral tribunal and the documents submitted to it shall be kept confidential. After finishing the arbitral process, the arbitral tribunal shall release to the parties to the dispute its final report within 120 days from the date of its composition. In case of urgency, the arbitral tribunal shall aim to issue its report to the parties to the dispute within 60 days from the date of its composition. The final report of the arbitral tribunal shall become a public document within 10 days after its release to the parties concerned.

Under Article 10 regarding the third parties, this provision states that any party having a substantial interest in a dispute before an arbitral tribunal and having notified its interest in writing to the parties to such a dispute, the "third party" shall have an opportunity to make written submissions to the tribunal. These submissions shall also be given to the parties to a dispute and may be reflected in the report of the arbitral tribunal. In case that a third party considers that a measure already the subject of an arbitral tribunal proceeding nullifies or impairs benefits accruing to it under the Framework Agreement, such party may have recourse to normal dispute settlement procedures under this Agreement.

Article 11 concerning about the suspension and termination of the

arbitral tribunal proceedings; where the parties to the dispute agree, the
arbitral tribunal may suspend its work at any time for a period not exceeding
12 months from the date of such agreement. For the termination of
proceedings, the parties to a dispute may agree to terminate the proceedings
of an arbitral tribunal established under this Agreement before the release of
the final report. In addition, before the arbitral tribunal makes its decision,
it may at any stage of the proceedings propose to the parties to the dispute
that the dispute be settled amicably.

The implementation of the recommendations and rulings of the arbitral
tribunal is provided in Article 12 which states that the party complained
against shall inform the complaining party of its intention in respect of implementation of the recommendations and rulings of the arbitral tribunal. If
it is impracticable to comply immediately, the party complained against shall
have a reasonable period of time in which to do so.

After examining through the provisions of arbitration procedures and
mechanism provided in the Agreement on Dispute Settlement Mechanism
between the contracting parties of China-ASEAN FTA, we can see that this
agreement gives the parties many alternative dispute settlement choices and
gives the right to arbitrate claims directly against any party when disputes or
conflicts arising under the Framework Agreement. Additionally, it gives the
parties the freedom to choose any arbitral institution to settle disputes
pursuant to Article 7, which from our point of views; it would certainly
meet the parties to the dispute's satisfaction because most people would
prefer to appoint the arbitrator from their local arbitral institutions rather
than international institutions. Thus, the dispute would definitely be settled
amicably and provide an effective and favorable outcome.

2. Arbitration Settlement and Arbitration Institution of In-vestment Dispute and Investment Arbitration Legal System in Thailand

Arbitration in Thailand is mainly governed by the Arbitration Act B. E.
2545 (2002), of which most parts follow the standards of the UNCITRAL

(United Nations Commission on International Trade Law) as a model law for arbitration. The Arbitration Act gives the arbitral tribunal broad powers and provides only limited scope for court intervention in the arbitration process. [1] In addition, the Arbitration Act addresses the enforcement of arbitration award and the procedural aspects of arbitration within the Thai legal system.

Another law that governs arbitration in Thailand is the Civil Procedure Code. The provisions concerning arbitration can be found in Article 210 to Article 222.

There are two types of arbitration in Thailand. The first one is called "in-court arbitration", and the second one is called "out-of-court arbitration".

The Thai Civil Procedure Code provides the provisions for an "in-court arbitration". This type of arbitration is conducted while a case is pending consideration by a court of first instance. The parties may agree to submit all or part of issues in dispute to one or more arbitrators for settlement. The Thai Civil Procedure Code provides rules for selection of arbitrators, fees, granting an award and filing the award with the court for purposes of execution. In addition, the court may be called upon to facilitate the arbitration by undertaking certain proceedings within its power, including summoning a witness, administering an oath or ordering the production of a document.

The Thai Arbitration Act B. E. 2545 (2002) provides the provisions for an "out-of-court arbitration". [2] According to the Act, the following requirements must be performed for a validity of the arbitration:

Pursuant to Article 11, an arbitration agreement shall be in writing and signed by the parties.

Pursuant to Article 17, the arbitral tribunal shall compose of arbitrators in an odd number. In the case where the parties determine the number of ar-

---

①   Norton Rose Group, Arbitration in Asia Pacific, Thailand January 2010, p. 2.

②   Baker & McKenzie, Dispute Resolution Around the World-Thailand, pp. 16~17.

bitrators in an even number, those arbitrators shall jointly appoint another arbitrator to be the chairperson of the arbitral tribunal.

Pursuant to Article 19, arbitrators shall be impartial and independent and shall have qualifications as specified by the arbitral agreement or, in the case where the parties appoint an institution established to settle disputes by arbitration, as specified by such institution.

Pursuant to Article 37, the award shall be made in writing and signed by the arbitral tribunal. If the arbitral tribunal consists of more than one arbitrator, the signatures of the majority of all members of the arbitral tribunal shall sufficient.

The Arbitration Act prescribes the rules governing the procedure as follows:

Pursuant to Article 29, within the period as agreed upon by the parties or as determined by the arbitral tribunal, the claimant shall state the facts supporting his or her claim, the points at issue and the relief or remedy sought, and the respondent shall state his or her defenses in respect of these particulars, unless the parties have otherwise agreed. In this regard, the parties may submit therewith relevant documents or lists of evidences referring to the documents or other evidences they intend to cite as evidence.

Pursuant to Article 30, the arbitral tribunal shall determine whether to hold hearings orally or in writing, or whether the proceedings shall be conducted on the basis of documents or other evidences.

The arbitral tribunal shall inform the parties, with sufficient advance notice, the date for hearings and inspecting of any objects, places or other documents.

All statements, defenses, requests, documents, or information submitted to the arbitral tribunal by one party shall be delivered to the others. Any expert reports or evidences on which the arbitral tribunal may rely upon in making its award shall also be delivered to the parties.

Pursuant to Article 31, if the claimant fails to deliver his or her statement of claim in accordance with Section 29, the arbitral tribunal must terminate the proceedings.

If the respondent fails to deliver his or her statement of defense, the arbitral tribunal must continue the proceedings. In this regard, the failure to deliver the statement of defense shall not be treated as an admission of the allegations of the claimant.

If any party fails to appear at a hearing or the appointed date or fails to produce any evidence, the arbitral tribunal shall continue the arbitral proceedings and make the award.

The above mentioned are the rules governing the procedure in accordance with the Arbitration Act. However, the parties may agree to use their own rules to govern the process for the arbitrations or they may select institutional rules to govern their arbitration. If the parties do not select a body of rules, the tribunal can conduct the proceedings in any manner it considers appropriate. In practice, if the parties do not select a body of rules, the tribunal is likely to look to an established set of rules as a model such as the rules of the International Chamber of Commerce (ICC) or the Thai Arbitration Institute (TAI)[①] or the provisions provided in the Arbitration Act as stated above. Other jurisdictions also have arbitration schemes which parties in Thailand may contract to use. This is particularly common with joint ventures where a third country is selected as the place of arbitration. International arbitration rules may be used, such as the Arbitration Rules of the International Chamber of Commerce and the *ad hoc* UNCITRAL Arbitration Rules. [②]

Regarding the arbitration awards, according to Article 35 of the Arbitration Act, it is required that the arbitral awards and other orders and rulings must be made by majority votes. If a majority cannot be obtained, the chairman of the arbitral tribunal must solely issue the award, order or ruling. Importantly, the arbitral award must be in writing and signed by the members of the arbitral tribunal or a majority thereof and must clearly state the reasons for the decisions, in order to make the awards to be valid and en-

---

① John King, Sally Wrapson and Kornkiat Chunhakasikarn, Dispute Resolution 2007/08. Volume 2: Arbitration-Thailand, p. 97.

② Baker & McKenzie, Dispute Resolution Around the World-Thailand, p. 18.

forceable.

For the enforcement of the awards, an arbitration decision may be submitted to the court for enforcement. The enforcement proceedings of an "in-court arbitration", and an "out-of-court arbitration" are quite different in some circumstances.

In the case of an in-court arbitration; after rendering an award, an arbitrator or arbitral tribunal is required to file the award with the court regardless of the parties' intentions to comply with its decision. If the court is satisfied with the legality of the award, it will render a judgment in accordance with the award. In the event one party fails to comply with the judgment, the other party can submit a petition to the court to execute the judgment by issuing a writ of execution, in accordance with the Civil Procedure Code of Thailand.

In the case of an out-of-court arbitration award, once the award is rendered by a majority of the members of the arbitral tribunal, the arbitrator's task is complete and the arbitrator is not in a position to submit the award to the court requesting confirmation of its contents. Unless otherwise agreed by the parties, a party may make a request to the arbitral tribunal to correct an error in an award, clarify a specific point in the award or make an additional award, within 30 days of receipt of the award. In addition, a party may apply to the competent court to set aside or revoke the award within 90 days of receipt of the copy of the award. [1] The court may set aside the award if the applicant can prove any of the followings: (Article 40 of the Arbitration Act)

(a) A party to the arbitration agreement is incapacity under the law applicable to that party;

(b) The arbitration agreement is not legally binding under the law to which the parties have agreed upon or, in the case where there is no such agreement, the law of the Kingdom of Thailand;

(c) A party who make the application was not delivered advance notice

---

[1]　Ibid. ,p. 19.

of the appointment of the arbitral tribunal or the hearings of the arbitral tribunal, or was otherwise unable to defend the case in the arbitral proceedings;

(d) The award deals with a dispute not falling within the scope of the arbitration agreement or contains decisions on matters beyond the scope of the submission to arbitration. If the decisions on matters submitted to arbitration could be separated from those not so submitted, only the part of award which contains decisions on matters not submitted to arbitration may be set aside by the court; or

(e) The composition of the arbitral tribunal or the arbitral proceedings was not in accordance with the agreement of the parties or, in the case where there is no such agreement, was not in accordance with this Act;

The court will also set aside an award if either:

The award deals with a dispute not capable of settlement by arbitration under the law.

The recognition or enforcement of the award would be contrary to public order or good morals.

In the event a party refuses to comply with an out-of-court arbitration award, the party seeking enforcement of the award is required to file a request with the competent court within 3 years from the date when the award can be enforced. In the event one of the parties to the arbitration is a Thai government agency, the Thai administrative court is the competent court for purposes of enforcement. [1] Upon receipt of the request, the court will hold an inquiry and give judgment without delay. According to Article 45, the decisions of the Court issues under the Arbitration Act cannot be appealed, except in any of the following circumstances:

(1) The recognition or enforcement of the award is contrary to public order or good morals;

(2) The order or judgment is contrary to the provisions of law relating to public order or good morals;

---

① Ibid.

(3) The order or judgment is not in accordance with the arbitral award;

(4) The judge who has tried the case gave a dissenting opinion in the judgment; or

(5) It is an order on provisional measure under Section 16.

An appeal against an order or judgment under this Act shall be made to the Supreme Court or the Supreme Administrative Court, as the case may be.

As I have stated earlier that the enforcement proceedings of an in-court arbitration, and an out-of-court arbitration are quite different. They are not only different in the enforced proceedings but also different in the governing law. While the enforcement of an out-of-court arbitration award is governed by the Arbitration Act 2002, the enforcement of an in-court arbitration award is governed by the Civil Procedure Code.

The entire above mentioned are the proceedings of the enforcement of a domestic arbitral award. The Thai court also allows an application to enforce a foreign arbitral award. Under the Arbitration Act, an award is binding upon the parties regardless of the jurisdiction in which it is made. Where the award is made in Thailand, the award will be enforced by the competent courts. However, if the award is made in a foreign jurisdiction, the Thai courts will only enforce the award if such an award is governed by a treaty, convention or international agreement to which Thailand is a member and only to the extent that Thailand agrees to be bound by such treaty, convention or international agreement. ① Therefore, due to the fact that Thailand is a party to the Geneva Convention 1927 and the New York Convention on the Recognition and Enforcement of Foreign Arbitral Awards 1958, arbitral awards conducted wholly or mainly outside Thailand involving any party which is not a Thai national may be enforced by the Thai court pursuant to those Conventions.

With regard to the enforcement of foreign arbitral award proceedings, it is the same as the enforcement of a domestic arbitration award, which is also

---

① Norton Rose Group, Arbitration in Asia Pacific, Thailand January 2010, p. 10.

governed by the Thai Arbitration Act. However, in order to enforce a foreign arbitral award under the Geneva Convention 1927 and the New York Convention on the Recognition and Enforcement of Foreign Arbitral Awards 1958, the award must also satisfy the requirements of those Conventions.

Up to this point, we can see that the court also plays a significant role in the arbitration proceedings. Apart from that I have stated above, the court can impose provisional measures to protect the parties' interests either before or during the arbitral proceedings. This provision can be found in Article 16 of the Arbitration Act.

Article 16 states that the parties to the arbitration agreement may, before or during the arbitral proceedings, request the competent court to impose a provisional measure in order to protect their interests. If the court considers that such request, if filed to it, is within its jurisdiction, the court shall consider the request. In this regard, the provisions of the law on court proceedings related therewith shall be applied *mutatis mutandis*.

If an order imposing a provisional measure has been given upon request of the party under paragraph one any such party fails to refer to the arbitration within 30 days as from the date in which the court having an order or within the period as prescribed by the court, such order of the court shall be deemed to be terminated upon the lapse of the aforesaid period.

With regard to the arbitration institutes, there are two main domestic arbitration institutes in Thailand. The first one is the Thai Arbitration Institute of the Alternative Dispute Resolution Office (TAI), which is governed by the Office of the Judiciary. TAI is the main arbitration body in Thailand. The role of the TAI is to facilitate the arbitration process; it does this through assisting with the selection of an arbitrator where necessary, by providing the necessary physical and human resources in conducting arbitration and by providing TAI arbitration and conciliation rules which govern the arbitration proceedings. The Second arbitration services are also provided by the Board of Trade of Thailand and the International Chamber of Commerce, Thailand (ICC Thailand). The Board of Trade has a set of rules which govern an arbitration conducted through it. The ICC Thailand applies the rules of arbitration promulgated by the International Chamber of

Commerce in Paris. [1]

Both of these are well respected, supervised by a diverse advisory board, have standard arbitration rules, and maintain a list of qualified and available arbitrators. Parties can nominate outside professionals as arbitrators, and most often elect to conduct the proceedings in English or Thai. Administrative costs and arbitrator fees for arbitrations conducted through the two arbitration institutes are quite reasonable and both have similar fee structures based on claim amounts. These fees are considerably less than those charged by many international institutes. [2]

The above mentioned is only a briefly introduction to the arbitration legal system in Thailand, which can be applied to any kind of dispute including, the investment dispute that seems to arise more and more due to the expansion and free access to the market with progressively liberalizing the investment regimes of China and ASEAN Free Trade Area (China-ASEAN FTA).

---

[1] Ibid. ,p. 4.

[2] John King, Sally Wrapson and Kornkiat Chunhakasikarn, Dispute Resolution 2007/08. Volume 2: Arbitration-Thailand, p. 95.

图书在版编目(CIP)数据

中国—东盟法律评论.第3卷.第1期/张晓君主编.—厦门:厦门大学出版社,
2014.10
ISBN 978-7-5615-5277-3

Ⅰ.①中…　Ⅱ.①张…　Ⅲ.①法律-中国、东南亚国家联盟-文集
Ⅳ.①D92-53②D933-53

中国版本图书馆 CIP 数据核字(2014)第 242375 号

厦门大学出版社出版发行

(地址:厦门市软件园二期望海路 39 号　邮编:361008)

http://www.xmupress.com

xmup @ xmupress.com

厦门市明亮彩印有限公司印刷

2014 年 10 月第 1 版　2014 年 10 月第 1 次印刷

开本:720×970　1/16　印张:22.25　插页:2

字数:384 千字　印数:1~1 000 册

定价:50.00 元

本书如有印装质量问题请直接寄承印厂调换